T0323723

Professionalization in the Creative Sector

This book seeks to better understand the processes and influences that have driven professionalization in the arts. It develops an analytical framework that examines how processes of professionalization that typically influence and shape work conditions and occupational status are, in the creative sector, augmented by atypical worker efforts and choices to self-structure their protean careers.

The book brings together a collection of works that explore the specific trajectories of professionalization in a variety of creative occupations as well as the formative processes that work across many creative occupations. In particular, the scholarship presented focuses on the interaction of three key variables: field growth and institutionalization, mutual benefit organization within fields and occupations, and the intervention of cultural policy to validate and foster professional support structures. In the broader context of expanding globalization, growing awareness of diversity, and tectonic shifts in technology, this volume unveils research-based implications for cultural policy, cultural workers, and cultural organizations.

This book will be of interest to researchers, creative professionals, as well as undergraduate and graduate-level students in the fields of arts administration and culture.

Margaret J. Wyszomirski is Professor Emerita of Arts Administration, Education and Policy at The Ohio State University, USA.

WoongJo Chang is Associate Professor of Arts and Cultural Management at Hongik University, Seoul, Korea.

Routledge Research in the Creative and Cultural Industries
Series Editor: Ruth Rentschler

This series brings together book-length original research in cultural and creative industries from a range of perspectives. Charting developments in contemporary cultural and creative industries thinking around the world, the series aims to shape the research agenda to reflect the expanding significance of the creative sector in a globalised world.

The Venice Arsenal
Between History, Heritage, and Re-use
Edited by Luca Zan

Managing Cultural Joint Ventures
An Identity-Image View
Tanja Johansson, Annukka Jyrämä and Kaari Kiitsak-Prikk

Public Relations as a Creative Industry
Elisenda Estanyol

Co-Leadership in the Arts and Culture
Sharing Values and Vision
Wendy Reid and Hilde Fjellvær

Cultural Work and Creative Subjectivity
Recentralising the Artist Critique and Social Networks in the Cultural Industries
Xin Gu

Advertising as a Creative Industry
Regime of Paradoxes
Izabela Derda

For more information about this series, please visit: www.routledge.com/Routledge-Research-in-the-Creative-and-Cultural-Industries/book-series/RRCCI

Professionalization in the Creative Sector

Policy, Collective Action, and Institutionalization

Edited by Margaret J. Wyszomirski and WoongJo Chang

LONDON AND NEW YORK

First published 2024
by Routledge
4 Park Square, Milton Park, Abingdon, Oxon OX14 4RN

and by Routledge
605 Third Avenue, New York, NY 10158

Routledge is an imprint of the Taylor & Francis Group, an informa business

British Library Cataloguing-in-Publication Data
A catalogue record for this book is available from the British Library

Library of Congress Cataloging-in-Publication Data
Names: Wyszomirski, Margaret Jane, editor. | Chang, WoongJo,
    1976– editor.
Title: Professionalization in the creative sector : policy, collective
    action, and institutionalization / edited by Margaret J. Wyszomirski
    and WoongJo Chang.
Description: Abingdon, Oxon ; New York, NY : Routledge, 2024. |
    Series: Routledge research in the creative and cultural industries |
    Includes bibliographical references and index.
Subjects: LCSH: Cultural industries. | Professional employees.
Classification: LCC HD9999.C9472 P76 2024 (print) |
    LCC HD9999.C9472 (ebook) | DDC 338.4/77—dc23/
    eng/20230526
LC record available at https://lccn.loc.gov/2023023763
LC ebook record available at https://lccn.loc.gov/2023023764

ISBN: 978-0-367-68624-6 (hbk)
ISBN: 978-0-367-68704-5 (pbk)
ISBN: 978-1-003-13869-3 (ebk)

DOI: 10.4324/9781003138693

Typeset in Sabon
by Apex CoVantage, LLC

Contents

Contributors

Editors

Margaret J. Wyszomirski, Ph.D., is Professor Emerita in the Department of Arts Administration, Education and Policy at The Ohio State University. She served as Staff Director at the 1990 Independent Commission on the National Endowment for the Arts and as NEA Director of Policy Planning, Research, and Budget.

WoongJo Chang, Ph.D., is Associate Professor and Chair of the Department of Arts and Cultural Management at Hongik University, Seoul, Korea. His research is focused on small arts organizations' entrepreneurial practices and how to support them.

Chapter Authors

Claudia J. Bach, M.A. has a professional trajectory that has entwined initiatives and research in support of individual artists since the 1970s. Her experience as an arts administrator led to her national consulting practice, AdvisArts, and she has served as adjunct faculty for Seattle University's Arts Leadership program since 2010.

Ayse Collins, Ph.D., is Associate Professor in the Faculty of Applied Sciences at Bilkent University. Her research areas include sustainability, equity in higher education, diversity, and social inclusion. She publishes in reputable social science journals in education, management, tourism, social diversity, and inclusion. She has also authored or co-authored numerous book chapters.

Patricia Dewey Lambert, Ph.D., is Professor and Director of Graduate Studies in Arts Management at the University of Oregon's School of Planning, Public Policy, and Management.

Chiara Carolina Donelli, Ph.D., is Assistant professor at the Department of Management, Ca' Foscari University of Venice, Italy. She combined academics with fieldwork as a consultant and project manager. Her research interests are collaborative governance and sustainability in the arts sector.

Ian Fillis, Ph.D., is Professor of Entrepreneurship at Liverpool Business School, Liverpool John Moores University. He has research interests in cultural entrepreneurship, small business, arts marketing, and creativity.

Ian Fraser, M.A., C.A., is Emeritus Professor of Accounting at the University of Stirling. Ian's primary research interests are in auditing, financial reporting, and corporate governance, and he has an interest in the valuation of art and artworks.

Ann Galligan, Ph.D., was Associate Professor and Fine Arts Coordinator in the Department of Cooperative Education and Co-Director of the Cultural and Arts Policy Research Institute at Northeastern University. Her teaching and research interests are in the areas of arts policy and education.

Javier J. Hernández-Acosta, Ph.D., MBA, is Associate Professor and Dean of the School of Arts, Design, and Creative Industries at Universidad del Sagrado Corazón in Puerto Rico. He is Founder of Centro de Economía Creativa, a nonprofit organization that supports the creative industries.

Youngaah Koh, Ph.D., is Assistant Professor of Arts Management and Arts Entrepreneurship at Miami University. Her teaching and research interests include undergraduate arts management education, arts policy and advocacy, and community-based arts, including arts education.

Boram Lee, Ph.D., is Senior Lecturer in Arts and Cultural Management, University of South Australia. She has a wide range of research interests in cross-disciplinary studies, covering the valuation of arts and culture and artists' career development.

Minha Lee, Ph.D., is Associate Professor at the College of General Education of Chung-Ang University, Seoul, Korea, and Chair of Korean Art Management Association. Her research interests include art and technology, artist branding, and audience experience.

Ruth Rentschler, Ph.D., is Professor of Arts and Cultural Leadership, UniSA Business, University of South Australia. She has published widely, usually with a focus on social inclusion in the context of the arts.

Rachel Shane, Ph.D., is Department Chair and Professor of Arts Administration at the University of Kentucky, Editor-in-Chief of the Journal of Arts Management, Law, and Society, and President of the Board of Social Theory, Politics, and the Arts.

Jung Yoon, Ph.D., is Postdoctoral Research Fellow at the Disability and Community Inclusion Research Center and the Centre for Social Impact at Flinders University. She focuses on individual and organizational professionalization in social enterprise management and social and disability policies.

1 Professionalization in the Creative Sector

Processes and Trends

Margaret J. Wyszomirski and WoongJo Chang

The Creative Sector as the Locus of Many Occupations

Art is, perhaps, as old as humanity. Art-makers have cultivated specific artistic skills, knowledge, and techniques across the millennia. Artists came to be regarded as artisans separated into different disciplines, each of which gave rise to numerous yet related artistic occupations characterized by working in different media, instrumentation, genres, or styles. While some artistic occupations were composed primarily of individual practitioners, others moved toward group efforts such as small ensembles or organized companies. Gradually, individual and organized art practices grew into art fields. Starting in the late nineteenth century, large and diverse strata of nonprofit arts organizations began to legally separate from those of commercial arts and entertainment businesses (Levine, 1988; DiMaggio, 1982). This split became the basis for a cultural hierarchy that was colloquially referred to as the high arts and the popular arts. Around the mid-twentieth century, as many nations founded government ministries or departments of arts and culture, various combinations of art-making activities came to be regarded as "the arts" (Berman, 1979). The establishment of government arts agencies not only provided funding, validation, and recognition for professional artists and professional arts organizations but also acted as an influential force for the institutionalization of art fields as employment structures for creative professionals.

Near the end of the twentieth century, the many distinctive disciplines, fields, and organizational forms began to be conceptually gathered into a phenomenon variously known as the creative sector, the creative and cultural industries, or the creative economy. Since the UK Department of Culture, Media and Sport (DCMS) announced its creative industries initiative in 1998, the idea of an arts- and cultural-based creative sector has spread across the globe, prompting ongoing debates about characterizing the overall grouping, determining what kinds of "creative" activity were included, and deciding how it could be meaningfully measured (Wyszomirski, 2008a). Clearly, the adoption of the creative sector concept has broadened our understanding of who works in the arts, thus expanding the occupational range in terms of

DOI: 10.4324/9781003138693-1

both substantive expertise and functional diversification. This provides a sectoral framework for our examination of professionalization in the arts and the changing state of professionalism in the arts.

The United Kingdom identified a list of 13 production clusters that became the touchstone for other nations and subnational levels of government to identify and map their own creative industries (DCMS, 1998, 2001). Notably, the U.K. listing did not include museums or heritage and preservation generally. Many other policy definitions of the creative sector have chosen to include museums and heritage or other "industries" in their frameworks. For example, international organizations like the United Nations Educational, Scientific and Cultural Organization (UNESCO) created an identification matrix that included many of the UK industries but grouped them into six clusters with an emphasis on both heritage and new media formats (UNESCO, 2009, p. 24). Additionally, UNESCO established a Creative Cities Network program that promoted urban and tourism development by assisting the growth and maturation of seven creative industries: Literature, Folk Arts and Crafts, Film, Music, Media, Design, and Gastronomy. The last of these is not always included in the composition of the creative sector.

Thus, the character and composition of the creative sector are likely to vary from one place to another depending on which creative industries are included in the working definition. As the local definition of the sector is subject to variation, so will the types and mix of creative occupations differ from place to place. Assuming a sectoral approach to the arts presents a broader sense of work opportunities for creative workers—across multiple types of employers, part-time jobs, multiple occupations, and ultimately multiple professions—all of which are arts-related. Hence, understanding the sectoral ecology of the arts is a fundamental building block of our understanding of the professionalization of the arts.

Figure 1.1 illustrates a general map of our understanding of the sector's current composition—a necessary baseline if we are to appreciate the variety of occupations and work opportunities that can be found in the creative sector. Unlike the overall structure of many other economic sectors, the core of the creative sector is composed of an unusually large group of workers who are self-employed or freelancers. The creative sector includes not only artists but also many individuals in arts-related occupations of an administrative and technical nature as well as intermediaries. Some studies estimate that as many as 80% of creative sector workers fall into the core category. The core of this sector is an employment locus for an unusually large number of creative workers who are individual, self-employed, and freelance artists, administrative and technical part-time and contract workers (see Chang, 2010). Figure 1.1 alerts us to the functional types of occupations possible—artistic, entrepreneurial, administrative, technical, and infrastructural. It also reminds us that working in the arts may not take the form of a stable, full-time job, but that a living wage may be assembled by individual creative workers from

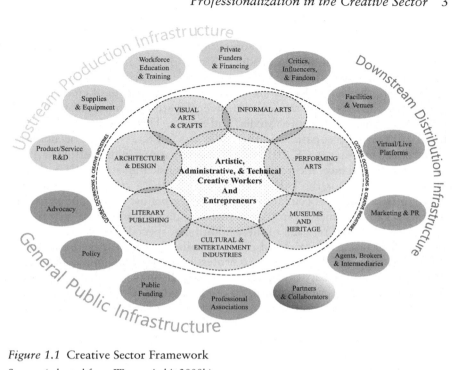

Figure 1.1 Creative Sector Framework
Source: (adapted from Wyszomirski, 2008b)

work among a number of nonprofit, commercial, and informal arts organizations and companies found in the seven industrial clusters of the second ring. Each of these industrial clusters includes a number of specific sub-industries. The outer ring represents various support structures that underlie the entire sector. Many of the individual workers of the sector's core are likely to combine their artistic work with part-time positions either in the second ring of industrial organizations or in the outer ring of infrastructure activities. Others may pursue a career that, over time, will move from one occupation and location within the sector to another. Figure 1.1 also identifies three dimensions of infrastructure: upstream production, general public support, and downstream distribution. Viewed from a policy, planning, and development perspective, Figure 1.1 can help explain how the ecological framework of the creative sector shapes the strategies creative workers employ to build work portfolios, sustain careers, and advance their professional practice.

Using this vision of the arts sector as a starting point, it is clear that the sector employs many and diverse occupations that function at differing levels of professionalism. Thus, it is worthwhile to get a sense of the range and variety of occupations that are included. For example, the U.S. National Endowment for the Arts (NEA) has long used a list of 11 types of artistic occupations to monitor and report on the artistic labor force. These range from actors, writers, musicians/singers, dancers/choreographers, designers, photographers, and architects to announcers, producer/directors, fine artists/animators, and other kinds of artists and entertainers (such as circus artists) (NEA, 1996). In comparison, the United Kingdom used a broader definition of creative occupations, as can be seen in the series of Blueprint studies commissioned by the U.K. Department of Culture, Media, and Sports. Three reports in this series listed 42 creative occupations in the visual arts (CCS, 2009), 42 occupations in the music industry (CCS, 2011), and 55 occupations in the performing arts (a composite of dance, theater, opera, and live music industries) (CCS, 2010). Neither the U.S. nor the U.K. inventories included a count for specialized genre or instrumental occupations, such as jazz pianist or symphony violinist; painter or ceramicist; tap dancer or ballet dancer; and visual art, music, or theater educator. Yet each of these additional, specialized occupations displays at least some indicators of professionalism, such as specialized education or training and the existence of professional membership associations.

Other types of occupations appear in these listings: administrative occupations such as arts administrator, box office and stage manager, and education manager, as well as production workers like designers of costumes, sets, and lighting. Intermediaries such as booking agents, critics, conservators, and gallerists are also listed. Using job titles as a proxy for occupation, the New Zealand Arts Council identified 12 occupations in the field of Literature or writing, which includes children's fiction writer, librettist, novelist, playwright, and reviewer, but omitted editor and publisher (Creative New Zealand, 2019). Relatively new occupations could also be added to the general list of creative professionals, such as website designer, chief information officer (museums), and film curator.

Professionalization, Field Institutionalization, and Self-Structuration

Professionalization, a process that institutionalizes authority, high social status, and economic rewards for members of selected occupational groups, has been an expanding social trend for decades. While the emergence of modernity saw the development of conventional professionalism for select occupations, such as doctors and lawyers, since the mid-twentieth century, an increasing number of occupational groups—for instance, social workers, paralegals, engineers, architects, and accountants—have sought to lay claim to the status of professionals. These groups created the benefits and structures of professionalism by founding organizations for collective action, advocacy, and self-regulation; developing standards of preparation, practice, and licensure; acquiring institutional validation and legal status; and mounting bids for economic exclusivity and societal recognition for their expertise and distinctive role. While traditionally, artists in Western societies were regarded as skilled artisans and supported through the patronage system, the modern emphasis on higher education opened a path to professionalism as did the formation of professional associations and/or unions. Arts professionals initially included architects, symphony musicians, and live theater actors. Most recently, cultural workers across the commercial and emergent nonprofit sectors have developed a more inclusive and diverse form of professionalism that we term "creative professionalism." Many other arts and arts-related occupations have arisen as the number of artists and arts organizations and businesses expanded, as cultural policy helped to shape field institutionalization—the expansion and structuration of both the nonprofit, creative arts fields and the commercial cultural industries—as occupations developed their capacity to manage risk and diversification, and the sector increasingly adopted digital technology. Most recently, creative professionalism has introduced additional attributes of professionalization through practices of entrepreneurial self-structuration.

Occupationally, artists have demonstrated an ambiguous social status—educated, skilled, and committed, but financially precarious, with unstable employment and uncharted career paths. Workers in art and arts-related occupations have struggled to gain professional recognition, even as some have acquired reputation and renown. With increasing access to both the intrinsic and instrumental benefits of the arts, the public has come to better appreciate the public value of the work of creative professionals. In recent decades, creative professionals have become more adept at constructing protean or portfolio careers out of a patchwork of freelance gigs and temporary projects, hybrid practices, and multiple occupations—thus exerting more control of their professional development while exercising free expression of their individual creativity (Menger, 1999, p. 571). Indeed, the recognition of the scope and variety of jobs encompassed within the creative sector has expanded the options for creative workers to be able to gain cultural capital and assemble work portfolios and careers within the sector.

Such changes in the capacity of creative workers to entrepreneurially pursue a living wage and to manage their careers within the broader frame of the creative sector alone could not advance professionalism in the arts. Larger changes in the organizational, social, and policy environment were also necessary to propel other forces conducive to professionalization in the arts. Three such developments emerged during the second half of the twentieth century: (1) the expansion and institutionalization of the nonprofit and creative arts fields and the commercial cultural industries; (2) a growing self-awareness of shared occupational identities and a quest for social status and economic sustainability that prompted collective action among many types of cultural workers; and (3) the establishment of national cultural policies and public funding for the arts.

Over the course of the second half of the twentieth century and the first two decades of the twenty-first century, the creative sector has been challenged economically, legally, and technologically on the global stage. The sector has navigated waves of new technology, industry conglomeration and out-sourcing, shifting financial resources, and politically driven governance to be refigured in the late twentieth-century knowledge and creative economy. The growth in the number of professional associations, unions, and other arts service organizations within each of the arts fields and around key cultural occupations furthered professionalization in the arts. These membership organizations provided much of the collective structure through which professional information and norms were disseminated, mutual benefit and self-governance were promoted, and individual professional identity was cultivated. Thus, in the emerging global economy, artists and arts-related workers across national, genre, and sector boundaries have increasingly come to recognize and advocate for themselves as a distinctive occupational class. Cultural policy innovations facilitated the expansion and proliferation of nonprofit arts organizations, resulting in a de facto nonprofit arts sector hospitable to professionalization. In different national settings, this evolution occurred at different paces, followed different paths in particular arts fields and disciplines, and came to embrace arts-adjacent occupations. The net result of the development of these new fields of organizational practice has been the emergence of creative professionalism.

Understanding the trajectory and impact of professionalization in the creative sector is critical to the future of arts and cultural management and significant for grasping broad social and cultural changes in society as a whole. Yet, evidence of creative sector growth and development is scattered across studies of art, theater, history of dance and opera, annuals of major private foundation programs in cultural philanthropy, biographies of artists and arts patrons, as well as the organizational histories of particular arts organizations and the histories of arts policies and public agencies. Consequently, it is difficult to piece together a systematic understanding of the interlocking processes of field institutionalization, occupational professionalization, and arts workers' self-structuration or to see the role of cultural policy in these transformations. Furthermore, the dramatic social, economic, political, and technological developments of the late twentieth and early twenty-first centuries have both complicated and facilitated the professionalization equation.

In this book, we seek to better comprehend the factors that have driven and continue to drive professionalization in the arts and arts-related occupations, both as a result of longitudinal processes and within the framework of the creative sector. In the broader context of expanding globalization, growing emphasis on diversity and democratization, and tectonic shifts in technology, we examine the ways in which field and industrial institutionalization, individual self-structuration, collective mutual benefit action, and changes in cultural policy have both reflected and propelled professionalism in the arts. We bring together a collection of studies that delve deeply into diverse aspects of professionalization in the arts and the creative sector and analyze the far-reaching implications for the future of cultural workers, arts organizations, cultural industries, and society as a whole. Despite decades of professionalization across occupations in the creative sector, the resulting professionalism is uneven, with some occupations moving closer to the conventional model of professionalism while others display more atypical patterns. Taken together, the scholarship in this volume grapples with the variegated results of professionalization across the creative sector and tensions between conventional professionalism and an emerging atypical creative professionalism, by focusing on the interaction of three variables: (1) field growth and institutionalization/structuration; (2) arts workers' self-structuration and mutual benefit initiatives; and (3) the intervention of cultural policy to validate and foster professional support structures. This volume widens the conceptual frame to accommodate the full range of occupations involved in the functioning of the creative sector and allows analysts to better see the proliferation, growth, and institutionalization of the range of arts organizations from nonprofits to for-profit entertainment and cultural businesses.

A Select Literature Overview

There is extensive but scattered literature pertinent to the subject of professionalization in the arts sector, including significant bodies of work in the fields of arts administration, cultural policy, cultural economics, the artistic labor market, and the sociology of professions. Much of this literature makes frequent mention of "professional artists" and "professional arts organizations" but seldom explicitly focuses on the processes or indicators of professionalization in the arts. Many scholars focus on the production processes of creative or artistic products, particularly concerning the experience and role of human capital. It is not uncommon for these literatures to assert that creative occupations cannot be regarded as professions because they lack the key attribute of exercising exclusive jurisdiction over the entry and career progress of their occupational members. Yet the rarity of standardized career paths has meant that a particular creative worker's diverse history of jobs in the creative sector enhances, rather than detracts from, their employability and helps to establish their creative professionalism (Bridgstock & Carr, 2013; Ashton, 2011). Two other persistent stumbling blocks to the study of professionalization in the creative sector have been weak requirements for formalized training/education and the precariousness of earnings from working in the arts. Artists who have earned a reputation for quality work are considered professional artists despite their different training and educational credentials. Similarly, multiple entry routes into creative sector occupations are accepted as legitimate paths to professionalization. Through protean careers and crossover artistic work patterns, artists and creative workers have become better able to assemble earning portfolios within the creative sector that approximate a living wage (Bennett, 2009; Bridgtock, 2007; Inglis & Cray, 2012; Markusen, 2006). Thus, the conditions creative workers must adapt to also impede the adequate study of the processes of professionalization in the arts.

This volume addresses lacunae, particularly from the perspective of cultural policy and arts administration. It argues that although occupations of the creative sector tend to present atypical professional profiles, they have become more professionalized since the mid-1960s and have developed innovative ways to construct many dimensions of professionalism. Much of the relevant literature appears within the individual chapters and helps inform the analyses of the evolution of key processes and structures of professionalism. Collectively, the chapter reference lists provide an extensive bibliography on the subject. A few of the chapters have assembled historiographies of key influencers of professionalization, such as the NEA or of a group of private foundations active in cultural philanthropy. Other chapters look at the impacts of unions or professional associations, and some chapters examine the cases of professionalism in small arts organizations, the additional challenges faced by disabled artists, or the emergence of specialized sub-professions within the arts management and arts education fields. Yet other chapters focus on the construction of a formal higher education curriculum for creative professionals or ongoing professional development programs, the growing emphasis on entrepreneurship, the creation of intermediary organizations, and the practice of self-structuration in careers and professions.

In addition, the majority of the inter-disciplinary literature on the subject appears in the form of journals of scholarly research, in public policy reports and documents, foundation and research institute reports, or as commentary in biographies about creative professionals or organizational histories of nonprofit arts organizations or entertainment and media businesses. With few exceptions, professionalism in the arts sector has not been systematically addressed in most of the literature, nor has a general framework emerged as a scaffold for furthering the discussion. By bringing together the research and analysis of a diverse group of scholars and practitioners, this collection builds on previous and related research to advance a cohesive understanding of the longitudinal trajectory, current and variable state, and future prospects of professionalization and professionalism in the creative sector.

There are three book-length works that are particularly germane to the topic of professionalism in the creative arts sector, which complements this volume. *Cultural Policy, Work and Identity: The Creation, Renewal, and Negotiation of Professional Subjectivities*, edited by Jonathan Paquette (2012), presents a collection of 11 studies from five Western countries to consider the intersection of cultural policy and professionalism through the lens of identity construction in arts, media, and heritage sectors. The book is particularly concerned with the power dynamics within cultural policies and how these interact with cultural hierarchies, institutional support systems, and professionalism in the arts. The presented case studies are valuable contributions, particularly in exploring the role of policy at the local level, and they provide useful cross-national insights into the processes of professionalization. The strength of the volume is its emphasis on the diversity and specificity of the case studies concerning the dimension of professional identity. In that focus, it provides an in-depth discussion of a dimension of professionalization that is not a major focus of this volume and yet works within a framework of cultural policy impact.

Creative Labour: Working in the Creative Industries (2009), edited by Alan McKinlay and Chris Smith, takes a labor process approach to explore career case studies of creative workers in the film, live theater, television, and new and interactive media industries. It traces the emergence, over the last 20 years, of the concept of the creative industries and how they have become a policy priority in the United Kingdom and spread to other countries like Germany, Sweden, and the United States. Although it explores the working conditions and labor practices cultural workers face, this work does not directly engage with the concept of professionalism. Instead, it briefly identifies ways in which creative occupations diverge from professional dimensions regarding control of professional entry and of required education and training credentials. The cases are particularly strong in their presentation of a view from inside specific commercial creative industries and in highlighting some of the ways creative workers deal with conditions of precariousness.

Another noteworthy collection of relevant case studies can be found in *Nonprofit Enterprise in the Arts* (1986), edited by Paul J. DiMaggio, which explores how the arts are produced and distributed in the United States. The cases examine the tensions between art for the public good and exigencies of the culture industries as they play out in nonprofits, private firms, government agencies, and the public imagination. Chapters delineate the basic organizational field form as the employment structures for many of the nonprofit arts industries and their importance to professionalization of arts occupations. Three chapters have proven to be particularly foundational: DiMaggio's "Cultural Entrepreneurship in Nineteenth Century Boston" (reprinted from DiMaggio, 1982); Richard Peterson's (1987) "From Impresarios to Arts Administrators: Formal Accountability in Nonprofit Cultural Organizations"; and Vera L. Zolberg's (1987) "Tensions of Missions in American Art Museums." The volume is particularly valuable for its attention to the importance of the nonprofit organizational form as a key factor in the institutionalization of nonprofit art fields and to the important role that public funding for the arts plays in the professionalization of the arts, particularly arts management.

These three books, each a collection of case studies, include conceptual chapters focused on select dimensions of working in the arts and creative sector professionalism, a taste of three disciplinary approaches to the subject, and a mix of national perspectives. Paquette is a Canadian political scientist, Smith and McKinlay are British management professors, and DiMaggio is an American sociologist. Taken together, the elements these three books explore present a wide-ranging sample of many facets, assumptions, and approaches that can be brought to bear on the study of working in creative arts and, more specifically, to the role of professionalism.

There is also a varied and dispersed body of articles and reports that present analysis and research on professionalism in general and professionalization in the arts and creative sector in particular. Since each of our authors provides a literature review pertinent to their study, here we would like to highlight some works that are foundational to the fields of arts management and cultural policy. Alper et al. (1996) explore the inequities in arts sector professionalism as evidenced by the mismatch between arts workers' education and attainments and their income levels. DiMaggio and Useem (1978) examine features of cultural workers' professional paths—notably, part-time and unstable employment and the lack of clearly defined career trajectories—that are seldom analyzed within the conventional framework of professionalization. Another body of academic literature, often rooted in arts administration and/or cultural sociology, has examined the work life, career, and social status of mostly artists (occasionally also of arts managers) to obtain a deeper understanding of the field structures and network systems (artworlds) in which professional arts occupations and workers operate (Becker, 1976; Caves, 2000; Dewey, 2004; DiMaggio, 1987; Shane, 2013). Some studies explicitly explore the experience of labor and economic issues within the creative industries using either the concept of professionalism (e.g., Deamer, 2020; Jeffri & Throsby, 1994, 2006; Throsby, 2001) or cultural theory (Banks et al., 2013). Many of these studies are written from the perspective of economics and typically draw on national labor statistics to support arguments that have been used in advocacy efforts to secure annual appropriations for public funding of the arts. Additionally, there are important works that explore the dimension of arts leadership and entrepreneurship (Essig, 2015, 2017; Rentschler, 2002, 2003), artistic reputation (Lang & Lang, 1988), and symbolic interaction in the social organization of the art world (Gilmore, 2009) though they don't treat these topics within the framework of professionalization.

The cultural economy, entrepreneurship, and the nonprofit sector have all garnered scholarly attention. Research on cultural economy has raised awareness of field structures and the role of agents (including unions, associations, and guilds) and drawn attention to working conditions in the gig economy, particularly the frequent lack of benefits for cultural workers (Morgan & Nelligan, 2018; Petriglieri et al., 2019; Wyszomirski & Chang, 2017). This literature includes policy-focused research reports commissioned by government agencies and private foundations (e.g., reports by the NEA, the Wallace Foundation, and Strategic National Arts Alumni Project). Various national arts agencies in a number of countries, including the United Kingdom, Canada, and Australia, have undertaken research on improving the economic conditions and creative productivity of individual artists (e.g., Jeffri & Throsby, 1994, 2006; Throsby, 2001). European Union Research Programs have sponsored studies of the work conditions and mobility of artists and the training of cultural managers in an effort to inform regional cultural policy following the promulgation of the Treaty of Maastricht in

1992, which formed the EU (e.g., Fisher, 2007). A series of NEA research studies that spans over 30 years has sought to interpret labor statistics for a core group of 11 arts occupations with regard to the number of workers, place of employment, and earnings. The first such NEA report on artists as a group in the general workforce was issued in 1970 as NEA Research Report #5 (Ellis, 1977).

Similarly, growing interest in arts entrepreneurship has stimulated attention to commonly recognized dimensions of creative professionalism, such as the training of arts workers and the structuration of the creative and cultural industries' (CCIs') occupational practices, and career self-management (Guo & Wyszomirski, 2019; Olson, 2018; White, 2017; Wyszomirski & Chang, 2017). This body of research has spurred studies on working in the commercial and cultural industries, such as film, broadcasting, music, theater, publishing, and videogames (e.g., Christopherson & Storper, 1986; Hang & Van Weezel, 2007; Khajeheian & Tadayoni, 2016; Peterson & Berger, 1971; Preece, 2011; Whitson et al., 2021; Zhao et al., 2013). Greater awareness of the relationship and interaction between the nonprofit arts sector and the commercial cultural industries has prompted scholars to examine aspects of professionalism, such as control over work products, intellectual property rights, and licensing as a revenue stream (e.g., Lessig, 2008; Menger, 1999; Towse, 2006).

The work collected in this volume builds on and extends this scholarship to develop an overarching understanding of the issues surrounding professionalism and moves toward a more integrated analytical framework that may prove useful for positioning future research in the field.

The Chapters

Collectively, the contributors to this book are uniquely positioned to understand the interlocking array of forces that shape professionalism in the arts. They are scholars and practitioners, each with a deep knowledge of specific art fields and artworlds, based in higher education institutions, especially in the fields of arts administration and cultural policy. In presenting their primary research and analysis, they draw on a broad and inter-disciplinary literature on professionalism, the history and development of arts and cultural policy, and the practice of arts management and organizational development.

In this volume, we approach the complexity of professionalism in the arts through three primary areas of concern: field structuration, collective action, and cultural policy. Part I, "Trends of Professionalization and Self-Structuration," explores a set of broad social, political, and economic forces that have shaped both the professionalization and the self-structuration of creative occupations during the past 60 years, such as the impact of national cultural policies and private foundation funding to professionalize creative occupations, a growing educational and training emphasis on strategic planning and entrepreneurship, and among creative workers, a growing practice of career and professional self-structuration. Part II, "Cases of Professionalization in Practice," explores cultural workers' growing self-awareness of shared occupational identities and interests in the context of the late twentieth-century global knowledge and creative economy. In-depth case studies tracking the professionalization of specific creative occupations or examining the impact of issues like blockchain technology or disability illustrate that there is no one route to professionalization but rather many unique, context-dependent paths. Throughout the volume, field structuration is dealt with as an important variable.

Part I: Trends of Professionalization and Self-Structuration

Part I of this volume takes on big questions. From a sectoral perspective, what are creative occupations? What are the characteristics of professionalization and professionalism in general and how have these characteristics diverged among creative occupations? If creative occupations tend to display incomplete or atypical professional structures, can these gaps be managed or filled in through less orthodox means? How do processes of organizational field institutionalization interact with processes of professionalization? How have public policy efforts, foundations' programs, collective action, and self-structuration practices both propelled professionalization and addressed the basic issues of economic precariousness and career uncertainty? How is professionalism displayed differently in fields that are organizationally institutionalized versus those that are characterized by self-employed artists and micro-enterprises? How might professional education and training be evolving to address the rise of the creative economy, the concept of the creative and cultural industries, and arts entrepreneurship?

Chapters in Part I address these questions and explore macro perspectives on multiple creative occupations and industries of the creative sector, as well as the ways in which those perspectives influenced processes, resources, and norms in multiple dimensions of professionalism. Collectively, Part I chapters consider the "big picture" within which individual creative occupations experienced professionalization. Some chapters assemble and analyze the historiography of a particular social or political actor on professionalization in the arts. Other chapters explore how individual artists and small arts organizations have learned to be the entrepreneurs of their own businesses and careers. Other chapters construct tools or curricula to assist in planning and making career choices to better prepare creative workers to help manage their own professional development. Taken together, the work presented in Part I moves us toward a better understanding of how atypical creative professions became more professionalized over the past 60 years and closer to an integrated conceptual framework on the complex mosaic of professionalism found in the arts today.

This chapter, Chapter 1, "Professionalization in the Creative Sector: Processes and Trends," presents an overview of this volume. It introduces key definitions and dimensions of professionalization and provides examples of the wide range of different arts and arts-related occupations that characterize the sector. It opens the discussion of how creative professions often present a profile that differs from models typical of other professions. The character and significance of the holistic creative industries concept are visualized as an aide to understanding the occupational range encompassed by the sector. Finally, the sequence of each chapter's focus is summarized providing an overview of the structure of this book.

Chapter 2, "Sustaining Atypical Professions: Professional Structuration in the Creative Sector," by WoongJo Chang and Margaret J. Wyszomirski, opens with a discussion of the range of types of occupations encompassed within the creative sector. It then moves to how the literature on the sociology of professions defines and distinguishes the concepts of professionalization and professionalism. It derives a set of basic indicators to be used in discussing how the character of these indicators can vary from their profile in more conventional professions. Next, the discussion focuses on six processes of professionalization that drive changes in the indicators of professionalization and, thus, the overall status of professionalism. The final section examines the various self-structuration practices artists have developed to help them address remaining gaps in the professional infrastructure of their occupations. The chapter concludes with the construction of a "Choice Matrix" that identifies the components to be considered and the strategic decisions creative professionals must manage in the processes of their professional development and artistic practice. These choices are particularly important for individual artists who are largely self-employed or self-manage protean careers. Specifically, this chapter explores both how classic dimensions of professionalism have adapted and how efforts at self-structuration have empowered individual artists who improvise or assemble the benefits that, in other professions, are likely to be collective support structures, practices, and processes.

In Chapter 3, "Cultural Policy Tools and Rising Professionalism in American Arts, 1963–1996," Margaret J. Wyszomirski focuses on how cultural policy has fostered the institutionalization of fields of professional practice and employment in the creative arts. She argues that professionalization was a part of the original mission and purpose of the establishment of the NEA. The chapter examines the role of the NEA in supporting the professional structuring of arts occupations: by underwriting the establishment of professional membership organizations that helped to develop professional networks, standards, and a growing number of nonprofit arts organizations. In turn, this led to an increasing number of institutions seeking to employ creative professionals as well as fostering professional identity formation through peer review.

Claudia J. Bach, in Chapter 4, "Passion and Profession: Individual Artists, Professional Development, and the Role of Foundations," delves deeply into the role private foundations played in the support and professionalization of artists, particularly with regard to the development of self-management skills and knowledge. She delineates the impacts of broad structural developments from the perspective of individual cultural workers, particularly the evolution of professional development training for individual artists, foundation-supported research on individual artist career development, and direct support programs and intermediary funding for the professional development of individual artists.

In Chapter 5, "The Dual Professional: The Artist/Manager in Small Arts Organizations," WoongJo Chang brings the broad perspectives explored in Chapter 2 to bear on dual professionalism in small arts organizations, with a particular focus on how individual cultural workers improvise their dual roles as artists and managers and create acknowledged professional productions while also acting as entrepreneurs of their own protean careers in the arts. Chang offers a timeline model of four possible policy interventions in the development cycle of a growing small arts organization that could foster further professionalism.

In Chapter 6, "Strategic Planning for the Creative Professional: A Curriculum Proposal for Career Development Design," Javier J. Hernández-Acosta looks at the efforts of university arts programs to incorporate entrepreneurship and business management into the curriculum for artists and cultural workers and specifically focuses on the academic experience of an entrepreneurship course for arts professionals. Recognizing that artists can be agents of change, he proposes a model that balances economic, artistic, and social objectives and concludes with an alumni profile that highlights the role of the artist as a creative agent, entrepreneur, connector, and agent of economic, cultural, and social change. Hernández-Acosta shows how an arts entrepreneurial curriculum can emphasize the cultivation of social value in artistic work. His proposed *Creative Professional Action Plan* can be seen as constituting a sixth portfolio within the Choice Matrix of Self Structuration developed in Chapter 2.

Part II: Cases of Professionalization in Practice

Part II presents a set of micro-level case studies that examine how macro-trends play out in particular occupations or focus on a specific dimension or issue of professionalization. These chapters deepen our understanding of how specific arts occupations have forged their paths toward professionalism. Each occupation is influenced not only by macro social, economic, and political trends but also by specific conditions in their artistic fields and/or functional specializations. The changes in the character of financial support structures or political funding structures can present technologically driven opportunities for individual artists while changes in the cultural policy environment may create the need for a new managerial sub-profession. Both may then drive changes in education and training as well as career paths. As new needs arise, new types of skilled workers or new forms of collective mobilization have developed and become institutionalized. Other chapters explore how a fractured organization field has given rise to fractured subprofessional groupings or how established professional expectations and norms have been adjusted to accommodate creative professionals who are disabled. The chapters in this section grapple with this complex and shifting terrain and examine how needs, threats, opportunities, and changing concepts of the public good have elicited professionalization responses.

In Chapter 7, "Actors' Equity Association and the Professionalization of the Acting Vocation," Rachel Shane examines the development of professional actors through unionization amidst field structuration (or institutionalization). In the twenty-first century, nearly every live theatrical production is controlled by policies set forth by Actors' Equity Association (created in 1919). Union institutionalization was a precondition for professionalization in the theatrical industry, which hinged on the union's ability to convince disparate theatrical venues to adopt similar policies. This homogenization enabled the union to leverage professional status for its membership. It took 80 years to establish Equity's authority over the vocation of acting in the United States.

In Chapter 8, "The Fractured Professionalization in Arts Education," Youngaah Koh and Ann Galligan demonstrate how the occupation of arts educator has been characterized by a number of sub-groups that have distinctive training and credentials, practice in different organizational settings, organize themselves into particularized professional associations, and followed different routes and progressions toward professionalization. They discuss the professionalism of these occupational fragments and track the development trajectory of the newest sub-profession—teaching artists. It explores the ramifications of this siloed professionalization, and how these have been shaped by both differences in policy attention and distinctive chronologies of field institutionalization.

In Chapter 9, "Cultural Value and Professionalization of Emerging Contemporary Artists," Ian Fillis, Boram Lee, and Ian Fraser examine the question of how the cultural value surrounding an annual contemporary art exhibition contributes to the professionalization of newly graduated artists. In order to understand how the various stakeholders of the contemporary art market interact, they drew on the range of sources involved in creating, sharing, and sustaining cultural value. They argue that this exhibition opportunity provided structural support that is often missing for young emerging artists.

In Chapter 10, "Strategic or Struggling? Professionalizing Philanthropy in Nonprofit Arts Organizations," Ruth Rentschler and Chiara Carolina Donelli examine the growth of philanthropy management as an administrative specialization within Australian nonprofit arts organizations as a response to an environment of diminishing public funding. As a new approach to securing private funds for arts organizations emerges in a policy context of privatization, there is a demand for new skills and a "whole organization approach."

In Chapter 11, "Performing Arts Center Managers: A Crucial Profession in Community Performing Arts Sectors," Patricia Dewey Lambert explores the distinctive role played by professional arts managers of large urban performing arts centers (PACs). PAC managers are central to the ecology of the creative industry and are active actors on the international stage. Professionalization of the PAC manager has occurred in the context of a proliferation of PACs in the United States since the mid-1980s. Lambert argues that PAC managers have developed a range of distinctive managerial skills beyond those traditionally characteristic of producing arts organization managers.

In Chapter 12, Ruth Rentschler, Boram Lee, Jung Yoon, and Ayse Collins present " 'I am a professional dancer': The case of professionalization in disability arts." This chapter examines the professional challenges that face both disabled artists and a professional dance company that employs them. They explore the professionalism of artists with disabilities by examining a set of attitudes and behaviors associated with a distinctive form of occupational organization. On the basis of a case study of an Australian dance theater that works with dancers with physical or intellectual disabilities, it investigates the enabling and inhibiting factors for professional value creation by artists with disabilities.

In Chapter 13, "Making a Buck Through Blockchain: Artist Entrepreneurship in the Artworld," Minha Lee explores the potential of blockchain technology to transform the visual arts industry, particularly for professional artists. Lee emphasizes the need for redefining the role and support structures for artists in the digital age. Blockchain's core principle of decentralization may enable a new market system that supports direct artist-to-collector transactions, empowering artists with more control over their financial rewards and fostering new business models.

Finally, in Chapter 14, the shutdown for the COVID-19 pandemic that started in March 2020 imposed multiple shocks on global society in healthcare, the economy, education, and the arts and culture sector. In the concluding chapter, "Epilog: Challenges for Creative Professionalism," the editors, Margaret J. Wyszomirski and WoongJo Chang, consider the possible impacts of the global pandemic and the accompanying social, political, and economic disruptions that are challenging and changing professionalism in the arts sector. Creative occupations are facing changing institutional fields, a shifting policymaking ecology, initiatives for greater diversity and inclusiveness, and the ongoing movement of the forces of technology and globalization that, taken together, are likely to significantly reshape arts professionalism.

In particular, a burgeoning array of digital, virtual, and information resources have diminished the role of conventional gatekeepers and made artistic production and dissemination directly accessible to diverse producers. We hope to contribute to the discussion of the importance and character of resilience moving forward in the post-COVID-19 era. We provide examples of arts sector responses by individuals, organizations, complex systems, and communities to the unprecedented challenges of recovering and adapting to the new normal. We suggest that dimensions of organizational resilience and a continuum of resilience goals may prove to be a useful framework for understanding challenges facing creative professionalism, creative professionals, and arts and cultural organizations.

As this volume goes to press, we are witnessing dramatic changes in real time. To meet the challenges of the future, we must attend carefully to what came before. It is our hope that this volume, poised at this unprecedented inflection point, is able to provide a depth of knowledge and perspective on professionalization that can help inform a healthy and vibrant ecology of the arts as we move forward.

References

Alper, N. O., Wassall, G. H., Jeffri, J., Greenblatt, R., Kay, A. O., Butcher, S. G. W., & Chartrand, H. H. (1996). *Artists in the work force: Employment and earnings, 1970–1990* (Research Division Report No. 37). Seven Locks Press.

Ashton, D. (2011). Media work and the creative industries: Identity work, professionalism and employability. *Education+Training, 53*(6), 546–560.

Banks, M., Gill, R., & Taylor, S. (2013). *Theorizing cultural work: Labour, continuity and change in the cultural and creative industries.* Routledge.

Becker, H. S. (1976). Art worlds and social types. *American Behavioral Scientist, 19*(6), 703–718.

Bennett, D. (2009). Academy and the real world: Developing realistic notions of career in the performing arts. *Arts and Humanities in Higher Education, 8*(3), 309–327.

Berman, R. (1979). Art vs the arts. *Commentary, 69*(5), 46–52.

Bridgstock, R., & Carr, L. (2013). Creative entrepreneurship education for graduate employability in the creative arts. *The CALTN Papers,* 8–35.

Bridgstock, R. S. (2007). *Success in the protean career: A predictive study of professional artists and tertiary arts graduates* [Doctoral dissertation, Queensland University of Technology].

Caves, R. E. (2000). *Creative industries: Contracts between art and commerce* (No. 20). Harvard University Press.

CCS (Creative & Cultural Skills). (2009). *The visual arts blueprint: An analysis of the skill needs of the visual arts sector in the UK.* The National Academy of Skills. https://static.a-n.co.uk/wp-content/uploads/2017/02/Visual-Arts-Blueprint-CCS.pdf

CCS (Creative & Cultural Skills). (2010). *The performing arts blueprint: An analysis of the skill needs of the performing arts sector in the UK.* The National Academy of Skills.

CCS (Creative & Cultural Skills). (2011). *The music blueprint: An analysis of the skill needs of the music sector in the UK*. The National Academy of Skills.

Chang, W. J. (2010). How "small" are small arts organizations? *Journal of Arts Management, Law, and Society, 40*(3), 217–234.

Christopherson, S., & Storper, M. (1986). The city as studio; the world as back lot: The impact of vertical disintegration on the location of the motion picture industry. *Environment and Planning D: Society and Space, 4*(3), 305–320.

Creative New Zealand. (2019). *A profile of creative professionals*. A Colmar Brunton Report. https://creativenz.govt.nz/-/media/Project/Creative-NZ/CreativeNZ/Legacy-Page-Documents/20052019_a_profile_of_creative_professionals_report_final.pdf

DCMS (Department of Culture, Media, and Sports). (1998). *Creative industries mapping documents 1998*. DCMS. www.gov.uk/government/publications/creative-industries-mapping-documents-1998

DCMS (Department of Culture, Media, and Sports). (2001). *Creative industries mapping documents 2001*. DCMS. www.gov.uk/government/publications/creative-industries-mapping-documents-2001

Deamer, P. (2020). Architectural work: Immaterial labor. In *Architecture and labor* (pp. 63–70). Routledge.

Dewey, P. (2004). From arts management to cultural administration. *International Journal of Arts Management, 6*(3), 3–23.

DiMaggio, P. J. (1982). Cultural Entrepreneurship in nineteenth century Boston: The creation of an organizational base for high culture in America. *Media, Culture and Society, 4*(1), 33–50.

DiMaggio, P. J. (Ed.). (1986). *Nonprofit enterprise in the arts: Studies in mission and constraint*. Oxford University Press.

DiMaggio, P. J. (1987). *Managers of the arts: Careers and opinions of senior administrators of US art museums, symphony orchestras, resident theaters, and local arts agencies* (Research Division Report No. 20). National Book Network, Inc.

DiMaggio, P. J., & Useem, M. (1978). Social class and arts consumption. *Theory and Society, 5*(2), 41–161.

Ellis, D. (1977). *Where artists live: 1970* (Research Division Report No. 5). NEA.

Essig, L. (2015). Means and ends: A theory framework for understanding entrepreneurship in the US arts and culture sector. *Journal of Arts Management, Law, and Society, 45*(4), 227–246.

Essig, L. (2017). Same or different? The "cultural entrepreneurship" and "arts entrepreneurship" constructs in European and US higher education. *Cultural Trends, 26*(2), 125–137.

Fisher, D. (2007). *Briefing paper on the implementation of article 151.4 of the EC treaty*. European Parliament.

Gilmore, S. (2009). Art worlds: Developing the interactionist approach to social organization. In *Symbolic interaction and cultural studies* (pp. 148–178). University of Chicago Press.

Guo, W., & Wyszomirski, M. J. (2019). Arts entrepreneurship in China: Exploring the professional career development model for Chinese emerging western classical musicians. *Journal of Arts Management, Law, and Society, 49*(3), 188–202.

Hang, M., & Van Weezel, A. (2007). Media and entrepreneurship: What do we know and where should we go? *Journal of Media Business Studies, 4*(1), 51–70.

Inglis, L., & Cray, D. (2012). Career paths for managers in the arts. *Australian Journal of Career Development, 21*(3), 23–32.

Jeffri, J., & Throsby, D. (1994). Professionalism and the visual artist. *International Journal of Cultural Policy, 1*(1), 99–108.

Jeffri, J., & Throsby, D. (2006). Life after dance: Career transition of professional dancers. *International Journal of Arts Management, 8*(3), 54–63.

Khajeheian, D., & Tadayoni, R. (2016). User innovation in public service broadcasts: Creating public value by media entrepreneurship. *International Journal of Technology Transfer and Commercialisation, 14*(2), 117–131.

Lang, G. E., & Lang, K. (1988). Recognition and renown: The survival of artistic reputation. *American Journal of Sociology, 94*(1), 79–109.

Lessig, L. (2008). *Remix: Making art and commerce thrive in the hybrid economy.* Penguin.

Levine, L. W. (1988). *Highbrow/lowbrow: The emergence of cultural hierarchy in America.* Harvard University Press.

Markusen, A. R. (2006). *Crossover: How artists build careers across commercial, nonprofit and community work.* University of Minnesota, Humphrey Institute of Public Affairs, Project on Regional and Industrial Economics, The Arts Economy Initiative. www.giarts.org/sites/default/files/Crossover_How-Artists-Build-Careers-Across-Commercial-Nonprofit-Community-Work.pdf

McKinlay, A. (Ed.). (2009). *Creative labour: Working in the creative industries.* Palgrave Macmillan.

Menger, P. M. (1999). Artistic labor markets and careers. *Annual Review of Sociology, 25*(1), 541–574.

Morgan, G., & Nelligan, P. (2018). *The creativity hoax: Precarious work in the gig economy.* Anthem Press.

NEA (National Endowment for the Arts). (1996). *Artists in the work force: Employment and earnings, 1970–1990* (Research Division Report No. 37). NEA.

Olson, A. M. (2018). *Closing the gap between education and career: A study of arts entrepreneurship curricula* [Master's thesis, University of Minnesota].

Paquette, J. (Ed.). (2012). *Cultural policy, work and identity: The creation, renewal and negotiation of professional subjectivities.* Routledge.

Peterson, R. A. (1987). From impresario to arts administrator: Formal accountability in nonprofit cultural organizations. In P. J. DiMaggio (Ed.), *Nonprofit enterprise in the arts: Studies in mission and constraint* (pp. 161–183). Oxford University Press.

Peterson, R. A., & Berger, D. G. (1971). Entrepreneurship in organizations: Evidence from the popular music industry. *Administrative Science Quarterly, 16*(1), 97–106.

Petriglieri, G., Ashford, S. J., & Wrzesniewski, A. (2019). Agony and ecstasy in the gig economy: Cultivating holding environments for precarious and personalized work identities. *Administrative Science Quarterly, 64*(1), 124–170.

Preece, S. B. (2011). Performing arts entrepreneurship: Toward a research agenda. *Journal of Arts Management, Law, and Society, 41*(2), 103–120.

Rentschler, R. (2002). *The entrepreneurial arts leader: Cultural policy, change and reinvention.* University of Queensland Press.

Rentschler, R. (2003). Culture and entrepreneurship introduction. *Journal of Arts Management, Law, and Society, 33*(3), 163–164.

Shane, R. (2013). Resurgence or deterioration? The state of cultural unions in the 21st century. *Journal of Arts Management, Law, and Society, 43*(3), 139–152.

Throsby, D. (2001). Defining the artistic workforce: The Australian experience. *Poetics*, 28(4), 255–271.

Towse, R. (2006). Copyright and artists: A view from cultural economics. *Journal of Economic Surveys*, 20(4), 567–585.

UNESCO. (2009). *The 2009 UNESCO framework for cultural statistics*. UNESCO Institute for Statistics.

White, J. C. (2017). Analyzing entrepreneurship in the US arts sector: Identifying arts entrepreneurs' demographics and shared characteristics. *Artivate*, 6(1), 8–32.

Whitson, J. R., Simon, B., & Parker, F. (2021). The missing producer: Rethinking indie cultural production in terms of entrepreneurship, relational labour, and sustainability. *European Journal of Cultural Studies*, 24(2), 606–627.

Wyszomirski, M. J. (2008a). The local creative economy in the United States of America. In H. Anheier & Y. R. Isar (Eds.), *The cultural economy* (pp. 199–212). Sage Publications.

Wyszomirski, M. J. (2008b). Field building: The road to cultural policy studies in the United States. In J. M. Cherbo, R. A. Stewart, & M. J. Wyszomirski (Eds.), *Understanding the arts and creative sector in the United States* (pp. 39–57). Rutgers University Press.

Wyszomirski, M. J., & Chang, W. J. (2017). Professional self-structuration in the arts: Sustaining creative careers in the 21st century. *Sustainability*, 9(6), 1035.

Zhao, E. Y., Ishihara, M., & Lounsbury, M. (2013). Overcoming the illegitimacy discount: Cultural entrepreneurship in the US feature film industry. *Organization Studies*, 34(12), 1747–1776.

Zolberg, V. L. (1987). Tensions of missions in American art museums. In P. J. DiMaggio (Ed.), *Nonprofit enterprise in the arts: Studies in mission and constraint*. Oxford University Press.

Part I

Macros Perspectives on Professionalism in the Arts

2 Sustaining Atypical Professions

Professional Structuration in the Creative Sector

WoongJo Chang and Margaret J. Wyszomirski

Introduction: The Occupational Range of the Creative Sector

Professionalism in the creative sector is atypical. While a distinction between amateur art-makers and professional artists is widely recognized, public perception of the professional status of artists is often indeterminate. Artists can be seen as lacking key attributes characteristic of professionals. Historically, the serious pursuit of an artistic career has been seen as a vocation rather than a profession. The core workers of the creative sector, the artists who are "the super-creative core of the creative class" (Florida, 2002, p. 69), have been viewed as skilled artisans who have a calling. Even though many artists cultivate a strong occupational identity and work commitment; assiduously pursue specialized, credentialed education and training; and assemble a progression of artistic jobs and achievements, society has been slow to accord them the social status of a publicly validated professional capable of making essential contributions to the public good.

Even before occupations in the creative sector began to professionalize, many of these occupations, particularly in the artistic core, were displaying characteristics that would influence how key indicators and processes of professionalization would develop. For example, the close relationship between specialized education and professionalization is broadly recognized. However, unlike the case in other occupations, "there are no occupational positions in art and culture with formal requirements for license or other authorization . . . [nor are there any] . . . occupational titles that are legally protected" (Svensson, 2015, p. 4). Nevertheless, the acquisition of specialized education through formal educational institutions has become "an increasingly important career factor" (Svensson, 2015, p. 6). Yet others have observed that significant artistic training continues to rely on quasi-apprenticeship experiences and learning from mentors (Greene, 2015; Rink et al., 2017). This suggests that the character of specialized education for creative professionals will rely more on processes of artistic development and less on scientifically based theory and research common to other professions. Similarly, Svensson (2015) notes "a strong commitment to a life as an artist and the competition for recognition serves as a more important motive to

DOI: 10.4324/9781003138693-3

participate in . . . [artistic fields] . . . than material awards and profit" (p. 7). The emphasis on symbolic rewards over economic rewards is thus a key factor in understanding how artistic occupations will tolerate more flexibility and greater variability of income and its sources as they experience professionalization. Thus, the atypicalness of creative occupations responded to certain market and field characteristics that would continue to influence the formation of atypical professionalism.

The occupational status of creative professionals has been further complicated by increasing public awareness that the arts are a cohesive sector composed of multiple, related creative and cultural industries, their workers, and their supporting infrastructures. An expanded conceptual framework is needed to understand the wide variety of artistic and arts-related occupations that populate this complex artworld ecology. As discussed in Chapter 1, Figure 1.1 illustrates that the creative sector is composed of three economic subsectors: the nonprofit and fine arts; the commercial cultural industries; and the often informal, community arts (PCAH, 1997). A number of distinct creative industries operate in each sub-sector, and some industries operate in more than one economic subsector. Each industry employs a variety of occupations at differing stages of professionalization. Furthermore, the entire creative sector draws on an array of infrastructural support and service systems which are home to a variety of arts-related occupations. Generally, occupations in the creative sector industries fall into six categories as indicated in Figure 2.1.

The first category consists of fine artists, musicians, writers, designers, performing artists, and other types of creators and performers. This group, whose members often lack the key markers of professionalism that we discuss later, has been widely studied (Americans for the Arts, 2021; NEA, 1996). It consists of individual artists whose considerable self-structuration efforts

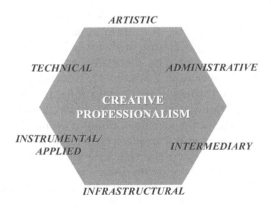

Figure 2.1 Creative Sector Occupational Range

have advanced their claims to professionalism. Self-structuration involves a variable set of processes that engage individual creative workers in drawing on both their entrepreneurial capabilities and the basic support structures of professionalization to assemble their own professional portfolios from artistic ambitions and skills, various income sources and sectors of employment, work-life balance, and educational resources. Many of the creative professionals in this category are

> characterized by a high share of freelancers and very small companies. A new type of employer is emerging in the form of the "entrepreneurial individual" or "entrepreneurial cultural worker," who no longer fits into previously typical patterns of full-time professions.
> (MKW Wirtschaftsforschung GmbH, 2001, p. 9)

A second category consists of individuals working in administrative or managerial positions in arts organizations and commercial entertainment companies including sub-specializations like a performing arts center executive director, a director of marketing, and a fund-raising or philanthropy development officer (DiMaggio, 1987). A growing set of technology specialists constitutes a third category of arts-related occupation, ranging from website developers and social media marketers to videographers and chief information officers. A fourth occupational cluster includes those engaged in instrumental and applied work, like arts educators and art therapists. A fifth category of arts-related occupations involves cultural intermediaries such as editors, critics, curators, agents, and gallerists. Finally, infrastructural occupations include, among others, policy advocates, staff members of professional associations, public administrators of cultural and heritage agencies, philanthropic cultural program officers, and makers of musical instruments and other relevant tools and supplies (CCS, 2009, 2010, 2011). The last five categories, arts-related occupations, have been less well-researched than artistic occupations. Some occupations exhibit more of the conventional characteristics of professionalism and tend to practice within highly institutionalized organizational fields. Paradoxically, workers in some of these arts-related occupations may be more likely to be perceived as more professional than artists themselves.

As a result of their ambiguous and contingent status, creative and performing artists, as well as some of those in other types of arts-related occupations, struggle with financial precarity in a labor market in which their knowledge, technique, skill, education, experience, practice, and commitment are insufficient to enable them to earn even a living wage, much less professional level compensation. Exploring the incongruities between the social and economic status of visual artists and their actual attainments, Jeffri and Throsby (1994) concluded that, although they possessed major hallmarks of professional standing, there is "still a lack of recognition by society at large of their social and cultural role, and an unwillingness to accord them the sort of respect as professionals that is shown to other professional groups" (p. 108). Thus, it is not unusual for artists and other types of arts-related workers to improvise a protean patchwork of freelance gigs, temporary projects, and/or hybrid economic, artistic, and/or occupational portfolios in lieu of full-time jobs, stable incomes, and predictable career progressions. As pertains to our concerns, the need for, the definition of, and challenges attendant to professionalization vary widely among creative sector occupational types and by conditions within the economic subsectors of practice. Thus, different levels of professionalization have been experienced by the core artistic occupations, as well as by other arts-related administrative, technical, cultural intermediary, infrastructural, and applied occupations. Figure 2.2 provides an overview of our analytical framework that combines the composition of the creative sector, the wide range of occupations within the creative sector, and the multiple processes of professionalization.

Indicators of Professionalization

Professionalism is the outcome of the processes by which an occupation acquires a set of characteristics (or indicators) that mark and legitimate it as a profession. Since the 1950s, scholars have been defining what traits indicate the professionalization of an occupation (DiMaggio, 1991; Greenwood,

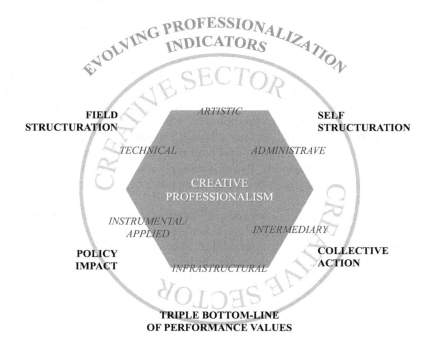

Figure 2.2 Analytical Framework: Processes of Professionalization Depicting on Occupations of the Creative Sector

1957; Hall, 1968; Jeffri & Throsby, 1994, 2006; Wilensky, 1964; Wyszomir-ski, 2006). Table 2.1 lists five conventional indicators of professionalization. The first is a specialized and credentialed university education (DiMaggio, 1991Greenwood, 1957; Jeffri & Throsby, 1994, 2006; Wilensky, 1964), which entails the transmission of a specialized body of knowledge and techniques of practice. Such knowledge and competencies are often formally acknowledged by legal instruments such as licenses, degrees, or certification. Professional credibility and authority were conferred by this specialized education. Typically, professionals thus anointed enjoy high social and economic status, and significant autonomy in practice. While specialized and credentialed higher education is a key indicator of professionalization, it lies outside the focus of this volume.

A second marker of a profession is that it provides full-time paid work sufficient to earn a living commensurate with the high level of education and training of its practitioners. This is at the top of Wilensky's list (1964), adopted by Hall (1968), implied by DiMaggio's (1991) acceptance of Wilensky, and included by Jeffri and Throsby (1994). This is perhaps the indicator that most starkly distinguishes conventional professionalism from the financial precarity that all too often characterizes atypical professionalism as seen in the creative sector.

Table 2.1 Indicators of Professionalization

Conventional Professionalization	Indicator		Effects of Field Structuration
Specialized and credentialed higher education	Education		
Full-time, stable, paid work with developed career paths	Income and work expectations		
Established network of mature professional associations	Professional associations		Increased density of inter-organizational contacts
Structures for public validation and protection	Public value		Increased flow information
Institutionalization of organizational field structures	Field structuration		Emergence of a center/periphery structure
			Generation of a collective definition of a given public
			Development of a triple bottom-line of public performance values

The third conventional marker is an established network of mature professional associations that arise from collective action by members of a given occupation (DiMaggio, 1991a; Greenwood, 1957; Hall, 1968; Jeffri & Throsby, 1994, 2006; Larson, 1977; Wilensky, 1964) for the purpose of advancing their common interests and cultivating a shared sense of calling and values. Professional values generally include a commitment to public service, a desire for autonomy, and a belief that self-regulation of professional practice is preferable to government regulation. This last is accompanied by an equally strong belief that the government should protect the profession's economic and authoritative exclusivity. According to Wilensky (1964), a key indicator of the professionalization of an occupation was that it sought some form of public protection or validation through "persistent political agitation in order to win the support of law for the protection of job territory and its sustaining code of ethics" (Wilensky, 1964, p. 145).

A growing number of professional associations serving the creative sector have organized themselves as platforms for professional self-governance through socialization instilled via professional norms and peer evaluation, and sometimes through the development of formal codes of conduct or ethics. Only a few creative occupations exhibit legally sanctioned protections for exclusive authority over their economic territory. However, a commitment to artistic and creative freedom is a broadly shared value of many creative occupations, especially since this value has, in the United States, a strong claim to the constitutionally based freedom of expression.

A fourth marker of occupational professionalism concerns a general quest for public validation and recognition and is key to legitimizing emergent professions (Jackson et al., 2006). Discussions of public validation often imply two different meanings. The first regards public validation as a concern for the role of the state in initiating, sanctioning, funding, and administering new and established professions. These forms of government action are often seen as regulatory and vary from one country to another. Differences arise depending on the chronology of professionalization and the role of the state in these processes as they are rooted in a country's history and institutional frameworks (Neal & Morgan, 2000). Public validation can also come from respected civic institutions, such as private foundations and community-based nonprofit organizations. Alternatively, many of the ways in which an emergent profession might seek recognition fall under the purview of its professional associations, such as acknowledging and enforcing licensing, developing certification and educational credentials, advocating for public funding for professional services in the public interest, and promoting legislation to protect the interests of professions and professional organizations in general.

In some countries such as the United States, the United Kingdom, Australia, and even South Korea, public validation for the creative sector has taken the form of arm's length funding from federal, state, and local government entities. This public funding has not only supported the production, distribution, and preservation of nonprofit arts and cultural activity but also broadened and deepened public access to and engagement with the arts. Thus, public validation, which entails the perceptions and expectations of the general public, is also shaped by financial support from government and private organizations, as well as by art criticism, media coverage, and awards and prizes (Jackson et al., 2003). As the economist, James F. English (2005) observed, the prestige of "prizes have always been of fundamental importance to the institutional machinery of cultural legitimacy and authority" (p. 37) and are now "perhaps indispensable to the institutional apparatus of cultural credentialing" (p. 41). In the United States and other advanced democracies, public validation is commonly accorded by a combination of government grants and awards; civic institution funding and recognition; policy, program, and/ or organizational evaluation; professional association activities; and audience valuation. This composite is now generally referred to as public value.

As seen in Table 2.1, we broadened the conventional list of indicators to include organizational field structuration or institutionalization, which is widely seen as inextricably intertwined with professionalization (DiMaggio, 1991; Peterson, 1986). Field structuration has dual meanings as a noun and as a verb. As a noun, field structuration serves as an indicator of professionalization in a field of "those organizations that, in the aggregate, constitute a recognized area of institutional life: key suppliers, resource and product consumers, regulatory agencies, and other organizations that produce similar services or products" and which constitute "the totality of relevant actors" (DiMaggio & Powell, 1991, p. 64). As noted in Figure 1.1 (in Chapter 1), other actors in this "totality" appear in the outer ring of the infrastructure of the creative sector, along with intermediaries between producers, distributors, consumers, collectors, and other actors within or across industries. In the creative sector, these institutionally defined clusters of similar types of organizations are variously referred to as "fields" (e.g., museums, concert dance companies, live theater, performing arts centers, or symphony orchestras) or as cultural industries (such as film, architecture, and fashion design). Each of the many fields or industries of the creative sector also acts as the primary employer of specialized professionals working in creative occupations. As DiMaggio and Powell (1991) note, "fields only exist to the extent that they are institutionally defined" (1991, p. 65). As such, the existence of a field is virtually a precondition to developing other indicators of professionalization. DiMaggio and Powell named this process of institutional definition "structuration." One might see the concept of the creative sector illustrated in Figure 1.1 as depicting the linkages and interactions between and among individual creative industries as well as the sectoral infrastructure, as a form of sectoral structuration. The exact composition of the creative sector will vary from one local situation to another (Wyszomirski, 2008). It is this process that is covered by the active sense of "field structuration," which refers to the dynamics of developing, adapting, and perhaps reshaping a field that will be further discussed in the next section on processes of professionalization.

Table 2.2 provides a summary comparison of how key indicators of professionalization tend to be displayed in conventional professions in contrast to how they manifest in atypical creative professions.

Table 2.2 Comparison of Professionalization Indicators: Conventional and Atypical

Conventional Indicators of Professionalization	Indicator	Atypical Indicators of Creative Professionalization
Specialized and credentialed higher education	Education	Occupationally specialized and increasingly credentialed higher education, but weak sense of sectoral cohesiveness and with need for entrepreneurial and digital skills
Full-time, stable, paid work with developed career paths	Income and work expectations	High degree of self-structuration as individuals manage artistic, financial, and career risks of protean work portfolios
Structures for public validation and protection	Public value	Emergent base of public value recognition subject to political threats
Established network of mature professional associations	Professional associations	Fragmented and relatively recent network of professional associations
Extensive organizational field institutionalization	Field structuration	Relatively recent, extensive organizational field structuration with strong element of self-structuration and recent emergence of triple bottom line performance markers

Figure 2.2 provides an expanded and comparative illustration of how the five indicators of professionalization manifest in conventional and atypical occupations in the arts. Since the mid-twentieth century, each of the conventional indicators has experienced progress toward greater professionalization, although this varies from one creative occupation to the next. Specialized and credentialed education has, perhaps, advanced the most but remains a work in progress, particularly as it adapts to changes that call for greater entrepreneurial and technical skills. Another subject only recently entering the curriculum is an understanding and awareness of the creative sector concept and how it could impact sectoral cohesiveness and opportunities. Progress on other indicators of professionalization, including professional associations, public value and validation, and field structuration, has all moved toward greater professionalization, but these are relatively recent cumulative developments.

Processes of Professionalization

For occupations of the creative sector, professionalization has been driven by six processes: (1) The strengthening and adaptation of conventional indicators of professionalization; (2) the development of field structuration and institutionalization; (3) the evolution of a triple bottom line (TBL) of performance values; (4) the impacts of public policy; (5) the undertaking of collective action efforts; and (6) significant individual investments in self-structuration. Figure 2.3 illustrates these six processes. Other chapters in this volume explore, through historical perspective and/or case studies, how the processes and indicators of professionalization have both influenced professionalism in the creative sector and responded to changing circumstances of working in the creative sector.

We start the discussion of processes of professionalization by considering the multiple activities that promote field structuration. This process essentially functions as an intervening variable that facilitates the acquisition of other indicators of professionalization and interacts with other professionalization processes. Through examining the case of museums, DiMaggio (1991) identified four effects that characterize field structuration in action:

1. An increase in the density of inter-organizational contacts;
2. An increase in the flow of information (among organizations in the field);
3. The emergence of a center-periphery structure (a distinction between leading and other organizations in the field);
4. The generation of a collective definition of a given field (of similar organizations).

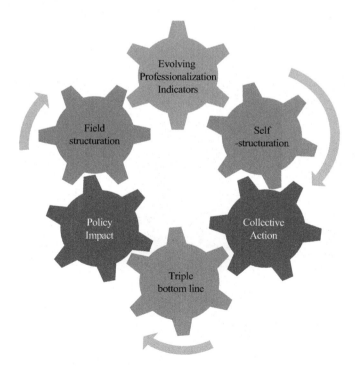

Figure 2.3 Six Processes of Professionalization

We add a fifth effect of field structuration that is displayed in the creative sector and that concerns the evolution of a set of performance values that have diffused and come to be widely accepted among organizational actors of the creative sector. This structure involved the construction of a triple bottom line (TBL) of performance values: artistic vitality, financial sustainability, and recognized public value (Wyszomirski, 2013).

Originally the TBL concept was developed with regard to the legitimation of cultural policy regarding public funding of the nonprofit arts (See Figure 2.4). The performance values evolved through the interaction of NEA efforts to politically justify arts funding; arts advocacy arguments advanced by arts service organizations regarding both the systemic needs and the public benefits of the arts, and efforts of nonprofit arts organizations to demonstrate their accountability to public and private funders. Evidence of each of these three values, presented in variable states of balance, helps to legitimate the societal value accorded to organizations and individuals operating within the sector and the products and services provided by the sector. The spread of these TBL values was facilitated by other processes of professionalization, particularly the impact of policy and collective action via professional associations. As such, the TBL can be considered another effect of field structuration. Furthermore, the TBL acts as a link between all five processes

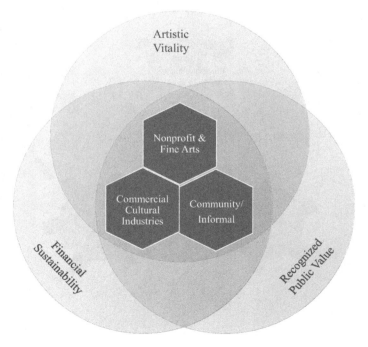

Figure 2.4 Triple Bottom Line of Performance Values for Creative Professionalism

of professionalization. As an effect of field structuration, TBL reflects the process of policy impact, has been disseminated via the collective action of professional associations, has become a value structure of public validation, and has helped to motivate self-structuration choices.

The overarching imperative that both individual workers and structuring institutions face is the need to establish and maintain a TBL. For artists who are self-structuring protean careers, meeting the TBL drives their endeavors. They seek to support themselves financially and to be recognized for their talent and contributions to society. For the institutions charged with shaping the creative sector landscape, the TBL defines the scope and raison d'etre of their missions. The TBL plays out differently in different subsectors. For instance, in the commercial creative industries, financial sustainability is the primary driver and both artistic vitality and public recognition are measured largely by earnings. However, they have faced challenges concerning their artistic standing as well as criticism over content deemed socially or morally offensive. In contrast, for the nonprofit arts, artistic vitality is the essential fulcrum around which financial sustainability and recognized public value strike a flexible balance. Community arts organizations, in turn, tend to emphasize public value by demonstrating diversity and participatory engagement, but struggle to surmount perceptions of amateurism or narrow cultural specificity. They pursue financial sustainability through bricolage, volunteerism, and entrepreneurship while relying less on earnings and grant support. Thus, specific organizations, creative occupations, and sub-sectors of creative practice have the flexibility to determine a balance that is feasible for each, rather than aim for a single, common balance point applicable for all.

The challenge of balancing a TBL also points to three significant deficiencies that professionalization in the arts has confronted. Both the financial bottom line and the recognized public value bottom line have necessitated atypical professionalization strategies. First, securing an adequate professional income has called on creative sector workers to take a larger role in self-structuring their occupations than is the case for more typical and organizationally structured professions. Second, given this financial precariousness, creative workers have often lacked the resources with which to organize and mobilize their collective professional support structures. Instead, the resources and motivation to do so have relied, in large part, on assistance from government and foundation grants that have helped support advocacy and other services offered by professional associations. Finally, the persistence of the romantic image of the artist required a long effort to reframe their image as a socio-economic asset. An unintended consequence of the "arts for art's sake" ethos seems to have required repeated efforts to demonstrate that creative workers (and the creative sector as a whole) could both provide intrinsic public benefits and make unique instrumental contributions to the public good. Thus, despite different TBL balance points among the three creative sub-sectors, professionalism describes the resultant state of an occupation that has acquired social legitimacy through the development and interaction of the indicators and processes of professionalization. Since professional status is a composite, it can experience uneven development among its components and is a dynamic construct subject to changing social, economic, cultural, and political conditions. It is this status of professionalism (or the lack of it) that plays a key role in demonstrating the value of creative workers to society's other social, economic, cultural, and political institutions. This chapter now turns to the examination of the efforts of individual creative workers, in pursuit of protean careers in the arts, to combine a variety of strategies, tactics, and building blocks to address inherent challenges and gaps in their professional structure with self-structuration efforts. These self-structuration efforts complement other conventional processes of professionalization to adapt professional indicators to shape a uniquely atypical creative professionalism.

Atypical Professionalism and Self-Structuration

Although professionalism in the creative sector shares many features with professionalism in other more established occupations, it also differs in significant ways. Indeed, "[a]rtists are an enigma: they challenge many of the accepted notions of what it means to be members of a professional group in this society" (Dubin, 1987, p. 25). Today, as a result of intensifying efforts to professionalize over the past eight decades, professionalism in the creative occupations is now a blend of five conventional processes plus a sixth highly customizable and atypical process of self-structuration. Beyond adaptations that accommodated particular social, economic, political, and work conditions, perhaps the most unique element of creative professionalism is the significant role self-structuration has come to play. This last feature, self-structuration, has been necessitated, in part, by the character of the creative sector labor market and by the nascent nature of the first five common processes of professionalization.

Professionalization is varied and uneven across the diverse and varied occupations that make up the creative sector, with each occupation having its own history of development. As Kooyman (2015) has observed: "It is difficult to analyze the sector as a homogenous group due to the fact that the Creative Industries—and within the individual sectors—there exists considerable diversity of occupational status" (p. 19). A major point to bear in mind is that forces of professionalization, entailing public and private income sources, support structures for arts entrepreneurship, expanded collective action structures, and a more recognized sense of the public value of the arts and of artists, have improved societal status for many creative workers. Yet, while accompanying improvements in income opportunities have developed, sufficient financial rewards continue to elude many in the creative sector. Instead, this circumstance remains evident despite the fact that many workers have extensive and specialized training in their fields as well as a commitment to lifelong learning. Recently, it has also become increasingly clear that not all creative workers have enjoyed the benefits of these improvements, particularly those marginalized by race, ethnicity, gender identity, sexual orientation, disability, religion, and other social identities.

The inadequacy or recent vintage of a full set of institutional support structures that elsewhere benefit conventional professions means that many artists and some arts-related workers face a situation in which few have single, full-time, stable jobs. Artists and other cultural workers have also faced the tacit expectation that they will be willing to trade economic wages for emotional and psychic satisfaction (Hesmondhalgh & Baker, 2010) and cultural capital (Bourdieu, 1986). Most artists work a succession of multiple, part-time jobs and/or take on temporary project work with a consequently low or unstable income. Many artists have to supplement their artistic income through "moonlighting" in non-arts job (Alper & Wassall, 2000). Historically, the indeterminate professional status of artists and creative workers may have limited their ability to contribute to the public good. However, by the 1990s, individual artists became more proactive in creating social value and pursuing public service as social change activists. It has become increasingly common for artists to position themselves as environmental proponents, champions of racial and cultural diversity and equity, and community organizers. Some undertake public arts commissions and programs for creative placemaking in urban planning (Markusen & Gadwa, 2010; Wyszomirski, 2017).

Furthermore, globalization and the rise of digital technology seem to have worsened the precarious situation of creative workers. Their precarity is further exacerbated by traditional beliefs about the nature of artists that intersect with the forces of globalization and the concomitant rise of the gig economy, tightening economic pressures, and the growing impulse of artists to engage in social justice activism. Yet, while the rise of digital technology has posed significant challenges, it has also presented unprecedented opportunities, such as unprecedented access to creation tools and the push to develop new skills and modes of creation and production. Researchers (e.g., Banks, 2007; Hesmondhalgh & Baker, 2010; McRobbie, 2007; Ross, 2004) have analyzed the experience of artists in the globally shifting political economies of culture, attending especially to the potential for exploitation of creative workers in the increasingly global gig economy. Since the 1990s, the conditions of cultural workers' "artistic (and informational) labor . . . have seen increasing casualization and short-term contract working" (Hesmondhalgh & Baker, 2010). Over this same period, digital production tools have become increasingly available and powerful. These developments have given rise to a new type of worker, the digital nomad (MBO Partners, 2020; Nash et al., 2018), while facilitating both a mobile labor force for industry and the potential for individual artists to reach broader audiences.

Still, for the workers in these gigs who tend to be younger, "work is irregular, contracts are shorter-term, and there is little job protection; career prospects are uncertain; [and] earnings are very unequal" (Hesmondhalgh & Baker, 2010, p. 34). Research has found that, in this environment, individual creative workers have learned to act as the entrepreneurs of their own careers (Beckman & Essig, 2012; Bridgstock, 2005; Chang, 2012; DeVos & Soens, 2008; Gold & Fraser, 2002; Wyszomirski & Chang, 2017). Professional development training, experiential learning, and, most recently, formal education have enabled individual creative workers to build sustainable, self-structuring portfolios that mix varied income streams, sectors of employment, artistic identities, and live-work demands. Such flexibility affords them both a sense of agency and relative creative freedom in structuring their career trajectory even as young artists are exposed to increased, and increasingly normalized, levels of financial precarity and life uncertainty (McRobbie, 2007; Wyszomirski & Chang, 2017).

A Protean Array of Self-Structuration Choices

Since the mid-twentieth century, conventional indicators of professionalization in the arts have strengthened and the effectiveness of field structuration has progressed, doing much to restructure the sector and make it more amenable to professionalization. Nevertheless, creative professionals, especially those most invested in their artistic occupations and identities, continue to face basic challenges in successfully building careers that are both creatively satisfying and financially sufficient. Cultural workers in a variety of artistic and arts-related occupations have come to approach self-structuration with a focus on "employability rather than job security" (Bridgstock, 2005, p. 41), seeking to meet this challenge with work and career patterns that encompass a changing mosaic of work in the arts (across the commercial, nonprofit, and community sub-sectors), non-arts employment, unemployment, and volunteer or unpaid work. While the particular patterns may differ from one artform or genre to another, as well as by the organizational and market features of each artworld (Ball et al., 2010; Becker, 1982; Menger, 1999), they are all driven by the same underlying social and market forces. These strategies, within the creative sector (and elsewhere), have been called protean careers. In the creative sector, it has also variously been referred to as cultural entrepreneurship (Ellmeier, 2003), career self-management (Essig, 2017), and portfolio careers (Gold & Fraser, 2002). The protean career concept intersects with the notion of an open range of career forms within and across organizations and fields that is termed the "boundaryless career" (Bridgstock, 2005; Greenhouse & Callanan, 2006; Tams & Arthur, 2010).

The concept of a protean career emphasizes the agency of the creative worker in the personal construction of his or her career (Ball et al., 2010; Bridgstock, 2005, 2012; Hall, 2004). Those pursuing protean careers are typically highly motivated, have a strong personal identification with their career, and approach it with a proactive attitude (Hall & Moss, 1998;

Wyszomirski & Chang, 2017). Cultural workers who adopt portfolio building strategies out of economic necessity (Alper & Wassall, 2000, p. 7) may
also be motivated by a wider range of perceived benefits, such as personal
self-fulfillment, a better balance between life and work, and creative autonomy, rather than externally determined career norms and financial security
(Briscoe & Hall, 2006; Greenhouse & Callanan, 2006). Research has found
that 79% of artists in a national survey engaged in self-employment because
they preferred not to work for someone else, and 58% found the flexible
schedules and independence attractive (NEA, 2019). Other researchers found
that, in spite of the challenges of self-structuring a sustainable profession,
many workers pursuing protean careers evinced high levels of satisfaction
and confidence in the value of their work (De Vos & Soens, 2008).

Furthermore, the possibilities for pursuing a protean career-building process had improved and broadened by the start of the millennium. The organizational institutionalization of various art fields has provided a larger, more
diverse, and widespread set of employing structures for creative workers in
many kinds of arts and arts-related occupations. Between 1980 and 2009,
investments from arts philanthropy and public funding for the arts helped to
support the dispersion of artists from historical cultural hubs and mega-arts
cities. Attracted by "affordability, amenities, space, and markets" and facilitated by new technologies and transportation systems that enabled distance
work, artists were enabled to practice their creative work and forge art-based
careers everywhere (Markusen, 2013, p. 490), including mid-size cities, small
towns, and rural communities. Similarly, as the number and geographic distribution of nonprofit arts organizations and their audiences expanded, the
opportunities for other arts-related occupations to thrive have also expanded.
Thus, the building blocks of self-structuring atypical creative portfolios have
become readily available in more communities across the country than they
were 50 years ago.

The core activities of an artist pursuing a protean career are professional
self-management and self-structuration, in which entrepreneurship and
business savvy enable creative work and talent (Essig, 2017; Wyszomirski & Chang, 2017). Creating a successful protean (or portfolio) career also
requires business skills that may be acquired in the academic realm, through
professional development, or learning on the job. Technical skills, as well as
teaching and management skills, and general competencies such as problem
solving, teamwork, critical thinking, and creative or innovative thinking are
also key to artistic success (e.g., Lena et al., 2014). The successful creative
entrepreneur is also likely to be a bricoleur (Chang, 2012, see also Chapter 5,
on Dual Professionalism, in this volume).

The process of shaping a protean career in the arts is likely to include
not only multiple jobs but also earnings from multiple economic sectors,
assembling various types of portfolios, creating across genres and mediums,
and accumulating the knowledge and experience of multiple occupations
and even pursuing multiple professions. There is now sufficient research

literature from many countries to allow us to distinguish a range of portfolio strategies and tactics that creative workers have developed to support themselves as they seek to further their art-making, reach audiences, and secure public validation. Three types of portfolios have frequently been discussed under the umbrella of a protean career consisting of a portfolio of jobs, a portfolio of hybrid artistic practices, and a portfolio of hybrid revenue sources. Individual creative workers may even combine and mix elements across these three types of protean careers. In addition, a fourth portfolio strategy—a portfolio of professions—can be assembled from combinations and/or sequences of various arts and arts-related occupations, each of which may be at a different stage of professionalization. All four types of portfolios call upon elements of business, entrepreneurship, and creative self-employment skills. A fifth, and essential, portfolio focuses on artistry and creative content. While alluded to in the hybrid artistic practices portfolio, the artistic component of self-structuration merits more detailed attention. This is the subject of Javier J. Hernandez-Acosta's Chapter 6, which presents a strategic planning process as part of a college curriculum for aspiring artists that is designed to structure a Creative Professional Action Plan. Thus, this chapter's discussion of self-structuration should be read in tandem with Chapter 6 as encompassing a full range of choices involved in this element of creative professionalism.

The Choice Matrix for Atypically Structured Creative Professions presented in Figure 2.5 provides a visual integration of many of the kinds of choices that are involved in pursuing and sustaining creative professionals. Many of these choices are not made just once, but are revisited and remixed across a creative career. Education, training, and professional development are recurrent choices that are part of a lifelong learning ethos. Formal education and training for artists have focused almost exclusively on artistic skills, knowledge, and technique, and are increasingly offered at higher education institutions. By the late twentieth century, courses in entrepreneurship began to appear in university curricula. In addition, technical skills, especially digital, computer-based, and Internet, have become ubiquitous and often self-taught.

A portfolio of jobs describes a work-life model in which multiple short-term gigs, freelance projects, moonlighting in the arts, and arts organization staff work might coincide or alternate with day jobs outside the arts, professional jobs in unrelated fields, or long-term gigs from grants or foundation support. This pattern, which takes the place of a full-time and stable job with a single employer (Wyszomirski & Chang, 2017) and is largely the rule for arts workers, has become an increasingly common practice among millennials in general. Artists often juggle this constellation of skills, networks, and income streams to create a viable and sustainable portfolio of jobs—a work-life pattern that is particularly common among artists compared to other professional or technical workers (Galligan & Alper, 2000, p. 190).

Artistic & Cultural Workers

Career Preparation

Artistic & Cultural Training/Skills Development	Tech Skills & Training	Entrepreneurial Training/Skills Development

Portfolio Building Blocks

Occupational Components Examples	Revenue Sources Examples	Economic Sector of Employment Examples
Artists—originator or performer	Sales of Artworks & Art Services	Non-Profit Arts
Arts Administrator	Royalties	Commercial Arts & Entertainment
Arts Teacher	Government Arts Grants & Commissions	Freelance Artistic Projects (any sector)
Arts Intermediary	Foundation Grants; Private Prizes & Awards	Private Self-employed
Arts Employment in Non-arts Settings	Licensing Fees	Community Arts

Life-work Balance Considerations

E.g., Further Advanced Study, Learn by Doing Experience, Spousal/Family Support, Family Care Responsibilities (such as having children, care of parents), Health Care Benefits, Pension Plans, etc.

Capacity for Portfolio Self Management

Protean Assemblage of Types of Portfolios

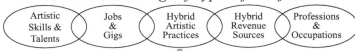

Artistic Skills & Talents — Jobs & Gigs — Hybrid Artistic Practices — Hybrid Revenue Sources — Professions & Occupations

Professional Support Structures

Atypically Structured Creative Professions

Figure 2.5 Choice Matrix for Atypically Structured Creative Professions

Another strategy artists have used to assemble portfolio careers entails interweaving hybrid economic practices across sectors or artistically multi-disciplinary practices (Galligan & Alper, 2000). This has grown out of, and in part because of, the blurring of boundaries both within and across arts fields. As artists have increasingly learned how to craft portfolio careers, they have also built beyond the portfolio of jobs model to expand their self-management abilities to develop a variety of interwoven, hybrid "crossover" practices both economically and artistically (Galligan & Alper, 2000; Markusen et al., 2006). Galligan and Alper have called for a shift in perspective from comparing artists to the general workforce to recognizing a "more dynamic relationship among the economic classifications of artists in various sectors of the workforce," as proposed by the American Assembly (Galligan & Alper, 2000, p. 156; see also American Assembly, 1997). Additional possible building blocks could include working with community arts groups (primarily for opportunities to broaden a repertoire or experiment with a new style or genre) or playing a part in community economic development or social benefit provision. Indeed, research has demonstrated that "when artists' work is seen and understood as contributions to the community, the public is more likely to be supportive of funding their work with tax dollars" and to develop a greater understanding of the public value of the arts (Novak-Leonard & Skaggs, 2021, p. 422).

As the portfolio of hybrid artistic practices illustrates, the phenomenon of artists working in multiple disciplines and/or with multidisciplinary collaborators has given rise to dynamic artistic hybrid practices. Multidisciplinary artists bring together a portfolio of artistic skills and talents that can be drawn from any of the creative industries commonly studied (Cherbo et al., 2008; DCMS, 1998, 2001; Mt. Auburn Associates, 2005). Markusen et al. (2006) reported that "an extraordinary 60% of responding artists in their study worked in more than one artform . . . [and that] interdisciplinary artists appear to enjoy greater opportunities to cross among sectors" than artists dedicated to a single discipline (p. 40). The 2016 study, *Creativity Connects*, notes that "an increasing number of artists are working in hybrid ways that defy discipline classifications" (CCINEA, 2016). It also reported that not only were more artists working in multi-disciplinary teams but also individually were "becoming proficient in multiple disciplines simultaneously . . . and bringing all that expertise together in a given work or series of projects" (p. 9).

Artists and creative workers are able to leverage the creativity, outside-the-box thinking, and orientation toward bricolage (Chang, 2012) that they bring to their creative work to the task of constructing sustainable, atypical professional careers through hybrid economic practices. "The workplace reality of most performing artists . . . involves freelance activity as well as employment in commercial and not-for-profit sectors" (Galligan & Alper, 2000, p. 176). Artists are effectively small business people who seek to leverage the resources available to them and their self-motivated creative activity to enhance their professional and reputational development while building financial sustainability (see NEA, 2008 for trends in 11 key artistic occupations). While few pursue all these practices at once, over the course of their careers, these hybrid economic practices have opened many opportunities for artists (Markusen et al., 2006).

For example, playwrights report assembling a self-structured work–life mix in which only 29.6% of their earnings are derived from dramatic writing. Additional related income is derived from the theatrical production of their plays (15%), script writing for television (9%), and writing for film (5.6%) (London et al., 2009). An additional 22% of their income comes from teaching and the remainder is non-arts-related earnings. Thus, their primary occupation, dramatic writing across three mediums, accounts for roughly 60% of their income. In addition, informal or community arts activities, though they rarely yield much income, do present opportunities for professional development and for generating social and cultural capital (Markusen et al., 2006).

A portfolio of professions describes a work-life model in which a creative worker pursues multiple professional roles (Wyszomirski, 2006; Wyszomirski & Chang, 2017). This third type of protean practice can allow artists to become "the producers of their own creative works" and thus to "function as multi-disciplinary professionals bridging the sectors of art, business, technology, policy, and education" (Bonin-Rodriguez, 2015, p. 3). For example, music professionals are likely to pursue protean careers by combining tactics from all five types of portfolios (Thomson, 2013). A musician might assemble a portfolio of professions that includes giving private lessons (self-employed) or teaching college classes (if they have the necessary academic background); sound engineering for live performances or in the recording studio (whether part-time or regularly); management of a music ensemble or a professional organization; and administrative roles such as concert organizer, venue manager, band manager, community center director, or booking agent. Similarly, dance professionals also display self-structured practices— often mixing working as a performing artist with being a choreographer, dance teacher, and/or company artistic director/manager (Bennett, 2008).

Thus, the overarching identity of such a music or dance professional is situated within their fields of music or dance but not limited to a particular job or set of jobs or a single professional identity. Rather, it crosses various functional, organizational, and economic contexts in the creative sector as they self-structure a personalized work-life balance. These varied roles, which comprise a portfolio of professions, certainly entail hybrid economic tactics and often open the door to hybrid, cross-genre artistic practices. Bonin-Rodriguez (2015) attributes cultural policy in the post-cultural war period as having "redefined U.S. artists' practices" as hybridization in a way "that aligns creative concerns with the organizational [management] demands as two aspects of one process" (p. 143).

Concluding Thoughts

Professionalism in the creative sector remains atypical and varies from one occupation to another. But indicators and processes of professionalization have progressed in ways that have strengthened the sector's professionalism while accommodating the values of artistic freedom and creativity. The institutionalization of many artistic fields and the power of the concept of a creative sector have expanded and diversified the employment opportunities available to creative workers and thus improved their earning capacity and their ability to make a living from their chosen occupation. Relatedly, financial and symbolic support from government arts agencies and from private foundations has awarded direct support to artists, fueled field structuration, and supported a growing network of professional associations and service providers. Government (and foundation) validation has conferred respect and recognition for the professionalism of workers in arts and arts-related occupations. Similarly, government and foundation actions have also fostered a general awareness of the public value of the arts and creative professionals.

Beyond strengthening the conventional indicators of professionalization, most of the institutional actors mentioned earlier have also collaborated with one another and with creative workers themselves to construct an additional, and atypical, process of professionalization—self-structuration. Given the range of these building blocks, creative workers are likely to thrive if they can cultivate—through education, experience, training, and/or networking—a capacity to be the entrepreneurs of their own careers. These self-structuration efforts act in addition to whatever occupational support structures underpin specific arts and art-related occupations as well as the entire creative sector.

As creative workers have become more adept at managing the versatility and risks that sustainable careers in the creative sector require, they have developed new ways of establishing and asserting creative professional identities that are hospitable to both specialization and multiplicity: from a professional jazz pianist to a multi-genre music professional and teacher; from a free-lance visual artist to an entrepreneurial arts market professional; from a ballet dancer to a performing arts and movement professional. Atypical creative professionalism has come to represent not conformity to a standardized model but recombinant adaptability that may not make creative careers easy but does make them more possible and legitimate.

References

Alper, N., & Wassall, G. H. (2000). *More than once in a blue moon: Multiple job holdings by American artists* (NEA Research Division Report No. 40). NEA, Seven Locks Press.

American Assembly. (1997, May 29–June 1). *The arts and the public purpose: The ninety-second American Assembly.* Arden House, Harriman, Assembly, Columbia University Press.

Americans for the Arts. (2021). *Artists in the U.S. workforce 2006–2020.* National Arts Administration and Policy Publications Database (NAAPPD). www.ameri cansforthearts.org/by-program/reports-and-data/legislation-policy/naappd/artists-in-the-us-workforce-2006-2020

Ball, L., Pollard, E., & Stanley, N. (2010). *Creative graduates creative futures.* CGCF Higher Education.

Banks, M. (2007). *The politics of cultural work*. Springer.

Becker, H. S. (1982). *Art worlds*. University of California Press.

Beckman, G., & Essig, L. (2012). Arts entrepreneurship: A conversation. *Artivate: A Journal of Arts Entrepreneurship*, *1*(1), 1–8.

Bennett, D. (2008). Dancer or dance artist: Dance careers and identity. *The International Journal of the Arts in Society: Annual Review*, *3*(3), 73–78.

Bonin-Rodriguez, P. (2015). *Performing policy: How contemporary politics and cultural programs redefined U.S. artists for the twenty-first century*. Palgrave Macmillan.

Bourdieu, P. (1986). The forms of capital. In J. Richardson (Ed.), *Handbook of theory and research for the sociology of education* (pp. 241–258). Greenwood.

Bridgstock, R. (2005). Australian artists, starving and well-nourished: What can we learn from the prototypical protean career? *Australian Journal of Career Development*, *14*(1), 40–47.

Bridgstock, R. (2012). Not a dirty word: Arts entrepreneurship and higher education. *Arts & Humanities in Higher Education*, *12*(2–3), 122–137.

Briscoe, J. P., & Hall, D. T. (2006). The interplay of boundaryless and protean careers: Combinations and implications. *Journal of Vocational Behavior*, *69*(1), 4–18.

CCINEA (Center for Cultural Innovation for the National Endowment for the Arts). (2016). *Creativity connects: Trends and conditions affecting U.S. artists*. https://www.arts.gove/sites/default/files/Creativity-Connects-Final-Report.pdf

CCS (Creative & Cultural Skills). (2009). *The visual arts blueprint: An analysis of the skill needs of the visual arts sector in the UK*. The National Academy of Skills, Creative & Cultural Skills.

CCS (Creative & Cultural Skills). (2010). *The performing arts blueprint: An analysis of the skill needs of the performing arts sector in the UK*. The National Academy of Skills, Creative & Cultural Skills.

CCS (Creative & Cultural Skills). (2011). *The music blueprint: An analysis of the skill needs of the music sector in the UK*. The National Academy of Skills, Creative & Cultural Skills.

Chang, W. (2012). Bricolage in small arts organizations: An artist's way of entrepreneurship. In G. Hagoort, A. Thomassen, & R. Kooyman (Eds.), *Pioneering minds worldwide: On the entrepreneurial principles of the cultural and creative industries*. Eburon Academic Press.

Cherbo, J. M., Vogel, H., & Wyszomirski, M. J. (2008). Towards an arts and creative sector. In J. M. Cherbo, R. A. Stewatt, & M. J. Wyszomirski (Eds.), *Understanding the arts and creative sector in the United States* (pp. 9–27). Rutgers University Press.

DCMS (Department for Culture, Media and Sport). (1998). *Creative industries mapping documents 1998*. https://www.gov.uk/government/publications/creative-industries-mapping-documents-1998

DCMS (Department for Culture, Media and Sport). (2001). *Creative industries mapping documents 2001*. www.gov.uk/government/publications/creative-industries-mapping-documents-2001

De Vos, S. A., & Soens, N. (2008). Protean attitude and career success: The mediating role of self-management. *Journal of Vocational Behavior*, *73*(3), 449–456.

DiMaggio, P. J. (1987). *Managers of the arts: Careers and opinions of senior administrators of U.S. art museums, symphony orchestras, resident theaters and local arts agencies* (NEA Research Division Report No. 20). Seven Locks Press.

DiMaggio, P. J. (1991). Constructing an organizational field as a professional project: U.S. art museums, 1920–1940. In P. J. DiMaggio & W. W. Powell (Eds.), *The new institutionalism and organizational analysis* (pp. 267–292). University of Chicago Press.

DiMaggio, P. J., & Powell, W. W. (1991). The iron cage revisited: Institutional isomorphism and collective rationality in organizational fields. In P. J. DiMaggio & W. W. Powell (Eds.), *The new institutionalism and organizational analysis* (pp. 63–82). University of Chicago Press.

Dubin, S. C. (1987). *Bureaucratizing the muse: Public funds and the cultural worker.* University of Chicago Press.

Ellmeier, A. (2003). Cultural entrepreneurialism: On the changing relationship between the arts, culture and employment. *International Journal of Cultural Policy, 9*(1), 3–16.

English, J. F. (2005). *The economy of prestige: Prizes, awards, and the circulation of cultural value.* Harvard University Press.

Essig, L. (2017). Same or different? The "cultural entrepreneurship" and "arts entrepreneurship" constructs in European and US higher education. *Cultural Trends, 26*(2), 125–137. https://doi.org/10.1080/09548963.2017.1323842

Florida, R. (2002). *The rise of the creative class, and how it is transforming work, leisure, community, and everyday life.* Basic Books.

Galligan, A., & Alper, N. (2000). The career matrix: The pipeline for artists in the United States. In J. Cherbo & M. J. Wyszomirski (Eds.), *The public life of the arts in America* (pp. 171–201). Rutgers University Press.

Gold, M., & Fraser, J. (2002). Managing self-management: Successful transitions to portfolio careers. *Work, Employment and Society, 16*(4), 579–598.

Greene, M. P. (2015). *Creative mentorship and career-building strategies: How to build your virtual personal board of directors.* Oxford University Press.

Greenhouse, J. H., & Callanan, G. A. (Eds.). (2006). *Encyclopedia of career development.* Sage Publications.

Greenwood, E. (1957). Attributes of a profession. *Social Work, 2*(3), 4–55.

Hall, D. T. (2004). The protean career: A quarter-century journey. *Journal of Vocational Behavior, 65*(1), 1–13.

Hall, D. T., & Moss, J. E. (1998). The new protean career contract: Helping organizations and employees adapt. *Organizational Dynamics, 26*(3), 22–37.

Hall, R. H. (1968). Professionalization and bureaucratization. *American Sociological Review, 33*(1), 92–104.

Hesmondhalgh, D., & Baker, S. (2010). "A very complicated version of freedom": Conditions and experiences of creative labour in three cultural industries. *Poetics, 38*(1), 4–20.

Jackson, M. R., Kabwasa-Green, F., & Herranz, J. (2006). *Cultural vitality in communities: Interpretation and indicators.* The Urban Institute, Culture, Creativity, and Communities Program. http://webarchive.urban.org/UploadedPDF/311392_Cultural_Vitality.pdf

Jackson, M. R., Kabwasa-Green, F., Swenson, D., Herranz, J., Ferryman, K., Atlas, C., Wallner, E., & Rosenstein, C. E. (2003). *Investing in creativity: A study of the support structure for US artists.* Urban Institute. www.urban.org/sites/default/files/alfresco/publication-pdfs/411311-Investing-in-Creativity.pdf

Jeffri, J., & Throsby, D. (1994). Professionalism and the visual artist. *European Journal of Cultural Policy, 1*(1), 99–108.

Jeffri, J., & Throsby, D. (2006). Life after dance: Career transition of professional dancers. *International Journal of Arts Management, 8*(3), 54–63.

Kooyman, R. (2015). Creative entrepreneurs: Cultural arts, "identity, perspectives, and dilemma". *International Journal of Economics, Commerce, and Management, 3*(9), 15–26.

Larson, M. S. (1977). *The rise of professionalism: A sociological analysis.* University of California Press.

Lena, J. C., Gaskill, S., Houghton, R. F., Lambert, A., Miller, A., & Tepper, S. J. (2014). *Making it work: The education and employment of recent art graduates.* Annual Report on the 2013 Strategic National Arts Alumni (SNAAP).

London, T., Pesner, B., & Voss, Z. G. (2009). *Outrageous fortune: The life and times of the New American play.* Theatre Development Fund.

Markusen, A. (2013). Artists work everywhere. *Work and Occupations, 40*(4), 481–495.

Markusen, A., & Gadwa, A. (2010). *Creative placemaking.* NEA. www.arts.gov/sites/default/files/CreativePlacemaking-Paper.pdf

Markusen, A., Gilmore, S., Johnson, A., Levi, T., & Martinez, A. (2006). *Crossover: How artists build careers across commercial, nonprofit, and community work.* Arts Economy Initiative, Project on Regional and Industrial Economics, Humphrey Institute of Public Affairs, University of Minnesota. www.hewlett.org/wp-content/uploads/2016/08/Crossover_HowArtistsBuildCareers

MBO Partners. (2020). *COVID-19 and the rise of the digital nomad.* https://s29814.pcdn.co/wp-content/uploads/2020/10/MBO-Digital-Nomad-Report-2020-Revised.pdf

McRobbie, A. (2007). *The Los Angelisation of London: Three short-waves of young people's micro-economies of culture and creativity in the UK.* https://transversal.at/transversal/0207/mcrobbie/en

Menger, P. (1999). Artistic labor markets and careers. *Annual Review of Sociology, 25,* 541–574.

MKW Wirtschaftsforschung GmbH. (2001). *Exploitation and development of the job potential in the cultural sector in the age of digitalisation.* European Commission.

Mt. Auburn Associates. (2005). *Louisiana: Where culture means business.* Office of the Lt. Governor. www.crt.state.la.us/Assets/OCD/arts/culturedistricts/reports/culturaleconomyreport.pdf

Nash, C., Jarrahi, M. H., Sutherland, W., & Phillips, G. (2018). Digital nomads beyond the buzzword: Defining digital nomadic work and use of digital technologies. In *Transforming digital worlds: 13th international conference, iConference 2018* (pp. 207–217). Springer.

NEA (National Endowment for the Arts). (1996). *Artists in the work force: Employment and earnings, 1970–1990* (Research Division Report No. 37). NEA.

NEA (National Endowment for the Arts). (2008). *Artists in the workforce, 1990–2005* (Research Report No. 48). NEA.

NEA (National Endowment for the Arts). (2019). *Artists and other cultural workers: A statistical portrait.* NEA.

Neal, M., & Morgan, J. (2000). The professionalization of everyone? A comparative study of the development of the professions in the United Kingdom and Germany. *European Sociological Review, 16*(1), 9–20.

Novak-Leonard, J., & Skaggs, R. (2021). American perspectives on public funding for artists. *Journal of Arts Management, Law and Society, 51*(6), 410–425.

PCAH (President's Committee on the Arts and Humanities). (1997). *Creative America: A report to the president by the president's committee on the arts and the humanities*. http://files.eric.ed.gov/fulltext/ED413276.pdf

Peterson, R. A. (1986). From impresario to arts administrator: Formal accountability in nonprofit cultural organizations. In P. J. DiMaggio (Ed.), *Nonprofit enterprise in the arts* (pp. 161–183). Oxford University Press.

Rink, J. S., Gaunt, H., & Williamon, A. (Eds.). (2017). *Musicians in the making: Pathways to creative performance*. Oxford University Press. https://snaaparts.org/findings/reports

Ross, A. (2004). Nice work if you can get it: The mercurial career of creative industries policy. *Work Organisation, Labour and Globalisation, 1*(1), 13–30.

Svensson, L. G. (2015). Occupations and professionalism in art and culture. *Professions & Professionalism, 5*(2), 1–14.

Tams, S., & Arthur, M. B. (2010). New directions for boundaryless careers: Agency and interdependence in a changing world. *Journal of Organizational Behavior, 31*(5), 629–646.

Thomson, K. (2013). Roles, revenue and responsibilities: The changing nature of being a working musician. *Work and Occupations, 40*(4), 514–525.

Wilensky, H. L. (1964). The professionalization of everyone? *American Journal of Sociology, 70*(2),137–158.

Wyszomirski, M. J. (2006). *Professionalization and portfolio careers in the creative sector: A conceptual framework* [Conference paper]. Social Theory, Politics, and the Arts Conference, Vienna, Austria.

Wyszomirski, M. J. (2008). The local creative economy in the United States of America. In H. Anheier & Y. R. Isar (Eds.), *The cultural economy* (pp. 199–212). Sage Publications.

Wyszomirski, M. J. (2013). Shaping a triple-bottom line for nonprofit arts organizations: Micro-, macro-, and meta-policy influences. *Cultural Trends, 22*(3–4), 156–166.

Wyszomirski, M. J. (2017, May 5–6). *Creative placemaking in New Orleans: Entrepreneurial leadership and policy momentum* [Conference paper]. 5th Biennial Pave Symposium for Entrepreneurship in the Arts at Arizona State University.

Wyszomirski, M. J., & Chang, W. J. (2017). Professional self-structuration in the arts: Sustaining creative careers in the 21st century. *Sustainability, 9*(6), 1035.

3 Cultural Policy Tools and Rising Professionalism in American Arts, 1963–1996

Margaret J. Wyszomirski

Introduction

Cultural policy in the United States has influenced many of the key indicators of professionalization in the nonprofit arts sector, particularly through the programs, policies, and procedures of the National Endowment for the Arts (NEA). The NEA's founding executive and legislative creators embedded a concern for enhancing the professionalism of the arts into the agency's mission. For the first 30 years of the agency's operation, the NEA fostered, supported, and supplemented the professional organizational and occupational support infrastructure of the nonprofit arts sector. It played an important role in the societal validation of the significance and social value of creative professionals by designing and relying on an elaborate system of expert review and peer advice that informed both the grantmaking and policymaking processes of the agency and recognized the authority and relative autonomy of creative professionals in setting professional standards and ethics. Through a variety of grant categories that developed in every program division of the NEA, it provided a public definition of who was an artist and channeled a significant amount of financial support to individual creative and performing artists by underwriting creative time, space, and project opportunities. Both directly and indirectly, the NEA facilitated the growth of professional networks, research, and information both about and for arts professionals, and promoted communication within and across fields. All of these activities advanced the professionalization of artists and arts-related occupations.

While the agency continues to be engaged in many of these activities to this day, it could be argued that 1996 marked the end of this wave of professionalization through cultural policy. By the mid-1990s, Congress had prohibited the agency from making most direct grants to individual artists and subtly diluted the professionalism of the peer review system by requiring the appointment of a layperson to each review panel. Since 1996, private foundations have taken a more active role in maintaining professionalism in the arts (Bach, Chapter 4) and self-mobilization efforts among artists and their professional associations. This chapter pays particular attention to how a concern for professionalism was embedded in the NEA's foundational

DOI: 10.4324/9781003138693-4

documents; to the role of cultural policy and NEA activities regarding arts service organizations (ASOs), especially professional associations, and to the purposes, procedures, and mechanisms of NEA grantmaking as forces of professionalization in the nonprofit arts sector.

Professionalism Concern at the Founding of the NEA

An extensive body of literature addresses the complex and long policy formulation process that culminated in the passage of the National Foundation for the Arts and the Humanities in 1965 and thus established the National Endowments for the Arts and the Humanities (Cummings, 1995; Larson, 1983). Relatively unnoticed in this literature is attention to the issue of professionalism. A close examination of two seminal actions were pivotal in articulating how a concern with enhancing professionalism in the arts was a key concern and purpose for the emergent arts funding policy. These were the 1963 release of the Heckscher Report on *The Arts and the National Government* (Heckscher, 1963) and the 1965 passage of the NEA enacting legislation (NFAH Act, 1965). Both these actions displayed an evident concern with professionalism and artistic excellence and with improving professional conditions of artists and arts organizations in America.

In March 1962, President John F. Kennedy announced the appointment of August Heckscher, Director of the Twentieth Century Fund, as the President's Special Consultant on the Arts with an assignment to assemble a report that surveyed the various programs, policies, and objectives of what the federal government was doing that affected the arts. It also gathered information about the needs, programs, and activities of individuals and organizations in the arts, and offered policy recommendations for appropriate federal actions. When the report was presented to President Kennedy in June 1963, he enthused that it would open up "how a new and fruitful relationship between government and the arts" might be advanced (Kennedy, 1963a).

On the very first page of the report, Heckscher emphasized that "the condition of the professional arts in the United States is not in all regards satisfactory" (Heckscher, 1963, p. 1). Throughout the 25-page report, he pointed out instances where professionalism in the arts was inadequate or in need of encouragement to sustain the arts and creativity at a level of excellence that could support "the well-being, the happiness, and the personal fulfillment of the citizens of our democracy" (Heckscher, 1963, p. 2). Heckscher pointed to a weak "cultural infrastructure" in which arts institutions were "inadequately supported and managed" (Heckscher, 1963, p. 1). The report called for government architecture that encouraged professional creativity through competitions, praised the recently issued "Guiding Principles for Federal Architecture" and its call to increase the use of professional architectural services and that paid architects adequate fees (Heckscher, 1963, p. 8). He noted that the lack of a federal central museum services system probably contributed to the "greatly varying character of professional care, preservation, accessibility and even knowledge of the art treasures belonging to the Government" (Heckscher, 1963, p. 13).

The *Heckscher Report* commented positively on progress in "recognizing the great educational potential of including performances by professional artists in the curriculum" (p. 15). It pointed out the relative scarcity of professional performing arts organizations and museum exhibitions worthy of representing the nation through international tours (Heckscher, 1963, p. 15). While favorably noting the Department of Labor's recognition of cultural workers for the first time in the 1961 "Occupational Outlook Handbook," it also bemoaned "the lack of adequate up-to-date factual and statistical information" on the arts because "professional organizations and associations of the arts have not had the resources to collect such information" (Heckscher, 1963, p. 18). The report observed that "the earning and income pattern of the writer and artist differs strikingly from that of most other professions and occupations" and argued that recognition of "the distinctive character of this income pattern would of [itself] go a long distance to remedy the artist's precarious economic plight" (Heckscher, 1963, p. 22). Heckscher went on to observe that artists and writers often found themselves unable to benefit from legitimate tax deductions available to other professionals and called for tax law and interpretation to "be consistently responsive to [the] characteristics of the creative artist's profession, both as a matter of equity and of the Nation's interest in the encouragement of the arts" (p. 24).

Finally, some of the most explicit comments on the state and importance of professionalism in the arts were voiced by President Kennedy in his statement establishing the President's Advisory Council on the Arts in fulfillment of a recommendation of the Heckscher Report. In this short, two-page statement (Kennedy, 1963b), President Kennedy used some form of the word "professional" eight times. He drew attention to a range of creative professions when he declared that private citizen members of the Advisory Council would be "drawn from civic and cultural leaders and others who are engaged professionally in some phase of the arts such as practicing artists, museum directors, producers, managers and union leaders." Despite over a thousand symphony orchestras in the nation, JFK noted that "only a comparatively few have serious professional status and offer a season of sufficient length to provide a living wage to performers" (p. 33). Most importantly, President Kennedy argued that he

emphasize[d] the importance of the professional artist because there is danger that we may tend to accept the rich range of amateur activities which abound in our country as a substitute for the professional. Without the professional performer and the creative artist, the amateur spirit declines and the vast audience is only partially served.

(p. 34)

The National Foundation for the Arts and Humanities Act of 1965 (NFAH Act, 1965), which established the NEA, incorporated this concern with fostering professionalization in the arts. The legislation spelled out the purposes, structures, powers, and procedures of the arts and the humanities endowments. Details regarding administrative standards and procedures for the NEA (NFAH Act, 1965, Secs. 952 and 954) repeatedly called for the "encouragement of professional excellence" and the meeting of "professional standards." It stipulated that labor hiring standards and working conditions for all professional performers and related or supporting professional personnel employed in projects or productions conducted by professional nonprofit arts organizations funded by NEA meet minimum compensation, health, and safety regulations. It authorized NEA grants-in-aid to cooperative efforts of state and local arts agencies that sought to strengthen the quality of arts available to their citizens through support of professional artists in community-based residencies as well as via support for professional staffing of arts organizations. It also authorized the NEA Chair to use contracts with or grants to state arts agencies to "raise the artistic capabilities of developing arts organizations," including staff development and technical assistance to improve managerial, business, and planning skills.

Clearly, President Kennedy and August Heckscher saw a need for greater professionalism and professional status for the arts as a goal for the projected new "administrative machinery relating to the arts" (*Heckscher Report*, 1963, p. 27). In numerous ways, the 1963 Heckscher Report and the attendant statements of President Kennedy echoed the declaration Heckscher had made in his earlier study of "The Quality of American Culture" prepared for President Eisenhower's *Commission on National Goals*. Speaking to Kennedy's predecessor and a Republican president, Heckscher identified the basic presupposition for maintaining the quality of American culture was understanding that "art is a matter for professionals" (Heckscher, 1960, p. 135).

The Concept of Explicit Administrative Classification as a Foundation for Professional Validation or Classification?

The NEA has acted as both a practical and symbolic agent of public validation and professionalization of the arts since its founding. A conceptual foundation for understanding this role and process rests upon the concept of "artistic classification systems (ACSs)" introduced by Paul DiMaggio (1987a). These ACSs are based on characteristics of production systems that influence the differentiation between different genres of artwork. These ACSs are "commercial classifications" that are market-based, "professional classifications" that are artist reputation based, and "administrative classifications" that stem from governmental actions. Within the administrative classification system, DiMaggio identified three forms of classification: ancillary, regulatory, and explicit. He observed that "public agencies that make grants to artists and arts organizations set out "explicit classifications of artistic work" (p. 452). Heikkinen expanded the idea of "explicit administrative classifications" beyond differentiations among artistic genres to encompass "all administrative categories of art" to include distinctions by "forms of art, types of audiences, or some other criteria" (Heikkinen, 2005, p. 329).

DiMaggio describes ACSs as "socially constructed" systems that "must be continually enacted in art worlds if they are to persist" (1987a, p. 441). Becker defined "art worlds" as "the network of all those people whose collective action is needed to produce a work of art" (Becker, 1982, pp. 34–35). When Becker refers to "people" this is not limited only to individual actors, but also includes organizational actors—whether public, private, professional or nonprofit. Thus, government agencies, such as the NEA, can be art-world players. Heikkinen demonstrated how the national arts agencies of Denmark, Finland, Norway, and Sweden acted as part of their art worlds using "administrative definitions [as] one factor in the process of producing societal definitions for 'art' and 'artists'" (p. 329). She specifically discussed administrative actions such as financial support for individual artists, the use of artistic quality as the main criterion for allocating support, decision-making by expert bodies responsible for peer evaluation of quality, and the central role of professional associations in these institutionalized processes of arts funding policy and practices.

A similar approach is taken here to explore the variety of explicit administrative classifications that were used by the U.S. NEA to foster greater professionalization in the arts—particularly those arts that were institutionalized in nonprofit production fields. Indeed, key definitional requirements for eligibility for public funding were nonprofit organizational status and artistic excellence for both individual artists and arts organizations. In contrast to Heikkinen's focus on how strong professional organizations of artists in the Nordic countries influenced official cultural policy, here the focus is on how cultural policy and its administration by the NEA influenced the growth and strengthening of professional associations and professionalism in the arts community.

Expert Review and Advice: Key Mechanisms of Professionalization

The NEA relied upon three layers of professional advice: the National Council on the Arts (NCA), the peer panel system, and the practice of contracting for knowledgeable site visit performance reviews. These layers of professional assessment were brought to bear at many points of the agency's grantmaking and policymaking processes. All applicants gained exposure to senior and established peers in their field; site evaluators both obtained a current sense of the field and augmented the paper application; the awardees benefited from the prestige of being recognized and funded; and the panelists deepened their awareness of and identification with their field and profession through the panel deliberations. The peer panel system thus stimulated a sense of professionalism among all of its various participants.

Initially, the NCA was composed of 26 members nominated by the President of the United States and confirmed by the Senate, selected from private citizens of expertise, distinguished service, achieved eminence, or professional engagement in the arts from among the major art fields (NFAH Act, 1965, Sec. 955(b)). Thus, the NCA was a multi-disciplinary, multi-professional panel that advised the Chair on policies, programs, and procedures and the review of applications for financial assistance (Sec. 955(f)). Over time, individual council members also served as advocates for the agency and for federal arts funding policy.

A second device was the practice of various NEA programs to also require the evaluation of live performances of select grant applicants via site visits. Site reviewers were consultants hired by individual agency programs to bring first-hand information about performance quality into panel deliberations. Site reviewers were expected to be knowledgeable in the field. For example, according to grant application guidelines for the Dance Program (NEA, 1993b), site visit evaluation was required and made available to the peer panels for choreographer fellowships, for dance company grants, and for dance presenting organization awards. While the agency selected the site visitors, grant applicants were asked to request a site visit by providing information identifying the performance(s) that they felt would show their work to its best advantage and in a format that showcased more than just one short work.

The most significant level of the expert review and advice was the peer panel system. Although barely alluded to in the NFAH Act of 1965, the peer panel system "developed into one of the most vital and central components of the [NEA's] grantmaking operations" (Galligan, 1993, p. 254). Panels have also served as a key administrative mechanism for bringing the expertise and experience of creative professionals into policymaking processes, especially within programs, and for building a sense of professional community within the many fields and occupations of the arts sector. Over time, the NEA's panel system grew into the largest, broadest, and most specialized peer evaluation system for the arts in the United States. Politically, the panel system informs grantmaking with expert advice and thus helps insulate the agency from charges of political interference with the work of artists and arts organizations (Masback, 1992, pp. 185–188). Collectively, the peer panel system became a visible demonstration of the principle of representativeness in arts policy funding, in both process and distribution. Peer panels legitimized NEA grantmaking decisions within the arts community and were essential to keeping the agency abreast of changing conditions and needs in specific arts fields and occupations. In turn, seeking the advice of artists, arts managers, and other creative professionals, the agency validated the expert knowledge and professionalism of the panelists and gave them a central role in decisions about grant awards for artists and arts organizations, in articulating and applying standards of artistic quality to allocating grant funding, and gave them a forum in which to raise art field and occupational concerns within the agency. Thus, the NEA panel system both validated professionalism throughout the nonprofit arts sector and legitimized the agency's arts funding policy with its primary stakeholders—the arts community, the public, and legislative officials.

The agency's enacting legislation did not specifically make peer panels a part of the NEA's structure. In Section 959 of the NFAH Act (1965), it merely gave the Chairperson the authority to "utilize from time to time, as appropriate, experts and consultants, including panels of experts." Initially, the National Council for the Arts acted as a de facto set of expert advisors to the Chairperson. However, the scope, scale, and specialization of programs, applications, and grant workload quickly grew beyond the capacity of the NCA to conduct detailed grant application review. This growth spurred the parallel expansion of the panel review system. For example, in 1969, the agency received approximately 2,000 applications that were reviewed by 79 panel members and consultants, leading to the award of 584 grants (NEA, 1970). By 1977, these numbers had grown as the agency received nearly 20,000 applications across 110 funding categories that were reviewed by over 300 panelists and resulted in over 4,000 grants (Wyszomirski, 1987, p. 208; NEA, 1978, p. 3). By 1989, the number of panelists had grown to nearly 800 as the NEA convened 103 panels (IC, 1990, p. 25).

All panels were composed of professional peers drawn from across the country and representing a mix of race, ethnicity, gender, genre, and artistic viewpoints. As a way of alerting the public to the expertise and stature of its panelists, the agency published a list of all panelists by panel in the NEA's Annual Report each year between 1966 and 1999, but not thereafter. Originally, panelists were appointed for multi-year terms. Another aspect of panel composition was occupational or professional diversity, which was particularly evident regarding panel composition for grant categories concerning major performing arts organizations, such as orchestras, dance, opera, and theater companies. For example, the 11 members of the 1987 Orchestra category panel (NEA, 1988, p. 129) included two different kinds of instrumental musicians, a union chapter president, four executive directors of symphonies of different sizes, a music director, a music critic, a member of a state arts council, and a lawyer serving on the executive committee of an orchestra. Similarly, the panelists on one of two dance company grant panels in 1992 (NEA, 1993a, p. 30) included the executive director of a city dance service organization; the executive director of a major modern dance company; the artistic director, choreographer, and composer of a postmodern dance company; a dance critic, a choreographer, a university dance professor; and the artistic director of a regional ballet company. Other panels included other creative occupations such as curators and conservators; arts educators, university arts professors, and teaching artists; filmmakers; public broadcasting producers and station directors; playwrights and directors; foundation directors and cultural program officers; designers, architects and urban planners; and staff members of national professional associations. Virtually every panel had a representative of a state arts agency. The occupational diversity of the professionals on these panels is a manifestation of the distinctiveness of the art worlds recognized by the agency's explicit administrative classifications in constructing its panel review system.

Although the term professional was not always used, other terms—artistic excellence, artistic merit, and expertise, as well as exceptional talent, distinction, and eminence—generally implied professionalism. Similarly, grant categories specified "professional" to describe the expectation of high organizational production values and operating capacity, as in grant categories for professional theater companies, professional choruses, and professional opera companies. Other grant categories and their panels were focused on reviewing applications designed to advance professional training and/or professional development. Excellence was the core criteria for grantmaking. The specialized expertise necessary to judge excellence was provided by artistic and managerial professional peers.

Since the panel system was so central to the operation of the NEA and to the coherence of the professional peer communities, the system was frequently the object of internal and external oversight (Galligan, 1993). The panel system was a topic of consideration in the Congressional reauthorizations of the NEA in 1968, 1973, 1980, and 1985 (Mulcahy, 1988). It was also addressed in the House Appropriations Committee report in 1979 (U.S. Congress et al., 1979), the Task Force on the Arts and Humanities in 1981 (Presidential Task Force, 1981), and the 1990 bipartisan Independent Commission (IC, 1990) and subsequent reauthorization. The NEA also conducted its own reviews of the panel system in 1978 (Jacob, 1979) and in 1987, in response to a 1985 Congressional reauthorization amendment requiring a detailed report on panel procedures and staffing (NEA, 1987b, p. 1). In other words, the agency and other oversight agents gave careful thought to the construction and management of this mechanism of explicit administrative classification.

While each of these reviews made recommendations on how the system might be improved and strengthened, each legitimated the importance and continuation of the panel system to the work of the Endowment. Perhaps the most important changes came in the late 1970s as a new chairman, Livingston Biddle, made two changes in response to the 1978 internal and the 1979 House Staff reports (Biddle, 1988). Both changes increased the role of expert panelists in the operations of the agency, thus recognizing the professional status of panelists and the importance of their expert knowledge to assuring the quality of the agency grantmaking (Galligan, 1993, pp. 257–260). In an attempt to include arts professionals in more of the policymaking processes of the agency, he added a layer of panels to each program. Originally called "policy panels" and later termed "overview panels," they were primarily comprised of panelists from each of a program division's grant panels. They were charged with providing guidance and advice to each program, as well as the NCA and the Chair, on funding priorities, future planning needs, and initiatives from a whole field perspective. Second, in an effort to bring new ideas and points of view into the grantmaking process, he decided to appoint panelists for only a one-year term, with possible repeats limited to three years in total. This resulted in the annual rotation of 40%–60% of all panelists each year (NEA, 1987b, p. 14). Over time, these periodic reviews helped legitimate both the agency and the professionalization of creative workers and organizational fields. Panels demonstrated agency attentiveness to both field and public representation and helped occupations strengthen their professional identities. By assembling and heeding the input of artistic professionals on the panels, the agency and its programs could be more responsive to changing needs of its arts constituency. Meanwhile, the service of arts professionals on panels nurtured "a large and growing body of professionals in each field who know how the panels work from their own experience as panelists" (NEA, 1987b, p. 14).

Supporting the Careers of Professional Artists

From its earliest years, the NEA was committed to supporting individual artists as constituting the core of the creative sector. Support for individual artists was a fundamental purpose of the agency's Congressional Commission, which declared: "It is necessary and appropriate for the Federal Government to help create and sustain not only a climate encouraging freedom of thought, imagination, and inquiry but also the material conditions facilitating the release of this creative talent" (NFAH Act, 1965, Sec 951(7)). Historically, discipline-classified program divisions had at least one direct fellowship grant category. Some programs, like Visual Arts, Literature, Theater, and Music, had multiple direct fellowship grant categories that targeted specific artistic occupations, such as solo recitalists and composers in music and playwrights or solo theater artists in theater. Additionally, many programs had individual artist project grants. Other types of grants to arts organizations provided individual artists with opportunities to work on commissions for new work, at artist residencies, or with space and facilities to develop new work (NEA, 1992). Added together, these grants provided significant financial support for individual professional artists to produce artwork, often at critical periods of their careers, and to reach larger audiences. For example, in FY1983, the NEA awarded 766 direct grants amounting to $6.7 million in artist fellowships, $27.1 million to arts organizations to provide artists with opportunities to develop their work and bring it to the public, $1.9 million to commission Art in Public Places, and $1.9 million in sub-granting programs for a total of $37.6 million (NEA, 1984b, p. 24).

The creation and funding of these programs are another example of explicit administrative classifications that were subject to peer review by recognized professionals. The 1969 Annual Report identified a total of 79 panelists and consultants who served the agency, including well-known artists such as choreographer Agnes de Mille, composer Aaron Copeland, visual artist Frank Stella, and conductor Julius Rudel, as well as *Village Voice* dance critic Deborah Jowitt and *NYTimes* chief art critic Hilton Kramer. Each grant category advanced the professionalism of individual creative and performing artists in three ways. Each defined a specific artistic occupation as a profession, eligible for public funding. For successful applicants, grants also identified awardees as examples of professionally validated excellence. Furthermore, the actual money award helped artists to earn a living from their professional artwork.

Direct fellowship awards for choreographers, creative writers, and visual artist of various genres were among the first grants awarded by the agency. In 1966, its first year of operation, the NEA awarded fellowship grants to 50 established novelists, poets, painters, sculptors, and composers. Between 1966 and 1993, over 11,000 artists received direct fellowship or project grants. Many went on to win other prestigious awards such as Guggenheim fellowships, Pulitzer prizes, and MacArthur "genius awards" (NEA, 1993a, p. 4). Direct support to individual artists took two forms—"buy-time" fellowships and artist project grants—each of which provided individual artists with broad freedom to focus on their creativity and were judged on the basis of the quality of the applicant's artistic record. Neither required a financial match from the artists. Project grants committed the artist to a specific project of their choice and were judged on the quality of both the artist's creative record and the quality of the proposed project. These were the most prized forms of public grant support because these awards granted artists maximum creative freedom and autonomy.

A longitudinal study of the visual arts program pointed to fellowship grants as "an expression of the Endowment's trust and belief in artists," as expressed in the freedom the award gave them to "decide what was right for them and to use their fellowship however they saw fit" (Brenson, 2001, p. 128). It also pointed out that the Visual Arts Fellowship program did a "superb job in finding gifted artists at the right time" (p. 128) in their career trajectory. The award of an NEA fellowship or grant was an important public validation of the selected artists. A 1993 NEA report presenting an overview of Endowment grant awards to individual artists presented testimonials as to the impact and significance these fellowships had on professional careers. For example, architect and architecture professor Thomas Hubka said:

[E]ndowment grants have definitely made a difference—they have shaped my entire professional life. They came at "crucial early stages of development" and were a "springboard to further grants, culminating in an award-winning book, NEH funded exhibits and a life-long interest in vernacular architecture."

(NEA, 1993c, p. 29)

Academy award winning documentary filmmaker Barbara Kopple recalled that

> receiving grants from the National Endowment for the Arts has been both a tremendous honor and essential to my survival. . . . For me, that grant meant more than money. It was an affirmation of the work that I was trying to accomplish. . . . I will always be grateful to the NEA for having that confidence in me.
>
> (NEA, 1993c, p. 33)

Visual artist Melissa Wren Miller described that when she applied for her first NEA grant, she

> had no gallery representative, few sales, no name recognition, and limited opportunities for my work to be shown. Perhaps just as valuable as the money—and the time and freedom it bought—was the crucial stamp of approval that the fellowship represented. On a personal level, it served as an extremely important confirmation of the value of my work and gave me the courage to carry on. On a professional level, the fact that I could now put "NEA Grant Recipient" after my name opened many, many doors. . . . Within three years of receiving the grant, I was supporting myself as a full-time professional artist. The work was represented by a gallery, being shown nationally, and receiving positive reviews in the regional and national press. A curator on the NEA jury panel that gave me the award continued to follow my work, and gave me my first major one-person museum show.
>
> (NEA, 1993c, p. 42)

Fellowship recipient, Pauline Oliveros, an acoustic and electronic composer, pointed out the personal and professional impact of three fellowship awards she received from the NEA, both directly and indirectly. She noted that

> the honor of the award has provided me with validation in my community. It has evoked dignity and respect for my profession. These awards have been key reference points in my career. The recognition from my peers is motivating. . . . My career has blossomed along with the network of community organizations that has grown throughout the years of the Endowment's existence.
>
> (p. 49)

Finally, Pulitzer Prize-winning playwright Wendy Wasserman remembered that

> the NEA grant I received gave me a sense of legitimacy as an artist. . . . I received it at a point when I was concerned about leaving the theater. . . .

The grant furthered my conviction that support for an artist, both financially and emotionally, is critical to the artist's belief in oneself.

(p. 67)

Clearly, individual artists felt helped and encouraged by NEA fellowships and often gained the confidence to see themselves as professional artists. Their professional identity was also reinforced and strengthened by the positive evaluations of the Endowment's three-layered peer review system. Thus, these multiple explicit administrative classifications advanced the processes of professionalization among many artistic occupations.

Arts Service Organizations (ASOs) and Professional Associations

ASOs exist to provide services to all parts of the creative sector—nonprofit, commercial, and informal or avocational. ASOs servicing the nonprofit arts subsector have played an important role in the growth and development of the Arts Endowment, in the shaping and implementation of national arts policy, in the mobilization and professionalization of creative workers, and in the institutionalization of individual fields of nonprofit arts organizations. Conversely, since its very beginning, the NEA has played an important role in the creation, expansion, and support of ASOs. Especially under the chairmanship of Nancy Hanks (1969–1977), the NEA strategically funded ASOs as a "patron of political action," mobilizing, strengthening, and coordinating its constituency from the top down by encouraging advocacy by these groups to "promote new legislative agendas and social values" (Wyszomirski, 1987, p. 230). In pursuit of budget increases for the agency, Hanks pursued an advocacy strategy that simultaneously allowed her to identify specific arts fields and their needs as a way to recruit specific institutional arts communities and their workers as advocates for agency growth and larger budgets. When these efforts secured larger appropriations, the targeted field as well as the entire arts community shared in the benefits of increased funding through larger and more numerous grant programs. In this mutually supportive effort, institutional fields and professional associations proved themselves to be valuable political allies of the NEA which, in turn, directed those funds to support growing institutional fields, creative professionals, and arts service organizations, thus strengthening the professionalism and support structures of the nonprofit arts industries.

The NEA deliberately evolved a policy regarding ASOs that involved two key components. First, virtually every program division earmarked funding via grant or cooperative agreement for services to the field. Between 1970 and 1994, aggregate funding awarded annually through the "Services to the Field" category accounted for between 5% and 9% of combined program and treasury funds appropriated to the agency (Wyszomirski, 1995, p. 54). This level of federal funding represented a significant public validation and commitment to building the infrastructure of professionalism in the arts. The second key policy component regarding ASOs is found in periodic assessment and deliberation of the purposes and performance of ASOs on an agency-wide basis. "Reports for Discussion" were prepared for National Council for the Arts (NCA) meetings in September 1973, August 1980, and November 1984 concerning the variety, functions, and characteristics of ASOs (Jacob, 1979; NEA, 1980, 1984a). Other agency discussions of the relationship between ASOs and the Endowment can be found in the *1986–1990 Planning Document* ((NEA, 1984b) and the *1980–1984 General Plan* (NEA, 1979). Although each of these reports acknowledged that the term "arts service organization" covered a wide variety of organizations, the analysis of each of these internal documents was based on a sample of ASOs that received NEA funding during a specified multiyear period. A recurrent definition held that ASOs "exist not to produce, present or preserve art, but to help others do so . . . [by providing] information, opportunities to communicate, advocacy, public education, professional and volunteer training, and various forms of technical, managerial, and support services" (NEA, 1984a, p. 109).

As late as 1997, a comprehensive list of ASOs was still lacking. This prompted a national report exploring "how the arts sector can and ought to serve public purposes" to call for better research and data-gathering "on support systems and organizations covering the commercial, not-for-profit, and unincorporated parts of the arts sector" (American Assembly, 1977, pp. 9, 31). In response to this call, a scholarly study was undertaken by Wyszomirski and Cherbo (2001) that reported finding 4,186 ASOs, which included international, national, regional, and local nonprofit membership organizations; unions, business leagues, and guilds; as well as honorary arts societies and volunteer and avocational membership groups. Of this universe, 710 were national membership organizations. Three hundred sixty-three of these were likely to be professional associations, business leagues, and unions whose members shared a sense of identity and pursued specific tangible interests. Thus, a rough approximation of the number of professional associations in the arts sector—commercial and nonprofit—would be between 300 and 350 in 2000. During the subsequent two decades, the specific number and composition of this list have seen additions and deletions, with a recent increase in national membership organizations (NMOs) that represent national members from particular racial, ethnic, and gender groups.

Of particular interest to the processes of professionalization of the arts and of arts occupations are three types of ASOs—(NMOs), direct service providers (DSPs), and unions. NMOs and DSPs are usually 501(c)3 tax-exempt, charitable organizations and therefore eligible for NEA funding. In contrast, unions are 501(c)5 tax-exempt organizations and, thus, ineligible for federal funding. Nonetheless, unions have collaborated with the agency and often had a membership on advisory panels and the NCA. Each of these three types of ASOs provides infrastructure elements for their members and the artistic fields with which they work. Membership associations may represent types of organizations (e.g., dance companies, symphony orchestras, or literary magazines and presses) or types of individuals (e.g., choreographers, composers, poets, or writers). Membership organizations may enlist members on an international, national, regional, or local basis. A few ASOs came into existence at the Endowment's initiative such as NMOs like Opera America, the National Association of Artists Organizations (NAAOs), and the Association of American Dance Companies, or DSPs such as the American Film Institute and the Theatre Development Fund (NEA, 1980, p. 68). National membership organizations are ASOs that exert a direct impact on the professionalization processes of arts occupations and also tend to be highly active in advocacy and public education activities.

Relatively few NMOs were founded before the establishment of the NEA. These included the American Institute of Architects (1857), the American Alliance of Museums (1906), the League of American Orchestras (1942), Music Critics Association (1956), and the Theater Communications Group (1964). Many NMO service organizations came into existence after 1965 and benefitted from NEA funding. NMOs proliferated as the number of nonprofit arts organizations and artists increased with the arts boom from the late 1960s to the mid-1980s. Concurrently, NMOs increased the capacity for effective mobilization and political advocacy in support of the NEA, public funding, and arts policy (Wyszomirski, 1995).

Many NMOs nominally represent member organizations, be they symphonies, theater companies, museums, or state arts agencies, but they also represent the specialized individuals who work in these member organizations. Thus, these associations serve to professionalize both organizational fields and occupational professions. Indeed, occupational groups often have affinity groups or subsections within these NMOs. For example, the American Alliance for Museums (AAM) lists 20 professional networks that its members may join. These networks include certain occupational groups such as curators, museum educators, or administrative staff who specialize in development and membership. It also has a network for museum studies designed to bridge field practitioners and academic museum studies programs (or museology). There is even an Independent Museum Professional Network for specialized museum professionals (e.g., consultants, freelancers, registrars, and exhibit designers) who make a career from multiple project positions rather than full-time work with a single museum. As another example, the National Assembly of State Arts Agencies (NASAA) represents the 56 state and territorial arts agencies, its leaders, board members, and staff. It has 12 peer groups that State Arts Agencies (SAA) personnel can join and which reflect their managerial and programming specializations—such as Folk/Traditional Arts Manager, Arts Education Manager, Community Development Manager, or Communications/Public Information Officer (NASAA, n.d.). These peer groups encourage communication and interaction as well as professional development opportunities and shared learning through specialized panels at annual conferences for occupations that could be characterized as semiprofessional. The professionalization of the managers of nonprofit arts organizations was also promoted by the NEA's expectation of paid, professional managerial staff as a grant eligibility requirement, and by periodic research studies on the training, careers, and professional status of arts managers (DiMaggio, 1987b).

NMOs provide some or all of the following services to their members: professional credentialing services, job postings, calendar services, and awards; professional development and technical assistance programs; conferences and other forums; publications; political and policymaking representation and coalition building; information gathering and research; public education efforts; and professional self-governance. Such activities and services help to strengthen professional identity and occupational communication as well as generate information about conditions and needs within the profession and occupational field. NMOs have also managed regranting programs funded by the NEA, thereby acting as policy implementation agents. The service organizations that are NMOs have developed a range of tactics and strategies to shape, promote, implement, and, at times, deflect policymaking. A few have even engaged in campaign activities to influence the election of particular public officials (Wyszomirski & Cherbo, 2001). Indeed, NMOs have become effective actors in the arts policy community, not only in the national arena but also in the state and local affairs. As such, they have demonstrated their capacity to maintain and advance the interests of their membership as well as support the public agencies that they work with and that demonstrate the public value of the arts. In mature professions, their professional associations provide many of these services for their members. Historically, many arts professional associations lacked the resources to support a full menu of support services for their members.

Direct Service Providers (DSPs) are another type of ASO that has been important to the professionalization of the arts. Unlike NMOs, DSPs are operating, rather than membership, organizations. DSPs complement professional associations to build up the support structures of organization fields and occupations, particularly where they are under-institutionalized. Whereas NMOs rely, at least in part, on membership dues to fund services, DSPs often offer their services to anyone in the profession or field either for a fee or by securing contracts and grants from arts agencies and/or private foundations. While some influential DSPs operate on a national scale, others play a major role at the regional, state, or municipal levels, depending on the structure of their respective fields or professions.

DSPs are nonprofit enterprises that undertake projects that may benefit an entire field but that are unaffordable or unavailable through membership organizations. Archival and preservation services in the film have been provided via the American Film Institute, and in dance by the Dance Notation Bureau and the NYC Public Library for the Performing Arts, which is a public organization. Some DSPs provide services to individual artists, often at the beginning of their career, such as Affiliate Artists, which seeks to help young artists who have completed their formal training to connect with audiences through intensive performing experiences, performance fees, and covered travel, administrative, and promotional costs (Netzer, 1978, pp. 138–139). Other DSPs provided services to individual nonprofit arts organizations at a fee and sometimes undertook contract work for federal, state, regional, or local arts agencies as well as private foundation arts and culture programs. Pentacle was a DSP established in 1976 at the initiative of the NEA to provide services for performing artists at critical stages of their careers (NCA, 1980, p. 68). They provide fiscal sponsorship as a form of administrative support to small and emerging dance groups, as well as representation for contracting and booking. They recruit and place college graduates and high school students as interns and trainees in administrative jobs at dance companies, thus providing the organizations with administrative personnel and the interns and trainees with work experience and a career opportunity (Pentacle, n.d.).

Certain artistic occupations—like visual artists, poets and authors, and composers—tend to work alone rather than in organizations. Historically, these occupations have been slow to develop mature organizational settings that structure and support their professionalism. The NEA fostered the organizational infrastructure of these fields by funding direct service providers that could provide professional supports and activities otherwise offered by professional associations. This process can be seen through the case of visual artists and the role of the NEA Visual Arts Program and the Comprehensive Employment and Training Act (CETA) during the 1970s and 1980s. Together, these federal programs were instrumental in bringing new kinds of direct service-providing organizations into existence to support the professionalism of visual artists and promoting the institutionalization of a field of nonprofit organizations that served the visual arts beyond commercial galleries and museums.

During the first 30 years of the NEA's operations, the agency undertook grantmaking activities focused on building the organizational infrastructure of many under-institutionalized organizational fields, including Visual Arts, Literature, Folk Arts, Media Arts, and Expansion Arts. For example, during these years, the agency made a concentrated effort to build up the organizational field for visual artists by fostering the creation and support of two grant categories—Visual Artist Organizations (VAO) and Visual Artist Forums (VAF). Visual Artists Organizations were often originated by or for artists to provide facilities for individual visual artists, such as studio space, exhibition and installation venues, and artist-in-residence opportunities. In 1973, the Visual Arts Program awarded a total of $50,000 to support a mere ten spaces (NEA, 1974, p. 318). By 1986, this grant category awarded 129 grants to 128 organizations totaling $1.874 million (NEA, 1987a). Of these 128 organizations, 120 could still be identified today even though approximately 20 had closed down. Of the 120 that could be identified, 11 had been established before 1965; 14 between 1966 and 1970, 81 were created during the 1970s; and 13 more between 1981 and 1984. VAOs continued to be a key funding category of the Visual Arts program through 1994.

The artist-in-residence idea has been widely used throughout the NEA. These programs were popular as devices both to provide artists with temporary employment and to increase contact between artists and audiences in local communities (Taylor & Barresi, 1984, pp. 208–213). Indeed, the artist-in-residence mechanism was regarded as so valuable to a thriving visual arts community that even after Congress prohibited most grants to artists, thus diminishing the visual arts program, the NEA established a new funding category for artists' communities in 2010 which focused on organizations that provided artist-in-residence opportunities. Historically, the efforts of the NEA to grow the universe of artists organizations and artist-in-residence opportunities were complemented by the art programs established under the CETA between 1974 and 1981 (Dubin, 1987, pp. 12–14). By 1979, the NEA was encouraging groups of artists to explore local CETA project positions. At the first national CETA arts conference in 1979, it was estimated that "as much as $200 million, maintaining 600 projects in approximately 200 locations had made CETA the largest funding source for the arts in the U.S." (Dubin, 1987, pp. 17–18). CETA residencies were helping the public to see artists as workers while providing artists with intermediary work positions that bridged the period between graduating from formal training and establishing careers. CETA positions also "gave artists the chance to learn new administrative skills necessary to negotiate the execution of their work in relation to clients' needs and demands" (Dubin, 1987, p. 34). Artists, with assistance from the MacArthur Foundation, also moved to organize a NMO—the Alliance of Artist Communities—in 1991. The Alliance was dedicated to representing the interests of artists and artist communities in preserving and cultivating this organizational field that was essential to both visual artists and creative artists in other occupations.

Similarly, the VAF category awarded 57 grants in 1986 that awarded $374,000 to enable artists to assemble with professional peers, teachers, students, and the public to debate issues, share information, and compare methods (NEA, 1987a, AR, p. 176). These grants supported the efforts of direct service provider nonprofit organizations in the publication of 22 national and regional, general, and specialized periodicals that informed artistic practice with criticism, commentary, and activities concerning contemporary art. These journals included well-known publications like *High Performance, New Art Examiner, Leonardo, Dialogue, Aperture*, and *Afterimage*. The Forums category awarded 25 grants to universities and colleges to support visiting artist programs, artists-in-residence programs, workshops, and seminars— thus encouraging academic institutions to add organizational support to the visual arts field beyond educational training. Contemporary art centers and galleries, regional and state arts agencies, and urban public art programs also hosted similar forums that facilitated the sharing of professional information and strengthened professional networking among visual artists. Thus, all of these administrative mechanisms—VAO, visual arts forums and artist-in-residency projects, and other DSPs—enhanced the professional infrastructure for professional visual artists.

Finally, unions are active across the creative sector and most were established before the NEA was created. These unions can represent a single occupation (e.g., Dramatists Guild for playwrights) or workers from a group of related occupations (e.g., American Guild of Musical Artists that represents dancers, opera singers, and choristers). The commercial entertainment industries are more unionized than the nonprofit creative industries, but some unions draw members from both the commercial and nonprofit arts organizations, such as the American Federation of Musicians (AFM), International Alliance of Theatrical Stage Employees (IATSE), or Actors Equity. Most of these are part of a larger coalition—the Arts, Entertainment, and Media Industry Coordinating Committee (AEMI) within the American Federation of Labor-Congress of Industrial Organizations (AFL-CIO) under its Department for Professional Employees. Large nonprofit performing arts organizations are most likely to be unionized. Members of these artistic unions tend to negotiate as individual organizations rather than through collective bargaining for their entire field. For example, the Metropolitan Opera negotiates worker contracts with 15 different unions, and its contracts apply only to the Met. In order to reopen after the COVID-19 shutdown, the Met had to negotiate new contracts with the AFM, IATSE, and AGMA, among others (Jacobs, 2021). Recently, new interest in unionization in the nonprofit arts has arisen among museum professionals as individual museums like the Whitney have voted to be represented by the United Automobile Workers Union (Moynihan, 2021). Unions, being 501(c)5 organizations, are ineligible for NEA grants, but they have been active in persuading the agency to integrate union work standards into grant guidelines for professional nonprofit performing arts organizations. In the process, the agency and the unions supported each other in their recognition of the professionalism of fields of arts organizations and the protection of individual performing artists. Shane's chapter in this volume on the evolution of Actor's Equity as a hallmark of professionalism for live theater actors provides more detail on this development.

Conclusion

As can be seen from the foregoing analysis, cultural policy, as designed and administered by the NEA, has been a crucial actor in the professionalization of artist and arts-related occupations in the United States. Indeed, a concern for raising the level of arts professionalism was embedded in the very creation of the agency. Using a strategy of explicit administrative classifications, the NEA developed a set of programs, grant categories, and procedural devices that fostered the careers of creative artists both directly and indirectly. Key among its procedures was a reliance on three layers of expert professional advice in grantmaking and program administrative policymaking. This system treated artistic quality as judged by professional artistic peers as the main criterion for the allocation of grant funding and fostered denser networks among occupations and fields of creative professionals. The case of the visual arts illustrates many of the key indicators of professionalization. Through direct support of individual artists in the form of "buy-time" fellowships and artist project grants, as well as artist residency opportunities, artists enjoyed creative freedom and autonomy as well as earned money for doing their artwork. Customization of similar efforts for other program divisions cultivated the professional infrastructure and support systems of other creative occupations. The NEA also underwrote the growth and strengthening of a variety of professional associations and direct service-providing organizations. The agency also worked with unions to improve economic and work conditions for creative professionals. Together, these activities gave form to and supplemented the collective action and mutual support typically provided by professional associations.

For the first 30 years of its operation, the NEA wove a supportive web of professionalization under the nonprofit arts sector in the United States. In doing so, the professionalism of many arts and arts-related occupations developed a more advanced state of professionalism. However, the process of professionalization is neither finished nor static. Some might argue that the arts in America experienced a shock of deprofessionalization when the NEA was prohibited from giving grant support directly to most artists in the mid-1990s. Others might argue that in response to this shift in cultural policy, private foundations and artists themselves were motivated to develop other means of supporting professionalism. Additionally, certain events and trends have demonstrated that professionalism in the arts now faces the challenges of dramatically changing conditions regarding equity and diversity, technology, and the COVID-19 pandemic. Hopefully, better understanding the momentum and methods of the twentieth-century trajectory of professionalization of the arts through cultural policy action can inform the design of new policy initiatives for the twenty-first century.

References

American Assembly. (1997, May–June 1). *The arts and the public purpose: 92nd American Assembly*. Columbia University Press, Arden House.

Becker, H. S. (1982). *Art worlds*. University of California Press.

Biddle, L. (1988). *Our government and the arts: Perspective from the inside*. American Council for the Arts Books.

Brenson, M. (2001). *Visionaries and outcasts: The NEA, congress, and the place of the visual artist in America*. The New Press.

Cummings, M. C., Jr. (1995). To change a nation's cultural policy: The Kennedy administration and the arts in the United States, 1961–1963. In K. V. Mulcahy &

M. J. Wyszomirski (Eds.), *America's commitment to culture: Government and the arts* (pp. 95–120). Westview Press.

Department for Professional Employees. (n.d.). *Arts, entertainment, and media industry coordinating committee (AEMI)*. www.dpeaflcio.org/aemi

DiMaggio, P. J. (1987a). Classification in art. *American Sociological Review, 52*(4), 440–455.

DiMaggio, P. J. (1987b). *Managers of the arts* (NEA Research Division Report No. 20). Seven Lock Press.

Dubin, S. C. (1987). *Bureaucratizing the muse: Public funds and the cultural worker.* University of Chicago Press.

Galligan, A. M. (1993). The politicization of peer-review panels at the NEA. In J. H. Balfe (Ed.), *Paying the piper: Causes and consequences of art patronage* (pp. 254–270). University of Illinois Press.

Heckscher, A. (1960). *The quality of American culture* (Goals for Americans: The Report of the President's Commission and National Goals and Chapters, Submitted for the Consideration of the Commission, pp. 127–146). Prentice Hall.

Heckscher, A. (1963, May 29). *U.S. senate, 88th congress, 1st session* (Document No. 28: The Arts and the National Government: Report to the Present Submitted by August Heckscher, Special Consultant on the Arts). U.S. Government Printing Office.

Heikkinen, M. (2005). Administrative definitions of artists in the Nordic model of state support for artists. *International Journal of Cultural Policy, 11*(3), 325–340.

IC. (1990). *A report to congress on the National Endowment for the Arts.* Independent Commission, Government Printing Office.

Jacob, E. (1979). *A study of the panel system of the NEA* [Unpublished report]. NEA.

Jacobs, J. (2021, May 13). "We are the met": Opera unions rally against pay cuts. *The New York Times.* www.nytimes.com/2021/05/2021/arts/music/Met-opera-protest-union.html

Kennedy, J. F. (1963a, June 10). *Letter to August Heckscher* (p. viii). The White House; Reprinted in *Heckscher report* (U.S. Senate Document No. 28).

Kennedy, J. F. (1963b, June 12). *Executive order 11112-establishing the president's advisory council on the arts.* www.presidency.ucsb.edu/documents/executive-order-11112

Larson, G. O. (1983). *The reluctant patron: The United States government and the arts, 1943–1965.* University of Pennsylvania Press.

Masback, C. A. (1992). Independence vs. accountability: Correcting the structural defects in the National Endowment for the Arts. *Yale Law & Policy Review, 10,* 177–204.

Moynihan, C. (2021). Workers at the Whitney move to form a union. *The New York Times,* p. C5. www.nytimes.com/2021/05/17/arts/design/whitney-museum-forming-a-union

Mulcahy, K. V. (1988). The politics of cultural oversight: The reauthorization process and the National Endowment for the Arts. In M. J. Wyszomirski (Ed.), *Congress and the arts: A precarious alliance?* (pp. 63–86). American Council for the Arts Books.

NASAA (National Assembly of State Arts Agencies). (n.d.). www.nasaa-arts.org/my-nasaa/about-peer-groups

NEA (National Endowment for the Arts). (1970). *Annual report 1969.* NEA. www.arts.gov/about/publications/1969-annual-report.pdf

NEA (National Endowment for the Arts). (1974). *Annual report 1973*. NEA. www. arts.gov/about/publications/197Swaim4-annual-report.pdf

NEA (National Endowment for the Arts). (1978). *Annual report 1977*. NEA. www. arts.gov/about/publications/1977-annual-report.pdf

NEA (National Endowment for the Arts). (1979). *General plan 1980–1984*. Office of Policy and Planning.

NEA (National Endowment for the Arts). (1980). Policy statement of the national council on the arts on service organization support. In *National council on the arts: Reports for discussion* (pp. 45–80). NEA.

NEA (National Endowment for the Arts). (1984a). Policy discussion paper on service organization support. In *National council on the arts: Reports for discussion*. NEA.

NEA (National Endowment for the Arts). (1984b). *Planning document 1986–1990*. U.S. Government Printing Office.

NEA (National Endowment for the Arts). (1985). *Annual report 1984*. NEA. www. arts.gov/about/publications/1984-annual-report.pdf

NEA (National Endowment for the Arts). (1987a). *Annual report 1986*. NEA. www. arts.gov/about/publications/1986-annual-report.pdf

NEA (National Endowment for the Arts). (1987b, October). *The panel study report*. Prepared in response to a Congressional Mandate. NEA.

NEA (National Endowment for the Arts). (1988). *Annual report 1987*. NEA. www. arts.gov/about/publications/1987-annual-report.pdf

NEA (National Endowment for the Arts). (1992). Assistance for artists. In *National council on the arts: Reports for discussion* (pp. 13–20). NEA.

NEA (National Endowment for the Arts). (1993a). *Annual report 1992*. NEA. www. arts.gov/about/publications/1992-annual-report.pdf

NEA (National Endowment for the Arts). (1993b). *Dance program application guidelines 1993*. NEA.

NEA (National Endowment for the Arts). (1993c). *Generation of fellows: Grants to individuals from the National Endowment for the Arts*. NEA.

Netzer, D. (1978). *The subsidized muse: Public support for the arts in the United States*. A Twentieth Century Fund Study. Cambridge University Press.

NFAH Act. (1965). National Foundation on the Arts and the Humanities Act (1965), Publ. L. No. 89–209, 20 USC, Chapter 26, Subsection Chapter 1.

Pentacle. (n.d.). *Pentacle*. www.pentacle.org/

Presidential Task Force. (1981). *Report to the president*. Presidential Task Force on the Arts and the Humanities. Government Printing Office.

Taylor, F., & Barresi, A. L. (1984). *The arts at a new frontier: The National Endowment for the Arts*. Plenum Press.

U.S. Congress, House of Representatives, Committee on Appropriations, & Surveys and Investigations Staff. (1979). *Report on the National Endowment for the Arts*. U.S. Congress.

Wyszomirski, M. J. (1987). The politics of art: Nancy Hanks and the National Endowment for the Arts. In J. W. Doig & E. C. Hargrove (Eds.), *Leadership and innovation* (pp. 207–454). Johns Hopkins University Press.

Wyszomirski, M. J. (1995). The politics of arts policy: Subgovernment to issue network. In K. V. Mulcahy & M. J. Wyszomirski (Eds.), *America's commitment to culture* (pp. 47–76). Westview Press.

Wyszomirski, M. J., & Cherbo, J. M. (2001). The associational infrastructure of the arts and culture. *Journal of Arts Administration, Law and Society*, *31*(2), 99–122.

4 Passion and Profession

Individual Artists, Professional Development, and the Role of Foundations

Claudia J. Bach

Introduction

Individual artists are the indisputable core of a vibrant and evolving creative culture. They are the generative source of new artistic works pushing new creative boundaries, and the carriers of artistic traditions interpreting and presenting works from the past. Artists are the wellspring for new, sometimes transgressive, explorations that stretch and reshape artistic genres and disciplines, and engage with new technologies. Opportunities for artists to pursue their creative work are shaped by numerous societal as well as personal factors. This chapter looks at the pathways to professionalization for individual artists that emerged and evolved in the United States. Our focus is from the 1980s into the first decades of the twenty-first century, a period of significant change in the culture at large.

New approaches to professionalization for American artists accelerated during the last two decades of the twentieth century. During the 1980s and 1990s, public funding for individual artists came under increased scrutiny in the United States. Political controversy led to restricted dollars from public arts agencies. As public policy shifted, philanthropic foundations stepped into new roles in support of artists. Indirect support for artists through nonprofit producing or presenting organizations, or professional associations, gave way to services directly reaching individual artists. Ideas about an artistic creator and their individual responsibility in shaping a professional career increasingly focused on entrepreneurial activity. New thinking emerged about artists' "career development" and "professional development" and spurred philanthropic and institutional responses to these concepts. A focus on business and managerial skills arose.

In this chapter, I look at interrelated elements in professionalization practices for independent artists in the United States, primarily from the late 1980s onward. I consider the practices of independent artists; explore research conducted on the needs, opportunities, and conditions of working artists; examine the expansion of professional development programs and pathways, all with attention to roles played by philanthropic foundations in these arenas.

DOI: 10.4324/9781003138693-5

Milestones in Research on Individual Artists

Research and related data on artists nationally were scarce until recently, as evidenced in Butler and DiMaggio's "Studies of Artists: An Annotated Directory" (2000), which looks back to the 1950s. Their research was conducted with support from the Pew Charitable Trusts and the National Endowment for the Arts (NEA), for the Center for Arts and Cultural Policy Studies at Princeton, as part of efforts to stimulate research on arts and cultural policy, including research on artists. Foundations, governmental agencies, artist-serving nonprofit organizations, academics, and practitioners in the field have all played roles in the emergence of research on artists. The 1965 launch of the NEA and the awarding of the first NEA Fellowships for artists in 1967 set the stage for inquiry into artists as a population, placing artists within the evolving scope of cultural policy (see Wyszomirski's Chapter 3 in this volume). Research at the NEA has focused more generally on arts participation and the economic impact of the arts and cultural industries.[1]

The Culture Wars of the late 1980s and 1990s, and the elimination of NEA Fellowships in 1995 and 1996, marked a period of political controversy and reduced public funding for individual artists. This created a new urgency for developing alternate avenues of support for the arts and artists. With that came the need for research to understand artists' needs and create advocacy tools. Foundations paid increasing attention to these concerns, as evidenced in reports developed for the MacArthur Foundation that examined issues of support for individual artists (Evans, 1994).

A group of like-minded funders began to coalesce (Kreidler, 2006). This period can be understood as a transition point with new, increasingly formalized networks, and new catalytic roles for foundations in research on, and support for, individual artists. Foundation program officers, public arts agencies representatives, and others engaged specifically with arts funding held their first conference in St. Paul in 1985. This led to the formation of Grantmakers in the Arts (GIA) in 1989, with individual artist support championed by a subset of funders. Many individual staff members in foundations brought deep personal investment as well as professional commitment to advancing this work on behalf of artists. During the 1980s, private sector arts grantmaking was elevated to the level of a conscious profession (Kreidler, 2006).

Two convenings were to prove pivotal in stimulating thinking and research on artists: Montauk Conference, held at the eastern tip of Long Island in 1986, and the Orcas Conference, held in the far northwest corner of Washington State in 1988. These conferences, sponsored by the New York Foundation for the Arts (NYFA) with seed funding from the NEA, brought together more than 200 artists, private and public funders, representatives of artist-centered organizations, arts institutions, advocacy groups, and research centers to explore "the creative support of the creative artist"

(Focke, 2015). Ruby Lerner, who would go on to be the founding director of Creative Capital, as well as 20 other artists, researchers, and thinkers, were commissioned to write papers to stimulate conversation and participation. Leadership from NYFA, the Pew Charitable Trusts, Arts and Humanities at the Rockefeller Foundation, and others note the influence of these conferences on subsequent directions for their own organizations, and for the field (Focke, 2015). Among those in attendance was Joan Jeffri, founder and director of the Research Center for Arts and Culture housed first at Columbia University and now at The Actors Fund. Jeffri's seminal 1989 *Information on Artists* (2015) examined work-related human and social service needs of artists across the country, beginning with data collected in the late 1980s in ten cities.[2]

The philanthropic community supported increasing research and also built new infrastructure in support of artists in the 1990s. A consortium of 38 funders, with original leadership from the Ford Foundation, supported a landmark national study on artists in the late 1990s that has shaped understanding of professionalization and artists, and served as a foundation in the creation of information and support structures over the subsequent decades. The Urban Institute's *Investing in Creativity: A Study of the Support Structures for U.S. Artists* (2003) remains an influential cornerstone in research on U.S. artists. The extensive list of foundation funders and partners includes many connected to the Montauk or Orcas convenings.

One of the most enduring influences of *Investing in Creativity* has been the definition of six dimensions of support for individual artists: (1) Validation; (2) demand and markets; (3) material supports; (4) training and professional development; (5) communities and networks; and (6) information. This framework identified the need for professional skills training along with acknowledgment of other professional needs from material supports, such as insurance, to professional connections within and beyond the cultural sector, information on copyright, and other legal protections. Many of the funders who supported the research subsequently integrated professionalization aspects into their support of artists, including Doris Duke Charitable Foundation (DDCF), William and Flora Hewlett Foundation, Rockefeller Foundation, and others.

Investing in Creativity led directly to the design and launch of a multi-faceted ten-year initiative, Leveraging Investments in Creativity (LINC), supported by many of the same funders. Founding president Holly Sidford, a leading thinker on support for artists, worked closely with the Ford Foundation as LINC took shape in creating "a philanthropic experiment in using information, money, strategy, and partnerships to effect change in the support system for artists in the United States" (Sidford et al., 2013). Between 2003 and 2013 LINC disbursed over $18 million to support national and local components, working with more than 100 partner organizations, and helping to activate a myriad of programs, projects, and related research

(Sidford et al., 2013), many of them evident throughout this chapter. An additional outgrowth of *Investing in Creativity* was the development of United States Artists and its national fellowship program in 2006, spearheaded by the Ford, Rockefeller, Rasmuson, and Prudential Foundations (United States Artists, 2023).

Artistic Dividend: The Arts' Hidden Contributions to Regional Development (Markusen & King, 2003) brought the entrepreneurial aspects and economic research dimensions of artists' careers into focus. Noted economist Markusen and her Arts Economy Initiative colleagues subsequently undertook a landmark study. *Crossover: How Artists Build Careers across Commercial, Non-profit and Community Work* (Markusen, 2006) was conducted for The William and Flora Hewlett Foundation, The James Irvine Foundation, and LINC[3] and greatly expanded understanding of the professional practices of artists in all disciplines.

As research on artists increased, gaps became evident. The Ford Foundation responded to concerns that Native artists and organizations were facing distinctive challenges and needs. A research initiative began in the early 2000s that culminated in the 2010 publication of *Native Arts and Cultures: Research, Growth, and Opportunities for Philanthropic Support*. This research led to the creation of a 501(c)3 philanthropic organization, Native Arts and Cultures Foundation (NACF), that was Native-led and exclusively focused on the preservation and promotion of American Indian, Alaska Native and Native Hawaiian arts and cultures nationwide (Native Arts and Culture Foundation, n.d.). Over 20 additional foundations joined the founding funder, the Ford Foundation, and today NACF provides direct grants to artists, a Mentor Artist Fellowship initiative, and other resources for Indigenous artists. Research, such as the Global Center for Cultural Entrepreneurship's 2010 report, supported by for the W.K. Kellogg Foundation, increased understanding of support and cultural entrepreneurship for Indigenous and minority artists (Snyder et al., 2010).

The Support for Individual Artists Committee of GIA has been one of the most active groups of funders within GIA for more than 20 years, serving as an advocate for research on artists. GIA commissioned an investigation into benchmarking of support for artists, beginning with "A Review of Scholarly Research on Artist Support" in 2012 (Brown et al., 2012). This review identified three primary subsections of support for artists found in previous research: monetary support (i.e., grants and awards); in-kind support with monetary value (such as residencies, insurance, or legal services); and intangible support. It is in this third category of intangible support that we find professional development training, information, and resources provided to artists by a variety of sources, from academic settings to local arts agencies, nonprofit organizations, and in some cases, directly from foundations (Brown et al., 2012). The initiative resulted in *A Proposed National Standard Taxonomy for Reporting Data on Support for Individual Artists* (Brown et al., 2014). Nine forms of "Professional Development and Sustaining Services" are noted: (1) Artist-in-Residence Programs; (2) Access to Networks and Markets; (3) Professional Training and Technical Support; (4) Subsidized Housing/Workspace; (5) Mentorship and Coaching; (6) Fiscal Sponsorship Services; (7) Information Access; (8) Legal Services; and (9) Subsidized Insurance (Brown et al., 2014).

A study in 2015 sought to revisit, expand on, and update the framework created by *Investing in Creativity* more than a decade earlier. *Creativity Connects: Trends and Conditions Affecting U.S. Artists* was led by the Center for Cultural Innovation (CCI), for the NEA, with additional support from the Surdna Foundation and DDCF (Center for Cultural Innovation, 2016). *Creativity Connects* identified four main socio-economic trends and their influences on artists including one of particular relevance to professional development: "Training and funding systems are not keeping pace with artists' evolving needs and opportunities" (Center for Cultural Innovation, 2016, p. 1). The study further states:

> Regardless of the entry point, the skills required to succeed as an artist today are not limited to mastering an art form or presentation technique. Increasingly, artists also need knowledge and skills in multiple areas of production, business, and social media, and must master the complexities and ambiguities of both making art and making a career in a contemporary world.
> (Center for Cultural Innovation, 2016, p. 20)

This research emphasizes how the practices and pathways of artists cannot be disconnected from larger systemic issues that create and constrain communities and opportunities.

Artists' professionalization has also been examined in relationship to academic training through the work of the Strategic National Arts Alumni Project (SNAAP). This research initiative was founded at the Indiana Center for Postsecondary Research at Indiana University, and launched with the support of the Surdna Foundation, other foundations, and in partnership with higher education institutions. For decades, BFA and MFA programs, and conservatories, were reluctant to embrace professional development and career skills as part of the curriculum. Such training and entrepreneurial approaches were often seen to carry a taint of the marketplace that distracted from, if not degraded, a focus on aesthetics and artistic skills and concepts (Bonin-Rodríguez, 2012; Dworkin, 2019). SNAAP research affirms that professionalization components and entrepreneurship are essential for artists (SNAAP, 2011, 2014; Johoda et al., 2016; Frenette et al., 2016). SNAAP studies provide a picture of expectations likely to guide future professional development training in post-secondary education:

> What do alumni say that their institutions could have done to better prepare them for careers? For alumni who are at least 30 years old,

and have worked in an arts-related occupation, they wish that their institution had taught them about the nuts-and-bolts aspects of work, including how to network and promote themselves, how to handle debt and budgets, how to manage the business concerns associated with their particular arts-based work, how to be entrepreneurial, and how to find jobs. These findings, based on arts alumni responding in their own words reinforce previously reported SNAAP results on a skills mismatch regarding the need for more entrepreneurial and business skills in postsecondary arts education.

(Frenette, 2019)

Research on individual artists began as disparate inclinations, spurred by individual researchers, foundations, and agency staff members tried to bring clarity and focus to support for artists. A body of literature, much of it since 1990 supported or driven by private foundations, now provides a richer and deeper understanding of artists' needs, and the mechanisms and methods that support professionalization for individual artists working in all disciplines. The term "artist" has expanded to be more inclusive over time. Amount of time devoted to artistic work; earnings from artistic work; reputation among the general public; recognition among other artists; quality of artistic work; membership in a professional artists' group or association; professional qualifications or educational credentials; and subjective self-identification as an artist were used to identify artists in the late 1980s (Frey & Pommerehne, 1989). Acknowledging the evolution of the term "artist" through the final decade of the twentieth century, Butler and DiMaggio (2000) focused on six forms of identification: (1) Membership in a professional artist group or association; (2) amount of paid time devoted to artistic work; (3) professional qualification; (4) reputation and recognition; (5) self-identification; and (6) directories. *Investing in Creativity* (Jackson et al., 2003) very intentionally acknowledged the diversity of artists as "all adults who have expert artistic skills; have received artistic education or training (formal or informal); attempt to derive income from those skills: and are or have been actively engaged in creating artwork and presenting it to the public" (p. 6). Jeffri (2004) pointed to three sources of definition for artists: the marketplace; education and affiliation; and self-identification and peer identification. Markusen's research (2006) included "anyone who self-defines as an artist; works as a writer, musician, visual or performing artist; spends ten hours or more a week on his/her artwork whether or not for income; and shares his/her artwork beyond family and close friends" (p. 7). The complexity of defining professional artists is noted in GIA's 2012 research. Income or time spent thresholds risk excluding marginalized populations of artists. Boundaries between professional and amateur, commercial, and independent artists are blurry, and often less clear among younger artists or within immigrant communities (Brown et al., 2012). The term artist and the role of self-identification have become increasingly inclusive.

Professional Development for Artists

Professional development opportunities for artists reflect the growth of institutional philanthropy's interest in research, and in building organizational structures to deliver assistance directly to a broad range of individual artists. We see how services and support for artists intersect with an emerging understanding of artists' needs and structural responses. Programs to assist artists with professional development emerged in tandem with the formation of the NEA, the growing number of state arts agencies, and the creation of nonprofit artist-serving organizations. By 1974, all 50 states had an arts agency that had operated for a year or more (GIA, 2015). Arts agencies and organizations began offering workshops and classes focused on marketing and business skills, looking for ways to support artists' ability to produce and disseminate their work. Public and private philanthropic support was emerging for professional tools and resources to address the needs of artists in a competitive marketplace. Professional development programs appeared with increasing frequency over subsequent years, underscoring a shift toward providing direct support to artists. These ranged from occasional "technical assistance" workshops or classes provided by arts agencies or nonprofits arts entities to the emergence of a new form of arts nonprofit: the artist-service nonprofit. These organizations developed with missions focused on the individual independent artist. From the late 1970s through the end of the twentieth century, we see the creation of notable organizations and programs that continue to have strong roles in professional development for independent artists. Foundations played a catalytic role, helping to launch or expand artist-service organizations especially in the 1980s and 1990s. Foundation-supported research informed the methods of delivery in these organizations, and foundation funding priorities had an impact on program design. Some foundations choose to have these entities administer grant programs for artists on their behalf.

Programs and services for artists continued to increase and adapt with the turn of the twenty-first century. In 2015, Essig and Flanagan inventoried 165 entities addressing acquisition of professional development skills for artists in *How It's Being Done: Arts Business Training Across the U.S.* The study identified programs or services providing planning skills, marketing, resource acquisition, fiscal literacy, relevant business law, and other topics. The authors define ten categories of training delivery methods: (1) Articles/podcasts/vlogs; (2) books; (3) facilitated conversations; (4) one-on-one consultation; (5) online resource library; (6) resources center; (7) seminar style class; (8) webinars; (9) workshops; and (10) various and other. The research also identified issues of access based on geographic location and concerns based on career stage (Essig & Flanagan, 2015). The Emily Hall Tremaine Foundation (EHTF) commissioned this study in advance of its initiative *Artists Thrive*. This initiative, launched in 2016 in support of artists (Artists Thrive, 2022), built on EHTF's commitment since 2002 to increase access to business development expertise, entrepreneurial skills, and related professional supports for visual artists (Emily Hall Tremaine Foundation, n.d.).

Four artist-service programs are examined here in greater depth: NYFA, Springboard for the Arts, Artist Trust, and Creative Capital. They provide a picture of the evolution of professional training programs and services for independent artists and also illustrate the deep engagement of foundations in exploring, encouraging, and experimenting in this arena. Numerous other noteworthy examples, past and present, exist. Arts councils, economic development offices, arts centers, community centers, schools, and other entities provide such services, often as an important if not central aspect of their mission. The entities profiled here are selected for their leadership roles and their continuing innovation and engagement with professional development services and resources for artists. All four were formed between 1970 and 1999 and continue to focus on individual artists as of 2023. They reflect both state-based and national scopes.

Delivering Professionalization Services: Four Examples

New York Foundation for the Arts (NYFA)

NYFA was established by the New York State Council on the Arts (NYSCA) as an independent nonprofit in 1971, catalyzed by a group of artists who were part of the New York City Department of Cultural Affairs. The purpose was to serve individual artists in New York State with resources, guidance, and funding for art projects. The state constitution prohibited NYSCA, a government agency, from distributing funding directly to artists. NYFA was set up as an intermediary, able to distribute monies provided by NYSCA as well as funds raised from other sources directly to artists. Under the leadership of Ted Berger from 1980 to 2005, NYFA's services and programs extended to serve artists throughout the United States, and even beyond its borders (Philanthropy News Digest, 2003). This includes a variety of physical and online professional development resources in addition to grant programs to support the creation of art for independent artists as well as small artist-centered organizations (NYFA, n.d.a).

A key program is NYFA Source, an extensive national online artist-focused resource, providing thousands of listings, accompanied by the option for individualized advice. It is built on the Visual Artist Information Hotline created in 1990 by the Marie Walsh Sharpe Foundation, in cooperation with the American Council for the Arts. Sharpe was originally the only funder of the Hotline, but in 1996, a consortium of funders joined to support the program, and management was transferred to NYFA and renamed NYFA Source (Peeps, 2001). In recent years, this online service of NYFA has been augmented by #ArtistHotline, a social media initiative to create online conversation around the professional side of artistic practice, and *The Business of Art*, an extensive online archive including articles, interviews, videos, and links focused on professional development topics (NYFA, n.d.b). NYFA has continuously provided artists with professional development training including workshops, panels, individual consultations, publications, in-depth training opportunities, and online resources. These now include an Artist as Entrepreneur Boot Camp, Immigrant Artist Mentoring Programs, an incubator program for a cohort of New York City-based arts startups, and the revised edition of a "how to" book compiling NYFA knowledge and experience (Cobb et al., 2011).

In order to permit artists and emerging arts organizations to raise funds from more sources, NYFA began its Fiscal Sponsorship program in 1976. It is one of the oldest such programs in the country, currently supporting more than 350 artists projects (NYFA, n.d.) in addition to providing the "umbrella" of 501(c)3 tax status, along with back office services, including payroll, and assistance in strategy development for fundraising. NYFA's services are supported through a mix of funds, including governmental support at the national, state, and city levels, as well as a few corporations. Foundations continue to play a pivotal role, with 20 foundations noted as supporters as of 2020, including the Doris Duke Foundation, Ford Foundation, Pollock-Krasner Foundation, EHTF, and Andy Warhol Foundation for the Visual Arts. This work is deeply dependent on such funding and built on relationships both long-standing and new.

Springboard for the Arts

Springboard for the Arts originated in 1978 as a program of United Arts and became an independent nonprofit in 1991 under the name Resources and Counseling for the Arts, to provide the arts community in Minnesota with management and consulting services. The name was changed to Springboard for the Arts in 2002 with a commitment to professional development services for self-employed artists, seeking to connect "artists with the skills, contacts, information and services they need to make a living and a life" (Springboard for the Arts, 2021). From its inception, it drew on community development models and a dedication to artists playing an integral role in communities. Low-cost individual consultations, workshops on professional development topics like "Marketing Your Artwork" or "Managing an Erratic Income," and attorney and accountant referrals were offered. Springboard also developed and administered an Artist Loan Fund as well as an Emergency Relief Fund offering up to $500 to artists dealing with career-threatening disasters (Springboard for the Arts, 2023a). Early support came from numerous regional sources, including the Jerome Foundation, McKnight Foundation, Target Foundation, as well as the Minnesota State Arts Board, and the NEA. Springboard has received consistent support from key foundation funders. It is interesting to note that longtime Springboard supporter, the McKnight Foundation, located in Minnesota, chose to focus its own arts grantmaking as of 2008 on working artists (Kunimatsu, 2014) suggesting the awareness and advocacy for individual artist support built by Springboard.

A steady growth of programs and services for and with artists has strengthened its role regarding economic and community development. Springboard has come to see its work as being integrally tied to building stronger communities, neighborhoods, and economies, with artists as valuable assets in that work (New Economy Coalition, n.d.). Their 2021 mission articulates this:

> Our work is about creating communities and artists that have a reciprocal relationship, where artists are key contributors to community issues and are visible and valued for the impact they create. We do this by creating simple, practical solutions and systems to support artists.
>
> (Springboard for the Arts, 2021)

Their work is guided by key principles that include illuminating the social and economic value that artists bring to every community, using the broadest definition of who is an artist, and a commitment to sharing tools to benefit as many artists as possible. Programs and services are categorized into six general areas: (1) Jobs and opportunities; (2) grants and funding; (3) professional growth; (4) health and wellness; (5) housing and spaces; and (6) resources. Professional growth tools include their *Works of Art: Business Skills for Artists*, a professional development curriculum that can be taken as a full series, customized, or presented as individual workshops, (Springboard for the Arts, 2023b) and one-on-one consultations with Artist Career Consultants, who are established artists with diverse experience and backgrounds. Artists can also access equipment, tools, and resources onsite, with some equipment available for loan (Springboard for the Arts, 2021).

Artist Trust

Artist Trust was founded in 1987 by artists and their supporters in Washington State to develop a new model to increase support for individual artists. The nonprofit was created to address dual needs of artists working in all disciplines: financial resources and information resources. Founder Anne Focke, who was involved with the Montauk and Orcas convenings and became the first Executive Director of GIA, intentionally sought to engage Artist Trust with other entities concerned with artist support, including NYFA.

Twenty initial $5,000 grants were distributed in 1987, and a newsletter with resources for artists was published. Programming during the first five years went beyond funding and information services to include building community understanding of the role of artists, as well as awareness of AIDS and issues of freedom of expression. In 1993, they added professional practice workshops for artists around the state on topics including *The Business of Being an Artist,* and in 1996 began co-sponsoring legal clinics for artists (Bach, personal archives). With the growth of the Internet, Artist Trust launched its website in 1999 and greatly expanded information on artists' opportunities and resources via new online tools. Artist Trust administered relief aid to artists after the 2001 Nisqually earthquake with funding from the NEA and the King County Arts Commission, strengthening its interest in emergency response. The following year, the organization moved into a permanent home and created a walk-in artists' resource center.

Professional development training expanded in 2003, when Artist Trust was one of four organizations that were awarded a two-year grant from the EHTF. Artist Trust developed the EDGE Professional Development Program, which initially focused on visual artists, expanding over time to a 50-hour training program for visual, literary, and film or media artists offered in a variety of formats over many years, including one-week on-site intensives, and through partnerships including a community college. Additionally, Artist Trust worked with The Longhouse Education and Cultural Center to create The Native Creative Development Program linking financial support with elements of EDGE professional development training. Other services have included an initiative to expand artists' health insurance supported by LINC and opportunities for regional dance artists to participate in professional development through a Dance/USA initiative (Artist Trust, n.d.; Bach, personal archives). Artist Trust was one of four artist-serving entities selected in 2012 by the Joan Mitchell Foundation to advance its initiative related to archiving and documenting older visual artists' work, Creating a Living Legacy (CALL) (Joan Mitchell Foundation, n.d.).

Current training opportunities at Artist Trust include practical instruction in business skills, led by established artists and arts professionals, a career-training series based on Artist Trust's long-running EDGE program, one-on-one meetings with staff regarding Artist Trust grant applications, and opportunities for artists and other stakeholders to discuss issues that directly impact the livelihood of artists (Artist Trust, 2023). Artist Trust's evolving professional development programs seek to equip artists to be self-sufficient creators of art, serving as a center and clearing house for artists' resources, and encouraging peer relationships and networks. Annual grant funding to artists has grown over the years, along with newer specialized funding opportunities, including a grant for Native artists, and grants focused on older women artists.

Creative Capital

Creative Capital began to take shape as an idea in the late 1990s. When it officially launched in 1999, it reflected the thinking and commitment of many partners eager to explore how artists could be supported with the same kind of opportunities as entrepreneurs in other sectors. A spirit of experimentation, drawing on the burgeoning tech sector, fueled its mission to reinvent cultural philanthropy and meet the needs of innovative artists across the country. Start-up funds were provided by 36 donors, mostly foundations, some of whom hoped that Creative Capital would serve as co-administrator or eventually administrator of their grant programs (Guay, 2012). The Andy Warhol Foundation for the Visual Arts provided founding support, and was joined by many other foundations, some of which continue their support to this day.

Creative Capital developed a four-component approach described by founding director Ruby Lerner as an "integrated, multi-faceted, and sequential system of support" (Hardymon & Leamon, 2010, p. 7). This takes the form of money to support the creation of the artist's project, connected to support for the artist by enhancing self-management skills. Additionally, support is provided for building relationships that could be sustained beyond the grant period, as well as support via Creative Capital's promotion of the project (Hardymon & Leamon, 2010). Over an extended time period, often three to five years, awardees engage with staff, participate in individual meetings with relevant colleagues, attend multiple meetings with a strategic planning coach, as well as consult with legal, financial, marketing, public relations, and web experts. An orientation meeting, artist retreats, and regional gatherings bring together awardees and build peer-to-peer networks as an integral aspect. Currently, each funded artist receives up to $50,000 in direct funding for their artistic project along with related career development services valued at $50,000 (Creative Capital, n.d.).

Creative Capital, with the Los Angeles Review of Books, published a series of pieces in 2019 that reveal a sense of this endeavor:

> Creative Capital's impulse to recast arts philanthropy as venture capitalism (albeit a patient and forgiving strain of it) was implicitly tied to the radical, democratizing promises of the internet—its potential for the free, DIY, networked distribution of artworks; its opportunities for gender- and color-blind interaction (lol); its infinite capacity for niche marketing—as well as the seductive techno-progressivism of startup culture. The organization was innovative in its aim to pair funding with professional support so that artists might develop financially sustainable, self-sufficient careers in the online era, and it was unique in hoping for a return on its investment (not to its donors but back to the fund).
>
> (Fateman, 2019)

This venture capital mindset reflected a shift in the way foundations approached philanthropy directed to individual artists. Many in the field see Creative Capital's creation as formative, with its emphasis shaped and supported by a consortium of foundations, and its focus on assisting artists to behave entrepreneurially. Pioneering approaches include maximizing the power of artist convenings and networks with resulting professional benefits (Cameron, personal communication, 2018).

Starting in 2003, Creative Capital reconfigured aspects of its professional development resources for awardees into programs accessible to artists across the country. In addition to online workshops, workshops became available in association with state and local arts organizations, foundations, artist collectives, nonprofits, fellowship programs, art schools, colleges, and universities nationwide permitting other entities to provide Creative Capital's respected professional development components. Creative Capital's relationship with some foundations is multi-dimensional as can be seen with the DDCF. In 2011, the DDCF asked Creative Capital to partner with them to launch and oversee the Doris Duke Performing Artist Awards Program. DDCF had been a major supporter of Creative Capital starting in 2000. They also provided lead funding for the MAP Fund starting in 2008 (originally known as the Multi-Arts Production Fund, created by the Rockefeller Foundation in 1988) an ancillary program managed by Creative Capital at that time (Whang, 2019). The Performing Artists Awards Program provided significant funding of up to $275,000 per selected artist. These funds were intended to support extended professional and artistic development, audience development, and retirement planning. Awardees were provided access to Creative Capital's professional development services, and DDCF offered an additional and untried element: funds to match contributions to artists' retirement accounts (Guay, 2012). This partnership with Creative Capital permitted DDCF to provide

> access and information to help artists understand and think about important non-artistic aspects of the Artists Awards grants. . . . This includes consulting to help artists understand and plan regarding taxes, financing and real estate . . . individually tailored, and long-range, to assist artists in thinking in terms of a sustainable career. To think beyond the life of the grant.
>
> (Cameron, personal communication, 2018)

These four featured organizations are far from alone in this work. Another noteworthy example is the CCI, founded in 2001 in California and today emphatically linking professionalization training with larger economic issues. CCI prioritizes helping artists realize financial self-determination, "attending to the needs of artists as a whole person and not just as producers of art" (Center for Cultural Innovation, n.d.) (Mirikitani, 2008). They believe that common cause with other sectors addressing similar financial struggles and tackling inequities built into existing systems of arts support is critical to making sustainable change in artists' lives (Center for Cultural Innovation, n.d.).

Roles and Modes

There is a complex interrelationship between artist-service organizations and foundations, not only as funders but also as thought partners. Shared research, attendance at GIA and other conferences, and a network of relationships link these organizations and foundations. We see a symbiotic relationship in the building of organizations to deliver professionalization skills and resources to artists. Some foundations have developed strong programs, interfacing directly with artists, while others continue to channel support through artist-service entities. At one time, direct support via grants and other assistance was thought to be too difficult to navigate for most foundations—legally and administratively—but this has become more of a question of priorities than roadblocks (Gehrig & Mittermaier, 2010). Today we see foundations exploring both direct and indirect means. The linkage of professional development training directly to grant funding grew after the publication of *Investing in Creativity*. It was acknowledged, if not broadly implemented, that financial support accompanied by relevant career skills training could maximize benefits to the artist. Many programs continue to experiment with ways to link training with financial support, and foundations are frequent champions for such endeavors. Artist-endowed foundations, such as those built on the estates of Andy Warhol, Lee Krasner, Robert Rauschenberg, Joan Mitchell, and many others, have emerged as important and active sources of support for independent artists. Research conducted by Christine J. Vincent has added significantly to our understanding of the role and potentials of this subsector of foundations (Vincent, 2011, 2013).

Social and cultural factors have had a strong impact on artist professional services and foundation funding priorities. Digital technologies shifted modes and methods of professional training, providing artists with expanded access to tools, entrepreneurial opportunities, and reducing the role of gatekeepers. The Internet greatly expanded access to fiscal sponsorship and evolving fundraising platforms such as Fractured Atlas (Fractured Atlas, 2023) and Shunpike (Shunpike, 2023), permitting artists to directly reach donors without the financial and administrative burden of creating their own 501(c)3 nonprofit. Artist support structures have responded to the huge cultural phenomenon of hip-hop, with some artists very successfully taking career paths disconnected from the nonprofit arts sector. We also see new efforts to find common cause with other professions, within and beyond the creative sector, and to build systemic change that can impact the professional aspects of an artist's career. The 2016 report, *Creativity Connects: Trends and Conditions Affecting U.S. Artists* (Center for Cultural Innovation, 2016), explores many of these factors, with a research framework built on the 2003 *Investing in Creativity* study. Foundations are increasingly attentive to what they hear from individual artists, as reflected by the 2020 decision by The Andrew W. Mellon Foundation (the largest supporter of the arts and culture in the country), announcing that its arts grantmaking would be reoriented entirely on issues related to social justice (Cascone, 2020). The giving priorities of foundations influence which programs and initiatives move forward.

Ben Cameron, president of the Jerome Foundation, holds a redoubtable vantage point in the field on the role of foundations and artist professional development. He served from 2006 to 2015 as the Program Director for the Arts at the DDCF, and previously held leadership positions with Theatre Communication Group, the Dayton Hudson Foundation, and served as director of the Theater Program at the NEA. He notes that foundations have supported highly structured as well as more flexible approaches to creating enhanced skill sets and that foundations are becoming more flexible in their support of artists. Over recent years, the Jerome Foundation "shifted more money to individuals. We knew that artists are less and less interested in working through nonprofits" (Cameron, personal communication, 2018). Cameron sees significant rethinking on artists and nonprofits in the past few years, and notes that the artistic impulse has found alternatives such as ensembles and collectives. The power of direct access via electronic distribution, an increasing emphasis on entrepreneurship, and the acquisition of related professional skills are at play. In a related shift, he notes a strengthening of artist-to-artist infrastructure, with artists now taking on the work of presenting and supporting each other (Cameron, personal communication, 2018).

Conclusion

Research on artists has provided a deeper and more nuanced understanding of the needs and challenges of individual artists, shaping responses from foundations and artist-serving entities. Affinity groups and partnerships have strengthened cultural philanthropy focused on artists. New insights and voices are influencing the engagement of funders, as well as guiding the design and delivery of professional development programs and tools. Artists' professional development practices today embrace management, business capacity, and artist entrepreneurialism, most often through nonprofit organizations serving artists, though sometimes directly through foundations' own programs. As we move through the 2020s, we see growing attention to flexibility, adaptability, and inclusiveness in programs and funding structures, and the importance of these traits to younger artists (Cameron, personal communication, 2018) and to the field at large.

The very idea of artistic practice is in a fluid moment, with new roles being shaped by artists. This includes artists' roles within organizations, and artists developing their own structures. These new structures may be intended to be short term or long term, nonprofit or not, and are often singularly focused on finding ways to produce and present their work. Patterns of work and monetary support have shifted toward a gig economy fed by new technologies. Artists have always resourcefully pieced together their careers via multiple sources (Markusen, 2006; Wyszomirski & Chang, 2017) and today this practice is occurring at a rapid rate in multiple sectors. As expectations and experiences change in the marketplace and society at large, it is likely to lead to different professional pathways, tools, and forms of support for artists.

The broad societal upheaval activated with the death of George Floyd at the hands of police, and the larger Black Lives Matter movement, has trained a spotlight on racial inequity, including its manifestations in the arts sector. Increasing attention and energy focused on challenging entrenched systems and mechanisms will undoubtedly result in changes in individual artist support. Funding and professional development programs for individual artists have actively wrestled with diversity, equity, and inclusion (DEI) for decades, but in recent years, we see new commitment and action. Both foundations and artist-serving organizations are making use of statements of diversity, equity, and inclusion to shape changes in program design, and to reconsider selection processes for competitive opportunities. A statement in an entity's public materials indicates awareness and is intended to hold them accountable in how they conduct and evaluate their work, including serving a more inclusive array of artists. The peer panel review process has been the dominant method used in selection of artists for support. This method is now acknowledged to reflect inherent systemic values and biases, and new approaches for selection of artists are being explored and implemented. One noteworthy effort is *RE-Tool for racial equity in the panel process* (Savage et al., 2018), a collaborative effort led by Jerome Foundation staff, catalyzed by a small group of arts philanthropists in 2015 with further support from the DDCF in 2017 (Savage et al., 2018).

Foundation funding continues to influence and amplify priorities. Nonprofit organizations and public agencies are attentive to foundation priorities as they seek, and are often dependent on, funding for professionalization programs serving artists. For some artists, entrepreneurially focused practices decrease interest and reliance on established pathways of philanthropic support. Such tensions will undoubtedly shape new methods and structures as artists, artist-serving organizations, and philanthropy navigate a dynamic set of conditions, and respond to the momentous changes resulting from the COVID-19 pandemic.

Communication was minimal among funders and providers of fledgling individual artist grants and professional development until the late twentieth century (Focke, 2015). Today, those with interest in this work have rich and varied opportunities to share research, experiences, strategies, and challenges to hasten experimentation and dissemination of best practices to benefit independent artists across the country. The intersecting roles of entities supporting independent artists are evident in the roster of the GIA Individual Artists Support Committee. Representation includes those with a longstanding mission and track record of individual artist funding, research, and professional development support.[4] We also see more recent additions, such as the ten-year-old Kenneth Rainin Foundation in the Bay Area, whose perspective as part of national leadership conversations on artist support is that "foundations are uniquely positioned to take risks, to work beyond a set of best practices that were designed to respond to the conditions and environment forty years ago" (Kenneth Rainin Foundation, 2019). This proactive approach took on new urgency in 2020, as reflected in a GIA blog post co-authored by a public funder and a private foundation director, entitled *A pandemic, a movement, and an agenda for change*:

> We must shift power and resources to ALAANA [African, Latinx, Asian, Arab, and Native American] (GIA, n.d.) communities, honor and center their leadership in organizing and designing programs, and center their voices in governance. . . . The COVID-19 crisis exposed the fault lines of this country, hiding beneath our business as usual frame, and has given us one of the most dramatic opportunities to seize the moment and the momentum to reimagine our systems and rebuild them equitably.
>
> (Johnson & Engstrom, 2020)

The groundwork has been prepared now for decades, with many significant areas of progress. New approaches build on a growing body of knowledge, analysis, and experimentation. Artists are more active than ever in defining and implementing new professional pathways, sometimes in partnership with foundations, public agencies, and nonprofits. The impact of the COVID-19 pandemic has dramatically transformed the landscape for artists, as well as the culture at large. Reliance on and innovative use of digital technologies is opening new forms of professionalization and creative opportunities for independent artists. Vital attention to issues of systemic inequities is causing reexamination of services and forms of support for individual artists by both artist serving organizations and foundations. New voices will shape the intersections of artistic passion, professionalization, and philanthropic support.

Acknowledgments

Many thanks to Ben Cameron, Susan Kunimatsu, Katie Oman, Katy Hannigan, and the many friends and colleagues with whom I've had the opportunity to discuss issues of support for individual artists over the decades. Research assistance was provided for this chapter by Erin Naomi Burrows, MA, MFA.

Notes

1 Since the 1990s, the NEA (2019) has produced valuable studies and reports looking specifically at artists, including *Artists and Other Cultural Workers: A Statistical Portrait* published in 2019.
2 Jeffri continued to expand on this research with studies in the series in 1997, 2004, 2007, 2008, and 2011, and numerous other publications on artists.

3 Markusen's further research on artists and professional issues includes *Native Artists: Livelihoods, Resources, Space, Gifts* (Rendon & Markusen, 2009).
4 Membership as of June 2020 included representation from the Jerome Foundation, New York Foundation for the Arts, Arizona Commission on the Arts, Artist Trust, Center for Cultural Innovation, Doris Duke Charitable Foundation, Creative Capital, Montana Arts Council, Native Arts and Culture Foundation, Artplace America, Surdna Foundation, and Ford Foundation.

References

Artist Trust. (2023). *Professional development.* http://artisttrust.org/professional-development/

Artist Trust. (n.d.). *Professional development.* http://artisttrust.org/professional-development/

Artists Thrive. (2022). *About us.* Artists Thrive. http://artiststhrive.org/history

Bonin-Rodríguez, P. (2012). What's in a name? Typifying artist entrepreneurship in community based training. *Artivate: A Journal of Entrepreneurship in the Arts, 1*(1).

Brown, A., Brown, A., & Bach, C. (2012). *A review of scholarly research on artist support.* Grantmakers in the Arts. www.giarts.org/sites/default/files/Review-of-Scholarly-Research-on-Artist-Support.pdf

Brown, A., Carnwath, J., & Bach, C. (2014). *A proposed national standard taxonomy for reporting data on support for individual artists.* Grantmakers in the Arts. www.giarts.org/sites/default/files/Proposed-National-Standard-Taxonomy-for-Reporting-Data-on-Support-for-Individual-Artists.pdf

Butler, D., & DiMaggio, P. J. (2000). *Studies of artists: An annotated directory.* Princeton University, School of Public and International Affairs, Center for Arts and Cultural Policy Studies.

Cascone, S. (2020). Mellon Foundation President Elizabeth Alexander tells us why America's biggest funder of culture is shifting its focus to social justice. *Artnet News.* https://news.artnet.com/art-world/mellon-foundation-social-justice-grants-1891607

Center for Cultural Innovation. (2016). *Creativity connects: Trends and conditions affecting U.S. artists.* www.arts.gov/sites/default/files/Creativity-Connects-Final-Report.pdf

Center for Cultural Innovation. (n.d.). *CCI: Mission, history, & now.* http://cciarts.org/mission_history.html

Cobb, P., Ball, S. L., & Hogan, F. (Eds.). (2011). *The profitable artist: A handbook for all artists in the performing, literary, and visual arts.* Skyhorse Publishing Inc.

Creative Capital. (n.d.). *About the creative capital grants.* Creative Capital. http://creative-capital.org/award/about

Dworkin, A. (2019). *The entrepreneurial artist: Lessons from highly successful creatives.* Rowman & Littlefield.

Emily Hall Tremaine Foundation. (n.d.). *Art overview.* Emily Hall Tremaine Foundation. http://tremainefoundation.org/art.html

Essig, L., & Flanagan, M. (2015). *How it's being done: Art business training across the U.S.* PAVE Program in Arts Entrepreneurship, Arizona State University. www.americansforthearts.org/sites/default/files/pdf/2017/by_program/7.%20How%20It%27s%20Being%20Done%E2%80%93Arts%20Business%20Training%20Across%20the%20U.S.pdf

Evans, R. (1994). *Playing Diaghilev.* MacArthur Foundation.

Fateman, J. (2019). *Art matters now: 12 writers on 20 years of art: Johanna Fateman on the founding of creative capital.* Los Angeles Review of Books (LARB). https://lareviewofbooks.org/article/art-matters-now-12-writers-on-20-years-of-art-johanna-fateman-on-the-founding-of-creative-capital/

Focke, A. (2015). Imaginary needs and a raucous caucus: Creative support for creative artists. *GIA Reader, 26*(1). www.giarts.org/article/imaginary-needs-and-raucous-caucus

Ford Foundation. (2010). *Native arts and cultures: Research, growth, and opportunities for philanthropic support.* www.fordfoundation.org/media/1758/2010-native-arts-and-cultures.pdf

Fractured Atlas. (2023). *Fiscal sponsorship.* Fractured Atlas. www.fracturedatlas.org/fiscal-sponsorship

Frenette, A. (2019). In their own words: Arts alumni describe what postsecondary institutions could do better to prepare them for future work and education. *Strategic National Arts Alumni Project (SNAAP): DataBrief, 7*(4). https://mailchi.mp/4c53ff38aac1/snaap-databrief-august-294063?e=554d89d1f1

Frenette, A., Miller, A., Martin, N., Gaskill, S., & Tepper, S. (2016). *Institutional connections, resources, and working across disciplines: What arts alumni are saying.* Strategic National Arts Alumni Project (SNAAP) 2016 Annual Report. https://snaaparts.org/uploads/downloads/Reports/SNAAP-Annual-Report-2016.pdf

Frey, B., & Pommerehne, W. (1989). *Muses and markets: Exploration in the economics of the arts.* Blackwell.

Gehrig, C., & Mittermaier, I. (2010). *Toolbox on making grants to individual artists: Dispelling the myths and barriers.* GIA 2010 Web Conference Series. www.giarts.org/2010-Web-Conference-Series/Toolbox-On-Making-Grants

GIA (Grantmakers in the Arts). (2015). Support for individual artists timeline. *GIA Reader, 26*(1). www.giarts.org/article/support-individual-artists-timeline

GIA (Grantmakers in the Arts). (n.d.). *Why GIA uses the acronym ALAANA.* Grantmakers in the Arts. www.giarts.org/why-gia-uses-acronym-alaana

Guay, A. (2012). In support of individual artists. *GIA Reader, 23*(1). www.giarts.org/article/support-individual-artists

Hardymon, F., & Leamon, A. (2010). *Creative capital: Sustaining the arts.* Harvard Business School.

Jackson, M., Kabwasa-Green, F., Swenson, D., Herranz, J., Jr., Ferryman, K., Atlas, C., Wallner, E., & Rosenstein, C. (2003). *Investing in creativity: A study of the support structures for U.S. artists.* Urban Institute. http://webarchive.urban.org/UploadedPDF/411311_investing_in_creativity.pdf

Jeffri, J. (2004). Research on the individual artist: Seeking the solitary singer. *Journal of Arts Management, Law & Society, 34*(9), 9–22.

Jeffri, J. (2015). *Information on artists [1989, 1997, 2004, 2007, 2008, 2011].* www.icpsr.umich.edu. www.icpsr.umich.edu/web/NADAC/studies/35585/versions/V1

Joan Mitchell Foundation. (n.d.). *Creating a living legacy (CALL).* Joan Mitchell Foundation. http://joanmitchellfoundation.org/artist-programs/call

Johnson, E., & Engstrom, R. (2020). *A pandemic, a movement, and an agenda for change.* Grantmakers in the Arts. www.giarts.org/blog/covid-19/pandemic-movement-and-agenda-change

Johoda, S., Murphy, B., Virgin, V., & Woolard, C. (2016). *Artist's report back: A national study on the lives of arts graduates and working artists.* BFAMFAPhD.

com. http://bfamfaphd.com/wp-content/uploads/2016/05/BFAMFAPhD_Artist sReportBack2014-10.pdf

Kenneth Rainin Foundation. (2019). *Further together: Helping artists thrive* [Video]. https://vimeo.com/374478572

Kreidler, J. (2006). From neolithic prehistory to the classical era: Grantmakers in the arts 1983–1998. *GIA Reader, 17*(3).

Kunimatsu, S. (2014). *Supporting individual artists: Five funder profiles.* GIA Reader. www.giarts.org/article/supporting-individual-artists-five-funder-profiles

Markusen, A. R. (2006). *Crossover: How artists build careers across commercial, nonprofit and community work.* Project on Regional and Industrial Economics, Humphrey Institute of Public Affairs, University of Minnesota. www.giarts. org/sites/default/files/Crossover_How-Artists-Build-Careers-Across-Commercial-Nonprofit-Community-Work.pdf

Markusen, A. R., & King, D. (2003). *The artistic dividend: The arts' hidden contributions to regional development.* Project on Regional and Industrial Economics, Humphrey Institute of Public Affairs, University of Minnesota. www.giarts.org/ sites/default/files/The-Artistic-Dividend.pdf

McKnight Foundation. (n.d.). *Our approach.* http://mcknight.org/programs/arts/ our-approach/

Mirikitani, C. (2008). *Business of art: An artist's guide to profitable self-employment.* Center for Cultural Innovation.

Native Arts and Culture Foundation. (n.d.). *We believe native arts and culture: Who we are.* Native Arts and Cultures Foundation. www.nativeartsandcultures.org/

NEA (National Endowment for the Arts). (2019). *Artists and other cultural workers: A statistical portrait.* NEA.

New Economy Coalition. (n.d.). *Springboard for the arts.* https://neweconomy.net/ organization/springboard-for-the-arts/

NYFA (New York Foundation for the Arts). (n.d.a). *Home.* NYFA. http://nyfa.org.

NYFA (New York Foundation for the Arts). (n.d.b). *Business of art.* New York Foundation for the Arts. www.nyfa.org/business-of-art

Peeps, C. (2001). *Profile.* Grantmakers in the Arts. www.giarts.org/article/profile-0

Philanthropy News Digest. (2003). *Theodore S. Berger, executive director, New York Foundation for the Arts: Helping the arts and artists recover in the wake of 9/11.* Philanthropy News Digest (PND). https://philanthropynewsdigest.org/newsmakers/ theodore-s.-berger-executive-director-new-york-foundation-for-the-arts-help ing-the-arts-and-artists-recover-in-the-wake-of-9-11

Rendon, M., & Markusen, A. (2009). *Native artists: Livelihoods, resources, space, gifts.* Project on Regional and Industrial Economics, Humphrey Institute of Public Affairs, University of Minnesota. https://www.giarts.org/sites/default/files/ NativeArtistsLivelihoodsResourcesSpaceGifts1209.pdf

Savage, E., Baylon, J., Breaux, P., Blythe, F. J., Brennan, M., Cachapero, E., Shindé, G., Hsieh, K., May, K., Navas-Nieves, T., Preston, J., & Silver, D. (2018). *Annotated guide to re-tool racial equity in the panel process.* Jerome Foundation. www. jeromefdn.org/sites/default/files/2018-10/Re-Tool_2018.pdf

Shunpike. (2023). *What is fiscal sponsorship.* Shunpike. https://shunpike.org/ what-is-fiscal-sponsorship/

Sidford, H., Mandeles, H. L., & Rapp, A. (2013). *Leveraging investments in creativity: Cornerstones.* Leveraging Investments in Creativity.

SNAAP (Strategic National Arts Alumni Project). (2011). *Forks in the road: The many paths of arts alumni*. Strategic National Arts Alumni Project, Indiana University. https://snaaparts.org/uploads/downloads/Reports/SNAAP_2011_Report.pdf

SNAAP (Strategic National Arts Alumni Project). (2014). *Making it work: The education and employment of recent arts graduates*. Strategic National Arts Alumni Project. https://snaaparts.org/uploads/downloads/Reports/SNAAP-2014-Annual-Report.pdf

Snyder, C., Binder, M., Girdner, A., Mitchell, J., & Breeden, L. (2010). *Cultural entrepreneurship: At the crossroads of people, place, and prosperity*. Global Center for Cultural Entrepreneurship. https://nasaa-arts.org/wp-content/uploads/2017/03/Cultural-Entrepreneurship-report.pdf

Springboard for the Arts. (2021). *Thrive as an artist, connect to artists*. Springboard for the Arts. http://web.archive.org/web/20210617233046/https://springboardforthearts.org/

Springboard for the Arts. (2023a). *Personal emergency relief fund*. Springboard for the Arts. https://springboardforthearts.org/additional-resources/personal-emergency-relief-fund/

Springboard for the Arts. (2023b). *Professional development overview: Business skills training for artists*. Springboard for the Arts. http://springboardforthearts.org/professional-growth/overview/

United States Artists. (2023). *About, history*. United States Artists. http://unitedstatesartists.org/about

Vincent, C. J. (2011). *Artist-endowed foundations, their charitable purposes and public benefit: Selections from the study report*. The Aspen Institute. www.aspeninstitute.org/wp-content/uploads/files/content/docs/pubs/artist_endowed_foundations_public_benefit_monograph_2012.pdf

Vincent, C. J. (2013). *The artist as philanthropist: Strengthening the next generation of artist-endowed foundations* (Study Report Supplement 2013). The Aspen Institute. www.aspeninstitute.org/wp-content/uploads/2016/07/AEF-Study-Report-Supplement-2013.pdf

Whang, V. (2019). *Diving into racial equity: The MAP fund's exploration*. Animating Democracy, Americans for the Arts. https://mapfundblog.org/wp-content/uploads/2019/12/Diving-into-Racial-Equity_MAP-AD.pdf

Wyszomirski, M. J., & Chang, W. (2017). Professional self-structuration in the arts: Sustaining creative careers in the 20th century. *Sustainability*, 9(6). http://dx.doi.org/10.3390/su9061035

5 The Dual Professional

The Artist/Manager in Small Arts Organizations

WoongJo Chang

Introduction

Small arts organizations (SAOs) comprise more than 80% of the arts sector (Chang, 2010), yet SAOs form and operate "mostly under the philanthropic radar" (Kitchener & Markusen, 2012). Despite growing recognition of their significance, SAOs receive a small fraction of the funding awarded to larger organizations, remaining undervalued, undercounted, and understudied (Chang, 2010, 2011; Sidford, 2011; Staub & Thatcher, 2003; Wali et al., 2001). The lack of appreciation and failure to accurately account for the strategies, activities, and contributions of active SAOs reflects and perpetuates the chronic underfunding these organizations face.

Of necessity, SAOs typically develop alternative forms of structural support and their leaders adopt innovative organizational practices, such as bricolage and dual professionalism, which, to a greater or lesser extent, diverge from those of conventional businesses and larger arts organizations. These departures from the norm can lead funders and the public to view SAOs and their leaders as less professional despite the high quality of their productions and the professional status and accomplishments of the individual artists and managers in the organizations. As Kitchener and Markusen found, funders "heavily favor large arts organizations over small" (2012, p. 6), in spite of the fact that SAOs are widely influential and numerically dominate the arts sector.

Arts organizations operate in a dual modality: Artistic creation is carried out by product or content professionals while managerial tasks, that is, the business of running the organization, are the province of organization professionals. In larger organizations, these two interlocking but distinct spheres of expertise and practice are typically carried out by differently specialized individuals. This duality especially pertains to the leadership structure, which is typically shared by two people, one of whom oversees the artistic activities, and the other, the business end. The dual modality of this leadership structure appears to have evolved in response to arts organizations' need to balance artistic mission with financial sustainability (Peterson, 1986). However, largely due to economic constraints, in SAOs, the responsibilities for

DOI: 10.4324/9781003138693-6

both artistic and business leadership are often undertaken by a single individual. So, many actors, painters, poets, musicians, and graphic designers, who devote their time to SAOs as artists, also serve in the capacity of managers. Indeed, in the current trend of portfolio careers, "slasher," an emerging term for "artist/manager," is being used to describe these new dual professionals (Chang & Park, 2015; LearnVest, 2013; Wyszomirski & Chang, 2017). This has resulted in a blurring of the traditional boundaries between amateur and professional (Missingham, 2009) as these dual professionals enact an expanded and more creative vision of professionalism.

In this chapter, I seek to understand the phenomenon of dual professionalism in SAOs, with a particular focus on how the cultural workers involved come together to build vibrant arts organizations in a nonprofit arts sector that offers a paucity of financial and structural support (Kreidler, 1996). These individual cultural workers improvise their dual roles as artists and managers and create acknowledged professional productions while also acting as entrepreneurs of their own careers in the arts. In their pursuit of artistic excellence, a diverse group of freelance workers respond to the challenge of occupational uncertainty and income insecurity to transform the understanding of professionalism across the arts and reconfigure the institutionalization of the creative sector. Here, I offer a close examination of one SAO, Available Light Theatre (AVLT) in Columbus, Ohio, and its team of dual professionals, in order to discover how they are able to leverage, individually and collectively, their cultural and social capital to access information, networks, and resources, as well as identify artistic and organizational opportunities, in an effort to establish credible claims to professional status. In light of my findings, I argue that in successful SAOs, it is the dynamic triad of the personal attributes of its leaders, its agile organizational structure, and its public-facing artistic productions that are reshaping the intersection of public culture and professionalism. Thus, I advocate for broader recognition of the unique and uniquely professional contributions that SAOs and their leaders bring to the public arena.

The concept of "professional" varies according to cultural, social, and governance contexts. Though generally understood to be an attribute of an individual who has completed specialized training and earned official certification from the government or a professional organization, professionalism in the arts context manifests in three distinct dimensions: (1) As the specialized skills and knowledge that an individual in a particular occupation possesses (personal professionalism); (2) as the artistic quality of the product (product professionalism); and (3) as an attribute of an organization that maintains high, and broadly recognized, standards of excellence both artistically and organizationally (organizational professionalism). Thus, the concept of professionalism is elastic in that it can refer to the individual, group, or product, and multidimensional in that it is variously used to describe an individual's bona fides, way of conducting business, affiliations, and social status, or an organization's mode of operating and the quality of its artistic output (Van De Camp et al., 2004; Wyszomirski & Chang, 2017). It is important to account for each of these interconnected dimensions as we seek to understand the challenges and opportunities posed by the intersection of structural constraints with the emergence of dual professionalism in SAO leadership.

Dual professionalism has emerged in SAOs in response to evolving economic and social exigencies. In the face of increasingly constrained funding streams, segmented audiences, and the proliferation of technological tools for arts production and business management, nonprofit arts organizations must meet a triple bottom line of artistic vitality, financial sustainability, and public value (Wyszomirski, 2013) in order to be viable players in the cultural sector. As I have argued elsewhere (Chang, 2012), many SAOs have adopted the unconventional practice of bricolage or a "making do" attitude (Chang, 2012; Lévi-Strauss, 1967), in which leaders fill both artistic and managerial roles on an ad hoc basis, regardless of their specialized training in one or the other areas. An SAO typically stakes a claim to being a professional organization by fostering a diverse team of artists and managers who practice dynamic collective entrepreneurship to creatively configure artistic production by adopting agile dual roles, cutting-edge technology, bricolage, and on-the-job learning. This has proven to be a strategy that allows resource-constrained SAOs to meet all three bottom lines and successfully produce acknowledged professional work.

Nevertheless, it can be challenging for an SAO to thrive in the highly contested territory of artistic and managerial professionalism. For funders, the perceived professionalism of an SAO is critically determined by the official qualifications of its staff. Thus, an individual artist or arts manager might have spent years gaining and honing their skills and knowledge and be perceived as fully professional by their peers in the arts world, yet when they take on multiple roles in an SAO be perceived by funders and the public as less than professional, due to a mismatch between their specialized training or credentials and those conventionally expected for their organizational role. By the same token, a larger arts organization might enjoy the mantle of professionalism in the public eye regardless of the status or specific professional qualifications of its organizational leaders. For example, a large, established cultural organization that hires a leader with no arts background from the financial or political spheres in order to capitalize on their connections will likely incur no loss of regard as a professional arts organization because other members of the organization are professionally qualified artists and managers.

In this chapter, I seek to challenge the (often implicit) assumption by funders, policymakers, and the public that insufficient specialization of labor within an SAO indicates a lesser personal, product, and/or organizational professionalism. Instead, funders and policymakers would be well-advised to craft support structures for dual professional artist/managers who are creatively and effectively responding to the shifting economic and social realities of our globalized world. Thus, in order to foster healthy growth in the nonprofit arts sector, proactive policy initiatives are needed to support and further the self-organizing institutionalization that dual professional artist/managers are effecting in the SAO world. In fact, the self-structuration practices of individual artists, who are managing protean careers in the arts (Wyszomirski & Chang, 2017), are already expanding the concept of professionalism in the arts to include the unconventional practice of bricolage (Chang, 2012), a focus on both artistic vitality and financial sustainability, and, most recently, a centering on public value (Wyszomirski, 2013).

How the multiple dimensions of professionalism are understood by funders, policymakers, and the public, and how they manifest in the nonprofit arts sector, can be seen with particular clarity in SAOs, which tend to have a precarious financial base. Through an in-depth case study of the AVLT, a small theater in Columbus, Ohio, I show how an SAO manages and sustains artistic and organizational professionalism by stepping outside perceived and conventionally understood bounds and adopting creative, on the ground, practices that reconfigure professionalism to be artistically vibrant, socially sustainable, and economically scalable. In what follows, I use data I collected from 2008 to 2011 (Chang, 2011), with follow-up research in 2015, 2017, and 2022, to present my case study of AVLT, painting a thick description (Geertz, 1973) of the transformative emergence of dual professionalism in this SAO's diverse workforce, and examine the implications of the organization's success and acknowledged professionalism for the arts sector. In the conclusion, I use what I have learned from AVLT to propose a preliminary model for three points in an SAO's development at which it might benefit from supportive interventions by potential funders, such as public arts agencies, private businesses, or foundations. I conclude by advocating for broader recognition by funders and the public of the value of the uniquely professional business and artistic practices of SAOs that are productively reshaping the intersection of arts professionalism and cultural institutions in the public arena.

The Case Study: Available Light Theatre

AVLT in Columbus, Ohio, was, and continues to be, one of the most successful SAOs in the city and surrounding area and has been praised by peers and audiences for being professional, independent, and inspiring. According to the company's mission statement (which has been substantively consistent over the course of my research), members envision themselves as engaging their community "by staging provocative works that examine our culture, expose its shortcomings, and reveal the beauty of humankind" (Available Light Theatre, 2022). AVLT's productions include original shows written by local artists, as well as contemporary works and reinterpreted classics.

Since its beginnings in 2002, the theater has grown dramatically in terms of its budget size, the number of productions, and especially its audience base. Founded in 2002 as BlueForms Theatre, restructured and renamed in 2004, AVLT was incorporated as a nonprofit 501(c)3 in 2009. The company's annual budget grew from approximately $40,000 in the 2008–2009 season to $165,417 in 2013 (according to AVLT's IRS Form 990-EZ). With 11 board members and 15 company members, as of March 2015, the theater had gained a prominent place in the Columbus community.

AVLT has been acclaimed for the entrepreneurial practices of its mostly part-time and volunteer workforce. AVLT claims to be "a fellowship of artists dedicated to building a more conscious and compassionate world by creating a joyful and profound theatre" (Available Light Theatre, 2022). In 2014, the company launched the YACHT (Young Artists Creatively Hustling for Theatre) Club, a group of young volunteers led by a company member who initially joined the company as an unpaid intern and later became a stipend-receiving staff member. Since 2010, AVLT has been using a small office in the Riffe Center building in Columbus, where eight other SAOs share facilities such as a conference room and rest rooms. However, its members usually prefer to gather in Luck Bros, and consider this local coffee shop to be their headquarters. This gives them the opportunity to involve any members of the community who might be interested. Although most of the company members received a stipend or minimal honorarium for their work, their contributions of time and talent to AVLT far exceed any financial compensation they receive. In the following section, I consider AVLT's successful deployment of its diverse workforce of dual professionals.

Workforce Structure

AVLT's workforce consists of three levels: two staff members who receive a monthly stipend, company members who receive a nominal compensation per performance, and board members who volunteer their time and skills without any compensation. Matt Slaybaugh and Michelle Whited (she is now Michelle Dranschak and emeritus) were the two paid staff in 2010. From June, 2015 to the end of 2021, as former artistic director and executive director, Slaybaugh spent roughly two-thirds of his time on managerial tasks regardless of his official role. Thus, he was an artistic professional who, of necessity, became an organizational professional. As the quintessential dual professional bricoleur, Slaybaugh was involved in almost every aspect of AVLT's creative and business endeavors, including the design and management of the company's interactive website. Whited, AVLT's only other full-time stipend-receiving member during the period of my initial fieldwork, originally joined the company as a costume designer and actor. Although she still filled these roles, she also took on tasks in operations, marketing, and fundraising. In addition to Slaybaugh and Whited, there were two other members who participated in every production: the box office manager and the production manager or resident sound designer. However, they were only paid per each performance they worked and did not receive a regular paycheck (Matt Slaybaugh, personal communication, April 2, 2015). Other company members received minimal compensation for acting and partici- pating in specific productions. They also undertook administrative tasks as needed, though they were not paid for this work. Board members contrib- uted their skills, labor, and time without compensation. In addition, it was not uncommon for volunteers from the local community, some of whom considered themselves amateur artists, to pitch in on both managerial and artistic tasks.

It is certain that with only two paid full-time workers and two paid event workers, AVLT would have difficulty carrying out all of the managerial tasks required for putting on eight to nine productions per season. It would also be impossible for the organization to meet the managerial workload, such as tasks involving financial and legal expertise, with only the paid staff. However, AVLT company and board members, as bricoleurs, all share in the necessary work, creatively leveraging their skills and resources to meet the organization's mission. Thus, the case of AVLT prompts us to consider the slippage between public and institutional perceptions of professionalism in the arts and the actual, if reconfigured, professional practices enacted in SAOs. We must consider the contribution of all members of an SAO's workforce— artists, managers, and technical experts, both paid and volunteer—to achieving the triple bottom line of artistic vitality, public value, and financial sustainability (Wyszomirski, 2013). In particular, as we see with AVLT, the self-structuration activities (Wyszomirski & Chang, 2017) of individual art- ists often, in their work with SAOs, lead them to adopt roles and rely on bricolage practices outside their professional training.

In the following subsections, I delve into how the members devoted their time to AVLT, the multiple roles volunteers undertook, and the ways in which the day job-supported portfolio careers of the company's artists contributed to the theater's recognized artistic excellence. The collaborative and collec- tive entrepreneurship of AVLT's dual professionals effectively positioned it as a serious and professional-level player in the theater world while revamping conventional notions of professionalism in the arts.

Time and Compensation

One of the conventional measures of a person's professionalism is the amount of time that person spends working at their profession, as well as how much they are compensated for that time. Wilensky (1964) suggests that an important characteristic of professionalism is full-time employment in the profession. To measure AVLT company members' time and compensation, I designed a Workload Survey that recorded what they got paid and tracked the hours that members devoted to the company each week.

In the summer of 2010, on a blank calendar for an eight-week period, AVLT members filled in how much time they spent working for the company and briefly described their activities. In addition, to support members' participation in this research and to confirm their entries, I conducted a spot-check phone survey with each participant twice a week during this eight-week period. In this phone survey, I asked members the following three questions: (1) What were you doing in the last 30 minutes? (2) How long have you been doing it? and (3) What will you be doing in the next 30 minutes? Lastly, at the conclusion of the eight weeks, after the participants had turned in their marked calendars, I interviewed the company members individually in order to create a work portfolio for each of them, which I then cross-referenced with the survey results. I found significant agreement between their calendars and their later recollections.

In addition to the Workload Survey, I interviewed company members again, as well as board members, guest artists, audience members, donors, volunteers, and professionals in public agencies and sponsoring companies. I conducted most of these interviews in 2010 and followed up with selected members in 2015. Furthermore, to get a full picture of members' work across managerial and artistic tasks, I shadowed many of them and attended and observed almost every event and performance of the company for two seasons between 2009 and 2011. I also examined company documents, primarily using virtual ethnography (Hine, 2000), such as the company website, emails, web-based project management tools, and social media. In addition, I conducted five focus group discussions with company members on issues of professionalism and their experiences with working with AVLT. These methods allowed me to understand the unique and complex picture of the workforce at this small theater.

The findings from the Workload Survey in 2010 showed that members spent almost as much time at AVLT as they did at their day jobs, even though they received far less than the state's minimum wage for their services to AVLT, or often received no compensation at all. AVLT members spent, on average, 30 hours and 38 minutes per week working for the company. However, during the survey period, the four AVLT members who received regular compensation (either a stipend or pay for every performance) earned $56 for working these hours or an average of $1.87 per hour. More specifically, during the survey period, the artistic director earned $5.71 per hour, the production manager earned $3.14 per hour, and the operations manager earned $1.24 per hour. Considering that the Ohio minimum wage in 2010 was $7.30 per hour (Ohio Department of Commerce, 2010), that members put 75% of full-time hours into the theater, and that AVLT is one of the most acclaimed theater companies in the region, it is an understatement to say their compensation was strikingly low. Thus, AVLT depended heavily on donated time and talent to realize its mission of producing professional quality theatrical performances.

Finally, the issue of employee benefits was of concern to all company members. As successful as AVLT was, no one, including the two full-time employees, received benefits. Some members had health insurance from their day jobs, purchased it privately, or were insured through their families. Others simply did without. The lack of health coverage kept some members from seeking or accepting fulltime employment at AVLT. In one focus group, a member joked that they had decided to produce "Food Play," a play about organic foods, because they all needed to learn more about eating right; "we have to [stay] healthy because we can't afford to get sick" (personal communication, October 6, 2010). With the passage of the Affordable Care Act in March 2010, and its subsequent implementation, this issue has been somewhat mitigated since many more Americans have gained access to affordable healthcare.

Bricoleurs and Volunteers

AVLT achieved professional quality theatrical productions through what I have elsewhere called the "bricolage in collective entrepreneurship" (Chang, 2017) of its volunteers and minimally compensated staff and company members. The concept of bricolage originated with Claude Lévi-Strauss (1967), who describes the practice of overcoming shortfalls in financial, material, and human resources by repurposing and creatively redeploying the resources at hand. The resources and tools available to SAOs are heterogeneous and always finite, and not necessarily specialized for any given individual project. The successful SAO leader is a "jack-of-all-trades who accrues tools and competencies" through repeated entrepreneurial disruptions of conventional constraints (Chang, 2017). In contrast to larger organizations' conventional institutional structure of internal specialization of labor and expertise, SAOs such as AVLT are entrepreneurial enterprises that deploy the ad hoc tactics of collective bricolage, "modes of action that began as loose improvisations and innovations . . . [to build] an organizational strategy of collective entrepreneurship" (Chang, 2017).

Although most of AVLT's bricoleurs were artists who jumped in as needed to carry out managerial tasks, there were also cases of company and board members with technical and professional skills, but without acting backgrounds, who jumped in as artists when the need arose. The results of the Workload Survey indicated that even artists at AVLT typically spent more than 50% of their time at the company carrying out administrative tasks, although they had little prior managerial training. In fact, the artistic director Matt Slaybaugh and operations manager Michelle Whited reported that more than 80% of the time they spent working for AVLT was spent on managerial tasks. Furthermore, in the spirit of collective entrepreneurship, board members who had nine-to-five professional jobs elsewhere frequently stepped in when managerial tasks required more specific expertise. Although not tracked by the Workload Survey, these board members devoted significant time and effort to AVLT, reporting in the individual interviews that they spent from one hour to 10–12 hours per week, depending on the season and the show. Far from just attending the monthly board meetings and showing up at the events and shows, board members lent not only their external professional expertise to accomplishing managerial tasks but also their cultural capital of professionalism to the organization's social legitimacy. Therefore, in considering the development of the organizational professionalism of an SAO such as AVLT, it is important to take into account the time and effort board members, who by law cannot be financially compensated, volunteer toward the realization of the organization's mission and its reputation for artistic and professional excellence.

Many board members at AVLT shared the administrative tasks with company members, and even some artistic tasks, including acting. (A former board member, e.g., even starred in a one-man play, "A Xmas Carol," that he adapted and wrote.) Serving on what they referred to as a "working board," board members functioned as the administrative body of AVLT, taking on roles usually filled by the hired staff in large arts organizations. For example, one board member, who worked as a senior account executive at a major marketing and advertising firm, oversaw AVLT's marketing plan; another board member was a former CEO of a major advertising company in Columbus and also contributed to AVLT's marketing. The former chair of the AVLT board was also a lawyer. One board member worked in, and another ran, an IT company. They all contributed their professional expertise (marketing, PR, accounting, law, and information technology) to the operations of AVLT, establishing benchmarks for professional administrative practices at the company. My findings from the interviews reveal that although board members were not paid, the administrative and professional expertise that they brought to AVLT was crucial for the SAO to function as a professional organization. Therefore, the workforce at AVLT, as is likely at many SAOs (Chang, 2017), was composed of a heterogeneous group of entirely or partially volunteer bricoleurs whose collective entrepreneurship built a small, community-based arts organization that was widely esteemed for its artistic merit and professionalism.

Technology and Opportunity

Digital tools have streamlined and potentiated many aspects of the artistic and managerial work in SAOs. Technology offers arts entrepreneurs an expanded palette of opportunities to produce professional artistic work and streamline managerial tasks. The workforce of an SAO is able to both accomplish more with the aid of technological tools and facilitate the efficient use of individual members' volunteered services. Indeed, at AVLT, the effective uses of technology by managers and artists have become crucial for stabilizing the balance between the organization's mission and its financial resources, enhancing its creative vitality, and thereby assuring its success. Their use of tools such as tax and project management software, for example, guided them through basic managerial tasks while image, video, and social media apps put the power of professional tools into the hands of AVLT's creative bricoleurs.

Social media, in particular, has been a boon for SAOs, vastly enhancing their advertising reach. Members of AVLT were among those proactively pioneering the use of this then-new technology. The board member in charge of finances attributed the theater's success to members' active embrace of the potential of social media. As he said, "We have technology- and social-networking savvy people, [which has] been an important part of Available Light's success" (personal communication, July 15, 2010). One of AVLT's frequent guest directors added that social media has dramatically reduced AVLT's budget for marketing and even allowed the company to more easily reach out to the public beyond its niche market (personal communication, September 21, 2010).

However, easy access to affordable technological applications and hardware has also blurred the distinction between an amateur hobby and professional craftsmanship, eroding societal perceptions of the value of rigorous artistic training. When seemingly professional results can be so quickly produced with the help of computers, when the technical and expressive skills of artistry that once took a lifetime to attain can be achieved after a few tutorials with the right software, and when marketing skills that used to require years of training and experience can be replaced by a kid with a smartphone, what does it mean to be a professional in the arts sector (Hodsoll, 2009; Keen, 2007; McCarthy & Ondaatje, 2002; Mercadex International, 2002)? While the software tools that have become available over the last decades give artists, amateur and professional, powerful palettes of tools previously unimaginable and undeniably shape the content and delivery of the works produced with them, they cannot provide the element of human creativity. Similarly, as Greffe observed, "digital technology influences the contents of artists' products as much as the environment in which artists work" (2004, p. 80). In addition, digital business management practices are creating an environment in which artists create works that, in turn, also influences the shape of those works. Yet, the confusion of tool with creation and the mismatch between public perceptions of professionalism in the arts and actual creative practices reveal the contested definition of art that underlies the question of professionalism that SAO bricoleurs and their digital tools pose.

In this environment, the dual professionalism of AVLT's leaders and members further enhanced the creative, or atypical, professionalism potentiated by digital technology. For example, stage designers were able to use the animation tools in commonly available presentation software (such as Apple's Keynote) to create dynamic, moving stage lighting and backdrops. The SAO also heavily depended on web-based applications to compensate for its lack of human and financial resources. In addition to its established website, www.avltheatre.com, AVLT made extensive use of two web-based project management tools: Basecamp.com and Backpackit.com. They also used free applications, such as Doodle.com, to schedule their events and meetings, Quickbook.com for bookkeeping, and Surveymonkey.com, for audience and market research. In addition, AVLT made extensive use of a wide range of social media, including Facebook, Twitter, Vimeo, and Instagram. AVLT fully exploited the range of new technological tools to facilitate both a flexible professionalism of dynamic bricolage and a productive artistic complexity as active members collectively brought their diverse social, cultural, technical, and entrepreneurial resources to the organization.

As can be seen in AVLT's case, the technological tools that have become increasingly available and increasingly powerful—for financial and project management, artistic production, and social media—facilitate artistic and managerial professionalism in SAOs, enabling workers to donate their services and realize their creative visions in efficient and cost-effective ways. Thus, the notion of professionalism as it applies to SAOs is both more complicated and necessarily more flexible than that applied to larger arts organizations, in which there are clear divisions of labor between individuals. The proof of professionalism is in the process and the product, rather than externally and restrictively defined markers of professional status.

Day Jobs and Portfolio Careers

My findings at AVLT are in line with the findings of other scholars and practitioners (Hyde, 1983; Ormont, 2005; Nelson, 2010; Throsby & Hollister, 2003). Most AVLT company members had a day job and received a token income from their night job at AVLT when they participated in productions. Nevertheless, most considered their work at AVLT, whether it was artistic or managerial, to be their main job. These members noted that they worked at their day jobs in order to support their night jobs. They were motivated by the desire to enhance the artistic quality of AVLT's productions, thereby enhancing the professionalism of the organization. Interviews, focus group discussions, and my observations revealed that most AVLT members had day jobs that were related to their theater work in one way or another. Throsby and Hollister (2003) also found that 43% of all artists had day jobs in an arts-related field, and arts professionals, especially those associated with SAOs, actively managed their portfolio careers. Some AVLT members taught theater at a middle school or high school or at an acting studio, and some freelanced in sound design or acted in commercials. One member worked in cosmetics at a department store where she could utilize her make-up skills, and in turn, she brought back to the theater knowledge about new products that are available in cosmetics. Their day jobs also provided learning opportunities for some artists to acquire managerial skills in marketing or accounting. In fact, company members emulated the marketing strategies they learned in their day jobs, with successful marketing results at AVLT. At times, day jobs even provided alternate sources of funding for AVLT, as in the case of one member who brought gift cards to sell from a department store where she worked; AVLT got to keep a small percentage of the sales. In addition, the day jobs that many members held helped them to network outside of AVLT and more affordably access critical resources in accounting and marketing, for example, and even bring in new board members. By successfully managing their day jobs and their portfolio careers, all AVLT members contributed to the company's artistic viability and managerial competency, thereby building the organization's professionalism.

While SAOs are usually unable to meet conventional, reductionist definitions of organizational professionalism, the concept of the portfolio career can help us understand the occupational professionalism that individual artists and managers bring to the organization (Evetts, 2010; Wyszomirski & Chang, 2017). AVLT's success demonstrates the ways in which professional legitimacy can be collectively constructed from the bricolage of its members' professional connections, certifications, and entrepreneurial skills. In this way, we see that artists and arts managers, who must of necessity build self-structured portfolio careers (Wyszomirski, 2006; Wyszomirski & Chang, 2017), are professionals engaged in managing and growing a fully professional organization.

Artistic Quality and Public Value

AVLT produces value and contributes to the public good through the consistently high artistic quality, performance level, and production values of their productions. While some of AVLT's workforce was full-time, and others were part-time or volunteers, I gathered in the interviews that everybody concerned with AVLT was equally committed to the quality of the plays and the integrity of the message—and this was the measure of the theater's professionalism used by both company members and audiences. In addition, the managerial work that went into delivering each production and sustaining the organization itself was critically important. Most AVLT members made a distinction between artistic professionalism and managerial professionalism, believing that they were professional at least in creating the arts, though they might sometimes be more amateur at managing the company. Regardless, AVLT members have an overarching, common goal to strive for challenging and provocative works that are artistically professional and perceived to promote the public good.

Despite the multidimensionality and context dependency of the term professional, members of AVLT, both full-time and part-time, and both paid and volunteer, did not doubt that they were professionals and that their company was a professional theater, an opinion that supporters and audiences of AVLT shared wholeheartedly. In focus group discussions with company members, they admitted that they may not qualify as conventional professionals. Nevertheless, they described the quality and community benefits of the shows AVLT produced as professional and did not want their productions to be perceived as amateur. Comments from members include: "Community actors would tell you that they're amateur actors, but they have a professional level of skills"; "Amateur kind of leaves a bad taste in my mouth"; "We choose things that are far more challenging for us to do in our professional works than we would in a [non-professional] situation" (focus group discussion, December 16, 2011). While AVLT's artists and managers may not have always conformed to conventional definitions of professionalism, the theater itself was regarded as professional in the local community. The reason many audience members gave for their regular attendance was the quality of the shows that AVLT produced. Their responses included "[AVLT is] top-notch," "professional," and "even more professional than a long-established, regional professional theater company in Columbus" (personal communication with company, May 2010). Clearly, AVLT members do believe in and enact professionalism in both individual occupational terms and in overall organizational capabilities and their belief is reflected in the quality and recognized public value of the company's productions.

Conclusion

The presence and prevalence in the cultural sector of SAOs, which of necessity devise novel responses to material constraints, continue to blur the traditionally accepted line between professionalism and amateurism in the arts (Missingham, 2009). While it is the mission of any public arts organization to meet a triple bottom line of artistic vitality, financial sustainability, and public value (Wyszomirski, 2013), in SAOs, dual professionals create an organizational and artistic professionalism that is greater than the sum of its leaders' (perceived) professional attainments. When individual members, whether artists or managers, adopt dual roles as artists *and* managers to ensure the SAO's economic health and creative vigor, and thus its organizational professionalism, they are able to create a professional product that enhances the public good. Figure 5.1 illustrates the relationship between dual professionalism, the levels of professionalism, and the triple bottom line. Through their personal professionalism as dual professionals who practice bricolage, the artists and managers create an organizational professionalism of artistic vitality, on the one hand, and financial sustainability, on the other. These, in turn, lead to the creation of new public value in the productions, the message, and the venue for creativity.

I have argued here that, in the face of constraint, the practices of dual professionals represent an expanded and more creative vision of professionalism and contribute to reshaping our understanding of the intersection of professionals, cultural institutions, and the public. In this chapter, through the case of the AVLT, I have shown how an SAO can position itself as a company, whose professionalism is recognized by both funders and the public, by creatively and flexibly developing its leaders' professionalism in both the artistic and managerial realms. AVLT has achieved recognition as one of the premier

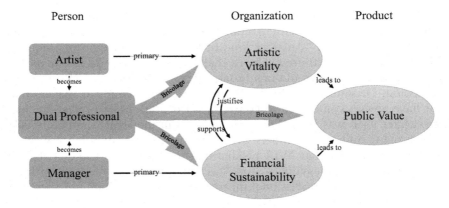

Figure 5.1 Dual Professionalism, Types of Professionalism, and the Triple Bottom Line

professional companies in its region by refusing to stay within the constraints of conventional professionalism and effectively deploying cutting-edge strategies and technologies to enact a dynamic creative, or atypical, professionalism. Notably, they have welcomed and fostered a diverse workforce of dual professional bricoleurs who, with board members and local community supporters, donate (all or much of) their labor and professional skills to practice a dynamic collective entrepreneurship. AVLT's deployment of dual professionalism has resulted in the steady growth of its professional capital and suggests a model of organizational development that may be widely applicable. Thus, I offer a sketch of an SAO's timeline of organizational development and suggest strategic interventions that potential funders, such as public arts agencies, private businesses, or foundations, might make to best foster the organization's growth (see Table 5.1).

In the first phase, SAOs often start small, as a single-person business or informal startup, without board members or any intention to be incorporated as a 501(c)3. While funding is always an issue, at this point the most important role for publicly funded arts agencies, which are tasked with fostering the arts as a social good, is to provide support by offering workshops, training, and mentorship in arts management and business. Individual artists, already bricoleurs in their artistic pursuits, can and should be trained in the skills of collective entrepreneurship and practices of dual professionalism necessary to build a financially viable organization able to produce and market professional works of art. Creative Capital in New York provides one model for potential funders for effectively supporting and advocating for local artists (Hardymon & Leamon, 2010).

SAOs in the second phase of organizational development have grown to have marketing, accounting, or legal issues that require expertise, planning, and often incorporation as 501(c)3s. Public arts agencies can support SAOs

Table 5.1 SAO Developmental Phases

Phase	1	2	3
Characteristics	Small startup or single artist, informal, not seeking 501(c)3 status	Growing, formalizing, seeking 501(c)3 status	501(c)3 organization on path to becoming established
Need/public arts agency intervention	Skills and guidance, training in collective entrepreneurship, development of dual professionalism	Financial and legal expertise, marketing support, community connections, organization building, planning grants	Leverage nonprofit status to create reliable funding streams, grantsmanship assistance, sponsorship networking

at this stage by connecting them with entrepreneurs in wider networks of business, financial, and legal professionals. It may also be that a planning grant would be beneficial to the organization at this time. For instance, AVLT benefited greatly when its first president, Artie Isaac, brought with him his personal and business networks from his former day job as CEO of a marketing company. Further, he recruited additional board members who also volunteered their professional services as financial, accounting, marketing, and legal experts. In the absence of a key person such as Isaac, SAOs can alternatively acquire contacts from public arts agencies. Networking with major players who possess legal and business acumen in the local community is thus a productive second point of intervention for an aspiring 501(c)3 SAO. In addition, public arts agencies should guide SAOs in the early phases of their development to avoid relying on the skills, drive, and charisma of one talented dual professional bricoleur. Rather, the emerging SAO can be guided to ensure that not only the vision but also the ability to realize that vision is distributed among a team of dual professionals.

In the third phase, once an SAOs is incorporated as a 501(c)3, it can take advantage of its nonprofit status to access expanded opportunities for funding in the form of individual donations, grants from public arts agencies and foundations, and sponsorship from for-profit businesses. In fact, obtaining and maintaining nonprofit status and applying for new grants or sponsorship is a marker of an SAO's organizational professionalism. However, it is time-consuming to secure nonprofit status and attract new funders and sponsors. SAOs need more efficient ways to document their activities for these funding pursuits. AVLT's artistic director Slaybaugh expressed frustration with repeatedly preparing similar documents with only slightly different formats, saying, "it's not worth the money and time" (personal communication,

February 21, 2011). Existing public arts agencies streamlined the funding search and application process for SAOs by aligning with regional arts philanthropy, such as Cultural Data Project by PEW (later DataArt project by SMU) (SMU DataArts, 2023). This has enabled an SAO to develop their base documentation once and then customize it for each grant package and would, in turn, effectively generate a pool of applicants that funding entities could access as they develop their funding and support programs for SAOs.

Professionalism in the arts context manifests in three distinct dimensions: (1) As the specialized skills and knowledge that an individual artist or manager possesses (personal professionalism); (2) as the artistic quality of the product (product professionalism); and (3) as an attribute of an organization that maintains high, and broadly recognized, standards of excellence both artistically and organizationally (organizational professionalism) (see Figure 5.1). The case study of AVLT demonstrates that the product professionalism of this organization arises from the synergistic intersection of its individual members' self-structured artistic endeavors (personal professionalism), its agile organizational structure (the management strategy of dual collective entrepreneurship), and its public-facing artistic productions. I have explored how SAOs are differently professional; how their alternative professionalism gets recognized, or not, by the public and funders; and what policy interventions might help SAOs to more effectively position themselves as professional. Further research is needed to more fully understand all these dimensions of how best to support SAOs in thriving. This research would likely result in broader recognition by funders and the public of the value of the uniquely professional business and artistic practices of SAOs that are productively reshaping the intersection of arts professionalism and cultural institutions in the public arena. By any holistic measure, being a professional in the SAO world is to be personally, tenaciously, and sustainably dedicated to the arts through focusing not only on one's own self-structured artistic endeavor but also on the dual-track collective entrepreneurship of organizational artistic production and management.

References

Available Light Theatre. (2022). Our mission. *Avltheatre.com*. https://avltheatre.com/about-avlt.html

Chang, W. J. (2010). How "small" are small arts organizations? *Journal of Arts Management, Law, and Society*, 40(3), 217–234.

Chang, W. J. (2011). *Small arts organizations: Supporting their creative vitality* [Ph.D. dissertation, The Ohio State University].

Chang, W. J. (2012). Bricolage in small arts organizations: An artist's way of entrepreneurship. In G. Hagoort, A. Thomassen, & R. Kooyman (Eds.), *Pioneering minds worldwide: On the entrepreneurial principles of the cultural and creative industries* (pp. 46–49). Eburon Academic Press.

Chang, W. J. (2017, October 13). *Collective entrepreneurship & bricolage in the arts: The case of a jazz house concert organization.* Paper presented at the 43rd

International Conference on Social Theory, Politics, and the Arts at the University of St. Thomas, Minneapolis, MN.

Chang, W. J., & Park, S. (2015, December 11). *Portfolio careers in arts management: From arts managers to arts entrepreneurs.* Paper presented at the 41st International Conference on Social Theory, Politics, and the Arts at the University of South Australia, Adelaide, Australia.

Evetts, J. (2010). Professionalism and management in public sector: Challenges and opportunities. In A. Langer & A. Schröer (Eds.), *Professionalisierung im nonprofit management* (pp. 33–44). VS Verlag für Sozialwissenschaften.

Geertz, C. (1973). Thick description: Toward an interpretive theory of culture. In *The interpretation of cultures: Selected essays* (pp. 310–323). Basic Books.

Greffe, X. (2004). Artistic jobs in the digital age. *Journal of Arts Management, Law, and Society, 34*(1), 79–96.

Hardymon, G., & Leamon, A. (2010). *Creative capital: Sustaining the arts* (Case 810–098). Harvard Business School.

Hine, C. (2000). *Virtual ethnography.* Sage Publications.

Hodsoll, F. (2009). Cultural engagement in a networked world. *Journal of Arts Management, 39*(4), 280–285.

Hyde, L. (1983). *The gift: Imagination and the erotic life of property.* Vintage.

Keen, A. (2007). *The cult of the amateur: How today's internet is killing our culture.* Doubleday, Currency.

Kitchener, A., & Markusen, A. (2012). Working with small arts organizations: How and why it matters. *Grantmakers in the Arts Reader, 23*(2), 5–12. www.giarts.org/article/working-small-arts-organizations

Kreidler, J. (1996). Leverage lost: The nonprofit arts in the post-Ford era. *Journal of Arts Management, Law, and Society, 26*(2), 79–100.

LearnVest. (2013). Portfolio careers: Is the latest work trend right for you? *Forbes.* www.forbes.com/sites/learnvest/2013/02/27/portfolio-careers-is-the-latest-work-trend-right-for-you/

Lévi-Strauss, C. (1967). *The savage mind.* University of Chicago Press.

McCarthy, K. F., & Ondaatje, E. H. (2002). *From celluloid to cyberspace: The media arts and the changing arts world.* RAND Corporation.

Mercadex International, Inc. (2002). *Face of the future: A study of human resources issues in Canada's cultural sector.* Cultural Human Resources Council. www.culturalhrc.ca/sites/default/files/research/CHRC_Face_of_the_Future_-_Findings-2002-en.pdf

Missingham, A. (2009). Music and the expressive life. In S. Jones (Ed.), *Expressive lives* (pp. 75–82). Demos.

Nelson, R. (2010). *How to start your own theater company.* Chicago Review Press.

Ohio Department of Commerce. (2010). *State of Ohio minimum wage.* http://com.ohio.gov/laws/docs/laws_MinimumWagePoster2010.pdf

Ormont, R. (2005). *Career solutions for creative people: How to balance artistic goals with career security.* Skyhorse Publishing, Inc.

Peterson, R. A. (1986). From impresario to arts administrator: Formal accountability in nonprofit cultural organizations. In P. J. DiMaggio (Ed.), *Nonprofit enterprise in the arts* (pp. 162–183). Oxford University Press.

Sidford, H. (2011). *Fusing arts, culture and social change: High impact strategies for philanthropy.* National Committee for Responsive Philanthropy. www.ncrp.org/wp-content/uploads/2016/11/Fusing_Arts_Culture_and_Social_Change-1.pdf

SMU DataArts. (2023). *Our history: Data-driven by design.* https://culturaldata.org/about/history/

Staub, S., & Thatcher, E. (2003). *Small organizations in the folk and traditional arts: Strategies for support.* Fund for Folk Culture.

Throsby, D., & Hollister, V. (2003). *Don't give up your day job: An economic study of professional artists in Australia.* Australia Council for the Arts. https://australiacouncil.gov.au/advocacy-and-research/dont-give-up-your-day-job/

Van De Camp, K., Vernooij-Dassen, M. J., Grol, R. P., & Bottema, B. J. (2004). How to conceptualize professionalism: A qualitative study. *Medical Teacher, 26*(8), 696–702.

Wali, A., Marcheschi, E., Severson, R., & Longoni, M. (2001). More than a hobby: Adult participation in the informal arts. *Journal of Arts Management, Law, and Society, 31*(3), 212–230.

Wilensky, H. L. (1964). The professionalization of everyone? *American Journal of Sociology, 70*(2), 137–158.

Wyszomirski, M. J. (2006). *Professionalization and portfolio careers in the creative sector: A conceptual framework.* Paper presented at the 2006 STP&A Conference, Vienna, Austria.

Wyszomirski, M. J. (2013). Shaping a triple-bottom line for nonprofit arts organizations: Micro-, macro-, and meta-policy influences. *Cultural Trends, 22*(3–4), 156–166.

Wyszomirski, M. J., & Chang, W. (2017). Professional self-structuration in the arts: Sustaining creative careers in the 21st century. *Sustainability, 9*(6), 1035. www.mdpi.com/2071-1050/9/6/1035

6 Strategic Planning for the Creative Professional

A Curriculum Proposal for Career Development Design

Javier J. Hernández-Acosta

Introduction

The world needs more creative professionals—artists who create symbolic value in the visual, performing, literary, and musical arts, whether as digital content or as tangible products, and who work collaboratively across disciplines. Professional arts and cultural work have evolved over the past decades parallel to the development of the field, mostly in response to changes in the social and economic environment, in ways that present new challenges to artists' creativity in reaching their audiences and, above all, crafting a dignified and sustainable creative life. These changes have been aligned with both the evolution of arts management and cultural policies. Some authors have identified multiple stages in the evolution of the discipline through the focus of academic programs since the 1960s, including the integration of aspects such as technology, cultural policy, and entrepreneurship (Varela, 2013; Brkić, 2009). On the other side, Bayardo (2008) suggests at least three periods of cultural policy that affects artists and cultural agents: culture as general ways of life, culture as cultural industries, and, finally, the focus of culture as development. Although patronage used to be an important way of subsidizing the arts, in recent years, unpaid work has become an important aspect promoting precariousness in cultural work (Brook et al., 2020, p. 572). Unfortunately, a substantial group of artists seems to self-subsidize their work, mostly because of "the enthusiasm" that Remedios Zafra describes as the "Achilles heel" of creative work (2018, p. 15).

In this chapter, I seek to understand the creative professional as the central figure in the creative economy and provide a framework to strengthen their career development, starting during their university years. While it is evident that the cultural and creative industries have grown and evolved and have potential for further growth (Buitrago & Duque, 2013), it is nonetheless difficult for artists to fully apprehend the value they create for the economy. While scholars and arts sector leaders recognize the creative economy's financial potential, the precarity of a career in the arts and cultural sector remains a constant (Abbing, 2008; Banks, 2017). In recent years, the term "creative entrepreneurship" has been used both to re-brand artist self-employment

DOI: 10.4324/9781003138693-7

activities and as an alternative to institutionally remunerated employment, that is, focusing on the creation of cultural and creative ventures to participate in the creation of wealth and economic development.

Over the last three years, I have taught cultural and creative entrepreneurship at the undergraduate level and done consulting work with creative professionals. The research presented is based on these experiences. During that period, approximately 150 students participate in the undergraduate academic course. The course was incorporated into the study plan of the degree in film and as an elective for students in the Visual Arts, Theater, Music, Photography and Dance programs. Also, close to 90 established professionals participated in the pre-incubation programs. These programs, offered outside the university and oriented to graduates and professionals, represent the first stage of business training before further stages of incubation (already operating) and acceleration (growth strategies). These two complementary audiences reflect the importance of the proposals in this chapter. Although the emerging professional had already recognized that they lacked entrepreneurial and managerial skills that were not taught at universities, most college students didn't recognize, at the beginning of the course, the importance entrepreneurial and planning skills can have in their careers. As an observation, most students didn't know the structure and occupational profile of their arts sector before the course. After they came to understand the relevance of self-employment and career development through data, the students' engagement in the course rose.

The profiles of the participants in these courses and trainings have been very diverse, including undergraduate students in a variety of arts disciplines, as well as in communication, design, media and humanities, professionals making a living from creative work and looking to expand their income, and professionals who combine their creative artwork with other professions or occupations. Unfortunately, they are limited by lack of access to necessary channels, strategies, and resources for achieving artistic production (Bilton, 2017, p. 28). Richard Caves (2002) has argued on the important challenge that represents the gap between creation and production in the arts and media industries.

This scenario takes us to universities, which bear the main responsible for those weaknesses in arts and cultural workers. We can argue that universities have not incorporated into their educational models an understanding of the new realities and changes in the labor market, especially in the arts and creative sector. The digital revolution has disrupted business or work relationships, including the creative economy (Bilton, 2017, p. 193), and engendered greater instability in work conditions and worker benefits. We can expect the digital revolution and artificial intelligence to continue to change job profiles and eliminate, redefine, or create new professions (Bakhshi et al., 2015, p. 3; Davies et al., 2020). As a result of these changes, autonomy for cultural workers has become necessary to their opportunities for success beyond the issue of work satisfaction. For this reason, universities and accreditation bodies need to reflect on how curriculum provides resources for a clear and critical understanding and the implications for arts professionals, notably the students' acquisition of the necessary tools to address these challenges after graduation.

The Evolution of Professionals in the Creative Economy

It is important to analyze how the cultural workers' profiles have evolved over time. The starting point should always be the artist as the atom of the creative economy. Artists and creative professionals provide the main input behind the cultural and creative industries. Throsby (2008) elaborates four concentric circles to explain and support this view, including creative arts as the core of the model, followed by levels of cultural and related industries. They represent a figure that creates value through a combination of talent, passion, context, symbolic value, and social impact. Gaztambide-Fernández (2008) provides a broad context of the social role of artists, presenting three main roles: "civilizer," the "border crosser," and the "representator" (p. 233). While the first role is related to the pursuit of beauty and "arts for the arts' sake," the role of border crosser pursues questioning and challenging the audience as a way to promote social transformation. Finally, the role of representator seeks to amplify the perspectives of a broader sector of society that goes beyond the artist (Gaztambide-Fernández, 2008).

However, over time, the individual work of artists began to require a middleman figure that added value to the chain by bringing that creative work efficiently to the audience (Caves, 2002). This led to the creation of the administrator or cultural manager. As an occupation, the arts manager operates as a facilitator who builds bridges between artists and their audiences through managing resources and communication (Paquette & Redaelli, 2015). This new occupation emphasized the importance of managerial skills such as marketing, human resources, finances and accounting, and operations management.

The beginning of the millennium brought a new look to cultural work from an economic perspective. The emergence of the discourse of cultural and creative industries adds a new management dimension focused on creating financial value through the cultural and creative entrepreneur. That figure, which is sometimes the artist himself, creates not only content but also wealth. According to Chang and Wyszomirski (2015), arts entrepreneurship could be defined as a management process through which cultural workers seek to support their creativity and autonomy, advance their capacity for adaptability, and create artistic as well as economic and social value. This definition addresses the broad approach that should be used for the arts, integrating the combination proposed by Beckman and Essig (2012) of a focused-on venture creation and on the habits of mind.

Today, artists and cultural workers must deal with technological evolution, labor market transformations, and trade and migration flows, among others. Also, some countries have experimented with a reduction in governmental cultural budgets that promotes a new approach to economic sustainability. This scenario drives cultural workers into having to address a new balance between the roles of artists, managers, agents, and entrepreneurs. It is very difficult to think of four separate roles (artist, manager, agent, and entrepreneur). A certain degree of integration between these roles and responsibilities is necessary to achieve what could be described as the new creative professional.

The Challenges of the New Creative Professional

Creative professionals have a great opportunity to become social, economic, and cultural change agents. Their talent contributes to preserving traditions for the enjoyment of future generations, and they are also the basis of many of the entertainment and leisure experiences. Also, artists play a key role in critiquing the conditions of society and providing new vision and perspective on how society could be. They are a support resource for traditional industries and have a key role in creating content, which in turn represents the basis of the entire digital revolution and social networks. However, there are many challenges to achieve this endeavor.

The problem of recognition and dignification of creative work remains (CODECU, 2015). The rigor in the training and development of these professions is not always recognized, and many times, creative professionals end up in other occupations due to a prejudice against earning a living from the arts. Frenette and Dowd (2020, pp. 2–6) identified multiple factors affecting the ability of arts graduates to stay in the field. For example, variables such as gender (female), race (black), and higher student debt make those graduates most unlikely to stay in the arts. Interestingly, some students increase their chances of staying in the arts by pursuing the path of the generalist, which includes a double major (inside and outside the arts) which expands the number of artistic occupations in which they can work. These patterns support new opportunities for academic programs to incorporate additional skills, experiences, and resources, not to mention the importance of addressing gender and racial equity.

But not all challenges in the creative professions are related to the external perception of society of the lack of opportunities for financial sustainability. There is the problem of excess supply (Menger, 1999, pp. 566–569) since a significant number of artists and creative professionals will not stop producing as a response to low demand because their intrinsic motivation is very high. Although this is positive for society, in economic terms, an increase in supply almost always results in reduced prices. Similarly, there is the challenge of few or no entry barriers since anyone can perform, or at least try to, without training, an academic degree, or experience. Finally, the challenge of business models should be highlighted since a large part of creative production consists of public goods. For example, much audiovisual and music content on social media, despite the option to receive royalties from advertising, will never capture its total value because of the complexity of these models. To understand this concept of total value, it is important to address all the dimensions that have been discussed by authors such as Throsby (2001) and Holden (2004), especially for dimensions of non-use value that includes historic, identity, and option value, among others. Recently, the COVID-19 pandemic and the transition to digital distribution for most artists and organizations have made it more visible that the main digital platforms' buying power has put a lot of pressure on the economic sustainability of the arts sector. This is what Chris Bilton (2017) has described as a "process of reintermediation" (pp. 11–14). While the digital revolution removes some of the large conglomerates (such as Time-Warner, Disney, and Deutsche Grammophon) that have controlled media industries, new platforms emerged (such as Netflix, Spotify, YouTube, and Facebook), limiting the revenue model for authors, filmmakers, and musicians. In other cases, as in the experience of visual arts, people can enjoy (or consume) an art exhibit at a gallery without having to purchase the tangible product, the actual artwork. In conclusion, it can be argued that there is a gap between creating and capturing value in the arts and creative sector, in which a high productivity is not necessarily translated into revenue streams.

All these challenges are realities that the arts and creative activities have long experienced. However, the training of these creative professionals has rarely attempted new methodologies or approaches to address these challenges. The environment of the artworld requires that creative professionals in the labor market, and those in training, develop a new professional profile that fits that context. Based on this premise, a general structure for this new profile will be proposed, something that both individuals and institutions could adopt in their programs or careers.

Toward a High-Impact Creative Graduate

To address the challenges discussed earlier, it is important to define the multiple roles that can exist within a professional profile that arts students at universities should develop through the curriculum. To better address these career development challenges, a proposed curriculum is based on these four roles: the professional as a creator, as an entrepreneur, as a connector, and as a social agent (Figure 6.1). This graduate profile is envisioned as concentric circles, considering that each level interact with each other since they could be considered prerequisites for the previous. To reach this profile, individual strategic planning for the creative professional will be proposed in the next section as a set of activities and reflections needed to advance their professional career. This component of the curriculum aims to prepare creative professionals with strategic choices, types of knowledge,

Figure 6.1 Creative Graduate Profile

and a toolkit of considerations with which to address the four components as described earlier.

The first ring represents the artistic or creative work domain. It is about artistic or creative excellence. That has been education's main focus for centuries and should be maintained in the future. Without a mastery and a focus on excellence in visual arts, performing arts, literature, music, film, design, and its derived activities, artists will not be able to achieve the expected impact. That includes not only creation but also criticism as a complementary activity that promotes growth.

After mastering an artistic or creative discipline, it is important to understand and be able to develop an entrepreneurial mindset. It has been noted in research on artists' occupations that creative professionals are very dependent on self-employment (Alper & Wassall, 2006). For example, in Puerto Rico, 45% of artists (using the same definition as of the National Endowment for the Arts in the report *Artists in the Workforce*) are self-employed while in the rest of the occupations (non-creatives) self-employment represents only 12% (Hernández-Acosta & Gómez-Herazo, 2020, p. 6). Not being aware of the importance of entrepreneurship will increase the chances of not being able to develop artists' full potential.

We live in a historic moment where technological development has facilitated closing the gaps between disciplines, and even creating some new ones. Similarly, creativity is becoming a competitive advantage for many traditional industries. Therefore, creative professionals must be ready to connect with other disciplines and industries. For example, many musicians have a clear expectation of their future work through live performances. However, they are not necessarily aware of the opportunities of collaborating with other artistic sectors such as dance, theater, and literature. But beyond art, there are great opportunities in other creative industries such as video games, film, advertising, and animation. Finally, a much broader field of action that transcends the creative economy could be considered, such as tourism, health, and well-being, or information technologies. So, when discussing the importance of connection, one can think of three levels: with other artistic sectors, with other creative sectors, and with other industries outside the arts and cultural sector. The intra- and inter-industry connection is the key to a true creative economy.

Finally, creative professionals must have a further purpose of transforming the social, political, economic, and cultural conditions of a community, city, country, or region. To achieve this role of social agents, each creative professional should have a clear expectation of how their work helps solve sustainable development problems and objectives. This is the reason why training must contemplate those key questions that guarantee that creative work does not operate in a vacuum, far from the external environment's conditions. Following this model, these four rings must represent the alumni's profile in any artistic or creative discipline academic program.

These professionals need to develop new possibilities for their creative work. Although creative professionals generate the main input of important innovations, it is often seen as an exception and not as the norm. A much more comprehensive training is needed, where the development of creative talent is aligned with training in disciplines related to its final outputs or products. Unfortunately, academic structures at universities are generally based on disciplines, such as social sciences, humanities, business, natural sciences, and education, among others. Although some extracurricular activities and programs try to address the issue of interdisciplinarity, "academic silos" still make it difficult to provoke this interaction (Uribe, 2012, pp. 14–24).

Creative work has at least four main outputs: tangible products, digital content, services, and experiences (tourism and event production being its main formats). Activities such as film, animation, video games, mobile apps and web development, advertising, publications, cultural tourism, and their complementary products, concerts and festivals, among many others, should be more integrated into artistic training. The sustainability of arts disciplines depends largely on providing creative professionals with direct access to the tools to develop the products or experiences that will reach their final consumer. If artists are kept isolated from these practices, their role will be that of employees instead of leaders or entrepreneurs. To address this important issue, universities should innovate in the academic structures to facilitate this interdisciplinary approach (Staley, 2019, pp. 12–21).

In contrast, I propose the idea of a more balanced *talent/output* approach, where there is a close interaction between the arts, tourism, audiovisual products, event production, content creation, animation, and advertising, all on a basis of entrepreneurial mindset and project management. To give an example, a visual artist must have early interactions with graphic design, advertising, and animation, just as a dancer must relate to theater, animation, health, education, and music and event production. On those activities lie many of their economic performance possibilities, so it is up to the academic programs to address this by design. As a final idea, a quote from Julio Cortázar's *Libro de Manuel* (1972) could apply to this proposal: "A bridge is a man [or a woman] crossing a bridge" (p. 78). This quote suggests that arts and creative work is the action of use or consumption beyond its simple creation, reaffirming that creative work materializes when their work reaches their audiences or customers through products, services, or experiences. Therefore, it is a duty for these professionals to have the tools to achieve it.

Strategic Planning for the Creative Professional: The Toolbox

To contribute to this creative professional's development, a strategic planning exercise is proposed. This tool has evolved based on its implementation through the courses across six semesters. The toolbox is based on a series of five questions to determine (1) the mission behind creative work; (2) the identifying elements for professional differentiation; (3) clear business models or revenue streams; (4) how to grow a personal brand; and (5) how to establish a viable action plan for their development. To put it simply, I am referring to the why, what, where, how, and when. For each of these questions we identify four factors, which represent a total of 20 (5 × 4) for the strategic planning exercise of the creative professional (Figure 6.2). As a visualization tool,

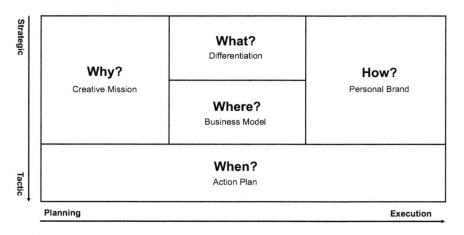

Figure 6.2 The Creative Professional Canvas

a canvas similar to other tools available to entrepreneurs is presented. This will allow us to understand the role of each of the five components from an axis that goes from planning to implementation and another axis that goes from strategic to tactical aspects.

Why? The Creative Mission

Normally, mission or vision statements are discussed in business courses in the context of companies, but this also applies to individuals. It is important to be clear on the things that motivate our work and project toward the future. To help students reflect upon this, we propose considering the following factors:

1. Influences: Many artists or creative professionals begin practicing their disciplines guided by external references, sometimes within the family, by people close to their communities or by professionals they admire. It is important to reflect on these figures that have so much weight on artists' work. Their experiences could serve artists as role models, precautions, continuities, or new ways of addressing old concerns.
2. Territory: Creative work does not occur in a vacuum. Rather, it usually occurs in the surroundings of cities or regions with specific social, economic, and cultural contexts. It is important to understand that context and all the dimensions of impact that we will generate in our communities. The city implies an interaction/collaboration/competition dynamic that is an essential part of the ecology of the cultural and creative economy. Deciding what kind of impact artists seek to generate is part of each professional's creative mission.
3. Cultural policies: One of the important characteristics of cultural agency is how each asset becomes a cultural policy agent. Cultural policies include aspects such as identity, diversity, equity, collaboration, education, decentralization, and artistic innovation, among others. If artists are cultural policy agents, they must decide which of these objectives they can contribute from.
4. Sustainable Development Goals (SDGs): The United Nations has identified 17 goals that must be met by 2030 if we want a more equitable, healthy, and fair society (United Nations, 2015). That reference represents a global effort to which the creative sector must be aligned. The framework, which includes 17 goals and 169 targets, addresses the main global challenges, including poverty, education, gender equality, climate change, peace, economic growth, and the reduction of inequalities, among others. Creative professionals can take advantage of this framework to align some of these goals into their interests and ideas. Considering the importance of social and community impact as part of the role of cultural agents, at least in the context of Latin America, this framework could become an easy access for students to understand sustainability challenges. United Nations' sustainability goals address the component of artists as social agents as described in the graduate profile.

This first component of the cultural mission is of great importance in the context of Latin American countries. In the highly complex social and political context of the region, heritage and arts management had a vital role in strengthening diversity and cultural identities in most communities in Latin America. This context gave birth to the *cultural agent*, a new professional role in the cultural ecosystem. As described by Doris Sommer (2006), it represents those who "create social change through creative practices" (p. 1). The cultural agent responsibilities go beyond management to include community development, education, and advocacy, reason to be considered as a cultural policy agent. For this reason, answering the why represents a starting point for the creative professional.

What? Professional Differentiation

A reality of artistic and creative work is the great challenge of standing out in such a saturated market. The digital revolution and the platforms that emerged from it facilitated an almost infinite availability of creative contents. As an example, the *Orange Economy* report states that 100 minutes of content are uploaded on YouTube every minute (Buitrago & Duque, 2013). On the other hand, it is estimated that 40,000 new songs are uploaded daily on Spotify. Imagine the complexity of achieving a space in the mind, time, and/or electronic devices of our audiences. To address this, it is important to develop a strategy by combining four factors. If innovation is the intersection between things that seem to be of a different nature, as Johansson and Amabile (2017) describe it in their book *The Medici Effect*, then this can represent a useful planning tool. The combination of these next four elements (Sector, Activity, Cause, and Opportunity) could help articulating a strategy.

5. Sector: Artists start with a decision to work in creative sector, which generally entails a discipline-based natural baseline. At some point, each artist has decided to become a musician, filmmaker, blogger, fashion designer, actor, or writer. That's the field of action on which each hope to achieve that level of excellence and mastery. But to get to the next step, it is necessary to understand the production dynamics in each sector.
6. Activity: Within each sector, there is a production chain that links training, artistic creation, production, circulation, promotion, distribution, consumption, conservation, and criticism. This is not a unique formula; it varies according to the sectors. Artists must reflect on which activities they can engage in to add value. Let's use the audiovisual sector as an example. Filmmaking is a complex creative activity that combines executive production, directing, editing, sound, coordination, lighting, photography, set dressing, and other technical areas. Although they may want to understand and exercise all these roles, identifying an area of expertise could help to achieve differentiation and more professional opportunities.

7. Cause: This is the moment to incorporate the elements of the mission. Beyond creative work, artists should always look for an element of transformation, whether social, political, community, educational, environmental, or gender equality. The nature of arts is transformative, through social, political, and educational dimensions. For this reason, the creative professional should incorporate this expectation of impact as part of their differentiation strategy.

8. Opportunity: Finally, if the above three factors are intrinsic, the fourth involves analyzing the external environment and trends. There are many changes in the creative economy. The digital revolution, the emergence of *on-demand* platforms, artificial intelligence, robotics, video games, gamification, cultural tourism, creative placemaking, etc. are trends that represent the final ingredient of a professional differentiation strategy.

Where? The Business Model

As a profession, creative work requires finding ways to secure financial sustainability. It is necessary to identify revenue streams so that creative professionals do not have to migrate to other fields to ensure their livelihood. It is a very common practice for creative professionals to self-subsidize their artistic work with revenue streams from other fields, but the important thing to achieve is that most of their time is dedicated to their art. These four components of a personal business model seek to present the main outputs that translate into revenue streams for creative work, in order to generate income that brings them closer to economic sustainability. Artists also require a deep understanding of the production dynamics and market trends of their sectors in order to translate their main outputs into revenue streams.

9. Products/tangibles: Many industries such as arts and crafts, industrial design and fashion are based on the sale of tangible goods. Other sectors such as publishing and visual arts still maintain a high portion of their revenue in the sale of products. Similarly, service or experience industries also have a great opportunity to cross borders between tangible and intangible, for example, through merchandising products. This has been a constant practice in film, music, and some events. Also, tangible products have been present in the heritage sector through *souvenirs*, and even in music through the physical recording as an object, sometimes as a collection item.

10. Digital content: The digital revolution has promoted a dematerialization of the cultural product. Music recordings, movies, games, illustrations, and books have become or been born as digital files. This raises major changes in terms of accessibility, copying (legally or illegally), and forms of monetization. Although it keeps evolving, the large platforms have been implementing income-generation models through royalties, synchronization, and through fractioning the value of the product according

to its use. The success of these revenue strategies requires understanding and keeping up to date with these changes.

11. Experiences: The cultural and creative economy has a strong experience component. Participation in museums, concerts, galleries, historic sites, festivals, celebrations, and gastronomy is mainly based on experiences. In these cases, the user reaches the point of cultural consumption and in most cases interacts with other consumers. The design and development of experiences are vital resources to generate revenue streams in the creative industries.

12. Services: In many cases, cultural and creative ventures have additional revenue streams through offering services to other institutions or companies. This practice in the business environment is known as B2B (business to business), although it may involve nonprofit entities or the government in the cultural and creative sector. Graphic designers and content creators, artists, photographers, and other professionals can find a sustainable and necessary source of income by providing services to entities to complement their artistic work. Revenue streams related to services could be the result of identifying opportunities in other industries such as education, wellness, tourism, and community projects. This will also require understanding process related to design, implementation, and assessment of projects.

The key to understanding these four alternatives of revenue streams for the creative industries lies within the need to create combinations to reduce creative professionals' financial vulnerability. In many cases, it is very difficult and risky to rely solely on one revenue stream. Artists need to innovate to sustain their creative production. The actual business model is completed with the perfect combination of revenue streams that are aligned to the artist's strengths and resources and those which represent value-added for customers and audiences.

How? Personal Brand

In most cases, the creative professional is his or her own brand. This is of great importance for the creative ecosystem since professionals tend to be serial entrepreneurs. For example, the publication *Emprender un futuro naranja*, from the Inter-American Development Bank (IDB), mentions that the lifetime of creative ventures is 2.44 years on average (Luzardo & Gasca, 2018, p. 64). Similarly, it argues that 60% of entrepreneurs have failed on previous venture. This leads us to a very iterative profile, where the company is primarily a vehicle through which the creative professional generates the expected impact. Beyond failure, these changes in the artists' ventures also represent an evolution of their projects as the entrepreneurs' ideas and priorities change. Academic programs and professional development experiences must ensure that creative professionals develop a personal brand beyond their businesses. This will greatly contribute to trust, continuity, and growth. For this reason, this component of the model proposes four key factors (4Cs) for the development of personal branding.

13. Contents: A creative professional grows based on their work. Social networks have awakened a new approach to digital identities that cannot be put aside. Creative professionals must ensure that they have a constant digital presence by creating content.
14. Community: Social networks have also allowed us to expand learning communities that were previously limited to physical outreach. Every professional must identify the communities they want to get involved with and which might be interested in their artistic or creative proposal. These relationships also shape the creative professional's personal brand.
15. Collaboration: A culture of cooperation is vital in the creative world. To expand their outreach, artists must transcend individuality to create, strengthen, and maintain networks with our creative ecosystem, but also through new relationships outside the creative industries. Collaboration works best when based on equity and mutual benefit. It is important to take care of these relationships and understand their benefit for the ecosystem.
16. Consistency: The personal brand is always anchored in fundamental values that must include solidarity, ethics, innovation, and commitment. Therefore, consistency is a fundamental resource for the creative professional since it remains in the other's mind. Consistency is needed in content creation, in the interaction with communities, and in collaboration.

When? The Action Plan

One of the great challenges that professionals face in creative industries is finding ways to have economic sustainability based on their artistic or creative work. The historical trend toward self-employment makes it very difficult to find a linear path in the development of their professional career. In addition, many creative professionals do not take advantage of their college years to create this experience portfolio. To the contrary, they consider those years as an opportunity to remain isolated from the labor market's reality. It is true that training years tend to be driven by excellence, and technical development, but the reality is that not getting involved with the ecosystem in those years could later delay their chances of success. That is precisely the idea of this phase: to propose some strategies to facilitate that transition. The importance lies in the fact that many creative professions' alumni expect to have immediate access to the labor market, and when they fail, many of them move to other professions or occupations in order to generate income. Once there, many will permanently leave the arts and creative work.

An explanation behind this phenomenon could be related to the practice of the portfolio in creative professions. Unlike many other disciplines, a university diploma or credential does not guarantee access to the labor market in the arts and creative economy. This is more common in professions such as engineering, accounting, and law, where diplomas, licenses, and certifications are used as a synonym of quality standards for employers. In the cultural and creative industries, this access is based on a portfolio of experiences, jobs, and projects that demonstrate the professional's growth and development, including variables such as versatility, consistency, networks, prestige, peer recognition, innovation, and diversity.

Now, the main challenge in building that portfolio is in the effort and time it requires. Many times, it will mean getting involved in projects that will not have financial compensation and that require a large investment of time. The problem is that this can become a vicious circle that can be difficult to escape. Whether in the arts, media, or design, a creative professional could spend decades in a portfolio-building strategy without being able to monetize from their work. This is what I call the "artistic or aesthetic portfolio paradox." This suggests that employers, companies, or collaborators of the creative ecosystem will constantly appeal for unpaid work under the argument of getting exposure or enriching the artists' portfolios. Awareness of this practice should be a key objective of academic programs, making emerging artists conscious that decisions on accepting unpaid work should be aligned with their goals and objectives and not a default practice.

For this reason, artists can't wait for graduation to start thinking about how to get a financial return on creative work. The only way is to advance as much as possible during that time at the university (a privileged space in terms of networks and resources) to build that portfolio. To achieve this, the four factors of this component include products, peers, projects, and people.

17. Products: Every creative profession has its final products, understood as works of art, songs, recordings, scripts, designs, short films, videos, publications, etc. For the purpose of the exercise, we will call them products, although it is known that some are services or experiences. It is important to start documenting and exhibiting these works early. It is possible to think that, in the early stages, these works do not necessarily have market quality; however, as part of the portfolio, it is important to show evidence of artistic and creative maturity. Therefore, one should apply an entrepreneurial approach to launching fast, using this as an opportunity to assess the response from our audiences and continue to improve skills and outreach strategies. Waiting for a scenario of complete self-satisfaction could delay the development of our professional portfolio.

18. Peers: One of the main access channels to the labor market in the creative industries are peers. To the extent that a creative professional builds, develops, and strengthens networks with colleagues, their chances of success will increase. When we are talking about peers, we mean all creative industries, not only those in the specific discipline they work in. The only

way to build networks is to get involved with the ecosystem and connect with people. It is important to identify the existing formal and informal events and platforms that bring creative professionals together. You have to attend, introduce ourselves, interact, and keep in contact. At the university, it is necessary to identify student associations or groups that connect with these professionals. Similarly, it is important for universities to understand these processes and incorporate them into students' co-curricular experiences. Otherwise, they would be contributing to keeping them within the academic bubble, something that will have a long-term negative effect.

19. Projects: Although artists often think of individual development, projects are the best strategy to advance on the two factors above. On many occasions, projects can achieve greater brand recognition than individual work. Therefore, managing these projects will allow for a better association with creative professionals, something that will open opportunities in the future. When talking about projects, we refer to collective initiatives with a short-, medium- or long-term reach. Sometimes, some of these projects do not have a financial outcome. Upon graduating from university, every creative professional must have carried out between three and four collective projects that have produced events or products with outreach in different market segments. Artists will not always have a leading role in projects; sometimes, it is about collaborating in colleagues' and organizations' initiatives.

20. People: Another key indicator for a professional-in-training is the reach they have to the stakeholders or consumers of their creative sector. It must be remembered that these consumers can be individuals or representatives of organizations, the government, or companies. The best way to make these connections is through the personal brand discussed previously, and a defined strategy on how to achieve them. Artists must determine who these people are, what their networks are, and how they are going to reach them. Similar to peers, they have to go out, introduce themselves, interact, build relationships, and maintain them.

Consideration of these 4Ps (product, peers, projects, and people) is a basis for a professional strategy as early as the moment emerging artists start college. In fact, I would propose it as an exercise for the first semester of the first academic year and to work on it year by year. Also, it could be worked as a set of actions for each one. The main importance of the work plan is the need to close the creation or production gap that affects creative industries. The hypothesis behind this approach is if students could start addressing their artistic portfolio earlier in the career, and by design, better opportunities could be pursued after graduation. In general, it is important to think of professional development as a long-term and ongoing exercise. However, the earlier they begin to set and work toward these goals, the more progress they will have achieved before entering the labor market. For many of the creative professionals, their portfolio will be the main source of their personal brand. Therefore, the best time to start is now.

Conclusion

In this chapter, I propose a series of exercises or reflections to be incorporated into academic courses or support programs for professionals in the arts and creative industries. It has been the result of several years of testing and iteration due to the constant assessment. The sustainability of artistic work requires an element of professional identity that is proposed through the figure of the creative professional. This allows students and emerging artists to see the output of their artistic work from an interdisciplinary perspective. Above all, the creative professional model seeks to be a tool for the early stages, reflecting the complexities of the career path in the arts.

Universities face the challenge of updating their curriculums. While it is true that liberal arts education focuses on the development of soft skills, it is important to combine the area of specialization with the ability to perform in professional settings. On many occasions, accreditation requirements do not leave room for curricular innovation. This requires us to be creative in how we incorporate these elements into the curriculum. While the proposal in this chapter is based on an undergraduate course, forms of application can also be identified through existing courses or through support services such as career development offices.

The application of business concepts to the arts still poses some challenges because of the different theoretical and disciplinary frameworks. For this reason, the five-question model (why, what, where, how, and when) can serve to simplify its adoption by faculty and students. Similarly, the arts graduate profile of the artist as a creator, entrepreneur, connector, and social agent requires an interdisciplinary approach that adds another challenge to art programs. The experience of the cultural agent role in Latin America presents an opportunity to be replicated in other contexts. The artist as an agent of change is a necessary approach, considering that cultural work does not occur in a vacuum of local context and needs for change. Incorporating these reflections at an early stage of college education contributes to a much more holistic artistic training.

This exercise could be considered a preliminary one that requires further validation and development. Many of the concepts used, such as differentiation, personal branding, and business models, among others, still require further questioning about the right way to be applied to the arts. Similarly, the wide diversity inside the cultural and creative industries concept sometimes makes an absolute generalization impossible. Each artistic and cultural activity (visual, performing, literary, music, etc.) has its own production dynamics that are important to consider. However, within those complexities, it is important to continue to identify and develop practical tools that could be applied in classrooms, career counseling, and professional consulting so that creative professionals can be better prepared to structure and sustain their careers.

References

Abbing, H. (2008). *Why are artists poor? The exceptional economy of the arts.* Amsterdam University Press.

Alper, N., & Wassall, G. (2006). Artists' careers and their labor markets. In V. Ginsburgh & D. Throsby (Eds.), *Handbook of economics of art and culture* (Vol. 1). Elsevier.

Bakhshi, H., Benedikt Frey, C., & Osborne, M. (2015). *Creativity vs robots.* NESTA. https://media.nesta.org.uk/documents/creativity_vs._robots_wv.pdf

Banks, M. (2017). *Creative justice.* Rowman & Littlefield International.

Bayardo, R. (2008). Políticas culturales: Derroteros y perspectivas latinoamericanas. *RIPS: Revista de Investigaciones Políticas y Sociológicas, 7*(1), 17–29.

Beckman, G., & Essig, L. (2012). Arts entrepreneurship: A conversation. *Artivate, 1*(1), 1–8. https://artivate.org/artivate/article/view/2/1

Bilton, C. (2017). *The disappearing product: Marketing and markets in the creative industries.* Edward Edgar Publishing.

Brkić, A. (2009). Teaching arts management: Where did we lose the core ideas? *Journal of Arts Management, Law, and Society, 38*(4), 270–280.

Brook, O., O'Brien, D., & Taylor, M. (2020). "There's no way that you get paid to do the arts": Unpaid labour across the cultural and creative life course. *Sociological Research Online, 1*(18). https://journals.sagepub.com/doi/pdf/10.1177/1360780419895291

Buitrago, F., & Duque, I. (2013). *The orange economy.* International Development Bank.

Caves, R. E. (2002). *Creative industries: Contracts between art and commerce.* Harvard University Press.

Chang, W., & Wyszomirski, M. J. (2015). What is arts entrepreneurship? Tracking the development of its definition in scholarly journals. *Artivate, 4*(2), 11–31. https://artivate.org/artivate/article/view/4

CODECU (Comisión para el Desarrollo Cultural). (2015). *Hilando voluntades: Cultura para la equidad, la diversidad y el emprendimiento.* Comisión para el Desarrollo Cultural. https://estadisticas.pr/files/BibliotecaVirtual/estadisticas/biblioteca/267489708-Informe-Final-de-la-Comision-para-el-Desarrollo-Cultural.pdf

Cortázar, J. (1972). *Libro de manuel.* Alfaguara.

Davies, J., Klinger, J., Mateos-Garcia, J., & Stathoulopoulos, K. (2020). *The art in the artificial: AI and the creative industries.* NESTA. https://pec.ac.uk/assets/publications/PEC-and-Nesta-research-report-The-art-in-the-artificial.pdf

Frenette, A., & Dowd, T. (2020). *Careers in the arts: Who stays and who leaves?* SNAAP Special Report, Strategic National Arts Alumni Project. https://snaaparts.org/findings/reports/careers-in-the-arts-who-stays-and-who-leaves

Gaztambide-Fernández, R. (2008). The artist in society: Understandings, expectations, and curriculum implications. *Curriculum Inquiry, 38*(3). https://doi.org/10.1111/j.1467-873X.2008.00408.x

Hernández-Acosta, J., & Gómez-Herazo, C. (2020). *Profile of artistic occupations in Puerto Rico*. Inversión Cultural. www.inversioncultural.com/labcultural

Holden, J. (2004). *Capturing cultural value: How culture has become a tool of government policy*. Demos.

Johansson, F., & Amabile, T. (2017). *The Medici effect, with a new preface and discussion guide: What elephants and epidemics can teach us about innovation* (Rev. ed.). Harvard Business Review Press.

Luzardo, A., & Gasca, L. (2018). *Emprender un futuro naranja: Quince preguntas para entender mejor a los emprendedores creativos en América Latina y el Caribe*. Inter-American Development Bank. https://publications.iadb.org/es/emprender-un-futuro-naranja-quince-preguntas-para-entender-mejor-los-emprendedores-creativos-en

Menger, P. (1999). Artists labor markets and careers. *Annual Review of Sociology, 25*, 541–574.

Paquette, J., & Redaelli, E. (2015). *Arts management and cultural policy research*. Palgrave Macmillan.

Sommer, D. (2006). *Cultural agency in the Americas*. Duke University Press.

Staley, D. J. (2019). *Alternative universities*. Amsterdam University Press.

Throsby, D. (2001). *Economics and culture*. Cambridge University Press.

Throsby, D. (2008). The concentric circles model of the cultural industries. *Cultural Trends, 17*(3), 147–164.

United Nations. (2015). *Transforming our world: The 2030 agenda for sustainable development*. https://sustainabledevelopment.un.org/content/documents/21252030%20 Agenda%20for%20Sustainable%20Development%20web.pdf

Uribe, C. (2012). *La interdisciplinariedad en la universidad contemporánea: Reflexiones y estudios de caso* (Vol. 1). Editorial Pontificia Universidad Javeriana.

Varela, X. (2013). Core consensus, strategic variations: Mapping arts management graduate education in the United States. *Journal of Arts Management, Law and Society, 43*(2), 74–87.

Zafra, R. (2018). *El entusiasmo: Premio Anagrama de Ensayo* (1st ed.). Editorial Anagrama.

Part II

Case Studies of Professionalization in Arts Occupations

7 Actors' Equity Association and the Professionalization of the Acting Vocation

Rachel Shane

Introduction

In the late 1800s, a group of actors came together and dreamed of establishing "a professional association which aims to assume such magnitude as to make membership in the association tantamount with membership in the profession" (McArthur, 2000). Original attempts at organizing such an association were considered failures. Actors found that their association had little influence over the powerful business structures that controlled the theatrical industry at the turn of the twentieth century. Thus, while originally opposed to unionization, actors found that in order to gain control over their own profession, they would need to follow in the footsteps of the musicians and stagehands—their theatrical counterparts—in the creation of a union designed to represent their own interests. Since its creation in 1919, Actors' Equity Association (AEA) has successfully established and maintained its role as the gatekeeper to professional status in the acting profession within the theatrical industry in the United States. In the twenty-first century, AEA represents over 50,000 actors and stage managers in the United States. The union negotiates and administers over 30 different theatrical contracts—including Broadway, Disney, resident theaters, cabarets, and casinos. Nearly every live theatrical production is controlled by policies set forth by AEA. The path to create such an authoritative association took 80 years of aggressive control over the entry and practice of the vocation of acting in the United States.

Over the course of 80 years, Actors' Equity was successful in creating interchangeable organizations across the theatrical sector by making the industry dependent on Actors' Equity for the vital resource of acting talent; by reducing the number of visible alternative organizational models in the field; and by increasing the reliance on specific credentials. Once Equity had established itself as *the source* for professional actors, the field was forced to conform to the union's standards of operation. Similarly, as Equity was effective in homogenizing large sections of the industry—Broadway, regional theaters, and stock—operational alternatives diminished for the remaining theatrical factions.

DOI: 10.4324/9781003138693-9

In order to investigate the professionalization process of actors, it is necessary to consider how the union came to be organized and embedded within the broader theatrical industry in the United States. For Actors' Equity, there were two primary waves of structuration. The first wave focused on the establishment and growth of the union, the development of the basic structures of the union, the diversification of its base, and the institutionalization of its practices within the field. The second wave of structuration centered on validation of the profession and the establishment of support structures that shape the contemporary theatrical field and profession.

First Wave of Structuration

In order to successfully create influence within the theatrical industry, the first wave of structuration had to establish a unified voice for actors. Through unification, Actors' Equity (or any union) has the ability to generate and control working conditions, environmental concerns, and compensation rates. By steering the climate, constraints, and compensation of actors, the union is able to pressure theatrical venues to adopt similar policies and practices. This, in turn, shapes the operations of the broader industry leading to similarity and uniformity. This process, called institutional isomorphism, describes how organizations come to resemble other institutions under the same set of environmental conditions (DiMaggio & Powell, 1983). In the case of AEA, the homogenization of the field created an environment that allowed the union to define and determine professional status for actors.

In order for institutional isomorphism to take place, institutionalization within the field where the organization exists must occur—meaning, before actors can professionalize, the theatrical field must institutionalize. The institutionalization process is defined by four characteristics: (1) Increased interaction among organizations within the field; (2) the emergence of patterns of domination and coalition; (3) an increase in information load; and (4) the development of a mutual awareness of the organizations in the field (DiMaggio & Powell, 1983). All four of these elements occurred during the formative period of the theatrical industry between 1880 and 1919. Prior to this time, the theatrical industry in the United States was largely undeveloped. The control and coordination of the field were haphazard. There were theatrical houses in major cities as well as road shows touring to various communities; however, there was little synchronization between theatrical venues, production creation, financing, or the obtaining of talent.

By 1870, the theatrical industry began to take on a more formal structure. During a time dubbed "the industrial revolution of the theatre," the theatrical industry experienced a centralization process, which consolidated the coordination and control of the national theatrical industry in New York City (Poggi, 1968, p. 27). The centralization was accomplished by two organizations—first, the Theatrical Syndicate, and later, the Shubert Brothers. These companies controlled multiple levels of the theater industry: venue owner-ship, theatrical production, and tour booking.

Between the years 1895 and 1910, the Theatrical Syndicate systematically expanded its control over theater venues—first in New York and then nation-wide. At the height of its power, the Theatrical Syndicate was responsible for booking productions into over 700 theater houses across the country, which created "a centralized national theatre system" (Bernheim, 1932, p. 67). This systemic coordination of the Theatrical Syndicate radically restructured the hiring of actors. For the first time in U.S. history, hiring for nearly every actor in the country was controlled by two men at the Syndicate. This extraordi-nary change was the impetus for actors to consider a formalized establish-ment of an institution that represented their interests.

In 1896, a small group of actors came together and formed the Actors' Society of America (ASA) to challenge the control of the Theatrical Syndi-cate and protect the actors' interests. The constitution of the Actors' Society, adopted May 19, 1896, asserted: "It shall be the duty of this Society to dis-criminate between responsible and irresponsible managers and to assist its members in securing contracts with responsible managers only" (Harding, 1929, p. 10). The actors in the group theorized that if they could create an agreement among the leading and most profitable actors of the time, those actors could then negotiate their own dates and terms with the theaters. This would, thereby, ensure actor independence which was contrary to the The-atrical Syndicate's requirement of exclusivity to the Syndicate. A proposed agreement was created by the ASA which stated that, as "both artistically and pecuniarily the good of the many is being subordinated to the profit of the few," an association was to be formed "for the promotion and protection of an independent stage in this country" (Hapgood, 1901, p. 32).

Notably, the ASA initially opposed the idea of unionization and sought to create a coalition that would represent actors without an alliance with organized labor. In fact, ASA's leadership fought to overcome the fears of potential members that ASA membership meant unionization. The Actors' Society's Monthly Bulletin was even published with the statement: "This is not a trades union but a professional association which aims to assume such magnitude as to make membership in the association tantamount with mem-bership in the profession" (McArthur, 2000). Despite its aims, the Actors' Society was never able to establish itself as a legitimate representative or negotiating entity for actors.

After 16 years of domination, the Theatrical Syndicate's monopoly was challenged by the emergence of a new theatrical production company, the Shubert Brothers. The Shubert Brothers' entrance into the theater business was welcomed by the venue managers and workers of the industry as a method of weakening the Syndicate's power over the theater industry. At first, unlike the Theatrical Syndicate, the Shuberts did not mandate exclu-sivity of the managers and actors with whom they worked. However, this entrance strategy soon changed, and both companies operated similarly, which effectively angered theatrical managers and actors.

Spurred by the poor working conditions and low wages proffered by the two theatrical monopolies, coalitions among other theatrical employees began to form. Specifically, the American Federation of Musicians (est. 1896) and the International Alliance of Theatrical Stage Employees (est. 1993) both organized as labor unions to protect musicians and stagehands, respectively. These unions subsequently joined the American Federation of Labor (AFL) before the turn of the twentieth century.

Meanwhile, since the ASA had found little success in negotiating with theatrical producers, the membership voted to suspend the organization in 1912. However, some members of the ASA felt there was still a fight worth fighting. Thus, a new organization concerned only with the *economic* grievances for actors was proposed. "The same meeting which heard the death sentence pronounced upon the Actors' Society of America witnessed the birth of a new organization which was to become the Actors' Equity Association" (Harding, 1929, p. 12). After several years of failed negotiations with theatrical producers, Actors' Equity aligned itself with the AFL and began fighting for recognition as a labor union.

During this first wave of structuration, the industry begins to show the four signs of institutionalization as described by DiMaggio and Powell (1983). First, through the organization of a complex system of booking productions into theaters across the nation, the Theatrical Syndicate, followed by the Shuberts, increased interaction among theater companies as required by the institutionalization process. The formerly independent theaters were now more aware and interested in the happenings at other theater companies. Second, patterns of coalition and clear dominant structures formed. Specifically, independent theaters aligned with the Theatrical Syndicate and later made a choice between the Syndicate and the Shuberts. Additionally, groups began to form in order to represent specific interests against other coalitions (e.g., ASA vs. theater producers). Third, the information available in the theatrical industry was becoming more abundant and more formalized. Fourth, theater managers, actors, and theater producers came to understand their role in the larger common theatrical enterprise. This is clearly seen in the attempts of the theater managers, actors, and producers to organize groups with their competitors that served their common professional interests.

Several key elements of the first wave of structuration are noteworthy when discussing the professionalization of actors. First, in the 1800s, it was common to have "actor-managers" in the theater industry. However, as the actors developed a coalition and moved toward unionization in order to negotiate with the theater managers and producers, actor-managers were forced to choose a side. This restructuring of the theater industry during this period triggered the disappearance of the vocation of actor-manager. The loss of this duality within the industry created allegiances—you were an actor or a theatrical manager—which led to competing interest entities.

Second, the theatrical industry centralized in New York City with a substantial touring component. Productions were often created in New York City and sent on the road to the venues. This new structure mimicked the industrial revolution—the creation of the product was centralized and then the product was nationally distributed. The centralization of the industry during this time period is a primary basis for the creation of the union as a national organization rather than local or national (like their music and stagehand counterparts).

Finally, and perhaps most importantly, during this time period, actors began to consider themselves part of a larger profession. While the actors' first attempt at forming a representative organization failed, the process opened the door to the notion of professionalization. The subsequent formation of the union, AEA, was intended to protect an actor's profession and standing in legitimate theater. Correspondingly, the incentive offered to actors who joined was the preservation of their art and the protection of their standing as a "legitimate" actor (as opposed to a vaudeville actor or a burlesque performer).

The conclusion of the first wave of structuration followed the successful 30-day Actors' Equity strike of 1919, which garnered the union's official recognition as the actors' negotiating organization within the industry.

Second Wave of Structuration

The second wave of structuration centers on the validation of the profession through successful expansion and the establishment of support structures that shape the contemporary theatrical field and profession. Once a field is institutionalized, the next step in the process is one of isomorphic change—the organizations within the industry begin to become more and more similar. This process is key in order for the actors to professionalize within the industry. The 1920s and 1930s proved to be a significant period of a homogenous shift in theatrical history—indelibly etching the subsequent structure of the industry. AEA took hold of the industry between 1919 and 1924 through a successful strike and adaptation of union contracts, which garnered the union's official recognition as the actors' negotiating organization within the industry.

The underpinning for what would become the theatrical industry's structure for the second half of the twentieth century and well into the twenty-first century was solidified during the early to mid-1900s through field development. DiMaggio and Powell (1983) assert that the copying of organizational structure is a method for institutions to secure legitimacy within an industry. This process occurs first in commercial theaters and then replicates in other types of theaters as the industry expands beyond commercial production.

Commercial Theater

For most of the nineteenth century and into the early twentieth century, theater in the United States was largely considered commercial. In the commercial theater, employees (the actors, director, and the ushers) were paid. By the 1910s, the Shuberts had overtaken the Theatrical Syndicate in terms of the majority of theater ownership nationwide. This marked the end of the Syndicate's monopoly on commercial theater ownership. Additionally, a good number of producers were in opposition to the Syndicate and Shubert model of commercial touring;[1] yet, most joined with the Shuberts eventually. Within just a few short years, the Shuberts controlled the theatrical resources.

The middle of the twentieth century brought discord to the commercial theater industry. Producers complained about rising costs and Equity pushed for the development of benefits seen in other unions, specifically a pension plan. Tense negotiations throughout the 1950s led to a Broadway shutdown in 1960 in what producers called an actors' strike and what Equity called a producers' lockout. Either way, Broadway was dark. The shutdown of 1960 would be just the first of three strikes throughout the decade.

While a tense relationship between actors and producers dominated the commercial industry during the 1950s and 1960s, another considerable alteration to the commercial theater occurred. The Shubert Organization ceased its production of theatrical shows. The family that had so clearly controlled the industry for decades was now no longer investing in commercial theater productions. During the 1950s and 1960s, the Shuberts did not produce any shows. And blamed their withdrawal on Actors' Equity.

However, Actors' Equity was not, legally, the cause for the Shubert's withdrawal from the producing business. In 1950, the Shubert Organization was brought up on charges by the U.S. government of violating the Sherman Antitrust Act. The government alleged that the Shubert Organization conspired to restrain trade and commerce and monopolized the theatrical industry. The Shubert Brothers lost the battle against the government and were forced to divest their role in theatrical booking and sell off ten of its theatrical venues. Nonetheless, the Shuberts remained the largest single theater owner and operator in the country. In commercial theater outside of New York City, Actors' Equity set its aim on unionizing stock theater companies.[2] Correspondingly, stock theaters created collective bargaining organizations (organized by type of stock) in order to represent itself in negotiations with Equity. This development was key to Equity's hold outside of New York City.

Noncommercial Theater

In the early twentieth century, noncommercial theater (also known at the time as "Little Theatre") began to develop. It was divided into two distinct forms: professional and amateur. In the professional noncommercial theater, participants would be paid; however, there was no expectation that the production as a whole would create a profit. In the amateur noncommercial theater, participants were volunteers (such as community groups or university theaters), and the production was not expected to make a profit. Some of the first attempts at noncommercial theater were initiated by professional directors and actors who worked in the commercial environment yet were dissatisfied with the ideals of the commercial theater and their economic obligation to create profit—perhaps at the expense of art.

The structure of the noncommercial theater was vastly different from that of the commercial theater. In the commercial arena, a producer would attempt to run a show as long as possible. If a show ran an entire season or more, it was a success, and a producer could recoup the capital he invested in the show and make a profit. But those who created the noncommercial entity did not have the desire to run a show in perpetuity. Rather, in the noncommercial theater, producers would seek to present numerous opportunities for artists and audiences throughout a theatrical season. In this system, called a repertory system, productions would run for a set number of weeks regardless of their level of success. Thus, if a show was scheduled for a five-week run and it sold out every night for those five weeks, it would still be closed at the end of the run, even if the producers could sell more tickets. Likewise, if a show was a failure and was losing money every night it remained open, it would still complete its pre-set run.

Noncommercial theater took many forms. The following sections outline how Actors' Equity came to influence these types of theaters.

Noncommercial Amateur Theater

In addition to the noncommercial professional theaters, the first 30 years of the 1900s saw the rise of the noncommercial amateur theater movement. These theaters included community theaters such as the Pasadena Playhouse and the Cleveland Play House; municipal theaters financed by individual towns; university theaters; noncommercial stock companies; and rural theaters. In 1917, there were approximately 50 noncommercial amateur theaters; 500 in 1925; and over 1,000 by the end of the 1920s. Many of the community and stock companies operated on the notion of slow and steady growth in order to become noncommercial professional theaters, and a number succeeded in making this transition.

It was not long before Actors' Equity began to set its sights on these noncommercial theaters. In 1938, AEA created "The Little Theatre" contract, which was to be used to employ AEA members in these noncommercial productions. Although it was only utilized by a few companies, this did not indicate that few AEA members were working in these noncommercial venues. In fact, appearances by AEA members were commonplace; and, by the 1940s, Actors' Equity had begun formally charging its own members with violating union regulations by appearing without an AEA contract. Hearings were typically held and members were fined (generally suspended pending good behavior). By 1948, Actors' Equity was focused on the expansion of legitimate theater and commissioned a study entitled "A Prospectus: For Surveying the Legitimate Theatre in the United States" (Nathan Associates, 1948). The study contended that noncommercial theater was of primary importance for "its value as indicating the existence of theatre markets that might be reached by commercial companies" (Nathan Associates, 1948, p. 24).

Works Projects Administration

During the 1930s, in addition to the Little Theatres, as a depression-era relief effort, the Federal Government became a major producer of theater in America. The Federal Theatre Project (FTP), part of the Works Projects Administration (WPA), was designed to offer "free, adult, uncensored theatre" (Findlay & Bing, 1998, p. 9). The primary purpose of the FTP was to provide re-employment to theatrical workers. However, the project aimed to establish a theater that was essential to community life and would keep operating even after the FTP program was finished. As the FTP was organized, the question arose as to who could seek employment in these federally funded theaters nationwide. It was determined that in order to be employed in the FTP, artists had to show evidence of theatrical employment *or* had to be a member of a theatrical union (including AEA or the American Federation of Actors for Vaudeville and Variety). This decision set forth a critical norm that union membership was synonymous with theatrical professionalism.

NONCOMMERCIAL NEW YORK CITY THEATER

Post-Great Depression, the surfacing of alternative theater began with Off Broadway theaters, which emerged most notably in the 1940s. Starting first as an alternative to commercial theater and often presenting avant-garde and financial failures, by the 1950s, the Off Broadway theaters had largely become an established and stable aspect of the New York theater scene. Actors' Equity quickly worked to unionize these theaters and productions. By 1959, the League of Off Broadway Theaters and Producers was officially formed to act as a professional association and a collective bargaining institution to negotiate with Equity.

REPERTORY THEATER

Outside of New York, the 1940s introduced a new theatrical movement that would shift the center of the theatrical industry. The first nonprofit, resident, professional, repertory theater in the United States appeared in 1947. Theatre '47 (later Theatre '48, and so on) was launched by Margo Jones in Dallas, Texas (Berkowitz, 1997). Jones' contribution to the shifting face of the theatrical industry was significant. First, Jones incorporated her theater as a nonprofit. She recognized that this type of theater venture would be too costly to support through ticket sales alone and valued the community input from the volunteer board of directors. Second, Jones envisioned and encouraged the widespread establishment of theaters across the country: "What our country needs today, theatrically speaking, is a resident professional theatre in every city with a population of over one hundred thousand" (Jones, 1951, p. 131). This helped move the centrality and control of the theater industry out of New York City. Third, Jones structured her theater into a subscription format, where the audience would buy tickets to all of the productions that the Theater produced in a season. Fourth, Jones produced classics and new plays (this was quite different from the summer stock standard of producing past Broadway hits). Finally, all references to Theatre '47 referred to it as a "professional" company. Jones paid the actors who worked for the theater, and there is at least one source (Landro, 1997) that indicates that Jones utilized Equity actors (although there do not seem to be any contractual ties to AEA). Unfortunately, Jones and her revolutionary company were short-lived due to her untimely death in 1955 (the theater closed in 1959).

Theatrical entrepreneurs were springing up in other cities as well. Nina Vance created an amateur company in Houston in 1947, later named the Alley Theatre. By 1954, with the encouragement of Jones, Vance converted the Alley into an Equity company. In 1950, Zelda Fichandler launched the Arena Stage in Washington, DC, as an amateur company. After one season, Fichandler converted the company to a commercial for-profit enterprise. However, the for-profit operation could not be sustained, and the arena was converted to a nonprofit organization. The paradigm, dubbed the Alley-Arena model (Berkowitz, 1997), of converting amateur companies into Equity companies was repeated in several other cities, including Oklahoma City with the Mummers Theatre, San Francisco with the Actors' Workshop, and Memphis with the Front Street Theatre.

These early professional repertory companies wanted to ensure employment to their artists. Therefore, they developed a system where they would contract actors to work for the entire season rather than per production. So, even if they were not being used in one particular show, the actor would still be paid his weekly salary. In exchange for the guarantee, actors were willing to accept a rate considerably lower than they would have in a commercial theater. However, the noncommercial theaters typically employed twice as many actors as the commercial venues. In the end, this system, while beneficial for the actors, proved to be a tremendous expense to the noncommercial repertory theater. In fact, operating these companies often cost more than operating a commercial theater. Combined with the fact that individual shows did not run long enough to recoup their costs, most noncommercial repertory companies were financially unsound.

The operational structure of nearly all of the professional theaters nationwide became very similar. Following the influential structure of Margo Jones' Theatre '47, companies organized as nonprofit corporations; ran entire seasons of productions; sold tickets via a subscription system; and often featured new or more experimental productions compared to the commercial theater of Broadway. By the mid-1960s, the resident theater sector had become organized enough to form a professional association. In 1966, the League of Resident Theatres (LORT) formed with 16 founding organizations. One of the primary goals of LORT was to serve as a collective bargaining agent with labor unions (including Actors' Equity) on behalf of its membership. The creation of such an association points to the institutionalization of the sector.

Structuration Duality

During the mid-twentieth century, the theatrical industry moved and morphed from commercial entities in New York City to nonprofit theaters across the country. This evolution can be examined through dual lenses: the changing goals of theater makers and supporters, as well as the expanding objectives of Actors' Equity. The following section discusses the driving forces in Equity coupled with the coinciding external initiatives that furthered Equity's mission.

Diversification and Proliferation

Recognizing the emergence of noncommercial companies, Actors' Equity established the "Non-Professional Theatre Committee" in the 1950s. This committee investigated all types of theater that were occurring throughout the country and made recommendations to the union as to how to proceed in unionizing the venues. It was interested in university theaters, community theaters, children's theaters, repertory theaters, and what it deemed "nonconforming" theaters. The latter were described as operating with Equity contracts but not with the desired form of employment for actors.

Within the year, the committee went on to create a proposed contract for repertory theater companies. The contract stipulated that a repertory theater must hire a minimum of five actors each year; employ those actors for a minimum of 26 weeks paying at least $75 per week; and produce a minimum of three productions. Additionally, Equity stipulated that repertory theaters could only produce one new or previously unproduced play without special permission from Equity—a notable stipulation since most unions only dictate the conditions of employment rather than the work itself. The guidelines of this contract, which was introduced in 1950, long before most repertory theaters were founded, likely influenced the structure of the field.

By 1953, Actors' Equity had authorized the Committee to Extend the Professional Theatre in order to carry out a new organizational objective: to generate employment opportunities for its membership through the creation of professional theaters.

The committee pursued its purpose through three main projects: women's club readings, university and college employment, and theater expansion in cities. The committee established a reading group in which Equity actors would perform selected readings for women's clubs. It also began courting universities and colleges in an attempt to convince the institutions to employ Equity actors to work alongside students. Lastly, the committee created a brochure entitled "A Theatre for Your City" that encouraged the creation of municipal theater operations in public settings. Over 3,000 of these brochures were sent to mayors, park commissioners, and chambers of commerce.

On the basis of the initial projects conducted by the committee, the group told the Equity council that the work involved was far more than could be expected from them as volunteers. Thus, in 1955, the committee recommended establishing a Department to Extend the Professional Theatre with paid staff. Equity would eventually create such a department but not until 1964. The first report, issued in 1955, of the newly created department stated its purpose as "seeking many avenues of employment in a changing theatre world. Broadway is no longer the Mecca of all professional theatre" (Actors' Equity Association: Records, Archive Box 30). The report continued by stating that the department's overarching function was the education of the public, government, and social services as to the differences between professional and nonprofessional theater: "Amateurs cannot learn from amateurs and the professional must take leadership" (Actors' Equity Association: Records, Archive Box 30).

The department operated with three primary goals in mind:

1. The development of new theaters to employ professional actors in the immediate and distant future;
2. The identification of areas that potentially could utilize the talents of the professional actor, but are not limited to the theater; and
3. Securing already existing professional theater operations in maintaining employment and extending seasons.

Consequently, the Department to Extend the Professional Theatre focused on the unionization of nonprofit theater companies, specifically focusing on new resident theater companies and the conversion of community theaters into professional theaters (Actors' Equity Association: Records, Archive Box 30).

While the department's focus was largely constructive and affirmed the desire of the union to create more professional opportunities for its membership, internal correspondence indicates that Equity officials were growing increasingly concerned with the success of non-Equity companies. Equity viewed these non-Equity theaters as problematic due to the competition that they would present for Equity companies.

As a result, Equity actively attempted to break the success of these companies. These efforts included trying to limit non-Equity companies' access to actors through methods including the manipulation of actors outside of the union ranks. Pointedly, Equity officials would attempt to coerce actors to leave productions. Documented cases included trying to convince members of sister unions (Screen Actors Guild and the American Federation of Television and Radio Artists) to resign from shows. Alternatively, Equity would attempt to force a theater to become an Equity house, often through the use of pickets or coercive media appeals.

As a result, some long-operating amateur theaters converted to operating under Equity contracts. This included one of the oldest community theaters in the United States, the Cleveland Play House (founded in the 1920s), which began operating under an Equity contract in 1958. Similarly, the Studio Arena in Buffalo, founded in 1927, became an Equity company in 1965. The Goodman Theatre, established in 1925, became an Equity repertory company in 1969. Also, Theatre Atlanta, which was formed in 1957 by the merging of several amateur companies, began operating under an Equity contract in 1966.

External Influences

The growth of new theatrical operations nationwide during the mid-1900s can also be partially credited to foundations whose funding interests included the performing arts. In 1957, the Ford Foundation's Arts and Humanities Program, under the direction of W. McNeil Lowry, sought to stimulate the regional theater movement. The Foundation believed that by providing seed money to companies, they could eventually assist them in becoming self-sufficient. The Ford Foundation began by studying the Alley Theatre, the Arena Stage, and the Mummers Theatre.

After the initial study, the Foundation "decided that increasing the availability of the arts to the American population was a legitimate extension of its social mandate, and that the resident theater movement was the great hope of the American theatre" (Berkowitz, 1997, p. 103). The Foundation began by providing travel grants that allowed directors of troubled companies to visit companies whose operations were more successful. By 1959, the Foundation had underwritten the payroll of four theater companies (the Alley, Arena, Actor's Workshop, and Phoenix) in order to see whether actors would be willing to commit themselves to repertory companies. By 1962, the Foundation committed $6.2 million in grants to nine theater companies. Over the next decade, the Ford Foundation's total arts giving averaged $9.5 million a year. In addition to direct gifts to theatrical organizations, the Ford Foundation established the Theatre Communications Group (TCG) in 1961 to serve as a national service in order to promote cooperation among U.S. professional, community, and university theaters.

The federal government also spurred the creation of theater companies during the 1960s. The government actively took strides to pave the way for artistic endeavors through the creation of the National Endowment for the

Arts and Humanities in 1965. Within one year of its creation, the National Endowment for the Arts (NEA) and the Federal Office of Education created theater companies. These companies were Equity theaters. The NEA's mission to develop professional nonprofit arts ventures converged with Equity's focus on developing unionized theater companies nationwide.

Between 1962 and 1969, over 170 noncommercial theaters and arts centers were built nationwide. Comparatively, Broadway was seeing a consistent decline of venues being utilized for legitimate theater (approximately 30 down from New York's all-time high of 76 in 1927). If professional theater had been a centralized industry in the first half of the twentieth century, it is no longer. Likewise, the role of Actors' Equity also expanded and diversified. It began to reposition itself from an institution that primarily battled commercial producers in Manhattan to one that sought to protect its membership in every state.

The professionalization process for theatrical actors reached its pinnacle in the middle of the twentieth century. The historical business structure of the theatrical industry was altered by governmental intervention while alternatives to commercial Broadway theater and road shows were developed. And for the first time in U.S. history, more than half of all theatrical employment for actors was based outside of New York City.

The development of the noncommercial theatrical industry offers convincing evidence that the phenomenon of institutional isomorphism existed. In the case of nonprofit theater, the homogeneity of the theatrical industry was propelled by three factors:

1. The financial support of the government and private foundations including the NEA and the Ford Foundation;
2. AEA's initiative for the extension of professional theater; and
3. The creation of professional associations (often created to negotiate with Equity).

Similar to the development in the commercial theatrical arena, the influence of Actors' Equity is crucial to the creation of analogous institutions. Moreover, this influence provides Actors' Equity with the authority necessary to define "professionalism" for actors. Correspondingly, this aligns with DiMaggio and Powell's (1983) definition of professionalization: "The collective struggle of members of an occupation to define conditions and methods of their work, to control 'the production of producers' and to establish a cognitive base and legitimation for their occupational autonomy" (p. 152).

Normalization

While the internal professionalization process of Actors' Equity was largely completed in the 1950s and 1960s, the final decades of the century solidified the union as the standard for professionalism within the field. Over the course of 80 years, Actors' Equity was successful in creating interchangeable organizations across the theatrical sector by making the industry dependent on Actors' Equity for the vital resource of acting talent; by reducing the number of visible alternative organizational models in the field; and by increasing the reliance on specific credentials. Once Equity had established itself as *the source* for professional actors, the field was forced to conform to the union's standards of operation.

DiMaggio and Powell (1983) contend that the professionalization process is intended to create "a pool of almost interchangeable individuals who occupy similar positions across the range of organizations and possess a similarity of orientation and disposition" (p. 152). Actors' Equity was interested in creating such a pool, but the union's focus did not lie so much on its own membership or individuals but rather on the industry. Herein, Actors' Equity sought to create a pool of almost interchangeable organizations that were similar in orientation, making them viable options for employment for its membership.

Similarly, as Equity was effective in homogenizing large sections of the industry—Broadway, regional theaters, and stock—operational alternatives diminished for the remaining theatrical factions. Thus, many of these companies no longer even attempted to organize professional associations in retaliation to Equity's demands; they simply conformed. Operationally, the theater companies began looking more and more similar due to the reliance on the credentials the union bestowed upon its membership. Moreover, a theater company could not employ "professional" union actors unless it met specific operational standards, not only in terms of salary but also in terms of facility structure, hours of work, and employment expectations. Additionally, Equity's influence became so dominant that these operational standards have also permeated theatrical institutions that do not utilize Equity members (e.g., no performances on Monday nights, dressing room requirements).

In the last decades of the twentieth century, Actors' Equity had firmly established itself within all aspects of the theatrical industry. Because of the union's success, few monumental struggles occurred in the 1980s and 1990s between Actors' Equity and producers in the theatrical industry. To be sure, there were contractual disputes, tense negotiations, and individual disagreements, but there were no strikes. Strikes were threatened; deadlines were missed; but, in the last two decades of the century, Equity actors never walked a picket line.

Systematically, the union worked for 80 years to unionize virtually every avenue of theatrical activity in the United States. By 1980, Equity had successfully normalized the use of Equity actors and firmly established the association between "Equity" and "professional" achieving its goal of creating an organization so authoritative that affiliation is "tantamount with membership in the profession."

Notes

1 The National Theatre Owners Association was formed in 1910 with approximately 1,200 theater venue owners who refused to align with either the Syndicate or the Shuberts.
2 Stock companies were located outside of NYC and presented popular or musical theater presented only in the summer months. Typically, the companies relied both on shows that were popular on Broadway and New York actors.

References

Actors' Equity Association. (1955). *Department to extend professional theatre report*. Records; Wagner 011; Box 30; Folder 2; Tamiment Library/Robert F. Wagner Labor Archives.

Actors' Equity Association. (1960). *Employment report*. Records; Wagner 011; Box 39; Tamiment Library/Robert F. Wagner Labor Archives.

Actors' Equity Association. (n.d.). Records; Wagner 011; Boxes 1–89; Tamiment Library/Robert F. Wagner Labor Archives.

Berkowitz, M. (1997). *New broadways. Theatre across America: Approaching a new millennium*. Applause.

Bernheim, L. (1932). *The business of the theatre: An economic history of the American theatre, 1750–1932*. Benjamin Blom.

DiMaggio, P. J., & Powell, W. W. (1983). The iron cage revisited: Institutional isomorphism and collective rationality in organizational fields. *American Sociological Review*, 48(2), 147. https://doi.org/10.2307/2095101

Findlay, J. A., & Bing, M. (1998). *WPA: An exhibition of works progress administration literature and art from the collections of the Biene Center for the Literary Arts*. Dianne and Michael Bienes Special Collections and Rare Book Library.

Hapgood, N. (1901). *The stage in America, 1897–1900*. Palgrave Macmillan.

Harding, A. (1929). *The revolt of the actors*. Quinn & Boden Company, Inc.

Jones, M. (1951). Theater for the future. *Southwest Review*, 36(2), 130–135.

Landro, V. A. (1997). *Theatres that work: A study of successful growth in small regional theatres in America* [Ph.D. dissertation, The Ohio State University].

McArthur, B. (2000). *Actors and American culture, 1850–1920*. University of Iowa Press.

Nathan Associates. (1948). *A prospectus: For surveying the legitimate theatre in the United States*. Actors' Equity Association: Records; Wagner 011; Box 12; Tamiment Library/Robert F. Wagner Labor Archives.

Poggi, J. (1968). *Theater in America: The impact of economic forces, 1870–1967*. Cornell University Press.

8 The Fractured Professionalization in Arts Education

Youngaah Koh and Ann Galligan

Introduction

The circle of arts educators has widened since the 1980s largely due to the paradigm shift from arts education to arts learning, which was a policy initiative of the National Endowment for the Arts (NEA). The terms "arts education" and "arts learning" carry similar yet considerably different connotations. Arts education has historically focused on formal, public education and put students at the receiving end of instruction. In contrast, the concept of arts learning places learners in the center as active actors who seek arts education in different venues, including schools and other community settings (NEA, 2002).

This broadened definition of arts education highlighted the significance of community-based arts education, which has been offered by arts and other organizations or by community members. This also helped expand the definition of arts educators from only certified classroom teachers and arts specialists who delivered a standardized curriculum in schools to community arts educators including teaching artists (TAs).

Against this backdrop, this chapter analyzes the different processes of professionalization of five different subgroups of arts educators. Specifically, it explores the ramifications of their professionalization, and how these have been shaped by both policy, and the different chronologies and characteristics of their fileld institutionalization. This chapter focuses primarily on arts educators in the United States but an international comparison is also offered. Moreover, it looks at the impact of the COVID-19 pandemic on the field of arts education and arts educator occupations, and their resilience in response to the disruptions to professionalization the pandemic has caused.

This chapter analyzes the different processes of professionalization of five different subgroups of arts educators. The first two are (1) full-time and part-time university professors and (2) full-time K-12-certified arts teachers. The last three are different types of community arts educators: (3) those who practice in organizational settings; (4) private, independent arts teachers; and (5) TAs. We utilize a set of indicators to examine the professionalization of each subgroup: (1) Their target learners and purpose of teaching; (2) their

DOI: 10.4324/9781003138693-10

teaching philosophy and pedagogy; (3) their training, education, and skill credentials; (4) their professional organizations; and (5) the government's role and impact on each subgroup. Discussion of each subgroup's teaching philosophy and pedagogy is important as they are closely related to educators' self-perceived professional identity.

Siloed Professionalization of Arts Educators

Among the aforementioned five arts educator subgroups, university professors are the only group that is widely accepted as a profession as per its sociological definition (Frederickson & Rooney, 1990; Moore, 1970; Wilensky, 1964). K-12 arts educators and the three community arts educator subgroups are typically considered semiprofessions, which require less lengthy education or rigorous training compared to university-based arts professionals (Etzioni, 1969; Greenwood, 1966).

The professionalization of university professors and K-12 arts teachers has been mostly standardized according to their respective occupations rather than as arts educators, particularly with regard to their target learners and purpose of teaching; teaching philosophy and pedagogy; and training, education, and skill credentials. Yet silos among artistic disciplines have persisted for arts educators in K-12 and higher education, which are shown through their professional organizations.

With regard to governmental involvement in the professionalization of arts educators in K-12 and higher education, public policy has the largest impact on these respective subgroups, in general. There is minimal arts policy that addresses arts education in higher education. Licensing and professionalization of K-12 arts education teachers have largely been the concern of the states' departments of education. The design and inclusion of the arts in core curriculum and their standards have been addressed by national, state, and local education and arts policy. Furthermore, in the 1980s and 1990s, arts policy acted as an advocate for and facilitator of a more consistent role for the arts in K-12 education.

This chapter thus focuses its analysis on the three subgroups of community arts educators. Community arts educator is a broad umbrella term that refers to arts educators who are not accredited or licensed to teach in formal education but serve learners of all ages in various venues. Because there is no clear, single definition of community arts educator, this chapter uses an inclusive approach and classifies them into three different subgroups: those who practice in institutionalized organizational settings, namely, nonprofit arts education program officers and museum educators; private, independent arts teachers; and TAs. They practice in and outside of school classrooms, in organizational settings such as nonprofit arts and community organizations, juvenile correction facilities, hospitals, as well as in private nonorganizational, for-profit settings. While TAs deliver arts programs that are offered by nonprofit organizations, they are addressed as a separate subgroup in this chapter due to their large presence in K-12 schools, unique professional identification as both artists and educators, and recent growth as an independent occupation.

Community-based arts programs have co-existed with formal education as supplementary in a form of community music schools since the settlement movement of the late nineteenth century. Through the establishment of settlement houses, such as Chicago's Hull House, grassroots efforts to bridge the gap between social classes by providing daycare, healthcare, and education, including in the arts, were made within communities.

Starting in the 1980s, community arts education programs began to be offered increasingly by nonprofit arts organizations, including museums. This was because public value of the arts emerged as a priority among them due to the declining arts participation rate among Americans (Sidford & Rabkin, 2014). To tackle this issue, arts organizations started outreach to nontraditional audiences within the community, including communities of color, marginalized communities, and people with disabilities. Outreach was mostly in the form of educational programs targeting community members.

Yet because not everyone felt welcomed in or had access to mainstream arts institutions, other community organizations started to offer arts education programs to increase their accessibility among diverse community members. Such venues included community centers, senior centers, hospitals, and correctional facilities, and targeted populations who had been historically marginalized and excluded from access to the arts due to socioeconomic, physical or mental, or other challenges.

Community Arts Educators in Organizational Settings

This chapter refers to nonprofit arts education program officers and museum educators as community arts educators who practice in institutionalized organizational settings. The former are a type of arts administrator (Hutchens, 1986) who plan and manage educational programming within arts and other organizations. Although nonprofit arts education program officers do not often engage in hands-on teaching, their teaching philosophy and pedagogy tend to be reflected in the planning and organization of education programs. Education programs in most arts and community organizations, with the exception of museums, are often instructed by TAs, who are employed by arts and other organizations on part-time contracts. TAs are addressed as a separate subgroup later in this chapter.

Meanwhile, museums uniquely employ mostly full-time educators who not only develop and deliver educational programming but also serve an important role as a bridge between visitors and art objects (Pitman-Gelles & El-Omami, 1988; Tran & King, 2007). This is due to the tendency of museums offering a variety of education programs related to their collections and exhibits, whereas other arts organizations offer general arts education programs. Museum educators organize educational programs, activities, and gallery tours and work with different units within a museum, such as exhibitions and marketing. There are virtually no counterparts for museum educators in orchestras, theaters, and dance companies. Given the large number of museums and their particular needs, museum educators thus have organized themselves as a distinct occupation (Weil, 1992). The case of museum educators highlights the institutionalized disciplinary silos that exist with regard to the professionalization of organization-based arts educators.

Target Learners and Purpose of Teaching

Community arts educators who practice in organizational settings work with a wide range of learners, from K-12 students, young children, adults, seniors, to individuals in correctional facilities. Because community arts educators teach in informal settings, the purpose of their teaching does not concern learners' mastery of skills and techniques. Rather, their focus is on providing learners with an opportunity to cultivate a transformative, empowering experience through the arts whether it be health, creative expression, or healing (Lawton & La Porte, 2013; Miller, 2020; Scher, 2007). The goal of many community arts educators is to help learners achieve a meaningful experience through which they are able to inquire about and reflect on their learning experience, and connect it with their real-life experiences and issues (Boyer, 2007; Hein, 2004; Koh, 2020; Tran & King, 2007; Vallance, 2004).

Whereas the purpose of many community arts education programs began with outreach to potential audiences, it has more recently evolved into engagement with the wider community. Most providers of community arts education thus consider themselves to be serving the whole community as opposed to only their constituents. Community arts educators often expect a public spillover of individual benefits into community development. Community development refers to community members working together to solve problems in the community and address community needs through their arts participation and learning (Kay, 2000).

Teaching Philosophy and Pedagogy

Due to their distinct teaching purpose, community arts educators who practice in organizational settings are not merely considered instructors but facilitators and participants who create a community of learners. Essentially, many community arts educators consider themselves agents of social change, use the arts as a "vehicle for activism" (NGCAE, 2019), and encourage learners to do the same.

Community arts educators are known to adopt public pedagogy, which is known to actively resist the idea of education as solely referring to institutionalized formal education. Public pedagogy is a "theoretical concept focusing on forms, processes, and sites of education and learning occurring beyond formal schooling and practices" (O'Malley et al., 2020, p. 1). More specifically, community arts educators implement a more democratic and pluralistic approach to art education than formal arts educators. This is because they seek to support a reform of the Eurocentric formal arts education paradigm and to tackle real-life social issues through artistic endeavors (Blandy & Congdon, 1987; Ulbricht, 2005).

Training, Education, and Skill Credentials

Community arts educators who practice in organizational settings come from different backgrounds that broadly concern the arts (content knowledge or aesthetics), general education, or arts administration. Over 73% of them hold a bachelor's or master's degree as their highest education credential in one of the three areas (Hutchens, 1986). An increasing number of degree and certificate programs in relevant areas such as community arts education, community arts, arts administration, museum studies, and museum education help college students and working professionals better equip themselves with the knowledge and skill sets that are needed for their career as community arts educators. The variety of higher education credentials that are displayed by community arts educators indicates an emergent professional norm characteristic of semiprofessionalized occupations.

The education and training that are required for community arts education program officers and museum educators are similar yet of different priorities. This is because the former are largely responsible for planning and organizing education programs, and the latter add actual instruction to the mix. Practical working experience, whether through internships or actual work experience in the field, is highly valued for both occupations (Bailey, 2006). For nonprofit arts education officers, knowledge in aesthetics or content knowledge, concern for community engagement and education, and managerial skills including fundraising and marketing have been regarded as necessary (Hutchens, 1986). For administrators who organize education programming in non-arts organizations, knowledge of the populations they serve, such as elders or youth, is beneficial.

Museum educators tend to be required to have similar skill sets with an addition of knowledge of pedagogy and learning theories. Specifically, these include (1) a master's level knowledge of art, as demonstrated by the study of aesthetics, art criticism, art education, art history, humanities, or studio art; (2) knowledge of pedagogy as demonstrated by the study of art education, museum education, philosophy of education, and more; and (3) the ability to teach with objects as sources of information, ideas, and aesthetic pleasure (Brigham et al., 1988; Tran & King, 2007). Program development skills, communication skills, and presentation skills are also known to be helpful for museum educators (Bailey, 2006)

Professional Organizations

The National Guild for Community Arts Education, which was established in 1937, is the only multidisciplinary national service organization that serves the wider community of community arts education providers. The Guild consists of over 300 institutional members including arts organizations, nonprofit organizations, and schools. Some community arts educator subgroups have organized themselves separately, for instance, as professional gatherings of museum educators or TAs.

The Guild has played a central role in providing community arts educators with an opportunity to share their knowledge and experience by hosting the annual Conference for Community Arts Education and through its quarterly publication, *Guild Notes*. The Guild also publishes occasional *Benchmark Data Reports* for purchase which offer information on staff and faculty compensation, instructional fees, and more. Moreover, the Guild offers a range of professional development programs that are intended to support its members with arts education for creative aging, youth development, and leadership.

Museum educators, meanwhile, have congregated separately within larger gatherings of visual arts educators and museums. They are represented in the National Art Education Association's (NAEA's) museum education division as well as many professional organizations serving museum professionals. These include the American Alliance of Museums, Visitor Studies Association, Museum Education Roundtable, the Group for Education in Museums, and regional museum education professional organizations.

With regard to publications, both nonprofit arts education program officers and museum educators publish their research and practice in academic journals in the relevant fields of arts education, arts management, and museums such as *Studies in Art Education, Journal of Arts Management, Law, and Society* (JAMLS) and the *Museum Management and Curatorship Journal*. Museum educators have their own separate publication, the *Journal of Museum Education*.

Government's Role and Impact on Community Arts Educators in Organizational Settings

Governments on different levels have increasingly supported community-based arts education since 1960s although their primary focus had been historically on formal education. While public grants and other measures do not directly support individual community arts educators, they assist arts and other organizations that employ community arts educators to provide a variety of education programs in the community. For instance, the NEA Expansion Arts program, which was launched in 1971, offered funding to schools and arts organizations to support community-based artists and arts organizations (NEA, 2001).

Yet it was NEA's arts learning initiative that was launched in 2003 that dramatically increased federal attention to community arts education, as discussed earlier in this chapter. With this new initiative, NEA introduced the Challenge America Grant program, which has funded community arts programs in underserved communities. NEA has also partnered with State Arts Agencies and other federal agencies, including Department of Education (DOE) through Arts Education Partnership; Department of Justice to provide arts programs for youth in detention and corrections; and Department of Housing and Urban Development. NEA also worked with National Guild of Community Schools of the Arts to help expand arts instruction in community schools for children and youth living in public housing outside of regular school hours. The National Guild of Community Schools of Arts later changed its name to the current National Guild of Community Arts Education, which reflected the organization's efforts to embrace a broader constituency from only schools to a wider field of community art education. Following NEA's lead, state and local arts agencies have also operated grant programs that supported arts organizations to either provide education programs for the community or engage in various partnerships, including with K-12 schools, to do so.

Private, Independent Arts Teachers

Studio-based arts education delivered by private, independent arts educators have been prevalent in the United States, particularly in the fields of music and dance education (Andrzejewski, 2009; Upitis et al., 2017) which, once again, highlights a disconnect among artistic disciplines. This is due to the tradition of learning to play an instrument in the Western canon through one-on-one studio teaching in music and a culture of dance competitions among private studios.

While private, independent arts teachers practice within their local communities, their work has not been typically considered a type of community arts education within the larger field of arts education. This is because the term, community arts education, has historically carried a strong connotation of an organizational context, and an emphasis on social change, access, and equity in the United States.

Terms such as freelance, private, independent, or studio arts teachers have been used to describe individuals who provide arts education in the community in non-organizational, for-profit settings. But independent arts teacher has become a more preferred terminology in the industry as the term conveys a notion of the educators' financial independence as business owners and entrepreneurs (Uszler, 1996). Most independent arts teachers either teach out of their home or own a studio, which is common for music and dance teachers.

Target Learners, Purpose of Teaching, and Pedagogy

A large portion of independent arts teachers instruct K-12 students and a small portion teaches young children and adult populations. Independent arts teachers seek out students who desire to acquire extracurricular arts education for merit and other purposes rather than those who seek supplementary education to formal education. The purpose of their teaching is often to help their students prepare for piano board exams or attain certificates of merit in the case of music education, or prepare for dance competitions in the case of dance education. Therefore, teaching performance and techniques in music or dance are the primary goals of independent arts teachers (Uszler, 1996).

As such, independent arts teachers' pedagogy focuses largely on the arts, particularly techniques and skills, and little on other educational components. There have been increasing voices from within and outside the independent arts teacher community that more knowledge of pedagogy and learning theories is needed for independent arts teachers. Critics of private arts instruction have called for a more holistic approach to teaching among independent arts teachers in order to encourage students' genuine appreciation for the arts and creativity (Andrzejewski, 2009).

Training, Education, and Skill Credentials

Most independent arts teachers have been trained in a conservatory style to become performers in their respective artistic discipline through a bachelor's or a master's degree (Uszler, 1996). In this style of training, great performers are believed to make great teachers. Pedagogy courses are often included as part of performance degrees but mostly concern learning about how to teach rather than training in an actual process of teaching (Uszler, 1996).

A key issue surrounding the occupation, which has been an unregulated one (Montemayor, 2008), is an ongoing debate around the need for a national licensure or certification program for independent arts teachers. Proponents of licensure or certification advocate for the occupation's potentially increased public recognition and validation. They also claim that such accreditation would be able to ensure that independent arts teachers have a balanced knowledge of their art forms and pedagogy (Heisler, 1995). However, opponents emphasize their independence as educators and that the art of teaching cannot be measured by standards (Uszler, 1996).

A number of community arts educators have self-organized into membership organizations that offer voluntary certification programs for independent arts teachers. Music Teachers National Association (MTNA) currently offers a certification program for independent arts teachers whose content addresses the arts, teaching practice, and business aspects. National Dance Education Organization (NDEO) and Dance Educators of America (DEA) respectively offer national certification programs for independent dance teachers which are the Certificate in Dance Education and an Advanced Teacher Certification.

Professional Organizations

It is questionable whether independent arts teachers can be considered a unified group of arts educators as many of them choose to operate independently as "islands" rather than a "continent" (Uszler, 1996, p. 8). The disciplinary silos as well as the disconnect among individual arts teachers due to the nature of their occupation are major contributors to this lack of a sense of unity among them.

Some independent arts teachers hold memberships in professional organizations while many others do not choose to do so. In the field of music education, there is no single professional organization that represents only independent music teachers but they are represented in larger professional organizations of music educators. These include the MTNA, the National Association for Music Education (NAfME), National Association of Teachers of Singing (NATS), National Guild of Piano Teachers, and the American String Teachers Association (ASTA). In the field of dance education, DEA is the only organization that represents studio dance teachers. DEA organizes dance tours throughout the country in which studios compete with one another. Some studio dance teachers hold memberships in the NDEO, which is the largest professional organization of its field serving dance artists, educators, and administrators.

Government's Role and Impact on Independent Arts Teachers

Because studio-based arts education mostly takes place in the informal or commercial sector, the government has not employed any support measures such as grants. Policy affecting this field has been typically related to independent arts teachers' business considerations, such as taxes and zoning regulations for those teaching out of their homes (Uszler, 1996).

Teaching Artists

TAs have become a widely used term to refer to artist-educators who choose to practice both in and outside of schools. A TA is generally known as "an artist for whom teaching is a part of professional practice" who earns income from their artistic practice in addition to their teaching (Rabkin et al., 2012, p. 7). While TAs are often broadly classified as community arts educators, they have rapidly grown as a separate occupation over the past decade due to their distinctive dual identification as both artists and educators and their large presence in schools. The field of teaching artistry first emerged in the 1980s amid the decrease in the offering of arts education in public schools, and arts organizations started sending artists to schools to help bridge the gap (Booth, 2015).

The growth of the field of teaching artistry is attributable to the increasing demand for arts education among a wide range of learners. In fact, TAs have played an important role to help mitigate the decline in formal arts education offerings and have contributed to the growing trend toward arts integration, or arts-in-education (AIE). Arts integration is the utilization of the arts in learning non-arts subject matters such as science, math, and English (Booth, 2015). The rising field of creative aging has also contributed to the increased demand for TAs and the effort to effectively train them to work with senior and adult learners (Boyer, 2007).

Target Learners and Purpose of Teaching

TAs work with a variety of learners from K-12 students, adults, to seniors in different venues including schools, afterschool programs, arts organizations, as well as correctional and senior facilities. Most of them are hired by non-profit organizations such as community schools, museums, and theaters, and teach at their employer's venue or are sent to teach in K-12 schools (Rabkin et al., 2012). Many TAs work full-time, often with three different employers, and practice in different venues as part of their portfolio career (Rabkin et al., 2012; Wyszomirski & Chang, 2017). The purpose of TAs' educational practice is mostly on providing diverse learners with access to the arts.

Teaching Philosophy and Pedagogy

The teaching philosophy and pedagogy of TAs are similar to those of other community arts educators who practice in organizational settings that stress access, equity, community engagement, and social change. TAs more often teach basic and fundamental skills rather than advanced skills in the arts, which is intended to inspire learners' long-term interest in and engagement with the arts (Rabkin et al., 2012). Their pedagogy also emphasizes "processes" that go into creating a quality artwork as opposed to the "products" (Rabkin et al., 2012, p. 8). TAs' pedagogy is known to focus on encouraging creative thinking and problem-solving skills among all learners while instigating their learning interests by utilizing a wide range of learning goals (Booth, 2015). This approach differs considerably from that used in formal arts education, which has been heavily focused on developing the skills and techniques of an artistic discipline, known as discipline-based arts education (DBAE) (Booth, 2015; Delacruz & Dunn, 1996; Greer, 1993). TAs have thus been assigned to teach AIE or arts integration programs in schools more recently. The priorities of TAs' approach to arts education are well noted in the Teaching Artist Manifesto (see Figure 8.1), which was introduced during the 2013 National Teaching Artists Guild (TAG) Conference.

Figure 8.1 Teaching Artist Manifesto (Teaching Artists Guild)

Training, Education, and Skill Credentials

As artist-educators, TAs come from arts and education backgrounds. Half of TAs hold a master's degree in an art form, one in eight hold a degree in education, and one in six have been licensed to teach by a state board of education, according to a national survey (Rabkin et al., 2012). With regard to qualifications of a TA, general consensus among stakeholders holds that "a balance should be struck between expertise in the artistic discipline and expertise in the matter of teaching" (Erickson, 2003, p. 137). However, there is considerable debate over how this balance can be struck. Many stakeholders, including TAs and administrators, do not believe that TAs need to be certified classroom teachers or have a graduate degree in education because of their unique pedagogy, which prioritizes learners' access to arts education and creativity.

Although there have been constant discussions of a need of a national certification program for TAs to formally accredit professionals in the field, one still does not exist. This is mostly due to the disagreement among stakeholders on what knowledge and skill sets are required of TAs. Young Audiences Arts for Learning, the largest arts-in-learning network in the country, however, offers a voluntary Teaching Artist Credential (TAC) program, through which the organization formally endorses seasoned TAs who are practicing in K-12 school-based residencies. The program requires credentialed TAs to embody excellence in four competency areas, which are preparation, artistry, planning, and instruction.

More recently, a number of universities have started offering undergraduate and certificate programs for working and prospective TAs. This is due to the growing demand among TAs for some sort of accreditation, which would help their work be more recognized and valued within the arts education community. Loyola University of Chicago and Minneapolis College of Arts and Design offer teaching artist undergraduate minor programs. Teachers College, Columbia University, and California State University, Los Angeles, are two of several universities that offer Teaching Artist certificate programs. Although the curricula for TA degree and certificate programs are not uniform, they concern elements of knowledge of the arts and pedagogy. Most programs also have a considerable emphasis on practicum or experiential learning.

Professional Organizations

TAs began to actively organize as a separate occupation in the early 2000s due to their increasing number in the field of arts education. Currently, there are a number of professional organizations, conferences, and a peer-reviewed journal in the field of teaching artistry. Notably, TAs are the only occupation within the field of arts education that has professionalized in an inclusive and multidisciplinary manner, whereas prevalent disciplinary silos are evident in other arts educator subgroups. This is due to the strong dual identity

TAs have as artist-educators rather than arts educators in their respective disciplines.

Two national professional organizations, TAG and Association of Teaching Artists (ATA), have led professional development and field-building initiatives through advocacy, honoring, convening, and resource sharing. TAG was founded in 2004 and offers resources for different stakeholders in the field of teaching artistry such as the Teaching Artists Asset Map and the Teaching Artist Pay Rate Calculator. The Teaching Artists Asset Map is an interactive, multilayered digital map that identifies individuals, organizations, and programs in the field across the country. The Teaching Artist Pay Rate Calculator is a tool that helps TAs determine and negotiate their hourly rate based on their location, living situations, experience, and employer.

ATA, meanwhile, was founded in 1998 as a TA advocacy organization serving the state of New York. It is most well-known for ATA Awards through which it recognizes distinguished TAs and their allies in the country. TAG and ATA were merged as TAG in 2020 to serve TAs in a more unified manner, and be more capable of representing its constituency and providing a wider range of services to its members nationally.

The first academic, peer-reviewed journal in the field, *Teaching Artist Journal*, was launched in 2003 by acclaimed TA, Eric Booth. The quarterly journal features not only articles on the practice, research, and theory regarding teaching artistry but also essays, reflections, and experiments. Booth also founded the biennial International Teaching Artist Conference in 2012, which was the first gathering of TAs on an international level.

Government's Role and Impact on Teaching Artists

While the TAs' independent growth as an occupation has been relatively recent, the model for teaching artistry evolved from the NEA's Artists-in-Schools (AIS) residency program which began in 1966. The AIS program was intended to provide employment opportunities for visual and performing artists as well as to increase arts education offerings to students for audience building purposes (Rabkin et al., 2012; Taylor & Barresi, 1984).

Whereas the artists in the AIS program were initially considered an addition to the school curriculum as enrichment for students, they gradually became part of the school curriculum as experts teaching arts subjects in the following decades largely due to NEA's policy efforts. In fact, a landmark NEA report, *Towards Civilization* (1988), played a key role in justifying this important policy shift. The report specifically called for the need for the arts to become a "basic part of education with a 'comprehensive and sequential' curriculum" (p. 12) and to develop standards that would be implemented by state education systems. It also called for arts education to "develop the skills for creativity and problem-solving, and acquire the tools of communication" among students (p. 5). The report was published as a direct response to the sweeping *Nation at Risk: The Imperative for Educational Reform* report

(National Commission on Excellence in Education, 1983) which led to a significant reform in the public school curriculum with a priority in, rigorous standards for, and testing of English, math, and science during the Cold War era.

Still, the U.S. government has mostly played a "facilitator" role in supporting the professionalization of community arts educators, including TAs (Chartrand & McCaughey, 1989). Over the years, governments on different levels have implemented policy tools, including grants and recognition mechanisms, which have contributed to the growth of the field of community arts education. While there are no public grant programs that directly benefit TAs on the federal and state levels, they support organizations and schools that employ TAs to deliver arts education programs in schools and the community. NEA grants supporting community arts education programs, which was discussed in the previous section, often support the employment of TAs.

DOE funds schools and nonprofit organizations through their Assistance for Arts Education Program (AAE) and AIE National Programs. The former provides funding for general arts education in K-12 schools with a focus on disadvantaged student populations and students with disabilities, and the latter provides arts integration or AIE programs. TAs have been actively utilized as instructors for AIE programs in schools.

On the state level, many states offer grant programs that support schools and arts organizations to employ TAs to enhance arts education offering to students. Furthermore, state TA rosters, which are administered by state arts councils, serve as important validation for TAs and increase their exposure to job opportunities in schools and community organizations. State arts councils usually, through a formal screening process, vet TAs based on their (1) mastery of their artistic discipline; (2) knowledge and expertise in pedagogy; (3) knowledge and expertise in arts integration and academic content standards; and (4) professionalism in communication, planning, and partnerships (Ohio Arts Council, 2022).

Professionalization of Arts Educators in South Korea

In this chapter, we offer a brief overview of the professionalization of arts educators in South Korea as a comparison to the United States' case. Arts educators in South Korea can be similarly categorized into the same five subgroups as those in the United States: university professors; licensed K-12 teachers; community arts educators who practice in organizational settings; independent arts teachers; and TAs. As with their American counterparts, the professionalization of Korean university arts professors and formal school arts teachers at the elementary and secondary levels has been mostly standardized. Licensed school teachers teach art and music, which are required in the elementary and secondary school curriculum. Licensed elementary school teachers are those who graduated from a public national university of education. Licensed secondary school teachers are those who either graduated with a bachelor's degree in education or completed credit hours for a Curriculum for Teaching Profession on top of their major in an artistic discipline from a university. All licensed elementary and secondary teachers need to pass a highly competitive teacher appointment exam to be placed in public schools.

Similar to their American counterparts, community arts educators in Korea work in and outside of schools, in organizational as well as private, for-profit settings. These include TAs. Community arts educators work with various learners from young children to seniors. As their American counterparts, the nature and pedagogy of community arts educators differ significantly depending on their work settings. Those who teach in public or nonprofit organizational settings tend to prioritize fostering of creativity among learners, whereas those in private, for-profit settings emphasize artistic skills and curricula.

Yet notably, on the policy level, whereas the U.S. government has assumed a facilitator role in the professionalization of arts educators, the Korean government has played an active role as an architect (Chartrand & McCaughey, 1989). Most policy decisions regarding arts education are made collaboratively between the Ministry of Culture, Sports, and Tourism (MCST) and Ministry of Education (MOE). Policies are administered by Korea Arts and Culture Education Services (KACES), a public agency and professional service organization under MCST, in cooperation with local governments. Other professional organizations participate in advocacy and conversations around policymaking.

Disciplinary silos exist among arts educators in Korea, as in the United States, in general due to the history and traditions of teaching or learning an artistic discipline. However, because of the strong role public policy has played in the professionalization of arts educators in Korea, more inclusive approaches to professionalization are shown in the field of arts education in the country than in the United States.

A public Arts and Cultural Education Instructor (ACEI) certification program is unique to Korea, which has qualified over 21,000 educators trained in a variety of disciplines to teach in state-run and public arts organizations including museums, performing arts centers, and libraries as well as the private sector (KACES, 2017). All public arts organizations are required by the government to employ at least one ACEI. ACEIs practice in not only teaching but also production, management, and administrative positions.

ACEI arts educators can work in nonprofit organizational or private, for-profit settings. Many of them serve a wide range of learner populations in arts organizations, welfare centers, military units, and correctional facilities, and with out-of-school youth and North Korean defectors in nonprofit settings. Others practice in the private, for-profit sector, which is a significant arts education market in Korea. They practice in *hagwons*, or private academies; private providers of arts education, including arts franchises and camps; or independently. Such private arts teachers tend to emphasize curricular theories and teaching philosophies rather than creativity (Shin & Kim, 2014).

TAs, meanwhile, play an important role to supplement and enrich arts education in Korean public schools. As their American counterparts, their pedagogy focuses on nurturing creativity and artistic capabilities rather than skills. TAs teach a variety of artistic disciplines in public schools, including traditional music, theater, film, dance, animation, craft, photography, and design.

The Korean government's architect role is highlighted in its latest support for TAs based on its acknowledgment of their contribution to the field of arts education. The culture ministry and local governments spent a total of 84.5 trillion won ($72 million) in 2020 to support arts education offerings in schools through TAs (KACES, n.d.). As of 2020, over 5,000 TAs serve in some 8,500 schools in 17 cities, according to KACES data (KACES, 2017).

Professional development of arts educators in Korea has been largely led by public policy, with KACES, a public agency and professional service organization, providing them with such programs. These include both in-person and online ArtE Academy, which provides training programs for TAs and courses for the ACEI certification program. Other professional organizations for different art educator subgroups and artistic disciplines provide professionals with networking, knowledge sharing, and advocacy opportunities.

Conclusion

The circle of arts educators in the United States has widened over the years largely due to the NEA's policy initiatives including arts learning. This has broadened the definition of arts education from solely formal education of school children to that within and outside of schools for a wide range of learners.

However, it is challenging to discuss the professionalization of arts educators in the United States as a single group as they have been rather siloed among the five different subgroups of arts educators: university professors; certified K-12 teachers; community arts educators who practice in organizational settings; independent arts teachers; and TAs. With the exception of community arts educators who practice in organizational settings and TAs, many of whom overlap, there are minimal interactions between the five groups. This is primarily due to differences in their venues of practice, education and training, and teaching philosophy and pedagogy, along with variances in the arts and education policies that affect each subgroup.

Division in the arts education community is another factor that hinders the professionalization of arts educators as a unified group. This is particularly shown between certified K-12 teachers and TAs, who both teach the arts in K-12 schools, though often with approaches that differ and sometimes conflict. There has thus been a strong, persisting claim from some certified arts teachers and arts specialists that TAs are unqualified to deliver the standards-based arts curriculum (Rabkin et al., 2012). In fact, State Education Agency Directors of Arts Education (SEADAE) defines those who are qualified to deliver standardized arts curriculum as only certified arts teachers, and considers the rest, including TAs, as providers of supplementary arts education (Richerme et al., 2012). This animosity toward TAs in the mainstream K-12 education community largely comes from a concern for the "long-term erosion of arts faculty positions in public schools" and that TAs represent a kind of "low-cost outsourcing" that enables the erosion (Rabkin et al., 2012, p. 16).

It is also important to note the disconnect between artistic disciplines as another factor that adds to the fractured professionalization among arts educators. Even within a given subgroup, arts educators of different disciplines do not tend to interact with one another. This is largely due to the term "arts education" being defined as a single realm by policy, whereas practitioners in the field have traditionally defined it by the respective artistic disciplines, such as art education, music education, dance education, and theater education. The training of artists has historically concerned development of craftsmanship through apprenticeships to master artists but evolved to include more theoretical matters once a more formal system of education was established.

On the policy level, the disconnect among relevant public entities regarding arts education is a major cause for the fractured professionalization in the field. Historically, the NEA has lobbied the DOE, chasing increased opportunities and support for the arts in formal education. During these occasions, NEA was often reactive to existing education policies. For instance, NEA's arts learning initiative was a response to the No Child Left Behind Act, which marginalized arts education in the K-12 curriculum. NEA's promotion of AIE or Science, Technology, Engineering, Arts, and Math (STEAM) was proposed as an alternative to a strong emphasis on Science, Technology, Engineering, and Math (STEM) in formal education (Galligan, 2014).

Moreover, the definition, professionalization, and growth of arts educator occupations have depended considerably on how arts and education policies have defined them. Essentially, arts educators possess an innate duality as artists and educators but their practice can be affected considerably by policy priorities. For example, TAs have provided students with arts education in K-12 schools since the 1960s. However, their recent growth as an occupation is attributable to their increased utilization in the instruction of AIE or arts integration in schools as per interests for such areas from arts and education policies. This made TAs' unique teaching philosophy and pedagogy more relevant in formal education.

Notably, the aforementioned fractures shown in the field of arts education in the United States can also be found in the Korean case. Whereas the Korean case features a relatively less disciplinary disconnect due to the existence of more influential arts education policy, the disconnect among arts educator subgroups and that on the policy level are evident. Like the NEA, the Korean culture ministry has mostly lobbied the education ministry for increased opportunities for the arts in formal education.

Nevertheless, other than university professors who are already considered professionals, the four semiprofessional arts educator subgroups in the United States have respectively undergone a process of professionalization. It is important to note that professionalization may not be an ultimate destination but a meaningful process for the four semiprofessional arts educator subgroups. It may be appropriate to conclude that these groups of arts educators professionalize to achieve professionalism rather than a professional status as per its sociological definition (Frederickson & Rooney, 1990; Moore, 1970; Wilensky, 1964). This chapter uses the term professionalism to refer to a "mechanism to facilitate and promote occupational change" (Evetts, 2013, p. 788). The ideology of professionalism is what has an appeal to semiprofessional arts educators, as having expertise and knowledge, power to define and access potential problems in the field, and collegial control of the field as opposed to hierarchical, bureaucratic control (Evetts, 2013).

Impact of COVID-19 and Arts Education Community's Resilience

The COVID-19 pandemic and subsequent societal shutdown in March 2020 profoundly disrupted economic activities and social interactions in the United States and worldwide, as well as exacerbated the existing systemic inequities that have affected marginalized communities, including racial minorities. The pandemic has disproportionately affected the arts and cultural sector, including arts education in schools and the community, when schools and organizations were unexpectedly forced to pivot to virtual learning. Moreover, many community arts education organizations encountered major budget cuts, which posed a challenge for them to meet the increased demand for the arts in the community to cope with the distress caused by the pandemic during this period (Wallace Editorial Team, 2020). The NYC Arts in Education Roundtable, as a result, launched the Arts Are Essential campaign in which they advocated for arts education funding and investment in the community (NYCAIE Roundtable, 2023). The U.S. government's extraordinary and unprecedented relief measures were temporary, due to its historical facilitator role, which would have long-term implications for the arts education community in the post-pandemic era. In contrast, the architect government of Korea has pursued more permanent policy changes concerning job security and benefits for artists and arts educators (MCST, 2022).

National service organizations have led efforts in the arts education community to provide discipline-specific resources to help educators transition to online learning. These included the NDEO, NAfME, and NAEA. More importantly, the aforementioned discipline-specific professional organizations, as well as those for community arts educators—namely the National Guild for Community Arts Education and the TAG—served as hubs for sharing resources such as workshops, trainings, and information. Professional associations also advanced ideas for furthering social justice in the arts education community.

Notably, the COVID-19 pandemic highlighted two valuable opportunities for community arts educators and TAs. First is the importance of flexibility and adaptability for individual arts educators, which enabled them to adapt to digital teaching media and thus helped increase their resilience in the face of the inevitable challenges posed by the pandemic. Furthermore, the fundamental value and importance of community arts education have become more widely recognized among the public because of the pandemic. They specifically relate to arts education as a means to help learners cope with and heal from trauma, tackle social issues, and be a conduit for social change while building community through the arts (Wallace Editorial Team, 2020). These purposes of community arts education differ significantly from skills- and knowledge-focused formal arts education and, thus, suggest that community arts educators may be expanding their skill sets moving beyond the pandemic.

References

Andrzejewski, C. E. (2009). Toward a model of holistic dance teacher education. *Journal of Dance Education, 9*(1), 17–26.

Bailey, E. B. (2006). Researching museum educators' perceptions of their roles, identity, and practice. *Journal of Museum Education, 31*(3), 175–197.

Blandy, D., & Congdon, K. G. (1987). *Art in a democracy*. Teachers College Press.

Booth, E. (2015). Something's happening: Teaching artistry is having a growth spurt. *Teaching Artist Journal, 13*(3), 151–159. https://doi.org/10.1080/15411796.2015.1029857

Boyer, J. M. (2007). *Creativity matters: The arts and aging toolkit*. National Guild of Community Schools of the Arts. https://nationalguild.org/files/resources/public/creativity-matters-the-arts-and-aging-toolkit.pdf

Brigham, D., Blume, S., & Knowles, P. (1988). Preparation for empowerment. *Journal of Museum Education, 13*(3), 8–11.

Chartrand, H., & McCaughey, C. (1989). The arm's length principle and the arts: An international perspective-past, present and future. In M. C. Cummings Jr. & J. M. D. Schuster (Eds.), *Who's to pay for the arts? The international search for models of support* (pp. 43–80). www.semanticscholar.org/paper/THE-ARM%27S-LENGTH-PRINCIPLE-AND-THE-ARTS%3A-AN-PRESENT-Chartrand-McCaughey/ee6e32d5d5e54a5801d5628ac32305b9085366e5

Delacruz, E. M., & Dunn, P. C. (1996). The evolution of discipline-based art education. *Journal of Aesthetic Education, 30*(3), 67–82. https://doi.org/10.2307/3333322

Erickson, K. L. (2003). The current state of teaching artistry. *Teaching Artist Journal, 1*(3), 135–143. https://doi.org/10.1207/S1541180XTAJ0103_03

Etzioni, A. (1969). *The semi-professions and their organization: Teachers, nurses, social workers*. Free Press.

Evetts, J. (2013). Professionalism: Value and ideology. *Current Sociology, 61*(5–6), 778–796. https://doi.org/10.1177/0011392113479316

Frederickson, J., & Rooney, J. F. (1990). How the music occupation failed to become a profession. *International Review of the Aesthetics and Sociology of Music*, *21*(2), 189–206. https://doi.org/10.2307/837023

Galligan, A. M. (2014). U.S. workforce policy builds up "STEAM". *CultureWork!*, *18*(2).

Greenwood, E. (1966). The elements of professionalization. In H. M. Vollmer & D. L. Mills (Eds.), *Professionalization*. Prentice Hall.

Greer, W. D. (1993). Developments in discipline-based art education (DBAE): From art education toward arts education. *Studies in Art Education*, *34*(2), 91–101. https://doi.org/10.2307/1320446

Hein, G. E. (2004). John Dewey and museum education. *Curator: The Museum Journal*, *47*(4), 413–427. https://doi.org/10.1111/j.2151-6952.2004.tb00136.x

Heisler, P. K. (1995). A theoretical comparison of certified piano teachers' claim to professional status with the sociological definition of profession. *International Review of the Aesthetics and Sociology of Music*, *26*(2), 239–249. https://doi.org/10.2307/837002

Hutchens, J. (1986). The emerging arts educator: A descriptive study of the education of the community arts administrator. *Studies in Art Education*, *27*(4), 174–185. https://doi.org/10.2307/1320913

KACES (Korea Arts & Culture Education Services). (2017). *Arts and culture education instructor certification system*. www.arte.or.kr/business/professional/license/intro/index.do

KACES (Korea Arts & Culture Education Services). (n.d.). *Teaching artists in schools*. www.arte.or.kr/business/school/tutor/intro/index.do

Kay, A. (2000). Art and community development: The role the arts have in regenerating communities. *Community Development Journal*, *35*(4), 414–424. https://doi.org/10.1093/cdj/35.4.414

Koh, Y. (2020). Achieving joy through community-based culturally relevant art education: A case study of Korean-American elementary students in the Midwest. *Journal of Cultural Research in Art Education*, *37*, 104–127.

Lawton, P. H., & La Porte, A. M. (2013). Beyond traditional art education: Transformative lifelong learning in community-based settings with older adults. *Studies in Art Education*, *54*(4), 310–320. https://doi.org/10.1080/00393541.2013.11518905

MCST (Ministry of Culture, Sports, and Tourism). (2022). *Establishing legal foundations to support teaching artists and increase their job security*. www.mcst.go.kr/kor/s_notice/press/pressView.jsp?pSeq=19324

Miller, J. B. (2020). Transformative learning and the arts: A literature review. *Journal of Transformative Education*, *18*(4), 338–355. https://doi.org/10.1177/1541344620932877

Montemayor, M. (2008). Flauto: An ethnographic study of a highly successful private studio. *International Journal of Music Education*, *26*, 286–301. https://doi.org/10.1177/0255761408096071

Moore, W. E. (1970). *The professions: Roles and rules*. Russell Sage Foundation.

National Commission on Excellence in Education. (1983). *A nation at risk: The imperative for educational reform*. http://edreform.com/wp-content/uploads/2013/02/A_Nation_At_Risk_1983.pdf

NEA (National Endowment for the Arts). (1988). *Toward civilization: A report on arts education*. https://files.eric.ed.gov/fulltext/ED300287.pdf

NEA (National Endowment for the Arts). (2001). *The National Endowment for the Arts 1965–2000: A brief chronology of federal support for the arts.* www.arts.gov/sites/default/files/NEAChronWeb.pdf

NEA (National Endowment for the Arts). (2002). *Learning through the arts: A guide to the National Endowment for the Arts and arts education.* NEA. www.arts.gov/sites/default/files/ArtsLearning.pdf

NGCAE (National Guild for Community Arts Education). (2019). *About the Guild.* https://nationalguild.org/about/about-the-guild

NYCAIE Roundtable. (2023). *Arts are essential.* NYC Arts in Education Roundtable. https://nycaieroundtable.org/advocacy/arts-are-essential/

Ohio Arts Council. (2022). *Welcome to the Ohio teaching Artist Roster.* Ohio Arts Council. https://oac.ohio.gov/Resources/Ohio-Teaching-Artist-Roster

O'Malley, M. P., Sandlin, J. A., & Burdick, J. (2020). Public pedagogy theories, methodologies, and ethics. *Oxford Research Encyclopedia of Education.* https://doi.org/10.1093/acrefore/9780190264093.013.1131

Pitman-Gelles, B., & El-Omami, A. (1988). Defining art museum education: Can we agree? *Journal of Museum Education, 13*(3), 21–23.

Rabkin, N., Reynolds, M., Hedberg, E., & Justin, S. (2012). Teaching artists and the future of education: A report on the teaching artist research project. *Teaching Artist Journal, 10*(1), 5–14. www.tandfonline.com/doi/abs/10.1080/15411796.2012.630633

Richerme, L. K., Shuler, S. C., & McCaffrey, M. (2012). *Promoting universal access to high-quality arts education: Roles of certified arts educators, certified non-arts educators, and providers of supplemental arts instruction.* The State Education Agency Directors of Arts Education. www.philasd.org/arts/wp-content/uploads/sites/144/2017/07/SharedDeliveryofArts.pdf

Scher, A. (2007). Can the arts change the world? The transformative power of community arts. *New Directions for Adult & Continuing Education, 116,* 3–11. www.calpresenters.org/uploads/7/9/5/6/79569060/272_ftp.pdf; https://doi.org/10.1002/ace.272

Shin, R., & Kim, J. (2014). A comparative cross-cultural examination of community art education programs in South Korea and the United States. *Studies in Art Education, 55,* 227–240.

Sidford, H., & Rabkin, N. (2014). *The public benefits and value of arts & culture: What have we learned and why does it matter?* A Report for Cuyahoga Arts & Culture. Grantmakers in the Arts. www.giarts.org/article/public-benefits-and-value-arts-culture

Taylor, F., & Barresi, A. L. (1984). *The arts at a new frontier: The National Endowment for the Arts.* Plenum Press.

Teaching Artists Guild. (n.d.). *Teaching artist manifesto.* https://teachingartists.com/teaching-artist-manifesto/

Tran, L., & King, H. (2007). The professionalization of museum educators: The case in science museums. *Museum Management and Curatorship, 22,* 131–149. https://doi.org/10.1080/09647770701470328

Ulbricht, J. (2005). What is community-based art education? *Art Education, 58*(2), 6–12. https://doi.org/10.2307/27696059

Upitis, R., Abrami, P. C., Brook, J., Boese, K., & King, M. (2017). Characteristics of independent music teachers. *Music Education Research, 19*(2), 169–194. https://doi.org/10.1080/14613808.2016.1204277

Uszler, M. (1996). The independent music teacher: Practice and preparation. *Arts Education Policy Review*, 97(3), 20. https://doi.org/10.1080/10632913.1996.993 5062

Vallance, E. (2004). Museum education as curriculum: Four models, leading to a fifth. *Studies in Art Education*, 45(4), 343–358.

Wallace Editorial Team. (2020). *Pandemic brings challenges (and opportunities) for arts education*. Wallace Blog. www.wallacefoundation.org/news-and-media/blog/pages/pandemic-brings-challenges-and-opportunities-for-arts-education.aspx

Weil, S. E. (1992). In pursuit of a profession: The status of museum work in America. In *Rethinking the museum and other meditations* (pp. 73–89). Smithsonian Institution Press.

Wilensky, H. L. (1964). The professionalization of everyone? *American Journal of Sociology*, 70(2), 137–158. https://doi.org/10.1086/223790

Wyszomirski, M. J., & Chang, W. (2017). Professional self-structuration in the arts: Sustaining creative careers in the 21st century. *Sustainability*, 9(6), 1035. http://dx.doi.org.proxy.lib.miamioh.edu/10.3390/su9061035

9 Cultural Value and Professionalization of Emerging Contemporary Artists

Ian Fillis, Boram Lee, and Ian Fraser

Introduction

In this chapter, we focus on newly graduated art school students. For them to become professional artists in the long-term, self-sustaining income-generating practices beyond selling their art are often required. We develop understanding of how a prestigious annual contemporary art exhibition contributes to building the professionalism of newly graduated art school students through promoting market production and consumption involving a number of interested stakeholders, including the exhibiting artists, the art schools, other partnering organizations with the institution where the exhibition is held, and the public. More specifically, by providing a level playing field, the exhibition acts as a platform or catalyst to professionalization of the newly graduated art school students (Lee, Fraser et al., 2018; Lehikoinen, 2018; Throsby & Petetskaya, 2017).

This exhibition creates a structured opportunity as a platform for career transition and development for newly graduated art school students to become emerging artists, something which has not been explored in the professionalization literature. There is a scarcity of such platforms not only in the United Kingdom but also in developed countries generally and so the provision of such intervention would be beneficial to emerging artists who tend to struggle for at least three years after graduation in developing their careers (Fillis et al., 2015; Lee, Fraser et al., 2018).

We position our thinking around Wyszomirski's (2013) notion of the triple bottom line of micro, macro, and meta policies as a way of understanding how the visual arts sector can move forward in a more integrated way. We investigate cultural value and professionalization of emerging contemporary artists using a case study approach of the Royal Scottish Academy's *New Contemporaries* exhibition, as an intervention in career transition and development of emerging artists. Most emerging artists tend to focus on the creation of their work and their own artistic integrity, exposure, and recognition, rather than on paying attention as to how they might integrate into the art market (Lee, Fraser et al., 2018). The student mindset developed during their time at art school is focused on the creative process, from idea generation

DOI: 10.4324/9781003138693-11

to experimentation with different techniques and styles, creating micro-level cultural value (Lee & Rentschler, 2020). To be professional is to assume that artists not only limit their practice to self-actualization but also enhance the benefits of their practice for the wider sector, as well as society itself. Our cultural value lens helps to uncover the different forms of value which contribute to achieving this triple-bottom line (Wyszomirski, 2013).

We also assess how created values lead the stakeholders in contemporary art to further involvement. Value emerges in both production and consumption through exchange and identity (Du Gay, 1997) as producers and consumers consciously and unconsciously acquire cultural and symbolic capital (Bourdieu, 1993). In order to understand how the different stakeholders interact, we assess how these activities of exchange create, share, and sustain cultural value. Some emerging artists' career development can be aided by entrepreneurial interventions and practices initiated by the artists themselves, as well as by other stakeholders, as they seek to achieve competitive advantage in the marketplace as their careers develop while, for others, it is the intrinsic focus and priority of their profession that sustains their careers (Wyszomirski & Chang, 2017).

We first discuss the definition of an artist and the attributes of professionalism in visual arts. The overarching cultural value concept is interrogated before we assess several value dimensions, for example, market and economic value, aesthetic, artistic, and experiential value, co-creation of value, social value, and brand value (Gokbulut Ozdemir et al., 2020).

Understanding Professionalism in Visual Art

According to UNESCO (1980), whether someone is an artist or not is dependent on self-assessment. Anyone can seek acknowledgment as an artist. Professionalism, however, entails certain attributes and implies externalities of the artistic activities. Jeffri and Throsby (1994) argue that the professional status of an individual artist must reflect the benchmarks set by (1) the marketplace (through earning income from working as a practicing artist); (2) the educational system (through having formally trained as an artist in higher education or through an association, union, or guild); and (3) the profession (through self-recognition and earning peer recognition). Professionalism in visual art is thus defined in terms of this three-way division (Jeffri & Throsby, 1994). However, there are only a few artists who would qualify in terms of the marketplace benchmarks, which assume a certain level of arts-related income.

Despite the substantial growth in the size and complexity of the contemporary arts market (Velthius, 2011), only a small proportion of artists make a living solely from their practice (Throsby & Mills, 1989; Jeffri & Throsby, 1994). Many emerging artists do not consider financial reward to be the main motive for their career choice (Lee, Fraser et al., 2018) and often hold multiple jobs, including non-arts-related work, in order to support their practices due to the precarious state of the visual arts market (Throsby & Zednik, 2010, 2011; Throsby & Petetskaya, 2017). As the artist develops his or her career, a portfolio approach to work is often required as he or she supports his or her artmaking by holding several other jobs that may or may not be art-related (Throsby & Zednik, 2011). Self-structuration through portfolio work is necessary in the arts more broadly, for example, in the arts and craft sector, where "liquid lives" often shape how the maker is able to create time and finances for the creative process (McAuley & Fillis, 2005). Income inequalities or variability are often witnessed and described by expressions such as "winners take all" or "superstar effects" (Frank & Cook, 1995). Yet artists are acknowledged to be much better educated than the labor force at large, and usually meet the customary professionalism benchmarks in terms of education.

Peer recognition or acceptance by the existing artistic community is recognized to be the most important indicator of professionalism for artists themselves (Jeffri & Throsby, 1994). Winning residencies, private commissions, public grants or prizes judged by peer review, public exposure, or recognition by critics all contribute to the perceived professional status of artists (Lee et al., 2017). Plattner (1998) claims that most artists believe peer recognition to be as important, if not more so, than financial success. Empirical work by Jeffri et al. (1991) and Throsby and Mills (1989), in the United States and Australia respectively, indicate that only a small proportion of artists would be entitled to professional status in terms of the three-way division (Jeffri & Throsby, 1994) indicated earlier. Yet the great majority of them would qualify based on education or training and/or peer evaluation alone (Jeffri et al., 1991). If, however, the conventional market-based definitions of professionalism are argued to be critical for professional recognition, an appreciation of art market mechanisms becomes necessary knowledge for newly graduated art school students.

Art and Its Market and Consumption Value

An appreciation of these art market mechanisms helps us to understand art's value associations. Hirschman (1983) has shown that the art market is distinctive due to artists' ideologies, often resulting in the rejection of the marketing concept and the notion of the customer. Some artists, however, do adopt marketplace practices and produce work that customers desire. With the contemporary art market, however, the situation veers toward self-orientation, although peer influences can also impact. Velthuis (2007, 2011) highlights the non-relationship between the market-price-focused capitalist and the intrinsically focused artist. Grampp's (1989) "nothing but" model views the art market as being similar to any other, one where artworks are (merely) economic goods or commodities. It can be argued, however, that a nothing but approach results in artworks being viewed as (merely) economic goods as opposed to those possessed of intrinsic value. By entering the art market for the sake of art rather than money, artists accumulate symbolic capital by establishing recognized brand names or reputations.

Bourdieu (2012) distinguishes between the commercial value of an artwork and the cost of producing and consuming it, with these costs having both sacred and social value. Consumption is where "meanings are made" (O'Reilly, 2005). Additionally, value emerges in both production and consumption through exchange and identity (Du Gay, 1997), through which producers and consumers consciously and unconsciously acquire cultural and symbolic capital (Bourdieu, 1993). Arts consumption value often relates to the viewer's experience of the art (Bourgeon-Renault et al., 2006). For some consumers, aesthetic and everyday consumption experiences are intertwined as they embrace art as part of their lives (Venkatesh & Meamber, 2008). Artistic and market value are diffused through art consumption (Botti, 2000), where the market system "actively places objects into communicative contexts and gives them visibility, thus creating and changing their cultural meaning" (Tharp & Scott, 1990, p. 47). Joy and Sherry visualize the way forward:

> The relationship between art and market can be rendered visible only by closely examining the actions of contemporary artists, art critics, and writers, and the efforts of gallery and auction house merchandisers. A market orientation is just one way of evaluating the activities of the art world. Art and market are not reducible to each other.
>
> (2003, p. 155)

When we are attracted toward an artwork, we experience aspects of fulfillment involving mental, sensual, and aesthetic arousal (Venkatesh & Meamber, 2008). Value is also created from art's written, verbal, and visual narratives. We encounter art both implicitly and explicitly as we are sold experiences and then consume them (Pine & Gilmore, 1999).

Understanding Cultural Value

Insight into these interactions can be assisted by viewing them through a cultural value lens. Although there is a lack of agreement on how we define cultural value, there is consensus on its active contribution to making change happen (O'Brien & Lockley, 2015). Crossick and Kaszynska (2014), for example, define cultural value as "the effects that culture has on those who experience it and the difference it makes to individuals and society" (p. 124). Cultural value can be conceptualized as a triangular relationship of intrinsic, instrumental, and institutional values (Holden, 2006, pp. 14–18).

The institutional value shapes institutionalization (the action of creating something as a norm or expectation in an organization or culture), which then enables those working therein to pursue careers and enjoy mobility between different organizations in their field (Fillis et al., 2022; Peterson, 1986). For this to occur, there needs to be an adequate number of organizations to provide employment opportunities; in the visual arts, this tends to be self-employment. Professionalization tends to be a similar process, but the focus is on the individual person. This relates to the artist's skills and their benchmarking, education and training, their sense of work identity, and an expectation of lifelong learning (Jeffri & Throsby, 1994).

The conventional interpretation of how culture is expressed is through systems of production and dissemination of cultural messages in products or services. At the same time, the need for an improved understanding of cultural value is now being emphasized. The problem is that research tends to principally adopt an instrumental, economic position in order to satisfy government concerns over funding and the measurement of value (e.g., Bonus & Ronte, 1997; Throsby, 2003), ignoring its intangible, qualitative, and subjective dimensions. However, methodological and definitional concerns surrounding the understanding of cultural value have stimulated critical work questioning existing underlying assumptions (e.g., Belfiore, 2002; Oliver & Walmsley, 2011). In contributing to improving understanding, we consider the cultural value of emerging contemporary artists exhibiting at an annual high-profile exhibition. The fact that cultural value effects change creates interest in its valuation (O'Brien, 2014). Cultural value can impact on our quality of life through its aesthetic context and the related social and psychological aspects of cultural capital (Geursen & Rentschler, 2003). Artists supply both a physical market, which shapes the art work's economic price, and a market for ideas, which determines its cultural price (Throsby, 2000). It is clear, then, that taking a purely economic approach to understanding cultural value will result in the omission of important contributing elements.

Explaining the Cultural Value of Contemporary Art

Value emerges from "the social pursuit of . . . meaningful distinctions . . . through the exchange of resources between actors" (Arnould, 2014, p. 130). However, with art, much more complex relationships are often involved. Building on Holbrook's (1999) consumer value dimensions and Bourdieu's (1993) symbolism, Throsby's (2001) six forms of cultural value (aesthetic, spiritual, social, historical, symbolic, and authentic) help us understand how value surrounds emerging contemporary artists and their art. Although the technical characteristics of the art are important (Marshall & Forrest, 2011), visual aesthetics and visual consumption also contribute to the value surrounding contemporary art (Schroeder, 2002). Perceived authenticity of artists' work also shapes brand value (Beverland et al., 2008) and consumers' experiences and intentions (Beverland & Farrelly, 2010). With emerging artists, however, the degree of authenticity can vary depending on how derivative or original the art is perceived to be. Their brand identity is also still developing with brand value shaped partly by the social and physical spaces between the artist and the place of creation (Schroeder, 2005). These highlight context and location issues that impact branding and how we interpret its value. The artwork is often created in a studio space, although when the work moves to a gallery, this then becomes part of the function of gallerists, whose space and reputation serve to legitimize and validate the artists exhibited. If the artist's work is exhibited in a museum, then the museum as a place, with its associated aura, influences the brand's value (Schroeder, 2009). This notion of brand value, of course, can also be manifested in other creative domains such as the performing arts in high-profile venues, or as part of an esteemed festival (Franklin et al., 2021). This broadening and enhancing of brand value can be viewed as a milestone for emerging artists, as they make an early move from exhibiting in their art school studio spaces to competitively earning a position in a professional venue with field rather than study peers.

In understanding the cultural value of contemporary art, we need to appreciate how our reception of an artwork involves both interpretation and realization as a form of co-creation (Fillis et al., 2023; Pongsakornrungsilp & Schroeder, 2011). We experience art both passively and actively as we consume through absorption and immersion, signaling the co-creation of value (Gronroos, 2012). We react to artistic value before we construct any intellectual or conceptual debate about the artwork in our initial viewing of an artwork in an exhibition as we are drawn toward it or dismiss it. In engaging with and consuming contemporary art, we also distinguish between extraordinary and ordinary experiences (Caru & Cova, 2003). Our experiences are a negotiation of the culturally constructed and interpreted symbols we identify and evaluate. Value is located in the arousal and pleasure experienced in a cultural environment where consumers can escape from daily routines (Miniero et al., 2014). The atmosphere or ambience of the cultural space also contributes to the perceived value of the experience (Goulding, 2000). It can be argued that these validated spaces and associated events are more valuable to emerging artists when compared to other forms of exhibition space such as a restaurant or café that also exhibits art, often for sale. In addition, corporate art collections and artist residencies in industrial settings introduce additional forms of value and aura while artwork in healthcare facilities adds a welcome diversion away from potentially stressful situations.

In consuming art as cultural objects, collections and residencies become conduits of dynamic meaning spanning the culturally constructed world to the individual consumer (McCracken, 1988). When an art object is located in a museum or gallery setting, this gives it an additional aura of value (Bjorkman, 2002). We do not normally enter this space blindly, given:

> the knowledge, the expectations, the mental schema, and the values that individuals bring to their experience of art. . . . When a cultural

object brings to the fore some of these assumptions held by individuals, a cultural interaction or positive encounter is said to have occurred.

(Duhaime et al., 1995, p. 356)

Holt (1995) helps us to understand how we engage with art and assess its cultural value, including assessing our subjective, emotional reactions to consumption objects, the integration or acquisition and manipulation of object meanings, and the classification of the cultural and personal meanings surrounding objects.

With art, the importance of intrinsic value or evaluating something "in itself" or "for its own sake" can exceed any other notion of value (De Gennaro, 2012). Boorsma (2006) identifies co-creation of value here:

The artistic experience is a rewarding value that consumers receive in return for their efforts to complete the work of art. This value is not created for the customer but created in cooperation with the customer.

(p. 78)

Venkatesh and Meamber (2008) view our engagement with art in terms of simultaneous production and consumption. Boorsma (2006) views art production and consumption as communicative acts, with value emerging through audience interaction. Who the audience is matters here, as value emerges long before public engagement, through peer and institutional influences when, for example, the artist is also the audience as a personal critic of the art.

With contemporary art, stakeholders interact directly and indirectly as they contribute to the production and consumption of art, and where symbolic meaning emerges (Lehman et al., 2018; McCracken, 1986). The symbolic consumption of contemporary art also constitutes part of its cultural value. Art's cultural value is expressed through involvement (Slater & Armstrong, 2010), with art consumers expressing different desires based on their perception of this value (Chen, 2009). McCarthy et al. (2001) expand upon the nature of the audience where artists and artwork interactions relate to the intrinsic aesthetic experiential benefits and the instrumental value of the arts, for example, in health, social, and economic terms. These outcomes have also been captured under the cultural value lens.

Visual artists are among the least well-organized arts occupations with little effective professional association representation or identity (Jeffri & Throsby, 1994). There are, however, some professional support networks and associations. Visual arts educators, for example, can make use of the National Art Education Association, which includes a wide diversity of all kinds of arts educators at primary, secondary, and higher education levels, as well as independent, individual arts teachers and those who teach in other kinds of institutional settings such as museums and community arts centers.

Designers can join the Chartered Society of Designers to help ensure that work is carried out to the highest professional standards. The Association of Illustrators maintains professional standards in the industry. Despite this, there is reliance not only on gallerists, agents, and collectors but also on the educational credentials the artists obtain, how they earn a living, and the role of public policy in assisting their career development, especially in terms of securing professional status. In order to assist in their professionalization, artists can apply for funding for residencies, fellowships, grants, and commissions. Obtaining an exhibition, either solo or as part of a group, also serves to enhance the artist's professional status (Throsby & Zednik, 2010, 2011; Throsby & Petetskaya, 2017).

Other possibilities for furthering professionalization include participation in art fairs and festivals in that they both provide additional visibility and achieve sales for the artist. There may even be additional kudos in the form of awards and enhanced peer recognition as a result of being selected to participate in the event. This then helps to extend our understanding of how the art market operates in effecting the attainment of professional status by bypassing gatekeeper controlling intermediaries who tend to operate a star system of quality control. Our case study insight of a launching platform for emerging artists provides additional insight into the growing number of structures, venues, and events, which are now available. Additional insight into the contemporary art market and its key values, stakeholders, structures, and processes is provided by Buck (2004) in a report, for Arts Council England, which aims to stimulate the economy for artists in the public and private sectors. The report covers essential insight into the mechanics of the market, the value of the art market, its characteristics, distribution, and supply chain issues, as well as the role of buyers and the future development of the market. It therefore provides additional insight into the role that public policy can play in the structuration of professionalization in the visual arts.

Institutionalization and professionalization reinforce each other through the establishment of those professional associations, which promote and socialize members to the expectations of the profession and any employing institutions (although most artists are ultimately self-employed). These associations provide information, networking opportunities, and ultimately mobilization for their members (Peterson, 1986). The art market, then, is not reducible to merely the market or the art standard but rather a combination of both that is further enhanced by the experience and the associated narratives of the artwork.

Methodology

The research site was the Royal Scottish Academy's *New Contemporaries* exhibition, an annual contemporary art exhibition in Edinburgh, showcasing the work of 60 selected graduates from five Scottish art schools in a ratio of one in seven of the graduating students in each school. Royal Scottish Academy is an independent membership-led organization, with over 100 Academicians and 30 honorary members. The aims of the institution include upholding the best practice in contemporary art and informing national debates on a range of visual, cultural, and educational issues as well as encouraging and supporting emerging artists. The institution's *New Contemporaries* exhibition is the only platform for new art school graduates in Scotland to progress in the early stages of their careers as artists beyond their degree shows. More specifically, by providing a level playing field, the exhibition acts as a platform or catalyst to professionalization of the newly graduated art school students (Lee, Fraser et al., 2018; Throsby & Petetskaya, 2017; Lehikoinen, 2018).

Interviews were held with a selection of the exhibiting artists, the majority with Bachelor of Fine Art degrees, prize-winning artists from previous years' exhibitions, other artists who had not been selected for the exhibition, the exhibition selection panel, institution staff, major prize givers, and visitors to the exhibition. Bonus and Ronte (1997) believe that only a small number of insiders can appreciate emerging artists' work. However, we challenge this view by investigating a wider variety of stakeholders. We asked each of the stakeholder groups a number of cultural value-related questions; for example, exhibiting artists (current and past) were asked about their participation in the exhibition, their long-term ambitions, the different types of value associated with their work, engagement or otherwise in the market, and the importance to them of attracting an audience. Some of the visual artists we researched tend to be able to distinguish between different audiences (those who view and engage with their work) and markets (those who purchase and collect it) while others are more focused on art making and are less engaged with the marketplace, at least before the career intervention of showcasing at the *New Contemporaries* exhibition. We also asked about the impact of their work and its validation, their reflections on the usefulness of the exhibition in developing their careers as artists and how this might be enhanced, the wider impacts of the exhibition, and the artists' relationship with the institution. Staff were asked about the value of the exhibition in relation to the wider aims of the institution and the impact of the exhibition on artists' careers and on the wider public, including its social value. Visitors—including first-timers, long-term attendees, and those who had purchased one or more of the exhibited works—were asked about their engagement with the exhibition.

Illustrative Findings

Professional value is created, consumed, shared, and sustained through the exhibition as a platform, and also through three major value stakeholders: the artist, the institution, and the public. This value is also shared over time with other communities and stakeholders.

Creation of Professionalism

An exhibiting artist revealed the challenges in the early stages of establishing the professional reputation of his art through his and others' actions (Holden, 2006; Preece et al., 2016):

> [T]he main dimension of value would be the actual chance to get to make it and to have the space to show it in because I can't show that in my living room at home . . . it's just getting the idea out and doing it and the value of speaking to people. . . . Maybe having it on my CV.
>
> (exhibiting artist)

The meaning of professionalism to the artists is also related to their own identity as a brand, as well as that of the artwork (Schroeder, 2009). This also demonstrates the value to the artist in market creation terms, with cultural value potentially increasing further once the artist let go of the work (Botti, 2000; Tharp & Scott, 1990):

> I don't like . . . that the artist holds the value rather than their artwork, but I think [that's] an honest perspective and the direction they've taken. . . . I think it's nice that an artwork can just go off and do something and have its own value.
>
> (exhibiting artist)

In the United States, research has found that audiences are often aware of an artwork but less aware of the artists or arts organizations behind it (McClellan et al., 1999). In order to build persistent presence in the market (p. 1), where visibility ultimately leads to survival, it is important for artists to engage with audiences at the personal level. This has led to the introduction of opportunities where artists can personally interact with audiences via consciously constructed exhibition tours, post-performance talks, and open studios, which thus both help the artist to acquire more visibility and provide enhanced authenticity for the artworks. Sjöholm and Pasquinelli (2014) similarly address the invisibility of contemporary artists as building personal brands is challenging as it concerns the recognition and validation of the artist (p. 13). Thus, fostering artists' awareness of branding effects is important in order that they might achieve a persistent presence given the temporal and episodic nature of their exposure to the market. McClellan et al. (1999) discuss the possible tactics that artists and arts organizations may employ, including adopting new marketing strategies, forming administrative alliances with other organizations, and creating programs that appeal to broader audiences. Nevertheless, they argue that persistent presence can only be achieved through recognition within the professional community.

Cultural Value of Emerging Artists Entering the Market

Expensive art does not necessarily mean better value, but it does indicate the artist's own sense of worth or status (Adorno & Horkheimer, 2007), as well as wider perceptions of its value. For emerging artists, there is no pre-existing market for their work. They may have a preconceived notion of its financial value or set a random price due to a lack of awareness of its value (Lee, Fraser et al., 2018, 2022). This lack of engagement with the market means that we need to re-conceptualize the concept of the market from the artist's perspective. It is a domain where making art, career development, reputation, and status are often valued more than sales and where these dimensions then contribute to the cultural value of the art and the artist.

Cultural Value Surrounding the Institution's Role in Hosting the Exhibition

Artists talked about the value of the institution in helping secure publicity, as well as being influential in launching their careers, acting as a catalyst in developing the value of their work, and reaching new audiences beyond the art school environment (Lee, Fillis et al., 2018; Fillis et al., 2022; Peterson, 1986). This supports the notion of the "art machine" as a means of cultural value creation (Rodner & Thomson, 2013, p. 66).

Intrinsic and Social Value Elements of Cultural Value

The director of a healthcare charity, which awarded prizes and purchased work for its own collection, talked about the ability of the art to "quite easily and cost effectively and quickly transform the healing space to create something . . . more familiar, less threatening" via the work's intrinsic values (Radbourne et al., 2010). An artist who had exhibited previously, and was selected for a major retrospective, reflected on the value created and shared, indicating its longitudinal worth: "The value isn't monetary . . . it's an emotional, more spiritual connection that you have with a piece that can't be quantified it's so personal to everyone who looks at it."

Cultural Value Through Co-creation and Sharing of Value

Cultural value was identified through interaction between stakeholders, the art itself, and the exhibition setting. The institution program coordinator also revealed how co-creation occurs (Pongsakornrungsilp & Schroeder, 2011):

> Making it a value to the artist while making it accessible to visitors who don't have the same understanding. . . . But saying, look this is what's coming out of art school and this is good, this is exciting and [having] gallery staff who are all artists themselves do . . . talks around a favorite

work. . . . I think it's valuable for people coming in to have . . . insight. . . . And just a . . . slight introduction . . . makes such a difference and I think that creates value, interpretation.

(program coordinator)

Co-creation also occurred between the artists and the institution through the provision of advice, encouragement, and engagement, which are crucial for professional development (Boorsma, 2006).

Contrasting Visitor Reactions to the Exhibition in Shaping Cultural Value

We identified a conflict between some visitors in terms of their perceptions of what constituted contemporary art (Danto, 2013). An older, conservative respondent reflected on what he viewed as the true meaning of art, and how this clashed with contemporary interpretations:

I think that there was a time when art was either paper, paint, canvas, steel, bronze. Now it's performance and it's bleeding into theater and theater bleeds into art. . . . My expectations were of more representative art and what I saw wasn't the kind of stuff I would hang and therefore it didn't get me excited. . . . There was no way I would go . . . to the people that I know, and I say "you've got to go to that" but that's because I've a very narrow set of tastes.

(exhibition visitor)

A regular visitor who collected art raised concerns about the professional quality of some of the work but thought that the exhibition was better than in previous years (Bonus & Ronte, 1997). This stimulated him to make a purchase. For this individual, the technical skill behind the production of the art was what impressed him the most, and which then shaped its value (Marshall & Forrest, 2011). A retired visitor's attendance was unplanned but resulted in a positive exhibition impression, although he had little inclination to make a purchase. He considered the role of the market and how people define art (Bourdieu, 1993) as influences on what is being produced. Authenticity concerns were also raised, which impacted the perceived value of the art (Beverland et al., 2008; Beverland & Farrelly, 2010).

The stakeholders in our study create, produce, consume, share, and promote cultural value to varying degrees, depending on their relationship with the art. Artists, for example, have a direct connection with the art but exhibition sponsors are often initially engaged in institutional relationships, with the artist relationship following on from this. The artist initially generates value through the creation of the idea behind the artwork and then enhances this, helped by the institution. Consumption of ideas from peers also informs how the artists themselves help create professional appreciation. Our data indicate that elements of heightened professional status are being experienced. This then results in additional cultural value and enhancement of the artist's brand and professionalism. The institution enhances the professionalism and brand value of the exhibiting emerging artists due to its prestigious status in the art world, acting as both anchor and broker of a professional network. It facilitates institutionalization of professional artists by acting as a platform for artists' career development, helped by marketing the artists and the exhibition itself.

Discussion

This annual exhibition provides opportunities for the selected artists to address all three of the Jeffri and Throsby (1994) benchmarks: opportunities for purchase of exhibited artworks, educational experience in competing and participating in the market, and recognition of one's peers through the selection panel review process. So, the annual exhibition provides a structured opportunity for the selected artists to engage in the processes of professionalization in all of its three aspects. The understanding of professionalism in visual art is still evolving as we acknowledge and move on from dominant economic interpretations to include experiential, co-created, socially impacting accounts (Lehikoinen, 2018). Our work has widened the conversation on professionalism of emerging visual artists more generally in setting up and clarifying the connection between creation, consumption, and cultural value. We also relate professionalism to experience and acknowledge the importance of social, symbolic, and sign context in moving beyond exchange and use value in understanding contemporary art as cultural value. We also build on the seminal work of Solomon (1988) in assessing how symbolic consumption, production, co-creation, institutional value, intrinsic value, instrumental value, and stakeholder interactions can contribute to enhancing understanding of professional arts creation and its cultural value.

In terms of the art market structure, the exhibition can be viewed at the center of a hub or network for cultural value creation and exchange, with the stakeholders as nodes on the network as shown in our conceptual framework (Figure 9.1). The exhibition not only showcases the artworks of newly graduated art school students but also offers most of them for sale. Our conceptual framework of cultural value creation also addresses the call by Preece et al. (2016) for a broader, socio-cultural perspective on value creation and the problematizing of value. Our cultural value research involves what O'Brien (2015, p. 210) terms "the opening up" of institutions and the drawing of attention to the geography of professionalism in relation to the location of the exhibition and the audience and artist catchment area (While, 2003). Collective audience experience and individual subjective experience also contribute to the recognition of professional value creation here (Kaszynska, 2015).

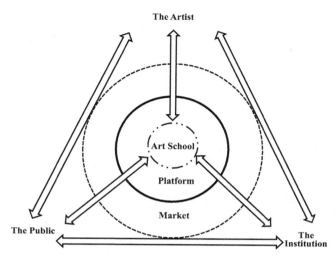

The Artist

Structures

- **Art School**
- **Platform**
- **Market**

Main Actors

The Artist – Professional Value Created (e.g. creation and sharing of the idea; career development, reputation, own sense of worth and status; enhancement of the artist's brand and professionalism)

Art School

Platform

Market

The Institution – Professional Value Shared (e.g. providing advice, encouragement & engagement; reaching new audiences; securing publicity, as well as being influential in launching the artists' careers)

The Public

The Institution

The Public – Professional Value Consumed (e.g. obtaining emotional and spiritual connection based on either viewing or purchasing the artworks at the institution)

Figure 9.1 Conceptual Framework of Cultural and Professional Values Creation and Consumption at the Platform

Rodner and Thomson (2013) deconstructed the validation process for contemporary art by re-visualizing its constituent elements and terminologies. In moving beyond Rodner and Thomson's symbolic and financial value, we have opened up the conversation on professional value by assessing its multiple sources. Rodner and Thompson's approach relies on all constituent members working together to generate value. Our research shows that this is often the case, but not always. Although Rodner and Thomson's (2013) art machine visualization is dynamic and stage-based, we have paid greater attention to multiple relationships and how to provide a platform to create professional value. We have built on their work by grounding stakeholder relationships within the domain of the visual art market. Our work contrasts with Rodner and Thomson (2013), Chong (2005), and Martin (2007) in that the institution serving as the initial platform enables instant access to other network members, rather than at some point in the future as the emerging artists' careers develop. In doing so, we visualize the bypassing or short circuiting of the longitudinal route to professional and cultural value creation. How we associate professional value with art depends on its market and non-market interactions. Some artists may proactively create a market and audience for their work while others hold strong artistic beliefs, negating any market conversation. They may, however, be later drawn in through necessity. We have seen that cultural value contains many facets, and not just economic dimensions linked to instrumentalism. Value can also lie in the spectacular (Debord, 1977; Penaloza, 1999), for example, in a blockbuster art exhibition. We can even visualize a circle of value involving culture, marketing, and consumption where meanings are made (O'Reilly, 2005). Art consumption then moves beyond Arnould's (2014) exchange and uses value to involve cultural knowledge and professional competency.

Conclusion

The notion expressed by Preece et al. (2016) of value being co-constructed, negotiated, and circulated is useful while we interrogate actual data relating to challenges in building professionalism and realizing the cultural value of emerging rather than established artists. They note that "the locus of control is . . . dispersed" and that some consumers are "more important than others in the valuation process" (p. 1377). With our research, the locus of control is very much with the institution at the early stages of the artists' careers, with control being superseded by the institution as facilitator or enabler (Peterson, 1986; Lehikoinen, 2018). The professionalism, which we find located around the contemporary art exhibition, challenges the belief that cultural value can only really develop once the artist's career has matured (Penet & Lee, 2014). Offering a platform via a prestigious art institution, as we have investigated here, acts as a catalyst to professionalization for emerging artists. Further events such as this across the sector would, we believe, contribute further to early career-stage professionalization. Understanding the professionalization process of emerging artists from the producer–consumer interface alone does not fully encapsulate stakeholder involvement (Preece et al., 2016). The visual arts value framework of Preece et al. is helpful in identifying how the artist receives support from a variety of stakeholders in order to build their professional status, but we do not necessarily view this as a process-led phenomenon. Our work moves beyond this perspective to also consider how subsequent cultural value is created, shared, and sustained, supported by the artist's professionalism. Preece et al. (2016) situate the artwork within a commercial context with support from the systematic intervention of a structured opportunity offered by the professional and private institution, which offers exclusive membership. While this is often the case, much contemporary art is not for sale or permanent if it is, for example, performative; this challenges the notion of professionalism set by the marketplace. The identification by Preece et al. (2016) of early champions of cultural capital resonates with our own work. It is not the art school, however, but the artist's first public exhibition that stimulates the more impactful marketplace interaction as the emerging artists become exposed to a wider audience for the first time. Our work informs theory and practice in the wider cultural landscape, including cultural entrepreneurship, which is critical to appreciating professionalism in visual arts (Fillis & Lehman, 2021; Wickham et al., 2020). We recommend that art school students graduate not only with artistic and creative competencies but also with a range of embedded entrepreneurial skills relating to networking, idea generation, and creativity in order to sustain their professional artist status. Along with Wyszomirski and Chang (2017), we also call for institutional, peer, and wider network support for artists as they seek to survive professionally, economically, and artistically.

This work was supported by the Arts and Humanities Research Council [grant number AH/L014750/1].

References

Adorno, T., & Horkheimer, M. (2007). The culture industry: Enlightenment as mass deception. In *Stardom and celebrity: A reader* (pp. 34–43). Sage Publications. https://doi.org/10.4135/9781446269534

Arnould, E. J. (2014). Rudiments of a value praxeology. *Marketing Theory, 14*(1), 129–133.

Belfiore, E. (2002). Art as a means of alleviating social exclusion: Does it really work? A critique of instrumental cultural policies and social impact studies in the UK. *International Journal of Cultural Policy, 8*(1), 91–106.

Beverland, M. B., & Farrelly, F. J. (2010). The quest for authenticity in consumption: Consumers' purposive choice of authentic cues to shape experiences outcomes. *Journal of Consumer Research, 36*(5), 838–856.

Beverland, M. B., Lindgreen, A., & Vink, M. (2008). Projecting authenticity through advertising consumer judgements of advertisers' claims. *Journal of Advertising, 37*(1), 5–15.

Bjorkman, I. (2002). Aura: Aesthetic business creativity. *Consumption, Markets and Culture, 5*(1), 69–78.

Bonus, H., & Ronte, D. (1997). Credibility and economic value in the visual arts. *Journal of Cultural Economics, 21*(2), 103–118.

Boorsma, M. (2006). A strategic logic for arts marketing: Integrating customer value and artistic objectives. *International Journal of Cultural Policy, 12*(1), 73–92.

Botti, S. (2000). What role for marketing in the arts? An analysis of arts consumption and artistic value. *International Journal of Arts Management, 2*(3), 14–27.

Bourdieu, P. (1993). *The field of cultural production: Essays on art and literature.* Polity Press.

Bourdieu, P. (2012). *The rules of art.* Polity Press.

Bourgeon-Renault, D., Urbain, C., Petr, C., Le Gall-Ely, M., & Gombault, A. (2006). An experiential approach to the consumption value of arts and culture: The case of museums and monuments. *International Journal of Arts Management, 9*(1), 35–47.

Buck, L. (2004). *Market matters: The dynamics of the contemporary art market.* Arts Council England. www.dacs.org.uk/DACSO/media/DACSDocs/news/Market-Matters-transcript.pdf

Caru, A., & Cova, B. (2003). Revisiting consumption experience: A more humble but complete view of the concept. *Marketing Theory, 3*(2), 267–286.

Chen, Y. (2009). Possession and access: Consumer desires and value perceptions regarding contemporary art collection and exhibit visits. *Journal of Consumer Research, 35*(6), 925–940.

Chong, D. (2005). Stakeholder relationships in the market for contemporary art. In I. Robertson (Ed.), *Understanding international art markets and management* (pp. 84–102). Routledge.

Crossick, G., & Kaszynska, P. (2014). Under construction: Towards a framework for cultural value. *Cultural Trends, 23*(2), 120–131.

Danto, A. C. (2013). *What art is.* Yale University Press.

Debord, G. (1977). *The society of the spectacle.* Black & Red.

De Gennaro, I. (Ed.). (2012). *Value: Sources and readings on a key concept of the globalized world.* Brill.

Du Gay, P. (Ed.). (1997). *Production of culture/cultures of production.* Open University, Sage Publications.

Duhaime, C., Joy, A., & Ross, C. (1995). Learning to "see": A folk phenomenology of the consumption of contemporary Canadian art. In J. F. Sherry Jr. (Ed.), *Contemporary marketing and consumer behavior: An anthropological source book* (pp. 351–398). Sage Publications.

Fillis, I., Lee, B., & Fraser, I. (2015). Measuring the cultural value of the royal Scottish academy new contemporaries exhibition as a platform for emerging artists. *Cultural Trends, 24*(3), 245–255.

Fillis, I., Lee, B., & Fraser, I. (2022). The role of institutional relationships in shaping the career development of emerging artists. *Arts and the Market, 12.*

Fillis, I., Lee, B., & Fraser, I. (2023). Creation and consumption experience of cultural value in contemporary art. In Y. Jung, N. Vakharia, & M. Vecco (Eds.), *The Oxford handbook of arts and cultural management* (Chapter 9, pp. 1–14). Oxford University Press.

Fillis, I., & Lehman, K. (2021). Art collecting as consumption and entrepreneurial marketing as strategy. *Arts and the Market, 11*(3), 171–185.

Frank, R. H., & Cook, P. J. (1995). *The winner-take-all society.* Free Press.

Franklin, A., Lee, B., & Rentschler, R. (2021). The Adelaide festival and the development of arts in Adelaide. *Journal of Urban Affairs, 44*(4–5), 1–26. https://doi.org/10.1080/07352166.2021.1909422

Geursen, G., & Rentschler, R. (2003). Unravelling cultural value. *Journal of Arts Management, Law, and Society, 33*(3), 196–210.

Gokbulut Ozdemir, O., Fillis, I., & Bas Collins, A. (2020). Developing insights into the link between art and tourism through the value co-creation lens. *Arts and the Market, 10*(3), 145–163.

Goulding, C. (2000). The museum environment and the visitor experience. *European Journal of Marketing, 34*(3–4), 261–278.

Grampp, W. D. (1989). *Pricing the priceless: Art, artists and economics.* Basic Books.

Gronroos, C. (2012). Conceptualising value co-creation: A journey to the 1970s and back to the future. *Journal of Marketing Management, 28*(13–14), 1520–1534.

Hirschman, E. C. (1983). Aesthetics, ideologies and the limits of the marketing concept. *Journal of Marketing, 47*(3), 45–55.

Holbrook, M. B. (1999). Introduction to consumer value. In M. B. Holbrook (Ed.), *Consumer value: A framework for analysis and research* (pp. 1–28). Routledge.

Holden, J. (2006). *Cultural value and the crisis of legitimacy: Why culture needs a democratic mandate.* Demos.

Holt, D. (1995). How consumers consume: A typology of consumption practices. *Journal of Consumer Research, 22*(1), 1–16.

Jeffri, J., Greenblatt, R., Friedman, Z., & Greeley, M. (Eds.). (1991). *The artists training and career project: Painters.* Columbia University, Research Center for Arts and Culture.

Jeffri, J., & Throsby, D. (1994). Professionalism and the visual artist. *International Journal of Cultural Policy*, 1(1), 99–108.

Joy, A., & Sherry, J. F. (2003). Speaking of art as embodied imagination: A multisensory approach to understanding aesthetic experience. *Journal of Consumer Research*, 30(2), 259–282.

Kaszynska, P. (2015). Capturing the vanishing point: Subjective experiences and cultural value. *Cultural Trends*, 24(3), 256–266.

Lee, B., Fillis, I., & Lehman, K. (2018). Art, science and organisational interactions: Exploring the value of artist residencies on campus. *Journal of Business Research*, 85, 444–451.

Lee, B., Fraser, I., & Fillis, I. (2017). Nudging art lovers to donate. *Nonprofit and Voluntary Sector Quarterly*, 46(4), 837–858.

Lee, B., Fraser, I., & Fillis, I. (2018). Creative futures for new contemporary artists: Opportunities and barriers. *International Journal of Arts Management*, 20(2), 9–19.

Lee, B., Fraser, I., & Fillis, I. (2022). To sell or not to sell? Pricing strategies of newly-graduated artists. *Journal of Business Research*, 145, 595–604.

Lee, B., & Rentschler, R. (2020). Cultural value in conflict. In K. Lehman, I. Fillis, & M. Wickham (Eds.), *Exploring cultural value: Contemporary issues for theory and practice* (pp. 51–65). Emerald Publishing.

Lehikoinen, K. (2018). Setting the context: Expanding professionalism in the arts—a paradigm shift. In T. B. Revelli & S. B. Florander (Eds.), *Careers in the arts: Visions for the future* (pp. 16–30). ELIA. https://issuu.com/elia-artschools/docs/nxt_publication_2018_careers_in_the

Lehman, K., Wickham, M., & Fillis, I. (2018). Exploring supply-side network interactions in the visual art production process. *Poetics*, 69, 57–69. https://doi.org/10.1016/j.poetic.2018.04.002

Marshall, K. P., & Forrest, P. J. (2011). A framework for identifying factors that influence fine art valuations from artist to consumers. *Marketing Management*, 21, 11–123.

Martin, B. (2007). How visual artists enter the contemporary art market in France: A dynamic approach based on a network of tests. *International Journal of Arts Management*, 9(3), 16–33.

McAuley, A., & Fillis, I. (2005). Careers and lifestyles of craft makers in the 21st century. *Cultural Trends*, 14(2), 139–156.

McCarthy, K. F., Ondaatje, E. H., Zakaras, L., & Brooks, A. (2001). *Gifts of the muse: Reframing the debate about the benefits of the arts*. RAND Corporation.

McClellan, A., Darlene Rebello-Rao, D., & Wyszomirski, M. J. (1999). Resisting invisibility: Arts organizations and the pursuit of persistent presence. *Nonprofit Management and Leadership*, 10(2), 169–183.

McCracken, G. (1986). Culture and consumption: A theoretical account of the structure and movement of the cultural meaning of consumer good. *Journal of Consumer Research*, 13(1), 71–84.

McCracken, G. (1988). *Culture and consumption: New approaches to the symbolic character of consumer goods and activities*. University of Indiana Press.

Miniero, G., Rurale, A., & Addis, M. (2014). Effects of arousal, dominance, and their interaction on pleasure in a cultural environment. *Psychology & Marketing*, 31(8), 628–634.

O'Brien, D. (2014). *Cultural policy*. Routledge.

O'Brien, D. (2015). Editorial. Cultural value: Empirical perspectives. *Cultural Trends*, *24*(3), 209–210.

O'Brien, D., & Lockley, P. (2015). The social life of cultural value. In L. MacDowall, M. Badham, & E. Blomkamp (Eds.), *Making culture count: The politics of cultural measurement*. Palgrave Macmillan.

Oliver, J., & Walmsley, B. (2011). Assessing the value of the arts. In B. Walmsley (Ed.), *Key issues in the arts and entertainment industry* (pp. 83–101). Goodfellow Publishers.

O'Reilly, D. (2005). Cultural brands/branding cultures. *Journal of Marketing Management*, *21*(5–6), 573–588.

Penaloza, L. (1999). Just doing it: A visual ethnographic study of spectacular consumption behaviour at Nike Town. *Consumption, Markets and Culture*, *2*(4), 337–400.

Penet, P., & Lee, K. (2014). Prize & price: The Turner prize as a valuation device in the contemporary art market. *Poetics*, *43*, 149–171.

Peterson, R. A. (1986). From impresario to arts administrator: Formal accountability in nonprofit cultural organizations. In P. J. DiMaggio (Ed.), *Nonprofit enterprise in the arts* (pp. 161–183). Oxford University Press.

Pine, J., & Gilmore, J. H. (1999). *The experience economy*. Harvard Business School Press.

Plattner, S. (1998). A most ingenious paradox: The market for contemporary fine art. *American Anthropologist*, *100*(2), 482–493.

Pongsakornrungsilp, S., & Schroeder, J. E. (2011). Understanding value co-creation in a co-consuming brand community. *Marketing Theory*, *11*(3), 303–324.

Preece, C., Kerrigan, F., & O'Reilly, D. (2016). Framing the work: The composition of value in the visual arts. *European Journal of Marketing*, *50*(7–8), 1377–1398.

Radbourne, J., Glow, H., & Johanson, K. (2010). Measuring the intrinsic benefits of arts attendance. *Cultural Trends*, *19*(4), 307–324.

Rodner, V. L., & Thomson, E. (2013). The art machine: Dynamics of a value generating mechanism for contemporary art. *Arts Marketing: An International Journal*, *3*(1), 58–72.

Schroeder, J. E. (2002). *Visual consumption*. Routledge.

Schroeder, J. E. (2005). The artist and the brand. *European Journal of Marketing*, *39*(11), 1291–1305.

Schroeder, J. E. (2009). The cultural codes of branding. *Marketing Theory*, *9*(1), 123–126.

Sjöholm, J., & Pasquinelli, C. (2014). Artist brand building: Towards a spatial perspective. *Arts Marketing: An International Journal*, *4*(1–2), 10–24.

Slater, A., & Armstrong, K. (2010). Involvement, Tate and me. *Journal of Marketing Management*, *26*(7–8), 727–748.

Solomon, M. R. (1988). Building up and breaking down: The impact of cultural sorting on symbolic consumption. *Research in Consumer Behavior*, *3*(2), 325–351.

Tharp, M., & Scott, L. M. (1990). The role of marketing processes in creating cultural meaning. *Journal of Macromarketing*, *10*(2), 47–60.

Throsby, D. (2000). Economic and cultural value in the work of creative artists. In E. Avrami, R. Mason, & M. De La Torre (Eds.), *Values and heritage conservation* (pp. 26–31). Getty Conservation Institute.

Throsby, D. (2001). *Economics and culture*. Cambridge University Press.

Throsby, D. (2003). Determining the value of cultural goods: How much (or how little) does contingent valuation tell us? *Journal of Cultural Economics, 27*(3–4), 275–285.

Throsby, D., & Mills, D. (1989). *When are you going to get a real job? An economic study of Australian artists*. Australia Council.

Throsby, D., & Petetskaya, K. (2017). *Making art work: Report for the Australian council for the arts*. https://australiacouncil.gov.au/advocacy-and-research/making-art-work/

Throsby, D., & Zednik, A. (2010). *Do you really expect to get paid? An economic study of professional artists in Australia*. Australia Council. https://australiacouncil.gov.au/advocacy-and-research/do-you-really-expect-to-get-paid/

Throsby, D., & Zednik, A. (2011). Multiple job-holding and artistic careers: Some empirical evidence. *Cultural Trends, 20*(1), 9–24.

UNESCO. (1980). *Recommendation concerning the status of the artist*. UNESCO.

Velthuis, O. (2007). *Talking prices: Symbolic meanings of prices on the market for contemporary art*. Princeton University Press.

Velthius, O. (2011). Art markets. In R. Towse (Ed.), *A handbook of cultural economics* (pp. 33–42). Edward Elgar Publishing.

Venkatesh, A., & Meamber, L. A. (2008). The aesthetics of consumption and the consumer as an aesthetic subject. *Consumption, Markets and Culture, 11*(1), 45–70.

While, A. (2003). Locating art worlds: London and the making of young British art. *Area, 35*(3), 251–263.

Wickham, M., Lehman, K., & Fillis, I. (2020). Defining the art product: A network perspective. *Arts and the Market, 10*(2), 83–98.

Wyszomirski, M. J. (2013). Shaping a triple-bottom line for nonprofit arts organizations: Micro-, macro-, and meta-policy influences. *Cultural Trends, 22*(3–4), 156–166.

Wyszomirski, M. J., & Chang, W. (2017). Professional self-structuration in the arts: Sustaining creative careers in the 21st century. *Sustainability, 9*(6), 1035.

10 Strategic or Struggling?

Professionalizing Philanthropy in Nonprofit Arts Organizations

Chiara Carolina Donelli and Ruth Rentschler

Introduction

This chapter examines the professionalization process in the performing arts, using the function of philanthropy, with case examples of how professional roles are developing from being a peripheral function to a central one. The professionalization process is occurring in the practice of philanthropy within Australian PAOs as the field struggles for financial sustainability with policy reforms to a greater or lesser extent. Using interviews, annual reports, and web analysis, the chapter reviews how professionalization has arisen in the arts due to the significant changes in institutionalized structures and roles that are sites of major arts manager employment. Occupations in performing arts management are coalescing around a new organizational funding and sustainability model amidst discontinuous global change. The changes profiled in this study examine what might be called national flagship PAOs, set amidst external and internal environmental shifts that have prompted reform of organizational funding and sustainability models, which, in turn, have led to the emergence and professionalization of philanthropic roles within arts organizations (which have also experienced a structural shift from government-funded organizations to hybrid nonprofit organizations). We lay out the complex explanation for this evolution that draws on resource dependency theory (RDT), new public management reform (NPM), and arts organizational practices that have generally moved from an impresarial to a managerial style and an ongoing need to rebalance their triple bottom line (Wyszomirski, 2013) in the face of changing service demands, multiple stakeholder scrutiny, changing audience demographics, and rising artistic production costs and values. In order to achieve our purpose, we investigate organizational structure and managerial roles, charting the changes occurring in them through the professionalization process.

Professionalization has arisen in the arts for a number of reasons, underpinned by the forces identified by RDT and how the organizational structure interacts with the evolution of the status of arts managers as agents of resource acquisition (via philanthropy) (DiMaggio, 1991; Pfeffer & Salancik, 2003), as discussed later. First, over the decades, exogenous factors, such as

DOI: 10.4324/9781003138693-12

economic downturns, decreasing public support, and government cutbacks (Daley, 2021; Palmer, 1996; Peterson, 1987) have put pressure on creating a viable and vital arts organization. For the arts sector, this has resulted in a decline in government funding for individual arts organizations over the last 50 years, exacerbated by the global financial crisis. This happened also in countries in which the arts have been considered a merit good with extensive financing from central governments (Fanelli et al., 2020). Hence, there is an ongoing lacuna and discontinuity in public funds to support nonprofit organizations (NPOs) (Dubini & Monti, 2018; Moldavanova & Goerdel, 2018; Weerawardena et al., 2010). This results in more competition for funds for PAOs, forcing them to change structures and managerial roles (Rossheim et al., 1995) in order to meet the needs of a turbulent, volatile global environment.

Second, endogenous factors have caused change to occur, such as increased demands for services to support communities, more scrutiny from stakeholders to manage service costs efficiently and effectively, and causing struggles that occur in NPOs between cultural and commercial imperatives (Rentschler, 2001), in addition to ensuring product quality (DiMaggio, 1987) in a sector hit harder by the global pandemic, COVID-19, than most others (Daley, 2021). These factors have caused the philanthropy function to evolve into a role with a place in the organizational structure, more or less formalized, depending on the organization type and the place in its evolution.

Third, in the 1980s, NPM government reforms spread throughout the Western world, resulting in initiatives that aimed to restructure the public sector (Halligan & Power, 1992; Kuipers et al., 2014), improving public service quality and cost efficiency. Arts organizations have been required to achieve sustainability through income diversity (i.e., by turning to philanthropy) (Donelli et al., 2023); new models of public–private partnerships (Brady et al., 2011); and the co-creation of value through audience centricity (Rentschler & Geursen, 2004). This resulted in the creation of mixed forms of governance (Schuster, 1998), suspended between private logics (expected to be autonomously funded) and public logics (expected to make the products fully and freely accessible for the public).

Fourth, some arts organizations have shifted from small, volunteer-led, amateur-run, informally structured organizations to larger, more formal structures that have been paralleled by the rise of arts managers who are educated in managerial roles. Peterson (1987), in his classic article, characterized the shift as that from an "impresarial [form of management to] arts administration" (p. 162). The impresario was led by artists who were without "schooling" and more "connoisseurs" and indeed "gentlemen" (as there were few if any women or people of ethnic backgrounds in these roles), whose style was "flattering" and "cajoling" the elite while behaving autocratically inside the organization (p. 162). In contrast, the arts manager is educated, a professional with specialized skills in management working in a formalized structure, and part of a network that seeks to continue to raise standards. Arts managers devote more of their time to management and less to artistry, which has been devolved to artistic paid staff (DiMaggio, 1987; Rentschler, 2001, 2015). Management has increasingly been recognized as a profession, with education being a core and specialized skill for managers, some of whom have specialized in philanthropy as a functional domain.

Furthermore, this process of change legitimized arts organizations, as policy processes also adopted new approaches to philanthropy as the political and socioeconomic context shifted (Wyszomirski, 2013). Within this context, philanthropy was one such role that became structured in different ways.

Drawing on historical and contemporary understanding of changes in the role of philanthropy from the performing arts in Australia, this chapter explores the complex landscape of professionalization of philanthropy focusing on one country. However, the lessons learned from Australia may well be of value to other developed countries seeking to benefit from philanthropy as a means to sustain their organizations in uncertain times. Hence, we answer the research question: How has the process of professionalization occurred in relation to philanthropy in terms of structure and managerial roles?

The rest of this chapter proceeds as follows. First, the professionalization process in the arts is defined; next, professionalization in the arts is examined before turning to the approach taken in this study. Third, the structure and roles of philanthropy in the performing arts are investigated. Finally, we discuss the implications of the professionalization in philanthropy structure and roles in the performing arts before our discussion and conclusion.

New Organization and New Professionalism: The Arts in Transition

New Public Management in the Performing Arts Sector

In the 1980s, NPM arose as a government initiative that aimed to restructure the public sector (Halligan & Power, 1992; Kuipers et al., 2014). The arts were not exempt from such NPM reforms and renewal. Hence, NPM is defined as an improvement in public service quality and cost efficiency. The implementation of NPM changes was introduced differently in different countries. In general, adopting NPM was meant to improve efficiency by using private sector management models, shifting from bureaucratic public administration to NPOs or hybrid organizations driven and managed with a performance focus.

By the 1990s, these trends became of interest in the cultural sector, with the Australia Council for the Arts, the government's arts funding and advisory body, requesting arts leaders to reorient their services to an audience focus, along with new skills and professions required in order to be able to attract different funding sources to supplement government income. Similar to other countries, such as the United States, the process of change in the funding structure of this organization took place at different levels (micro, macro, and meta processes) (Wyszomirski, 2013). In this chapter, diversity of funding sources relates to the growth of philanthropy, bringing in an additional funding stream and allowing donors to interact with the organization.

The fragile nature of the performing arts sector, theorized in Bauman and Bowen's (1966) classic cost disease theory, makes it even more important for those organizations to balance stakeholder needs to manage service costs efficiently and effectively while ensuring product quality (Rentschler, 2001). Participation in revenue diversity to ensure mission delivery is then a top priority for cultural organizations. It determines whether PAOs are able to achieve financial viability, postulated by NPM changes, through diversification of revenue portfolios and promoting greater organizational longevity (Carroll & Stater, 2008).

The Process of Professionalization

Professionalization is the process of "mobilizing professionals" to perform with a "service ethos," and by exercising "expertise on behalf of the common good" (DiMaggio & Anheier, 1990, p. 142). Professionalization is defined by classic sociologists such as DiMaggio (1987) as professions "self-organiz[ing] that enables practitioners of an occupation to defend the importance of their contribution and the legitimacy of their decision" (p. 52). Professionalization is perceived to be a cognitive, ideological, behavioral, and organizational (DiMaggio, 1987) process of change that leads to greater development in a profession or emerging profession, both for the people who lead the profession through their role in the organization and for the structure in those organizations. The cognitive part of professionalization is reserved for its learned function that affects the people employed in the organization. For example, while professionalism is usually reserved for professions in fields such as medicine, dentistry, or law, newer disciplines are putting in place the tenets of professionalization. The tenets of professionalization are: (1) Professions are guided by special knowledge; (2) knowledge is learned at university; (3) professional associations are key to guarding or guiding the profession in its standards and ethics; and (4) professionals should have a degree of autonomy in their professional work. The behavioral and organizational dimension to the process of professionalization is denoted by changing organizational structures and roles that are becoming more complex and formalized, requiring the employment of figures that have been educated in the functions of the profession and with specialized skills (e.g., philanthropy).

Professionalization in the Arts

In arts management, the emergence of the International Conference on Arts and Cultural Management (AIMAC) in 1996, the establishment of the journal, the *International Journal of Arts Management* in 1998, and the burgeoning of education in arts management throughout the 1980s have all led to the professionalization of the field (Evrard & Colbert, 2000). When DiMaggio (1987) first wrote about professionalization, it was argued that it was still incomplete as well as being "fraught with paradox" (DiMaggio, 1987, p. 20) and tensions. Key tensions remain between (1) the need for managerial control for the benefit of the organization and the need to live up to the standards of the profession; (2) managerial and creative orientations; and (3) formalization and centralization (Sandhu & Kulik, 2018). There has been an extensive literature that has emerged since DiMaggio (1987) wrote such words. In earlier decades, arts managers were held in low regard, with their skill sets unrecognized, perceived as failed artists, or diminished through an ingrained culture that saw the artist as supreme. For example, Peggy Guggenheim, an early twentieth-century international icon in the art world for the insight and foresight in collecting and exhibiting contemporary art before, during, and after the Second World War, when most other people in the world disparaged it, was not given full credit for what she achieved as a philanthropist and as an arts manager. Guggenheim had no tertiary education as there were no courses in arts management in those days. She did not bring a body of knowledge learnt at university, which is the harbinger of a profession. That came much later. However, it was also rare for women to be tertiary educated. Hence, she was self-taught, a type of amateur in the art world. Furthermore, the role was neither recognized for the skill set that it required, nor were the skills of women in professional positions given due recognition and visibility. For example, Mackrell (2018) says:

This was a period when the majority of collectors, critics and artists were male, when misogyny was still deeply ingrained in the culture . . . [seeing Guggenheim] belittle[d] . . . assum[ing] that her role in her gallery could involve little more than the signing of cheques . . . she was seen almost every day in her office, keeping vigilant control of her accounts, [but that] was taken as evidence that she had no creative vision of her own—that she was the daughter of the Guggenheim tribe, unable to separate money from art.

(p. 315)

In short, a professional role taken on by an enterprising and philanthropic woman, who owned, managed, and succeeded in running a gallery, also collecting and exhibiting contemporary art at a time when few others had the vision to see its worth, was undervalued. Her role was "crudely disparage[ed]" (Mackrell, 2018, p. 316). The attempts to diminish Guggenheim were strong and unrelenting. Similar issues were evident in Australia during this period (Rentschler, 2001). Women in Australia developed a distinctive pattern of philanthropy, adapting inherited traditions to their location and circumstances, with their role nonetheless marginalized by a masculinist or egalitarian notion of a welfare state (Swain, 1996).

As our study illustrates, things have changed in the art world, although tensions remain in the field.

For example, Rentschler (2001) examined the tensions between creativity as a leader and creativity in pursuing the artistic vision in art museums while Jeffri and Throsby (1994) investigated professionalization and the visual artist. Further, Suchy (2000) examined tensions between different kinds of leaders in art museums. These are only a few examples from a plethora of studies on the tensions that occur in the arts between seeking to achieve the aesthetic mission and the constraints of structure and role in the organization. However, they have spawned another strand of literature related to professionalization in the arts: that is, careers in the arts. DiMaggio (1987) first touched on this aspect of the topic. More recently, it has been examined by Bridgstock (2005) and Wyszomirski and Chang (2017), again by focusing on artists and the precarious nature of artistic careers. However, the key point is that artists are deemed to have a career that is worthy of examination, for which they are educated, and indeed, for which they are considered by some to be entrepreneurs or running microenterprises. Professionalization for philanthropy roles incumbents has been occurring alongside the professionalization for artists and indeed arts managers as career options widen in a burgeoning field. Although the research literature in this area is still generally limited, it is growing. Many scholars view this as a positive and necessary step towards further establishing philanthropy as a legitimate profession rather than simply as an amatourial activity (see Tempel et al., 1966).

The New Role of Philanthropy in Arts Organizations

NPOs have traditionally devoted a considerable amount of their time to resource acquisition in order to ensure mission delivery (McCaskill & Harrington, 2017). Benevolence and private donations of money for the public benefit are nothing new, rooted in the nature of the term philanthropy, emanating directly from the ancient Greek (Sulek, 2010), meaning goodness, benevolence, and goodwill toward fellow man. More recently, it is said to apply to "active efforts to promote human welfare" (Sulek, 2010, p. 199). It concerns the application of private means through money, time, goods, or effort to achieve public ends (Sulek, 2010).

Academic research has been dominated by motivational studies on individual donors (Bekkers & Wiepking, 2011; Van Slyke & Brooks, 2005) and corporate donors (e.g., Moir & Taffler, 2004). Motivational study has evolved into a new research stream studying how external factors can affect donation behavior, such as government support (Borgonovi, 2006; Brooks, 1999) and tax benefits (Donelli et al., 2022; Pharoah, 2011).

Shifting the focus from donors to recipient arts organizations, studies on philanthropy have been undertaken mainly in marketing, where potential donors have been seen as, and compared to, potential consumers (Sargeant, 1999) while management studies have mainly neglected the issue. After NPM reforms, new models, resulting from changing times and transformations in donor behavior, emerged (Radbourne & Watkins, 2015). Hence, philanthropy emerged as a concept that moved from the transactional (i.e., raising money) to one of shared value creation, which Drucker called *people development* (Drucker, 1995), examined here according to structure and roles.

Theoretical Framework

Resource Dependency Theory

RDT enables an organization to withstand immediate pressure for survival by obtaining external resources to ensure mission delivery and to design internal organizational structures to mitigate against the external threats the organization faces (Pfeffer & Salancik, 2003). As such, RDT is defined as bringing a different mix of capital to the organization (Hillman & Dalziel, 2003). Capital can include people in leadership roles with background and skills, personal affiliations, and relationships that collectively benefit the organization (DiMaggio, 1991; Dubini & Monti, 2018) by providing access to external resources that enable the NPO to meet its social mission. Role incumbents can use their combined capital to acquire resources for the organization (Froelich, 1999; Turbide, 2012), whether they are board members, members of the executive team (Ostrower & Stone, 2010; Radbourne, 2003), or indeed placed at a lower level in the organizational structure.

At the same time, access to new external resources can influence and be influenced by internal organizational structure, which in turn improves organizational positioning in order to meet its needs (Moldavanova & Goerdel, 2018; Weerawardena et al., 2010). In other words, external organizational resources combined with external stakeholder support to obtain them can influence internal organizational structure, influencing internal change (Valos et al., 2017). RDT can affect organizational structure and role as well as people's relationships inside the organization, providing support from the outside. Thus, RDT can help NPOs overcome resource deficiencies caused by external shocks (e.g., reduced government funding, economic crises, and global pandemics) while prompting internal organizational restructuring and the development of new role incumbents to meet changing organizational needs.

New Organizational Structures

Mintzberg (1979) was the classic advocate of the 1970s and 1980s on organizational structure, postulating its importance for examining formalization and centralization that created tensions between the loose–tight dimensions that were re-examined by Peters et al. (1982) in the 1980s. Sandhu and Kulik (2018) revisited organizational structure in their article on organizational structure and managerial roles, where they examined organizations in developed and developing nations. What is pertinent to our study is that the tension between formalization and centralization remains in PAOs today, despite NPM reform, as they struggle with how to restructure in order to obtain optimal structural configurations with the purpose to increase philanthropic income. These changes included the legal restructuring of arts organizations in order to encourage philanthropy, with more formalized and centralized roles emerging. Similar restructuring occurred in other Western nations (e.g., see Dubini & Monti, 2018; Donelli et al., 2022) as evidence of professionalization occurring in the arts.

The necessity of a whole of organizational commitment has been identified as one of the key elements for strategic success in philanthropy (Bönke et al., 2013; Radbourne & Watkins, 2015). Philanthropy is indeed best based on an entire organizational commitment to long-term relationships and sharing values with donors, both between donors and via organizations (Chong, 2009; Radbourne & Watkins, 2015), but functions are not always structured in order to co-create value.

Recent studies have shown that philanthropy roles are increasingly taking on more managerial functions than technical ones (Waters, 2008). In NPOs, with social and aesthetic missions, such as Australian PAOs, too tight a structure can stifle creativity, and too loose a structure can create chaos and confusion (Mintzberg, 1979; Suchy, 2000), sometimes leading to catastrophes such as organizational collapse. Further, organizational structure is based on the recognition that roles are the left hand and structure is the right hand (Chandler, 1962; Hatten, 1982; Mintzberg, 1979). Structure entails a complex combination of planned and emergent forces (Mintzberg & Waters, 1985), often used for strategy rather than structure and implemented at different times and in different ways in different organizations. The impact of different philanthropy structures on PAOs has a strong and direct impact on the development of professional roles within the organization.

Thus, arts organizations have been forced to diversify their funding mix, search for management efficiencies, and recognize that they operate in an increasingly competitive environment as they seek to serve their social and creative mission. In order to survive, arts organizations are seeking to attract philanthropic support, encourage donations, and generally diversify their funding. One example is the case of Italian opera houses, where legislative and structural change has put additional pressures on opera houses to seek funds from other sources and include external stakeholders inside their organizational structure through collaborative governance. Opera houses in Italy were in financial crisis. Thus, the Bray Law was introduced as a means of submitting opera houses with severe financial difficulties to a recovery plan. The plan encouraged forms of collaboration with stakeholders for revenue diversification, resulting in sustainability for the opera houses regarding financial and artistic performance (Fanelli et al., 2020). This was a form of professionalization caused by exogenous forces that caused internal restructuring and the creation of new managerial roles in Italian opera houses.

New Roles

Role theory sits at the intersection of individual and organizational behavior, providing a valuable framework for discussion in a chapter on organizational structural influences on managerial roles (Sandhu & Kulik, 2018) as they professionalize. Defining roles for incumbents enables arts organizations to better secure a future in turbulent and rapidly changing times (Rossheim et al., 1995). Definition of roles is pivotal to the success of arts organizations, with the role incumbent attending to the duties identified. Not identifying particular roles may constrain or limit organization growth. It has been observed that some arts managers can be change avoidants (Jeffri, 1980; Rentschler, 2001), thus imperiling necessary restructuring or the need to seek funds from diverse sources (Rossheim et al., 1995). Indeed, the effect of cultural funding policy shaped the performance expectations of arts managers as they learned to accommodate shifting public funding patterns. Policy interacted with exogenous political changes, shifting public management reforms (e.g., complex governance models involving multiple stakeholders and their demands), thus prompting NPO change and occupational professionalization (Wyszomirski, 2013).

Hence, there are different types of roles that managers may play, the configurations of which may provide for the emergence of certain structures that can maximize philanthropy for arts organizations (Mintzberg, 1979). The dimensions for roles generally focused on categories such as resources, style, performance, and ideologies, which in combination or separately produced models for managers (Rossheim et al., 1995).

The process of professionalization in arts organizations can be gleaned from the emergence of professional managerial roles that are shaped by rules constituted by role incumbents who also shape those roles (Mintzberg, 1979; Sandhu & Kulik, 2018). The emergence of philanthropy professionals is crucial for resource acquisition, as already demonstrated by DiMaggio for museum managers, as they dominated both reform efforts and fieldwide reorganization (DiMaggio, 1991). It is at the discretion of the role incumbents as to how they implement structural change in order to solve organizational problems. The structure literature examines organizational dimensions of formalization and centralization while the role literature investigates the incumbent, who performs a function to achieve the organizational mission (e.g., Schwartz, 1994).

Arts Philanthropy in Australia

Yet despite this general context, Australia has a unique cultural history that spans two worlds: Aboriginal heritage and new settlers. It has a long cultural tradition in Aboriginal arts, which has a 50,000 year history, with a relatively young performing arts sector, mostly established in the twentieth century. Before COVID-19, cultural activity made a substantial contribution to the Australian economy, contributing A$50 billion to Australia's GDP, comparable to the GDP share in the United States. It includes over A$4.2 billion from the arts. Expenditure on culture by Australian governments in 2012–2013 was $7 billion including over $1.3 billion on the arts (AMPAG, 2017). Against this background, philanthropic giving in the performing arts sector was growing (Daley, 2021). Revenue from donations, corporate sponsorship, and fundraising events in Australia grew by 15.2% in 2016, to a total of A$95.7 million (AMPAG, 2017). Income from single donations rose by 23.4%, and overtaking corporate sponsorship was the major source of private sector income (AMPAG, 2017). Overall, private sector support for the major PAOs contributed 17% of their total income in 2016, with 42% coming from performance income, 28% from government grants for core funding (federal and state), 3% from grants for specific projects/initiatives, and 10% from other sources (AMPAG, 2017). Such philanthropic contribution is even more central to organizational survival during and after a global pandemic.

History of the Performing Arts Sector in Australia

The foundation of the Australian major PAOs was in the mid-twentieth century, although there were commercially supported arts companies from the early days of European settlement. The 32 (28 in 2017) national, flagship PAOs, including dance, theater, opera, orchestra, and circus, were founded at the federal level and are supported by the Australia Council for the Arts.

Australia is part of a cluster of Anglo-Saxon countries (Hood, 1995), categorized by Pollitt and Bouckaert (2011), as core NPM countries. It was deeply affected by the wave of privatization that swept across the world during the 1980s–1990s, which was the most striking evidence of the NPM changes (Fenna, 2004). Hybridization was implemented extensively in Australia in many sectors (Fenna, 2004), including the largely public education and training and arts sectors, and the performing arts.

The performing arts sector was struggling to achieve financial stability (Donelli et al., 2023). Hence, the federal government commissioned Helen Nugent (Nugent, 1999) to undertake the first major national analysis of the status of the PAOs in Australia. This first report, dated 1999, had the aim of securing the future of the performing arts sector in Australia, which then represented 75% of all funding by the Australia Council for the Arts. Nugent not only recommended to ensure (per recommendation 2.3.1) that "the strategy of each company reflects its artistic capabilities and fundamental economics" (p. 8) but also prescribed to maximize (per recommendation 2.3.2) "private sector support, while minimising the use of resources and achieving best practice management" (p. 9).

Australian major PAOs mainly suffer from having philanthropy as a peripheral role (compared to other countries such as the United States or the United Kingdom) in their funding mix for two key reasons:

1. Australia is lacking a strong culture of philanthropy (Wiepking & Handy, 2015), with a background of a welfare state philosophy and a cultural disposition toward privacy. While there are many philanthropic institutions in Australia (such as trusts, foundations, and bequests), until recently there has been less of a habit of private philanthropic giving and less of a take-up of the opportunities for philanthropy by arts organizations due to a background of a welfare state philosophy hampering the development of individual giving.
2. There is a lack of professional staff and managerial skills for maximizing donations in Arts Organisations. Smaller companies, especially, cannot afford to invest in staff, which results in their not being able to optimize marketing and development income (Nugent, 1999, pp. 66–67).

Despite the positive levels of net assets achieved by PAOs as a result of the recommendations of the Nugent Report, by the twenty-first century, there was again a need for higher levels of private sector income to ensure the future of the performing arts sector in Australia. For example, the Opera Review (Nugent, 2016) identified the continuing gap between production costs and income earned in Australian opera. In the next section, we examine the extent to which the PAOs are making the transition into professionalization in philanthropy.

Empirical Analysis: Research Methods and Challenges

In order to interpret change in structure and roles in PAOs, a qualitative approach was used. This study examined 12 PAOs as cases in order to determine change across art forms and the process of professionalization in structures and roles. Case study analysis is considered an appropriate approach for interpreting development and change in organizations (Eisenhardt, 1989). The art forms in PAOs investigated were dance, theater, and opera, recognized for their national leadership and artistic excellence by the Australia Council for the Arts. The PAOs were selected to ensure a national perspective (see Table 10.1).

The 12 cases are NPOs (limited by guarantee). One is a hybrid organization (Melbourne Theatre Company), and three companies are still registered as statutory authorities (Queensland Theatre, South Australia Theatre Company, and State Opera South Australia). One theater is in the process of moving away from the current structure as a Statutory Authority to that of a private not for profit company. Data show an overall shift toward philanthropy in all annual reports examined, suggesting a general understanding of its importance.

Table 10.1 Organization Profile

Performing Arts Company	Location (State)	Type	Established
West Australian Ballet	Perth (WA)	Dance	1952
Melbourne Theatre Company	Melbourne (VIC)	Theater	1953
Opera Australia	Sydney (NSW)	Opera	1956
Queensland Ballet	Brisbane (QNL)	Dance	1960
Australian Ballet	Melbourne (VIC)	Dance	1962
Queensland Theatre	Brisbane (QNL)	Theater	1970
State Theatre Company	Adelaide (SA)	Theater	1972
State Opera of South Australia (SOSA)	Adelaide (SA)	Opera	1976
Sydney Theatre Company	Sydney (NSW)	Theater	1978
Opera Queensland	Brisbane (QNL)	Opera	1981
Bangarra Dance Theatre	Sydney (NSW)	Dance	1989
Black Swan Theatre Company	Perth (WA)	Theater	1991

The approach taken was to triangulate the data, using analysis of annual reports and interviews with key executives of PAOs. The CEO and chair's reports were scrutinized to identify the attention paid to structure, roles, and philanthropy. Data were analyzed thematically using a two-stage process of thematic identification aided by the use of the software package NVivo11. Annual reports have been used widely in both quantitative and qualitative research, as they are documents prepared by the CEO and the board as a statuary requirement, as institutions report to parliament and their stakeholders. Consequently, annual reports and interviews were used to understand the mission and values of the PAOs. Eleven semi-structured interviews were conducted with an interview guide based on the research questions and emerging issues from the literature (deMarrais & Lapan, 2003). The interviews were based on a few, broad, open-ended questions structured following four main themes: philanthropy, professionalization, structure, and roles, as well as demographic questions.

Findings From the Performing Arts Sector

Professionalization

From our analysis, a profile emerged of PAOs in relation to philanthropy's structural and role choices in a changing, turbulent world. For example, a word cloud was run over the CEO's reports of the 12 PAOs studied in the annual reports from 2017. It shows the prominence of words relating to philanthropy, such as "support," "donors," and "patrons," in the rhetoric of PAOs (Figure 10.1), illustrating the degree of formalization and centralization that is occurring in these companies. These words are evidence that philanthropy is occurring in all PAOs studied to a greater or lesser extent, with

Figure 10.1 Prominence of Philanthropy in Performing Arts Organizations

Source: Based on Annual Reports of 12 performing arts organizations in this study (2017)

larger font indicating the more important roles and structures (e.g., "foundation") while smaller font indicates less attention being paid to that role or function in some instances (e.g., "committed"). However, the extent of the process of professionalization in structure and role in the major Australian PAOs varies, as discussed later.

We will now analyze structure and role. While we analyze them separately, we recognize that there is overlap between the two functions.

Structure

Performing arts organizations (PAOs) are structured differently, with more or less formalization and centralization, depending on how philanthropy is valued in the organization. Indeed, with the exception of one case, all the organizations analyzed have at least one philanthropy roles in their struc-ture (either full-time or part-time). More centralized and formally structured philanthropy approaches included managers with philanthropic roles also in the leadership team and implementing organizational strategy together with the artistic and executive directors and the board. This implies considering philanthropy a core activity throughout the organization. For example, the annual reports of the Australian Ballet provide evidence that the centralized and formalized philanthropy team comprises 11 roles. These roles include the philanthropy director, philanthropy events manager, philanthropy ser-vice coordinator, major gift manager, state managers, and the chair of the Foundation who sits on the Board of Directors. For example, the philan-thropy director provides overall leadership and oversight of the different philanthropic functions inside the organization. In large, complex PAOs, they may coordinate larger, more diverse teams (e.g., marketing, finance, and administration) and discuss with the executive director and artistic director the specific needs for the season and plan an effective philanthropic strategy accordingly; the events manager organizes philanthropic events to attract and steward current donors to make them feel special while state manag-ers are responsible for different geographic regions of Australia, targeting and promoting different audiences and donors according to geographic and demographic differences.

From our analysis, it was clear from annual reports that PAOs are recruit-ing managers with specific philanthropy skills. They could be philanthro-pists themselves or have been working as philanthropy managers in different fields, such as charities, higher education, or sport. However, not all PAOs have the highly centralized and formalized structure and roles evident in The Australian Ballet. PAOs in the sector have made different strategic choices, which can be inferred from analyzing organizational structure. For exam-ple, in the case of a major theater company, our interview with a manager illustrates that philanthropy is a shared role with government relations and corporate sponsorship:

We operate under the development structure, so government, corporate sponsorship, and philanthropy are all run by the same area. So, the CEO spends a lot of time setting up the strategy, and then the director of develop-ment reports to the CEO and drives or creates the strategy, but the board comes back and gets regular updates from the CEO and the director of phi-lanthropy and is supported operationally by making a lot of contact with the board (Interview, theater company, 2018).

Hence, there is shared attention to the role of professional donor manager. Organizational structural importance given to philanthropy is shown in the attention given in the annual reports to donors and stakeholders in general, where a special section on philanthropy suggests accountability in the use of resources and identifies donors in the process of value creation.

We have done a lot of work to make donors feel connected and know where the money is going, and then that enables us to grow those donations.

Donations may have started at a low entry point but have become major donors (interview, dance company, 2018).

Such interviews infer that the structures in place in such PAOs create value to a higher degree than other structures where there is a shared role in place at a lower level of influence in the organization.

Role

As was seen under structure, most PAOs have at least one philanthropy roles (either full-time or part-time). As illustrated in the case of the Australian Ballet, there are a variety of role titles in relation to philanthropy as a managerial function. More widely in the PAOs studied, the range of roles and the responsibilities underpinned by the role may range from: new donor cultivation; stewardship of current donors; managing donor events or friends committees; liaison with board philanthropists and networks; coordinating various internal or staff members; and whole organization commitment (that might involve calling in the chair of the board and or artistic director to help close a donation deal). This speaks to the special skills and knowledge that the philanthropy management position requires. Or an alternative structural approach is to share the responsibilities but expect the philanthropy manager to be the coordinator of the whole organizational commitment.

Role incumbents' profile and education are coherent in the different organizational structures, consistent with a professionalizing performing arts sector, with all of them having a tertiary education qualification. What is different across the PAOs is the centralized and formalized structural positioning of philanthropy in the organization, the number of positions devoted to philanthropy, and the background and philanthropic skills of staff members. Board director roles were also examined in annual reports, as the board has a role in philanthropy, opening doors, chairing philanthropy subcommittees of the board, and mentoring executives in philanthropy in order to boost giving. Hence, there are commonalities across philanthropy roles that were identified from annual report analysis.

In all organization annual reports analyzed, the board of directors is equally balanced between women and men, demonstrating the gender diversity of the PAOs, as well as the change in diversity that has occurred since the middle of the twentieth century (DiMaggio, 1987; Mackrell, 2018; Rentschler, 2015; Radbourne, 2003). However, philanthropy roles on the board are still evolving.

All boards need to be balanced so we've got to be looking at gender balance and we've taken a look at skills balance. But we've not had a philanthropy person on the board for some time (Interview, opera company, 2018).

In all cases, annual reports provided evidence that there was at least one board member who either has previous experience in philanthropy or has been a major donor, as the dominance of corporations on boards illustrates.

Ethnic diversity was less obvious with the predominance of white, Anglo-American men and women on the boards of these PAOs. Further, it was less evident that artistic roles were represented on these boards. There has been significant criticism of them as they professionalized that they have overlooked the need for artistic roles to be represented on the board, due to the drive to attract business people to the board who can help raise money (see Rankin, 2018). Hence, professionalization is a complex process, driven by a variety of factors, including the need for resources as well as the need to respond to contextual shifts in what is important in structure and role.

Philanthropic activity may be the prerogative of single board members or external entities (e.g., through an external foundation or group of friends) without shared strategic directions within the organization. When roles are apportioned in this fashion, the PAO struggles more to achieve its philanthropic goals. For example, one interviewee in an opera company shared with us:

> At the moment it [the organization] employs five people: we have a CEO; we have a finance director; we have an executive officer; we have a wardrobe person and a stage manager . . . the rest are volunteers.
>
> (Interview, opera company, 2018)

In other cases, philanthropic roles may be assigned to a philanthropy coordinator located at a mid-level or low-level in the organizational structure. When the position was located at a mid- or low-level in several PAOs examined, the role was vacant for a year or not well defined within the structure. One interviewee offered this insight, claiming that confusion about role and lack of clarity in structure caused the organization to be unable to attract an enlarged donor pool:

> Who is responsible for philanthropy? Really it is in the hands of the board because there is no particular person there who looks after philanthropy. . . . Furthermore, she [the board member in charge] doesn't go out and find new people as donors. Her job is to service donors after the board or the CEO finds them. But unfortunately, she does not have time to seek new donors.
>
> (Interview, theater company)

Hence, sometimes philanthropy may have been the responsibility of a single board member rather than a paid staff member, with the role unable to be filled or to a specific role.

The people we interviewed in PAOs, such as at a state theater company and a state opera, both from a regional state, employ a mid- to low-level philanthropy coordinator or a sponsorship coordinator to support their activity. Indeed, in these organizations, philanthropy is addressed together with other roles, such as marketing and communications, providing role incumbents less time to undertake their philanthropic duties effectively.

In short, there are PAOs that are strategic, taking a whole of organization approach to philanthropy in structure and role. Such organizations are more successful in raising philanthropic income as they also perceive philanthropy as a whole of organization function. Others struggle with a low-level role and unclear structural responsibility and accountability, more likely behaving reactively and in a piecemeal fashion. Thus, they are not likely to be as successful in raising philanthropic income.

Discussion and Conclusion

In answering our research question, we found that the PAOs studied changed philanthropic structures and roles in response to exogenous and endogenous forces, in order to aid sustainability in a volatile context of resource constraints. This bipartite world is summarized in Table 10.2.

Despite these differences in structure and role identified in Table 10.2, philanthropy has shifted from a peripheral activity to being embedded in organizational structure but to different degrees, dependent on the level of organizational commitment by the allocation of role incumbents to the function. However, structural differences among PAOs reflect different institutional systems that vary among the cohort studied (DiMaggio & Anheier, 1990). While PAOs studied are heterogeneous in their degree of professionalization in regard to philanthropy, there are some clear lines between those that are more strategic and those that are struggling.

Whole of organization commitment was a key element of philanthropy being deemed strategic in our study, as in the literature (Daley, 2021; DiMaggio, 1991; Radbourne & Watkins, 2015). Role incumbents in strategic PAOs create engagement with stakeholders in a more holistic manner, given roles in the structure that are embedded in the executive of the organization. Thus, being strategic, they understand it is crucial for stakeholder engagement to occur at all organizational levels. Role incumbents in struggling PAOs are located at a low level in the organizational structure and are more likely to operate alone rather than see philanthropy as a whole organization function, thus limiting likely philanthropic success.

Nonetheless, there are commonalities in all PAOs studied, which demonstrate the growing complexity, formalization, and centralization in PAOs today. While this study took place in Australia, such changes have relevance across the performing arts world. Table 10.3 shows the commonalities identified in all the annual reports in regard to philanthropy, demonstrating the professionalization that is occurring in philanthropy roles in PAOs in Australia, albeit at different levels of commitment.

Table 10.2 Strategic and Struggling Arts Organizations Professionalization Characteristics

Characteristic	Strategic	Struggling
Governance ethos	All board members give	Some board members give
Legal status	Independent NPOs or companies limited by guarantee	Embedded in bureaucratic structures
Philanthropy, philosophy	Embedded and whole of organization approach to philanthropy	Piecemeal and limited to one person handling philanthropy
Professional autonomy	Direct access to the board	Limited low-level position without board access
Role incumbents	Senior executive	Junior coordinator or position vacant
Service ethos	Donors engage in the company: being part of a family; changing people's lives; donating to education in order to sustain the future of the arts. Donor pipeline is created, seeing "donations in action." Organization creates something tangible and worthwhile. Donors meet regularly with the company and take part in the life of the company. A committee or foundation (made up of donors) ensures a constant exchange between donors and organization.	Donations are direct to support the ongoing activity of the organization.
Exercise of expertise on behalf of the common good	Strategy is usually developed by the philanthropic director in the development team, revised by the executive team and approved by the board. More sophisticated ways of tracking donor behavior Donors give online and offline, especially when buying tickets.	Philanthropy strategy set by a single role or figurehead; there is no dynamic and continuous exchange between organizational levels.

Nonetheless, all PAOs have identified philanthropy as a structural norm, with role incumbents allocated to perform it in a centralized and formalized function at some level of organizational structure, with philanthropy discussed as a function in annual reports, demonstrating its value to the major PAOs studied.

Table 10.3 Philanthropy Commonalities in Arts Organizations

- Philanthropy is part of the structure of arts organizations.
- Philanthropy roles are discussed in arts organization annual reports.
- Board members have a role in donating to the company.
- Board members are on the board for their role skills and ability to network. Creative programming is in the hands of the artistic director; donors do not interfere.
- Donors' roles are acknowledged in annual reports.
- Gender diversity is present on boards with an overall equal number of men and women, in response to contextual pressures.
- Preponderance of corporate skills on the board (e.g., finance, accounting, consulting, marketing, stakeholder relations) to the partial exclusion of artistic skills.

The process of professionalization, which has infused the performing arts (e.g., compare with DiMaggio & Anheier, 1990; Peterson, 1987) in Australia, has increased competition for limited revenue sources brought on by a partial hybridization of the sector through NPM, and greater professionalization of organizational structure and role, requiring more skilled philanthropy professionals in more formalized and centralized structures. This is one manifestation of a broader shift in flagship organizations that started out as public organizations and are in the process of becoming hybrid organizations in order to provide them with the structure and role to accept other types of funding (e.g., Schuster, 1998), including philanthropy. As new roles emerge in philanthropy for individual creative workers (Wyszomirski & Chang, 2017), the roles played inside different organizations will continue to emerge and structures will continue to change.

References

AMPAG. (2017). *Arts nation: An overview of Australian arts.* Australian Major Performing Arts Group.

Bauman, W. J., & Bowen, W. G. (1966). *Performing arts: The economic dilemma.* The Twentieth Century Fund.

Bekkers, R., & Wiepking, P. (2011). A literature review of empirical studies of philanthropy: Eight mechanisms that drive charitable giving. *Nonprofit and Voluntary Sector Quarterly, 40*(5), 924–973.

Bönke, T., Massarrat-Mashhadi, N., & Sielaff, C. (2013). Charitable giving in the German welfare state: Fiscal incentives and crowding out. *Public Choice, 154*(1–2), 39–58.

Borgonovi, F. (2006). Do public grants to American theatres crowd-out private donations? *Public Choice, 126*(3–4), 429–451.

Brady, E., Brace-Govan, J., Brennan, L., & Conduit, J. (2011). Market orientation and marketing in nonprofit organizations: Indications for fundraising from Victoria. *International Journal of Nonprofit and Voluntary Sector Marketing, 16*(1), 84–98.

Bridgstock, R. (2005). Australian artists, starving and well-nourished: What can we learn from the prototypical protean career? *Australian Journal of Career Development*, *14*(3), 40–47.

Brooks, A. C. (1999). Do public subsidies leverage private philanthropy for the arts? Empirical evidence on symphony orchestras. *Nonprofit and Voluntary Sector Quarterly*, *28*(1), 32–45.

Carroll, D. A., & Stater, K. J. (2008). Revenue diversification in nonprofit organizations: Does it lead to financial stability? *Journal of Public Administration Research and Theory*, *19*(4), 947–966.

Chandler, A. D. (1962). *Strategy and structure: Chapters in the history of American industrial enterprises*. MIT Press.

Chong, D. (2009). *Arts management*. Routledge.

Daley, J. (2021). *Performing arts advocacy in Australia*. Australian Major Performing Arts Group. https://apo.org.au/sites/default/files/resource-files/2021-04/apo-nid312235.pdf

deMarrais, K. B., & Lapan, S. D. (2003). Qualitative interview studies: Learning through experience. In *Foundations for research* (pp. 67–84). Routledge.

DiMaggio, P. J. (1987). *Managers of the arts: Careers and opinions of senior administrators of US art museums, symphony orchestras, resident theaters, and local arts agencies* (Research Division Report No. 20). National Book Network, Inc.

DiMaggio, P. J. (1991). Constructing an organizational field as a professional project: US art museums 1920–1940. In P. J. DiMaggio & W. W. Powell (Eds.), *The new institutionalism in organizational analysis* (pp. 267–293). University of Chicago Press.

DiMaggio, P. J., & Anheier, H. K. (1990). The sociology of nonprofit organizations and sectors. *Annual Review of Sociology*, *16*(1), 137–159.

Donelli, C. C., Mozzoni, I., Badia, F., & Fanelli, S. (2022). Financing sustainability in the arts sector: The case of the art bonus public crowdfunding campaign in Italy. *Sustainability*, *14*(3), 1641.

Donelli, C. C., Rentschler, R., Fanelli, S., & Lee, B. (2023). Philanthropy patterns in major Australian performing arts organizations. *Journal of Management and Governance*, 1–30. https://doi.org/10.1007/s10997-022-09657-2

Drucker, P. F. (1995). *Managing the non-profit organization: Practices and principles*. Taylor & Francis.

Dubini, P., & Monti, A. (2018). Board composition and organizational performance in the cultural sector: The case of Italian opera houses. *International Journal of Arts Management*, *20*(2), 56–70.

Eisenhardt, K. M. (1989). Making fast strategic decisions in high-velocity environments. *Academy of Management Journal*, *32*(3), 543–576.

Evrard, Y., & Colbert, F. (2000). Arts management: A new discipline entering the millennium? *International Journal of Arts Management*, *2*(2), 4–13.

Fanelli, S., Donelli, C. C., Zangrandi, A., & Mozzoni, I. (2020). Balancing artistic and financial performance: Is collaborative governance the answer? *International Journal of Public Sector Management*, *33*.

Fenna, A. (2004). *Australian public policy*. Pearson Longman.

Froelich, K. A. (1999). Diversification of revenue strategies: Evolving resource dependence in nonprofit organizations. *Nonprofit and Voluntary Sector Quarterly*, *28*(3), 246–268.

Halligan, J., & Power, J. M. (1992). *Political management in the 1990s.* Oxford University Press.

Hatten, M. L. (1982). Strategic management in not-for-profit organizations. *Strategic Management Journal, 3*(2), 89–104.

Hillman, A. J., & Dalziel, T. (2003). Boards of directors and firm performance: Integrating agency and resource dependence perspectives. *Academy of Management Review, 28*(3), 383–396.

Hood, C. (1995). Contemporary public management: A new global paradigm? *Public Policy and Administration, 10*(2), 104–117.

Jeffri, J. (1980). *The emerging arts: Management, survival, and growth.* Praeger.

Jeffri, J., & Throsby, D. (1994). Professionalism and the visual artist. *International Journal of Cultural Policy, 1*(1), 99–108.

Kuipers, B. S., Higgs, M., Kickert, W., Tummers, L., Grandia, J., & Van der Voet, J. (2014). The management of change in public organizations: A literature review. *Public Administration, 92*(1), 1–20.

Mackrell, J. (2018). *The unfinished palazzo: Life, love and art in Venice.* Thames & Hudson Ltd.

McCaskill, J. R., & Harrington, J. R. (2017). Revenue sources and social media engagement among environmentally focused nonprofits. *Journal of Public and Nonprofit Affairs, 3*(3), 309–319.

Mintzberg, H. (1979). An emerging strategy of "direct" research. *Administrative Science Quarterly, 24*(4), 582–589.

Mintzberg, H., & Waters, J. A. (1985). Of strategies, deliberate and emergent. *Strategic Management Journal, 6*(3), 257–272.

Moir, L., & Taffler, R. (2004). Does corporate philanthropy exist? Business giving to the arts in the UK. *Journal of Business Ethics, 54*(2), 149–161.

Moldavanova, A., & Goerdel, H. T. (2018). Understanding the puzzle of organizational sustainability: Toward a conceptual framework of organizational social connectedness and sustainability. *Public Management Review, 20*(1), 55–81.

Nugent, H. (1999). *Securing the future.* Department of Communications, Information Technology and the Arts.

Nugent, H. (2016). *National Opera review: Final report.* Department of Communications, Information Technology and the Arts.

Ostrower, F., & Stone, M. M. (2010). Moving governance research forward: A contingency-based framework and data application. *Nonprofit and Voluntary Sector Quarterly, 39*(5), 901–924.

Palmer, I. (1996). Arts management cutback strategies: A cross-sector analysis. *Nonprofit Management and Leadership, 7*(3), 271–290.

Peters, T. J., Waterman, R. H., & Jones, I. (1982). *In search of excellence: Lessons from America's best-run companies.* Harper and Row.

Peterson, R. A. (1987). From impresario to arts administrator: Formal accountability in nonprofit cultural organizations. In P. J. DiMaggio (Ed.), *Nonprofit enterprise in the arts: Studies in mission and constraint* (pp. 161–183). Oxford University Press.

Pfeffer, J., & Salancik, G. R. (2003). *The external control of organizations: A resource dependence perspective.* Stanford University Press.

Pharoah, C. (2011). Private giving and philanthropy—their place in the big society. *People, Place & Policy Online, 5*(2), 65–75.

Pollitt, C., & Bouckaert, G. (2011). *Continuity and change in public policy and management*. Edward Elgar Publishing.

Radbourne, J. (2003). Performing on boards: The link between governance and corporate reputation in nonprofit arts boards. *Corporate Reputation Review*, 6(3), 212–222.

Radbourne, J., & Watkins, K. (2015). *Philanthropy and the arts*. Melbourne University Publishing.

Rankin, S. (2018). *Cultural justice and the right to thrive*. Currency House, Strawberry Hills.

Rentschler, R. (2001). Is creativity a matter for cultural leaders? *International Journal of Arts Management*, 3(3), 13–24.

Rentschler, R. (2015). *Arts governance: People, passion, performance*. Routledge.

Rentschler, R., & Geursen, G. (2004). Entrepreneurship, marketing and leadership in non-profit performing arts organisations. *Journal of Research in Marketing and Entrepreneurship*, 6(1), 44–51.

Rossheim, B. N., Kim, P. S., & Ruchelman, L. (1995). Managerial roles and entrepreneurship in nonprofit urban arts agencies in Virginia. *Nonprofit and Voluntary Sector Quarterly*, 24(2), 143–166.

Sandhu, S., & Kulik, C. T. (2018). Shaping and being shaped: how organizational structure and managerial discretion co-evolve in new managerial roles. *Administrative Science Quarterly*, 64(3), 619–658.

Sargeant, A. (1999). Charitable giving: Towards a model of donor behaviour. *Journal of Marketing Management*, 15(4), 215–238.

Schuster, J. M. (1998). Neither public nor private: The hybridization of museums. *Journal of Cultural Economics*, 22, 127–150.

Schwartz, S. H. (1994). Are there universal aspects in the structure and contents of human values? *Journal of Social Issues*, 50(4), 19–45.

Suchy, S. (2000). Grooming new millennium museum directors. *Museum International*, 52(2), 59–64.

Sulek, M. (2010). On the modern meaning of philanthropy. *Nonprofit and Voluntary Sector Quarterly*, 39(2), 193–212.

Swain, S. (1996). Women and philanthropy in colonial and post-colonial Australia. *Voluntas: International Journal of Voluntary and Nonprofit Organizations*, 7(4), 428–443.

Tempel, E., Cobb, S., & Ilchman, W. (Eds.). (1966). *The professionalization of fundraising: Implications for education, practice, and accountability* (New Directions for Philanthropic Fundraising No. 15). Jossey-Bass.

Turbide, J. (2012). Can good governance prevent financial crises in arts organizations? *International Journal of Arts Management*, 14(2), 4.

Valos, M. J., Maplestone, V. L., Polonsky, M. J., & Ewing, M. (2017). Integrating social media within an integrated marketing communication decision-making framework. *Journal of Marketing Management*, 33(17–18), 1522–1558.

Van Slyke, D. M., & Brooks, A. C. (2005). Why do people give? New evidence and strategies for nonprofit managers. *American Review of Public Administration*, 35(3), 199–222.

Waters, R. D. (2008). Applying relationship management theory to the fundraising process for individual donors. *Journal of Communication Management*, 12(1), 73–87.

Weerawardena, J., McDonald, R. E., & Mort, G. S. (2010). Sustainability of non-profit organizations: An empirical investigation. *Journal of World Business*, *45*(4), 346–356.

Wiepking, P., & Handy, F. (2015). *The Palgrave handbook of global philanthropy*. Palgrave Macmillan.

Wyszomirski, M. J. (2013). Shaping a triple-bottom line for nonprofit arts organizations: Micro-, macro-, and meta-policy influences. *Cultural Trends*, *22*(3–4), 156–166.

Wyszomirski, M. J., & Chang, W. J. (2017). Professional self-structuration in the arts: Sustaining creative careers in the 21st century. *Sustainability*, *9*(6), 1035.

11 Performing Arts Center Managers

A Crucial Profession in Community Performing Arts Sectors

Patricia Dewey Lambert

Introduction: Performing Arts Center Management as a New Arts Management Profession

This chapter discusses an emerging sub-profession of arts management, namely, leadership and management of a performing arts center (PAC). PACs around the world are found everywhere, from small community centers, to collegiate theaters and auditoriums to large urban facilities that contain multiple performance venues. Over the past five decades, this specialized field of professional practice has evolved from an occupation to a career to a profession. A few academic research and published studies relevant to this sub-field of arts management began to emerge in the early 2000s (Donnelly, 2011; Hager & Pollak, 2002; Micocci, 2008; Stein & Bathurst, 2008; Webb, 2004), and strengthened in recent years (Woronkowics et al., 2015; Lambert & Williams, 2017a) but this remains a distinct domain of professional arts management about which comparatively little is known (Lambert & Williams, 2017a).

The main focus of this chapter is on the role of arts management within a major urban presenting or hosting PAC in the United States, defined as a facility "with multiple users, where there is a management organization in place that activates a building with some combination of rentals, presented events, producing, and community programming" (Webb, 2004, p. x). These arts organizations differ from producing companies, which fund and create their own artistic work. In contrast, a PAC that hosts or presents the performing arts is an arts organization that "works to facilitate exchanges between artists and audiences through creative, educational, and performance opportunities. The work that these artists perform is produced outside of the presenting organization" (Hager & Pollak, 2002, p. 9).

PACs are key elements of a community's arts infrastructure, often serving to anchor cultural districts and support wide-ranging urban revitalization and economic development initiatives. Urban PACs often provide a well-subsidized home to the city's symphony orchestra, opera, and ballet and bring touring productions as diverse as comedy, commercial concerts, circus, international artists, and Broadway musicals to local audiences. The PAC

DOI: 10.4324/9781003138693-13

is expected to be a leader within the arts and culture sector and to support civic priorities. PACs explicitly exist to serve the public interest, whether they are structured as a public, nonprofit, for-profit, or hybrid entity. As a result of their organizational form, leaders of these organizations must have the capacity to work with government entities, a wide array of nonprofit arts organizations, and diverse community groups while constantly generating their own revenues as well.

Around the world, the performing arts sector has been one of the hardest hit by the recent COVID-19 pandemic and its economic impacts. In most communities, performing arts facilities were among the first businesses to close and the last to reopen. According to Andrew Recinos, president of the global Tessitura Network, presenting PACs have been the hardest hit within the entire performing arts sector because of their reliance on ticket sales and their extensive fixed assets (personal communication, October 29, 2020). Rebuilding a strong performing arts infrastructure in our communities will require exceptionally strong PAC leadership in the next few years.

This chapter begins by presenting the evolution of the urban PAC in the United States and explaining how these organizations function within the arts ecology of their communities. The chapter then discusses the crucial role of the PAC within the local creative economy. A detailed presentation of requisite competencies and skills of professional PAC manager includes discussion of professional development and certification in the field. The chapter concludes with an analysis of the ways in which professional PAC managers contribute to all dimensions of public support for arts and culture in their communities as well as serve a unique leadership role in facilitating the functioning of their local creative sector as a whole.

What Kind of Arts Organization Is a PAC?

The contemporary urban PAC first became visible in America's communities in the 1960s as a home for the local nonprofit arts organizations, typically the resident companies of the local symphony orchestra, opera company, and ballet company. However, by moving away from being the home of the traditional performing arts companies, the PAC has evolved in several stages to now lead "the way in ensuring that the performing arts have a place in the cultural identity and expression of citizens and communities worldwide" (Wolff, 2017, p. 21). Wolff (2017, pp. 35–40) contends that the evolution of PACs has taken place in four distinct steps, or "generations." Generation 1 was a home; generation 2 was a place; generation 3 was a community center; and generation 4 is a nexus. He argues that the contemporary generation 4 PAC is a sophisticated community resource that offers public value through its varied roles in eight main domains (see Table 11.1): place or home, destination or brand, showcase, partner, incubator, thought leader, educator, and innovator.

Table 11.1 Roles That Contribute to the Public Value of a Performing Arts Center (Adapted from Wolff, 2017, pp. 39–40)

Home. It is a place for the production and presentation of traditional and emerging arts and culture programs in appropriate facilities.

Destination. It is a place and a brand, recognized as a provider of excellent quality programs and activities in its facilities and throughout the community.

Showcase. The PAC confers legitimacy on a diverse array of programs by presenting new, different, and traditional arts and culture to the community.

Partner. The PAC recognizes that collaboration is an effective strategy to achieve shared goals. It invests resources in identifying and enabling partnerships.

Thought Leader. The PAC enables continuing evolution for the creative sector, in its art forms, business models, delivery systems and audiences. PAC leaders advocate for change and for support.

Educator. The PAC is a place to learn and celebrate exploration, diversity, and inquiry. PAC manager collaborate with others to develop and offer programs that provide access for youth, the underserved, and lifelong learners.

Incubator. The PAC enables new content development and supports emerging organizations by providing resources, facilities, technical support, and management guidance that facilitate success.

Innovator. The PAC encourages risk and exploration while managing exposure through strong governance and by developing leadership skills, tools, systems, and financial resources that support innovation.

The evolving civic engagement and community leadership role evident within urban PACs is also reflected in the *programming* decisions made by these organizations' managers. PACs are the main presenters of touring productions in local communities and are, therefore, an integral part of the live performing arts industry, both domestically and internationally. Since performance and educational programs are always at the core of the PAC mission, careful attention must be paid to balancing cultural presenting (the presentation of artistic work that requires a financial subsidy) with commercial presenting (where ticket revenue is anticipated to more than exceed the costs of presentation). For the current generation of PACs, "a shift is taking place in performing arts centers' identities from being bastions of culture to being urban connective nodes . . . [and] effective community-based cultural catalysts" (Micocci, 2017, pp. 82–83).

These changing community roles of PACs can be seen throughout the four main types of PACs found in the United States. The major metropolitan PACs, the focus of this chapter, serve a large urban region with one venue or multiple venues. These PACs feature diverse types of programming and community engagement initiatives. Funding varies in the levels of government support, nonprofit funding streams, and commercial revenues, and the governance and local politics associated with this type of PAC vary significantly. Mega-PACs, such as Lincoln Center and the Kennedy Center, possess identical structures and functions to those of the typical major metropolitan PAC but have a much larger scale of operations. In contrast, small market PACs tend to be community arts-based, with a mission and programming reflecting a smaller venue size and lower budgets. A wide array of PACs are also managed within colleges and universities. The collegiate PACs do not differ significantly from other PACs in their basic operations and programming, but they are distinguished by their academic mission, governance system, and funding streams (Lambert & Williams, 2017b, pp. 4–5).

This introduction to the community role and programming role of the PAC manager within the different types of PACs that exist can be further clarified by offering a snapshot of the diverse activities that take place within the major metropolitan PAC. The four major categories of PAC activities are (1) resident company performances, (2) other performing arts presentations, (3) community-focused events and activities, and (4) profit-making activities. A detailed listing of representative activities in these four categories is provided in Table 11.2.

The management structure of a major metropolitan PAC is in many ways similar to that of a large nonprofit arts organization. The most significant difference is the PAC's focus on "bricks and mortar assets as well as on guest services such as safety and security, food and beverage, and the general guest experience in the facility" (Lambert & Williams, 2017b, p. 7). A highly effective staff must be in place to attend to all of the activities listed in Table 11.2. Major administrative functions of presenting PACs include production (technical aspects, production management, stage management); rentals and booking; event services, and general facility operations (hospitality, security, housekeeping, concessions, etc.). All functions and operations of a PAC are led by a chief executive officer, who oversees financial management personnel, information technology systems and support, and the administrative staff

Table 11.2 Main Types of PAC Programming and Ancillary Revenues

Venue Programming	Ancillary Revenues
Resident company performances	Concessions and restaurants
Broadway series	Merchandise sales
International touring and presenting	Parking income
National/regional touring and presenting	Facility fees/user fees
Commercial concerts	Ticketing commissions
Family/kids programs	Equipment and utility charges
Lectures	Other for-profit activity
Community events	Labor charges
Conferences and meetings	Rental fees
Weddings, banquets, and receptions	Advertising
Other private events	Sponsorship
Other revenue rentals	

Source: Lambert & Williams, 2017a, p. 6.

of the organization. Many PACs have strong fundraising, marketing, and human resources departments, as well as large education and/or community engagement staff who support the organization's civic mission (Lambert & Williams, 2017b, pp. 6–7).

The PAC's administrative structure must align with the form of owner-ship and governance that exists in the umbrella organization that oversees the PAC. This umbrella organization can comprise many entities in a highly complex organizational structure, and significant variation exists in the form of ownership and governance of PACs throughout the United States. In fact, urban PAC oversight can be composed of several distinct layers. The PAC facility will be owned by an entity, which may or may not manage the PAC. Community oversight of the PAC may be provided by a different entity. And day-to-day operations of the PAC may be provided by one of these entities or by another group. Each of these entities may be any number of organiza-tional types structured as a public (government) entity, a nonprofit organi-zation, or a hybrid of the two. In practice, the structure of this oversight is unique to each community (Lambert & Williams, 2017c, p. 121).

Three major overarching types of PAC ownership and governance can be found in America's cities. The performing arts center can be run by or as a 501(c)3 nonprofit organization, it can be run by or as a cultural district or a cultural center, or it can be run by a division of a city, state, county, or region's government. Significant variation exists in the organizational form of day-to-day operations within these three types, reflecting the complex inter-play among models of ownership, governance, management, and operations (Lambert & Williams, 2017c, pp. 120–126). What is central to balancing the PAC mission and revenue generation goals is the set of decisions made by a community to operate the PAC directly, at arm's length, or independently. Ultimately, the business model that the PAC adopts may be that of a for-profit entity, a nonprofit organization, or a governmental (public) entity. The PAC may also use different business models for the different programming and revenue generation activities listed in Table 11.2.

Given the organizational complexity of the ubiquitous urban PAC, it fol-lows that a distinct set of core arts management competencies is required for the effective management of these organizations. In their communities, PAC managers provide leadership and advocacy for the arts sector as a whole. In their organizations, PAC executive staff work at the nexus of public admin-istration, nonprofit management, and for-profit entrepreneurship. Over the past five decades, a distinct sub-profession of arts management has emerged in this field.

Managing the PAC Within the Local Creative Economy

An excellent analytical framework for the creative sector was developed by Wyszomirski (2008). A revised and updated version of this schematic was introduced and discussed in Chapter 1 of this book as Figure 1.1. This illustration may be best understood as a variation of a nested rings model in which individual artists, other types of independent creative workers, and small entrepreneurs are located at the center. They are surrounded by a second ring of arts and cultural industries and a third ring of more peripheral and/or support activities. The schematic is particularly useful for analyzing the complex industrial structure of the creative sector in terms of the upstream production infrastructure, the downstream distribution infrastructure, and the general public infrastructure as the support system for the sector as a whole. To briefly clarify, the upstream production infrastructure provides equipment, services, private monetary capital, and human capital for the creative industries. The downstream distribution infrastructure connects the cultural industries to their markets and consumers. The general public infrastructure includes an emphasis on public funding, public policy, advocacy, and professional associations across the sector that supports the creative industries.

In comparison with other domains of arts management within the creative sector, the PAC manager is uniquely positioned to take an active role in supporting the workforce, industries, and infrastructure throughout the local creative economy. What this means in practical terms is that the PAC manager engages virtually all aspects of the upstream production infrastructure, the downstream distribution infrastructure, and the general public infrastructure. Indeed, the PAC bridges and connects the artistic core of the performing arts industry (artistic and creative expression) to a diverse array of industrial components of production organization.

With reference to Figure 1.1, the primary role of the PAC manager—at least at first glance—appears to be located in the "Facilities and Venues" sphere of the downstream distribution infrastructure, engaging most directly artistic, administrative, and technical creative workers in the performing arts. However, the PAC manager's role in the local creative economy requires these individuals to engage all of the other domains of the creative sector at various times. It is imperative to consider the PAC leaders' crucial roles in governance and in cultivating public or private coalitions in the arts and culture in their local communities. In the creative sector, PAC managers function essentially as network brokers who are allied with public goods, with artists as citizens, and with a highly diverse public audience.

As a result, the role of the PAC manager in the general public infrastructure and the upstream production infrastructure is just as important as it is in the facilities management role. In urban planning efforts, the arts and culture sector is frequently engaged for purposes of community, economic, and social development (Borrup, 2006; Evans, 2001; Landry, 2000; McCarthy et al., 2007). Metropolitan regions are continually ramping up their efforts to be viewed as a competitive creative city, and cultural amenities are called upon to attract and stimulate creativity and innovation. As a result, the PAC frequently becomes a central focus of urban cultural planning and development efforts, often serving to anchor cultural districts.

In the worldwide competitive environment to attract creative economy businesses and workers, policymakers, urban planners, and civic leaders alike recognize the important role of PACs in urban revitalization, development of cultural districts, and animating a downtown area or a neighborhood (Frost-Kumpf, 1998; Markusen & Gadwa, 2010; Stewart, 2008; Strom, 2003). Public awareness of PAC facilities' important contributions to the overall community and economy is increasing as PACs are expanding their role as urban competitive assets. Effective PAC leaders partner with urban planning and cultural affairs practitioners, as well as convention and visitors' bureaus, to enhance the quality of life for citizens, to support the creative vitality of the community, and to promote cultural tourism in the region. PACs are now considered to be destinations—regionally, nationally, and internationally. In addition, PAC leaders serve an essential role as a supporter, a collaborator, and a partner to local arts organizations and artists (Williams et al., 2017).

By serving the community as a legitimizer, an incubator, and a steward, the PAC possesses a tremendous opportunity and responsibility to support local arts organizations and local creative expression. In activating these three roles, the PAC can remain deeply engaged in and relevant to the local arts community. By extension, the PAC executive leader can promote a crucial community role in convening sector-wide leadership and advocating for the arts and culture sector within additional public-sector gatherings (Williams et al., 2017, p. 256).

In communities, large and small, across the nation, the PAC has the potential to support the local creative economy as a physical manifestation of a central gathering place in a community where the diverse domains of the upstream production infrastructure, downstream distribution infrastructure, and general public infrastructure can come together. It follows that the successful PAC manager must possess the requisite knowledge, competencies, and skills to engage the diverse creative sector specialists found throughout these domains. As the performing arts sector gradually recovers from the economic impact of the 2020–2021 COVID-19 pandemic, these professional competencies will be more important than ever.

PAC Leadership as an Emerging Arts Management Profession

In many ways, the emerging profession of PAC management has trailed the organic evolution of the role of PACs in America's communities from the 1960s to the present. As Steven Wolff (2017) convincingly suggests, the professional role of leading the PAC has changed significantly over the four generations of these institutions (home, place, community center, and nexus). Parallel to other specialized fields of arts management, the increasing complexity of this sub-profession now requires a much more expansive set of qualifications and experience than it did in prior decades. Like other areas of arts management, this sub-profession began with individuals who developed their field-specific knowledge and skills through years of on-the-job experience.

However, specialized training in PAC management is now required "due to public venues' highly complex business models, multimillion-dollar budgets, the demands of asset and capital project management, myriad software systems and other technologies used in these organizations, and the increasing complexity of booking, contracting, and event management operations" (Lambert & Williams, 2017b, p. 8).

Over the past half-century, the continually increasing demands placed upon PAC leaders for specialized knowledge and skills, education, and credentialing have led to a gradual structuration of this distinct sub-field of arts management. PAC management has followed the evolution of the four generations of PAC institutions as it has gradually progressed from an occupation to a career to a profession. Early leaders of PACs came from the field, often drawn from expert practitioners in booking, touring, presenting, production management, and technical direction. Their patterns of activities became framed as a distinct occupation that was necessitated by the establishment of PACs across the nation in the 1960s and 1970s. APAP was originally established in 1957 as the Association of Performing Arts Presenters and changed its name to the Association of Performing Arts Professionals in 2017. APAP has long been recognized as the national organization that supports the entire system of booking, touring, and presenting of live performing arts. Broad membership in APAP—including staff members of PACs—has grown significantly over the past 60 years.

As PACs took on more of the community responsibilities of place and community center (Wolff, 2017), often closely aligned with urban revitalization efforts in the 1980s and 1990s, arts management needs of a PAC became more structured. In this career phase of PAC leadership, related occupations required within PAC management became more hierarchically arranged, and pathways for credentialing and professional development began to emerge. Interestingly, professional PAC managers have not historically thought of themselves as arts managers. Instead, the professional structuration of this particular sub-field of arts management has grown within the context of professionalization of management of other types of public assembly venues, such as arenas, stadiums, and conference centers. The national professional association for these kinds of facilities is the International Association of Venue Management (IAVM)—initially International Association of Auditorium Managers (IAAM) then renamed International Association of Assembly Managers (IAAM)—which was founded in 1924. PAC managers comprise a specific professional group within the IAVM.

The IAVM has taken on a pivotal role in the gradual shift from PAC management as a career to a profession over the past several decades. Chapter 2 of this book clarifies key indicators of professionalization. As listed in Table 2.1, these indicators include specialized, credentialed higher education; full-time, stable, paid work with a developed career path; established professional associations; structures for public validation; and institutionalization of organizational field structures. Indeed, these indicators can be used to assess how PAC management is now perceived as a profession. University-trained experts are found in this field, in both university-level arts management education programs and more general facilities management programs. A growing body of research on PACs is appearing in an array of peer-reviewed journals and academic book publications, creating an ever-expanding body of specialized knowledge. In the United States, a robust national dataset called PAC Stats (see www.pacstats.com) serves as a benchmarking and performance measurement tool for PACs. The PAC sub-group within the IAVM provides networking and professional development opportunities through annual conference sessions and other communications. In short, the professional elite of PAC leadership have consolidated within the organizational field structure of the IAVM.

The foremost credentialing system that supports PAC professionalization is currently the IAVM's Certified Venue Professional (CVP) and Certified Venue Executive (CVE) programs. The CVE credential is a professional distinction that requires continuing professional development and recertification every three years. The rigorous certification process demands extensive professional experience and service, a written examination, and an oral interview. Venue management professional competencies across the sector are framed as managing operations, managing resources, managing people, and managing risk, as well as general leadership and management competencies (IAVM, 2014). A quick glance at the "Career + Learning" tab on the IAVM website (International Association of Venue Managers, 2014) provides valuable insight into both of these credentialing programs and an impressive array of other professional development initiatives underway by the professional association. These initiatives include a career center, mentorship program, college partnership program, books, webinars, conferences, meetings, newsletters, trade journals, and other resources.

Many pathways now exist for individuals to pursue a profession in PAC leadership. However, it is increasingly insufficient to rise in the profession solely through decades of work experience in the field. The complexity of the profession now requires knowledge acquired through a combination of university-level education, professional experience, professional credentialing, and continual professional development. The IAVM CVE credential has emerged as the designation of recognized professional achievement in PAC leadership, but the educational foundation for entering the field might range in university programs as diverse as arts management, music, theater, dance, theater technology, business, urban planning, nonprofit management, or facilities management.

As the PAC management profession continues to evolve in the Generation 4 PAC construct of nexus and beyond (Wolff, 2017), the field requires an increasingly nuanced set of arts leadership expertise. These competencies and skills are discussed in detail later. America's PAC is no longer just a performing arts sector business; it is now a civic leader and a thought leader in adding value and creating opportunities for the local community. The PAC serves as a convener and a learning environment within which new experiences are shared and new knowledge is created. PAC leadership increasingly emphasizes relationships, inclusion, relevance, sector-wide support, and participation within the community (Webb, 2017). "The cultural observer is now a cultural participant, and the performing arts product is now a process of audience engagement" (Williams et al., 2017, p. 240).

Competencies and Skills Required of PAC Leaders

As argued by Williams et al. (2017),

> the environment of rapid and turbulent change, shifting community expectations of the PAC, and a reconceptualization of what the public value of a PAC should be in its community calls for nothing less than transformational leadership on the part of the field's senior executives.
>
> (p. 242)

Although many of the contributing authors to *Performing Arts Center Management* (Lambert & Williams, 2017a) address this reconceptualization of a PAC's public value, Wolff (2017) discusses public value most concisely within his "Generation 4 PAC" construct. The evolving public leadership role involves a responsibility to serve the community as a destination, a showcase, and an incubator, educator, innovator, partner, and thought leader (see Table 11.1). In response to this new emphasis on public value, transformational leadership focuses on managing change within the organization to advance the PAC's ever-expanding role in the community.

The emerging role of the PAC as a leader in the community encompasses two roles. First, the PAC is a key element of the urban planning, facilities, and amenities infrastructure of the community. Second, the PAC serves to lead the local arts community as a legitimizer, an incubator, and a steward (Williams et al., 2017, p. 250). It follows that a diverse set of professional competencies is required of PAC managers in order to exercise transformational leadership in addressing these two key roles in the community. These professional competencies can be divided into two major areas: (1) PAC executive leadership and the community and (2) performing arts management in the PAC (Lambert & Williams, 2017b, p. 10). Whereas the first area of professional competency detailed later refers primarily to external relations and activities, the second area addresses a focus on internal relations and functions. In practice, however, these competencies are engaged across the internal and external domains of PAC leadership. The performing arts executive must possess the ability to seamlessly shift their application of management instruments as they interact with diverse stakeholders across the local creative sector, as depicted in Figure 1.1.

PAC Executive Leadership and the Community

As mentioned previously, PAC executive leadership requires management competency in all three spheres of the economy—the public, the nonprofit, and the for-profit sectors. This entails the capacity to smoothly adapt the type of management praxis that is exercised in public administration, nonprofit management, and for-profit enterprise to the particular situation of governance and operations of the facility that the PAC manager is engaged with on a day-to-day and hour-by-hour basis. Quite a balancing act is required to both serve the public (the PAC's public sector and/or nonprofit sector purposes) and promote profit-making programming and activities. The different operating rationales of the three sectors engaged in the ownership, governance, and operations of the PAC call for diverse sets of management expectations and norms, which are discussed in detail later.

Three general models of structuring the ownership and governance of the PAC in America's communities tend to exist. First, the PAC may be owned by a city, county, state, or regional government. If this is the case, it may be managed and operated either as or within a department or division of government, or it can be managed and operated as an independent nonprofit that reports to the government. Second, the PAC may be run by or as a cultural district or a cultural center. In this case, the PAC is often operated as an independent nonprofit organization within this entity. Third, the PAC may be overseen by or structured as an autonomous nonprofit organization. In this case, the PAC can be owned and operated as a community nonprofit. Alternatively, the city or region may own the PAC, but an independent nonprofit is set up to operate it (Lambert & Williams, 2017c).

Beginning with the umbrella organization involved in ownership and governance of the PAC, the PAC manager will most likely report to public oversight of some kind. This public administration role of PAC leaders will likely entail engagement in urban planning and economic development discussion, such as those that frame cultural district initiatives. PAC leaders have an important role to play as community-wide representatives of the arts and culture sector, including advocating for ongoing public support of creative sector initiatives and organizations. Advocacy activities also include tapping into state public alliances and partnerships, engaging with regional and national professional associations and arts organizations, and potentially negotiating across international borders and with foreign ministries. Therefore, although the public administration role of PAC leaders is primarily local, it can also involve a range of intergovernmental forums and actors.

With reference to Figure 1.1, the PAC manager must play an important role in representing the creative sector within the general public infrastructure, including engagement with advocacy, policy, public funding, and professional associations. The public role extends also into the upstream production infrastructure, in which the PAC manager will engage in activities such as providing research, information, supplies, equipment, funding, and training to the local creative sector as a whole. One of the most important public roles of the PAC manager is that of a partner, collaborator, and network broker within the community. The most evident of the PAC manager's responsibilities is to oversee the facilities and venues of the community within the creative sector's downstream distribution infrastructure. However, the public role of the PAC leader is likely far more significant within the general public infrastructure and the upstream production infrastructure.

With reference to the PAC roles depicted by Wolff (2017) in Table 11.1, the community relevance of the contemporary PAC nexus may be understood almost entirely in terms of its contribution to the public good. In this construct, the PAC manager's role is one of facilitating support for the creative sector's upstream and public infrastructure. The PAC leader serves to support the community's branding and creative placemaking efforts, partners with local arts organizations through providing a home and resources, and supports the creative sector as a whole through incubating projects, offering education, encouraging innovation, and serving as a thought leader. These responsibilities all require political acumen and strong advocacy skills to work with governmental entities, as well as a high capacity to form and support coalitions and alliances. Further, these public administration responsibilities demand sophisticated understanding of diverse governance systems, institutional structures, and functions of PACs.

In addition to the contributions of the PAC leader to the public good through full engagement in the creative sector, the PAC manager must also possess specific knowledge and competencies pertinent to his or her leadership role within the arts and culture community. For example, the PAC manager should engage in constant professional development activities to ensure knowledge of the changing context of performing arts management, changing audience behaviors and expectations, and approaches to audience development, arts education, and community engagement. And, with historic preservation and the visual arts frequently part of PAC building or renovation projects, it is very useful for PAC managers to also possess the capacity to program public art spaces and art galleries.

Performing Arts Management in the PAC

The organizational structure and personnel functions of a PAC typically look very similar to those in place at other professional nonprofit performing arts organizations. Successful PACs require strong marketing and communications, development, volunteer management, education and community engagement, and financial management operations. The main difference between producing organizations (such as the local symphony orchestra, opera, and ballet) and the presenting PAC is that the PAC books other organizations' arts performances rather than create its own. Although artistic personnel are not required for production, the PAC nonetheless maintains especially strong technical and backstage operations. The focus of PAC management in the local performing arts ecology is to provide the best possible venue and audience experience to the community for all of the arts programs and activities offered within the facility.

What this means in terms of performing arts management practice is that the PAC leader must possess expertise in both nonprofit and for-profit management because he or she is constantly working with resident nonprofit companies, commercial presenters, and local community groups engaged in the arts. A major focus of the PAC leader is on revenue generation through commercial presenting and ancillary revenues in order to meet the PAC mission of subsidizing resident company activities. Successful PAC leadership therefore requires strong financial management acumen and the capacity to develop both earned and contributed revenue streams.

Day-to-day operations in a PAC involve maintaining the quality of the facility (including areas like technology, housekeeping, building repairs, parking, and security systems), strategically overseeing the PAC booking schedule, processing and executing presenting contracts, managing communications and ticketing systems, complying with union contracts (especially IATSE, International Alliance of Theatrical Stage Employees, for technical personnel), and ensuring excellence in ongoing production management and stage management services for clients. Because the public mandate for the PAC is to provide support to local arts organizations, PAC management sees itself in service to the performing arts sector as a whole rather than seeking to directly promote its own artistic products and activities. That said, the communication, branding, and marketing functions of a PAC are very important to continually position the PAC as a destination in the community. Strong partnerships and continual discussions are required to ensure mutually supportive marketing and development functions within both the PAC and its separate resident companies. Tensions among the resident companies and the PAC often exist regarding performance scheduling and revenue generation activities.

The most significant area of performing arts leadership exercised by the PAC—and the one that has been given the least attention in research into this field—is that of arts programming and curation. For much of the past five decades, the main approach to this role used by PACs could be characterized as "managing the calendar." Due to its public role and mission, the PAC typically begins booking the season through a scheduling process in place with its resident companies. After these dates are booked, the PAC continues to fill in dates throughout the year in all the venues it oversees while meeting its dual mandate of maximizing earned income and expanding arts opportunities throughout the community. To do so, PAC staff participate in annual booking conferences (the Association of Performing Arts Professionals, as well as regional conferences), and they are contacted by booking and touring professionals and agents to secure dates that work with the touring artists' travel schedule. Beyond anecdotal evidence, very little is known of the decision-making processes that are used on a day-to-day basis by PAC staff to advance programming. Much more study of this function would be

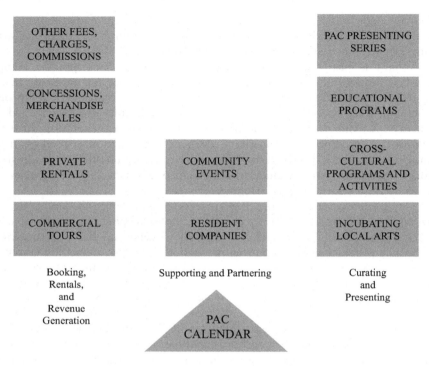

Figure 11.1 The Presenting PAC's Programming Balance

beneficial, especially given the significance of the PAC's increasing role in curating and presenting the arts in local communities.

With reference to Figure 11.1, the evolving role of PAC managers in programming performing arts within their communities should be given careful consideration. The balancing act involved in managing the calendar is complex. Most urban- and community-based PACs serve a public mandate to support resident companies and provide an important facility for community events and activities. Although this is a primary concern of PAC leaders, many other elements involved in programming and revenue-generating activities are required on an annual basis. To offset the expense of subsidizing resident company rehearsals and performances and other community-focused cultural engagement, the PAC must schedule and promote a wide array of commercial tours (such as Broadway series, comedians, and popular music) and must generate income from facility rentals, concessions, restaurants, merchandise sales, and other fees.

Because of the changing public expectations for the value that PACs will offer their communities, the role of PAC leaders in supporting, partnering, presenting, and curating cultural activities is increasing in importance. PAC leaders are expected to incubate and steward start-up (and amateur) performing arts groups. They partner with a wide array of community partners to develop educational programs for all demographic groups. And, increasingly, they curate their own PAC presenting series through carefully selecting, arranging, and scheduling performing arts programs that will enhance quality of life in their communities. In this sense, the role and responsibility of curation in PACs can be viewed as similar to those of the curation that takes place in a community's museum.

One particularly important dimension of performing arts programming pertains to the role of PACs in advancing cross-cultural and international understanding. Through partnerships and collaborations with specific racial, ethnic, and immigrant groups in a community, specific arts-based programming by the PAC can encourage processes of communication and dialogue across manifold differences. International touring and presenting also offer special opportunities for public education. Some very large PACs, such as the Kennedy Center and Carnegie Hall, consider international presenting as a crucial cultural diplomacy activity and as a way of providing their communities with a wider range of artistic choices.

For many American citizens, engaging with foreign cultures and identities is not an everyday occurrence. Artists visiting the local community from abroad may provide valuable insight into other cultures, including excellent opportunities for enhancing international relations. When touring artists from abroad visit a local community, PAC managers can partner with various organizations and schools to offer residents opportunities for international cultural interactions. PAC managers can also partner internationally in programs to enhance international understanding (e.g., with sister city organizations), and can serve a leading role in festivals that enhance cross-cultural understanding within the local community. The responsibility of international presenting requires managing a process that involves a network across multiple levels of government (e.g., for processing visas) as well as working with commercial agents, touring companies, diplomats, educators, and translators.

The performing arts management competencies required of the presenting PAC leader are, in sum, far more complex than they are in the nonprofit professional performing arts organization—which is the focus of most of the scholarship in arts management. The PAC leader must be able to run their own organization essentially as a nonprofit arts organization while in explicit service to public entities. The PAC manager must be able to equally engage with other nonprofit arts managers and with for-profit commercial booking and touring. With annual programming including performances as diverse as Broadway musicals, comedians, ballet, opera, symphony, international art forms, and circus-like spectacles, managing a PAC necessitates an extensive toolkit of performing arts knowledge, competencies, and skills. Indeed, serving as an artistic gatekeeper and a facilitator of creative expression requires that the PAC leader possess significant artistic knowledge and competency in artistic administration.

Analysis: The State of Professionalization of Performing Arts Center Management

This chapter presents PAC management to be an emergent sub-profession of arts management. Beginning with a history of the evolution of PACs in America's communities, the chapter profiled the diverse roles, functions, and types of PACs. The chapter introduced the essential role of the major metropolitan PAC and its senior leadership within the local creative economy, and discussed the development and structuration of PAC leadership as a profession. The requisite competencies and skills for PAC management were then addressed in detail.

The PAC management sub-profession may be particularly intriguing to the field of arts management because of its unique form of hybrid performing arts management praxis. Indeed, it is hard to imagine another area of arts management being called upon to contribute to provide a similar scope of public value and support to all domains of the creative sector. The successful PAC leader is called upon to participate in advocacy and policy discussions, engage in public administration to support civic goals, support the local non-profit and community-based arts scene, and provide entertaining and educational arts programming to local audiences. This field of professional practice clearly requires competency across public administration, nonprofit management, and for-profit business.

Ultimately, the crucial role of the PAC leader within the local arts and culture sector is that of an arts manager uniquely located in a position to support the creative ecology as a whole. The significance of this role cannot be overstated as the entire arts and culture sector seeks effective systems to recover from the 2020–2021 COVID-19 pandemic and economic downturn. As discussed previously with reference to Figure 1.1, the PAC leader is positioned to engage in the upstream production infrastructure and the general public infrastructure in addition to their obvious location within the downstream distribution infrastructure. In navigating across these domains of the creative sector, the PAC manager can contribute to all four dimensions of public support for arts and culture in the community: financial support, social support, professional support, and ideational support.

Wyszomirski (2002) argues compellingly that a complex and interdependent model of support for the arts and culture sector is required for a strong and sustainable creative economy. The community's PAC and its leadership have great potential to consolidate and amplify all four dimensions of support in this model. One of the primary roles of public PACs is to provide financial support to local arts organizations. The PAC is viewed to be an efficient way to pool resources in the community to provide an excellent home to resident companies for their performances. Through leveraging direct government funds and earned income—and, in some cases, private contributions and other forms of revenue—a successful PAC is able to provide significant financial support to local arts organizations.

The PAC's role in providing the second pillar of support—that of social support—is just as important. By consistently providing an excellent audience experience in well-maintained facilities that are event destinations in the community, generally positive public attitudes toward the arts can be strengthened. Effective communications and facilities services (hospitality, food and beverage, easy parking, user-friendly ticket purchasing, safe and comfortable setting, etc.) can go a great way in incentivizing arts participation and reducing perceived barriers to participation. Many PACs also have robust volunteer programs (ushering, concessions, gift stores, etc.) that provide excellent opportunities for increasing the community's social network of support for a vibrant arts and culture scene.

In the local community, the PAC can also provide extensive professional, ideational, and educational support. Well-trained and unionized technical directors and stagehands provide a safe and professional setting for all performing arts activities. The PAC typically offers technical advising and administrative support of various kinds to community-based organizations, and collects and disseminates valuable information among its community partners. Through being a thought leader, innovator, and incubator as it partners with others in the creative sector both locally and beyond, the PAC is providing extensive ideational support. This refers to "aesthetic or cultural ideas and norms [as well as] ideas and information about the sector that facilitate and support its ecology" (Wyszomirski, 2008, p. 228). Ongoing education of representatives from arts and culture organizations as well as the general public is likely one of the most powerful steps that PACs can take to continually strengthen the local creative economy.

It can, therefore, be argued that investment in professionalizing PAC management may provide an effective and efficient pathway for communities to strengthen their entire creative economy. In fact, PAC management provides a microcosm of the six areas of support needed to further professionalize arts managers throughout America's communities. These six areas, first articulated in *Investing in Creativity: A Study of the Support Structure for US Artists* (Jackson et al., 2003) are identified as public validation, demand and markets, material support, training, communities and networks, and information.

The areas of public validation and demand and markets both pertain to the pillars of financial support, social support, and ideational support. In the local arts and culture ecology, the PAC provides community-wide recognition of the value of the arts, and legitimizes public and private investment in arts organizations and creative activity. Through the professional facility offered by the PAC, local arts organizations can expect an excellent performance venue experience for their artists and their audience. By cross-promoting arts events and supporting marketing and ticketing activities, the PAC helps to build and expand the community's demand for arts participation. Similarly, by advancing the legitimacy and value of arts activities and artists in the public's eye, the PAC is helping to contribute to general ideational and social support for strong public funding of the arts and culture sector. In this context, for example, PAC leaders can raise the issue of living wage compensation to address income insecurity of artistic and creative workers in the community. The PAC has a responsibility to effectively articulate and demonstrate the public benefits of arts engagement and the creative sector's role in societal, cultural, and professional well-being.

As is evident in Figure 11.1, PAC leaders interact regularly with a highly diverse group of stakeholders in the creative sector. It can be argued that stakeholders from the general public infrastructure as well as private funders comprise a governance network within which the PAC must operate. Although the PAC serves the public, many other private sector interests must also be routinely addressed. Public validation is continually enhanced when the PAC communicates its "triple bottom line" social, cultural, and financial outcomes in the local community (Wyszomirski, 2013). Please see Chapter 2 of this volume for a discussion of the triple bottom line as an effect of field structuration.

The PAC's material support is perhaps most evident in the community. In anchoring cultural districts and providing the largest performing arts venue(s) in the community, the PAC provides extensive financial and physical resources that are needed for the performing arts production chain to function. This area of support involves employment of artistic, administrative, and technical workers. It also involves supporting the arts and culture sector as a whole through the provision of space, facilities, technology, equipment, materials, insurance, benefits, and expertise. The PAC can provide significant productivity advantages through pooling resources in a way that results in a leaner administrative and support infrastructure for the arts.

Three areas of support that PACs offer the community are difficult to distinguish from each other: training, communities and networks, and information. This area of support connects most directly with the upstream production infrastructure in the creative sector, as well as with the domain of professional associations in this schematic. In practice, however, this area of support contributes to the professional and ideational pillars of support that contribute to successful advocacy, policy, and public funding that is provided through the general public infrastructure. For example, a PAC may provide administrative services for numerous local arts organizations, as is the case with the Columbus (Ohio) Association for the Performing Arts. Another example is the Kennedy Center for the Performing Arts, which has been recognized for decades for its important activities nationwide in arts education advocacy and training.

In short, everything having to do with the provision of information and training through professional networks is a powerful tool that the PAC can use to strengthen the local creative sector. The profession's national association, the IAVM, already offers an impressive array of professional development and credentialing opportunities. The research, information, and management practices shared through this—and other professional associations in the arts—can be systematically shared by PAC managers with other creative sector stakeholders in the community.

This chapter has offered detailed insight into the professionalism process underway in PAC management. As this distinct profession continues to congeal as a sub-profession of arts management, it can be expected that the creative sector in America's communities will continue to strengthen. Indeed, the PAC executive can be viewed as a linchpin of smooth functioning across artistic production, performance venues, community enrichment, and public support for arts and culture. The PAC is positioned at the core of the local creative ecology, and deserves highly competent leadership to support creative vitality throughout America's communities.

References

Borrup, T. (2006). *The creative community builder's handbook: How to transform communities using local assets, arts, and culture.* Fieldstone Alliance.

Donnelly, P. (2011). Arts facilities: Schedules, agreements, and ownership. In M. Brindle & C. DeVereaux (Eds.), *The arts management handbook* (pp. 13–37). M. E. Sharpe, Inc.

Evans, G. (2001). *Cultural planning: An urban renaissance?* Routledge.

Frost-Kumpf, H. (1998). *Cultural district: The arts as a strategy for revitalizing our cities.* Americans for the Arts. www.americansforthearts.org/sites/default/files/Cultural%20Districts_0.pdf

Hager, M. A., & Pollak, T. H. (2002). *The capacity of performing arts presenting organizations.* The Urban Institute.

International Association of Venue Managers. (2014). *Venue management competency standards.* www.iavm.org/sites/default/files/images/iavm_venue_professional_competency_standard.pdf

Jackson, M. R., Kabwasa-Green, F., Swenson, D., Herranz, J., Ferryman, K., Atlas, C., Wallner, E., & Rosenstein, C. (2003). *Investing in creativity: A study of the support structure for U.S. artists.* Urban Institute.

Lambert, P. D., & Williams, R. (Eds.). (2017a). *Performing arts center management.* Routledge.

Lambert, P. D., & Williams, R. (2017b). The professionalization of performing arts center management. In P. D. Lambert & R. Williams (Eds.), *Performing arts center management* (pp. 1–19). Routledge.

Lambert, P. D., & Williams, R. (2017c). Ownership and governance of urban performing arts centers. In P. D. Lambert & R. Williams (Eds.), *Performing arts center management* (pp. 120–141). Routledge.

Landry, C. (2000). *The creative city: A toolkit for urban innovators.* Earthscan.

Markusen, A., & Gadwa, A. (2010). Arts and culture in urban or regional planning: A review and research agenda. *Journal of Planning Education and Research*, 29(3), 379–391.

McCarthy, K. F., Ondaatje, E. H., &Novak, J. L. (2007). *Arts and culture in the metropolis: Strategies for sustainability*. RAND Corporation.

Micocci, T. (2008). *Booking performance tours: Marketing and acquiring live arts and entertainment*. Allworth Press.

Micocci, T. (2017). Programming the performing arts: Balancing mission and solvency. In P. D. Lambert & R. Williams (Eds.), *Performing arts center management* (pp. 63–83). Routledge.

Stein, T. S., & Bathurst, J. (2008). *Performing arts management: A handbook of professional practices*. Allworth Press.

Stewart, R. A. (2008). The arts and artists in urban revitalization. In J. M. Cherbo, R. A. Steward, & M. J. Wyszomirski (Eds.), *Understanding the arts and creative sector in the United States* (pp. 105–128). Rutgers University Press.

Strom, E. (2003). Cultural policy as development policy: Evidence from the United States. *International Journal of Cultural Policy*, 9(3), 247–263.

Webb, D. M. (2004). *Running theaters: Best practices for leaders and managers*. Allworth Press.

Webb, D. M. (2017). Trends in the development and operation of performing arts centers. In P. D. Lambert & R. Williams (Eds.), *Performing arts center management* (pp. 45–62). Routledge.

Williams, R., Harris, K., & Lambert, P. D. (2017). Executive leadership for performing arts centers. In P. D. Lambert & R. Williams (Eds.), *Performing arts center management* (pp. 238–259). Routledge.

Wolff, S. A. (2017). The evolution of the performing arts center: What does success look like? In P. D. Lambert & R. Williams (Eds.), *Performing arts center management* (pp. 20–44). Routledge.

Woronkowics, J., Joynes, D. C., & Bradburn, N. (2015). *Building better arts facilities: Lessons from a U.S. national study*. Routledge.

Wyszomirski, M. J. (2002). Support for the arts: A 4 part model. *Journal of Arts Management, Law and Society*, 32(3), 222–240.

Wyszomirski, M. J. (2008). The local creative economy in the United States of America. In H. K. Anheier & Y. R. Isar (Eds.), *The cultural economy* (pp. 199–212). Sage Publications.

Wyszomirski, M. J. (2013). Shaping a triple-bottom line for nonprofit arts organizations: Micro-, macro-, and meta-policy influences. *Cultural Trends*, 22(3–4), 156–166.

12 "I Am a Professional Dancer"

The Case of Professionalization in Disability Arts

Ruth Rentschler, Boram Lee, Ayse Collins, and Jung Yoon

Introduction

Previous academic literature has largely overlooked professionalization in disability arts. There is little literature discussing the career progression of artists with disability. Many studies explore the therapeutic and recreational roles of the arts for people with disabilities rather than focusing on the arts as a career for such individuals. This study explores different roles and meanings of the arts for artists with disability. It also reviews the literature on professionalization and professionalism in the arts based on the general concepts introduced by DiMaggio (1987). The study aims to conceptualize professionalization in disability arts at the individual and organizational levels through qualitative analysis; 17 individuals are interviewed, including artists, artists' carers, and other internal and external stakeholders of an inclusive arts organization working with artists both with and without disability. The results from the study suggest three significant aspects of professionalization in the disability arts.

The findings indicate, first, that there are both commonalities and differences in professionalism between artists with and without disability. Thus, it is essential to broaden the definition of professionalism in the arts to encapsulate the particular characteristics of artists with disability (Bain, 2005; Svensson, 2015; Throsby & Petetskaya, 2017; Wyszomirski & Chang, 2017). Second, there are both inhibiting and enabling factors at both individual and organizational levels that influence the development of the professional careers of artists with disabilities. In particular, we find that inclusive arts organizations play multiple roles in the professional development of artists with disability. For instance, inclusive arts organizations create alternative educational pathways for artists with disability by providing professional skills training programs and workshops for those who are often unable to undertake tertiary-level education due to their disabilities, thus enhancing their career opportunities. Third, the study provides insights which suggest professional development strategies for artists with disabilities at the individual and organizational levels.

DOI: 10.4324/9781003138693-14

Professionalization

The terms professionalization and professionalism sometimes have been used interchangeably, but they are different concepts. Professionalization is the process of becoming professional (Pitman, 2012). According to DiMaggio (1987), "sociologists define *professionalism* as a form of self-organization that enables practitioners of an occupation to defend the importance of their contribution and the legitimacy of their decisions" (p. 52). DiMaggio (1987) also identifies two aspects of professionalization: (1) The ideological and cognitive capacity to establish the legitimacy of professional claims to authority, autonomy, and expertise; and (2) the behavioral and organizational means to provide a framework by which professionals can interact with their colleagues, learn and develop new ideas and reputations, and make public contributions in their field. In the past, the recognized professions mostly concerned vocational disciplines, such as engineering, architecture, law, medicine, and theology (Wyszomirski & Chang, 2017). In this chapter, we use the term professionalization in relation to disability arts becoming professional, as it encapsulates the process disability and the arts are undergoing. In the twenty-first century, however, the concept of the profession has been broadened to include the development of education and training and creative and social intelligence in less traditional areas, such as the arts and information technology (Collins et al., 2022; Wyszomirski & Chang, 2017). This study seeks to identify how the professionalization process was achieved in an inclusive arts organization, at both the individual and organizational levels.

Professionalization in the Arts

The process of professionalization in the arts is ambiguous because the definitions of the arts vary depending on whether interpretations are based on philosophical, sociological, psychological, economic, or historical perspectives (Currie, 2010; Fokt, 2017; Monseré, 2016). Despite these differences, there are recognized commonalities in different definitions of professionalization in the arts. The first commonality is education and training. The institutional definition has predominantly governed the professional status of artists who wish to be accepted as members of the art world (Fokt, 2017). The criterion for classification as a work of art is that it is appreciated by people acting for social institutions (i.e., the art world) (Dickie, 1974). For example, according to the Canadian Artists' Representation le Front des Artistes Canadiens (CAR-FAC), the conditions for acceptance as a professional artist require educational qualifications in the arts (Bain, 2005). The second commonality is career progression, which refers to a period in which an artist strengthens personal skills and knowledge to achieve a level of professional acceptance with a degree of commitment (Bain, 2005; Svensson, 2015; Throsby & Petetskaya, 2017). It also aims to generate a regular source of income for artists by gaining a grant or some other financial assistance for living by establishing artistic careers and professions in mainstream arts (Bain, 2005; Svensson, 2015; Throsby & Petetskaya, 2017). Being paid for one's arts practice entitles an artist to claim professional status regardless of whether the remuneration received amounts to a living wage or is paid by one employer.

The third commonality is act of creation, which includes individual freedom of artistic expression, creative production in an artistic form, and pursuing artistic activity beyond ordinary thoughts and behaviors (Bain, 2005; Svensson, 2015). The nature of creativity is intrinsically driven by the power of individual imagination (Bain, 2005). The last commonality is cultural capital, which means achieving recognition as a professional artist pursuing a more important social and cultural motive than material reward or profit (Bain, 2005; Wyszomirski & Chang, 2017). Professional artists tend to cultivate diverse perspectives and interpretations that contribute to enhancing their status as members of the social elite (Bain, 2005; Wyszomirski & Chang, 2017).

Over time, professionalization in the arts has come to entail obtaining (1) knowledge, technique, and the abilities of individual artists that indicate a certain level of specialization and performance, for example, as exhibited by a professional dance company; (2) the capacity and competency for organizational management and operations; and (3) an expectation of quality in the product produced and presented to audiences, for example, onstage performances (DiMaggio, 1987; Wyszomirski & Chang, 2017). All three dimensions of professionalization are ideally, but not necessarily, mutually reinforcing.

Professionalization in Disability Arts

Professionalization can create another level of artistic space in a variety of ways for artists with disabilities. Initially, the arts were offered through therapy, first, to people with disability to whom it was thought that it might prove beneficial either educationally or in terms of well-being; and, second, to people with disability unable to obtain employment. More recently, it has been offered with the aim of enhancing employment opportunities (Lee et al., 2022). Given a continuum of participation, the relationship between the arts and people with disability has moved from therapy to recreation to community arts to employment. These four components have enabled artists with disabilities to find places where they might belong, be trusted, and obtain recognition for their professional achievements. Engaging with the arts has become a means of generating change for people with disabilities (Collins et al., 2022; Fujimoto et al., 2013). However, career prospects for professional artists with disability remain challenging. This study, first of all, explores the professionalization of artists with disability by exploring different roles of the arts in disability. Two distinct roles of the arts in disability can be distinguished: disability and arts and disability arts. These two distinguishing roles are now discussed.

Disability and Arts

Disability and arts can be categorized in two ways theoretically, depending on the interpretation of artists' roles: the medical model and the social model. The medical model describes the conventional concept of disability as "an objective medical condition in need of treatment and rehabilitation" (Dirth & Branscombe, 2017, p. 414). In contrast to the medical model, the social model interprets disability as imposing a barrier or difficulty upon a person's environmental and social circumstances rather than resulting from medical diagnosis (Dirth & Branscombe, 2017).

The four categories of engaging with disability and arts are (1) therapeutic arts; (2) recreational arts; (3) community arts; and (4) disability arts (Richards et al., 2019; Sandahl, 2018; Solvang, 2012, 2018). Each category of disability and arts focuses on different goals and criteria in relation to how professional the artists and arts organizations are perceived to be. Therapeutic arts entail using art as a therapeutic intervention to analyze and/or comprehend clients or patients through a process of assessment, planning, implementation, and evaluation based on the medical model (Evans et al., 2017; Solvang, 2018). Therapeutic arts intervention has two main purposes: (1) Utilizing arts practice as an intervention component to treat a medical condition, such as psychological issues based on psycho-therapeutic theories; and (2) providing a valued social practice by applying the social model, which aims to create socially accessible environmental circumstances for artists with disabilities (Argyle, 2003; Dirth & Branscombe, 2017).

Recreational arts focus on the improvement of individual well-being by enhancing self-satisfaction, self-enrichment, self-expression, feeling of accomplishment, and social interaction through participation in arts creation in a positive environment (Chandler et al., 2018; Cohen-Gewerc, 2013; Solvang, 2018). The process of self-development through recreational arts unlocks the individuality of people with disability and enables them to explore various dimensions of themselves, with the aim of encouraging artistic outcomes (Cohen-Gewerc, 2013; Collins et al., 2022; Fujimoto et al., 2013).

Community arts create opportunities for developing artistic skills and expression within a group of individuals with disabilities, leading to transformative social change (Richards et al., 2019; Vick & Sexton-Radek, 2008). Sandahl (2018) states that community arts entail: "participating in meaningful community activities based on personal interests;" "working and earning a living wage;" "having relationships with friends, family and significant others;" and "being physically and emotionally healthy" (p. 83). Community arts tend to create a supportive and artistic environment for emerging artists with disability, thus facilitating their professional development.

Disability Arts

Disability arts is defined as an arts and cultural movement led by artists with disability with the objective of sharing their disability experience and culture as an artistic and expressive form (Sandahl, 2018; Solvang, 2018). Disability arts originated as a political agenda through protests for equal rights and pride in identity through disability (Stöckl, 2014). The disability arts movement became an ongoing activity of cultural expression to realize "unity and pride among disabled people" (Stöckl, 2014, p. 179). Disability arts are now institutionalized by inclusive arts organizations through artistic events in order to sustain the movement (Solvang, 2012). Nevertheless, art as therapy is still perceived to be the predominant role of the arts in disability, although professional artists with disability emphasize that they do not identify themselves as disabled persons who engage in art as therapy (Barnes, 2003). In disability arts, disability becomes a valuable and significant subjective asset, not a burden or problem to overcome (Sandahl, 2018; Solvang, 2012; Stöckl, 2014). Disability arts as a cultural movement has empowered artists with disabilities to express their demand to be "equal but different" creatively (Stöckl, 2014, p. 39). It is seen as a form of professionalism by artists with disabilities since they are considered to be artists primarily rather than people with disabilities. There is little literature specifically discussing professionalization in disability arts in terms of definition or career progression.

Research Approach

Case Study Setting: Restless Dance Theatre

Restless Dance Theatre Incorporated (hereafter, Restless), established in 1991, is a nonprofit organization located in Adelaide, a city of 1.3 million people in South Australia. Restless is an award-winning, contemporary dance company. It developed from a Carclew Youth Arts Centre project with a strong education character. Its mission is to present "unexpectedly real" dance theater works in multiple media in order to develop audience appreciation of the arts, nationally and internationally (Restless Dance Theatre, 2019). Restless is an integrated dance company, meaning that it works with dancers with and without disabilities, either physical or intellectual. Some dancers are in wheelchairs, others are partially blind while still others have intellectual disabilities. Restless creates collaborative "outstanding inclusive work informed by disability" with their artists enlivening and diversifying Australian dance (Restless Dance Theatre, 2016, p. 2).

One of their award-winning performances, *Intimate Space*, is a site-specific dance theater production that involves a series of experiential site-specific solo and duet works within a hotel. The sites include the hotel lobby, bedroom, kitchen, laundry, and bar, each of which represents a transient everyday business experience in a hotel. A group of ten audience members are simultaneously invited to become immersed in the sites, guided by an evocative soundscape and choreography delivered by performers of different physical and intellectual abilities. *Intimate Space* delivers challenging themes of visibility, authority, self-worth, and relationships *informed by* disability rather than being *about disability* (Restless Dance Theatre, 2019).

Intimate Space was extremely well received and enjoyed a sell-out season and five-star reviews for its novelty, creativity, and quality when it first premiered at the Adelaide Festival 2017, one of the world's major annual arts festivals and a curated preeminent cultural event in Australia. Subsequently, it was invited to the 2018 Bleach* The Gold Coast Festival, as well as the 2019 Seoul Street Arts Festival in South Korea, with both events boosting the national and international profiles of Restless. Table 12.1 illustrates the trajectory of *Intimate Space* together with selected critics' reviews.

Table 12.1 Trajectory of Intimate Space

Year	Stage	Location	Specification	Selected Critic Reviews
2017	Adelaide Festival	Adelaide, Australia	Curated national festival	"5 STARS. Innovative, potent, bold and beautiful, Intimate Space is an extraordinary and highly entertaining experience." *Limelight*, 3 Mar 2017.
2018	Bleach* Festival 2018 as part of the Commonwealth Games Arts and Culture Program	Gold Coast, Australia	Curated national festival	"*Intimate Space* is a beautifully crafted piece of theater—tender, witty, challenging, and whimsical." *Dance Australia*, April 10, 2018
2019	Seoul Street Arts Festival	Seoul, South Korea	Curated International festival	"An elegant and humorous performance, *Intimate space* was presented at the Seoul Street Arts Festival by 4 Korean and 8 Australian artists with disability. . . . it invites audiences to a hotel. . . . Such artistic exchange develops the capacity of individual artists as well as creating more opportunities for Korean artists to be showcased to international audiences." *Kukminilbo*, October 2, 2019

Table 12.2 Professional and Public Workshops

	Category	Specification	Age	Female/Male	With Disability	Without Disability	Total Number
Company membership by invitation only	The Company	Core dancers	18 to 35	17%	4	2	6
	Impulse	Young artists group	15 to 26	75%	7	1	8
	Junction	Graduates from Impulse	26+	40%	10	0	10
Public workshops	Central	A series of charged dance workshops	15 to 26	67%	13	2	15
	Links	A series of charged dance theater workshops	8–14	60%	10	0	10
	Total	5 Professional and public workshops			44	5	49

Table 12.2 summarizes the professional and public workshops provided by Restless, and their specification, target age range, gender distribution, and as to whether the participating dancers are with or without disability.

The core dancers in the company are 18 to 35 years of age while the younger dancers in Impulse are aged 15 to 26. Restless also provides an additional program for those who are 26 years of age or older, with the assistance of the federal government-initiated National Disability Insurance Scheme (NDIS), which provides financial support to individuals with disabilities.

Restless supports the professional development of their artists. From 2008 to 2016, Restless presented a *Debut: The dancers direct* series each year which presented five short works directed by the Restless Youth and Senior Company dancers with intellectual disability. *Debut: The dancers direct* provided an opportunity for the dancers to showcase their choreographed work and gain experience in directing while receiving guidance and direct feedback from their mentors. Restless also pays their professional artists who are invited as company members on a per project basis, and six out of 12 employed tutors are company dancers with disability (as of 2020). Some dancers with disabilities have moved on from Restless and are performing as independent artists at other dance or theater companies.

Key remunerated back-of-house staff include the artistic director, artistic manager, company manager, and development and marketing managers. The volunteer board of nine brings together skills in law, disability, education, community development, philanthropy, choreography, marketing, management, and festivals. The turnover is less than A$1 million per year;

nonetheless, the 2017 annual report includes a long list of supporters and sponsors, including government agencies, individuals, and businesses.

Restless believes that the individuality of their artists is a major strength of the company. They may not fit the stereotypical dancer image reflected by traditional and classic art forms such as ballet, but Restless considers that their different qualities create exquisite performance experiences that have the capacity to surprise audiences by "their astounding beauty and vigorous creativity" (Restless Dance Theatre, 2019). The Restless web site further states that:

> Restless has developed a way of working that produces unique, distinctive and striking dance through a process that nurtures the creative voices of the performers, artists and participants. We offer life-changing opportunities for young people through exposure to high quality arts experiences and significant professional development opportunities. Our hope is to continue to transform lives, touch audiences, inspire greatness and help to shift perceptions about disability well into the future.
>
> (Restless Dance Theatre, 2019)

Data Collection and Analysis

A case study provides an interpretive framework in a domain where there is little research and the phenomena under study are poorly understood (Eisenhardt, 1989; Fujimoto et al., 2013; Yin, 2014). A qualitative methodology is often used in order to obtain a deep and rich understanding of the context of the arts and disability. Interviews comprise the principal focus of this study. We interviewed volunteer board members, staff, artists, and industry leaders of Restless, with and without disabilities. Interviewee demographics are provided in Table 12.3. Each interview lasted around 45 minutes and was recorded and transcribed. Interviews were analyzed thematically, according to themes that emerged from the other sources including observations, related documents from web sites, media material, strategic plans, internal business materials, and annual reports, and the results were triangulated (Rentschler et al., 2021a, 2021b). These related sources illuminate how Restless introduced dance and disability to its industry leaders. This study was undertaken with university ethics approval. Restless Dance Theatre staff and dancers have approved this case study.

Findings

Professionalization in Disability Arts

The study finds three significant factors influencing the process of professionalization in disability arts at the individual and organizational levels: (1) Artistic development; (2) establishing both individual and organizational reputation and recognition; and (3) changing public perceptions by breaking down disability stereotypes.

Table 12.3 Profile of Interview Participants

	Category	Alias	Disability	Profession
1	Board member	Amy	No	Philanthropy manager
2	Board member	Celine	No	Academic
3	Board member	Nash	No	Lawyer
4	Board member	Sam	No	Lawyer
5	Industry leader	Lilly	Yes	Chair, inclusive arts organization, with disability
6	Industry leader	Vicky	No	CEO, inclusive arts organization
7	Industry leader	Janet	No	Former chair, arts manager
8	Industry leader	Mark	Yes	Director, disability arts related organization, with disability
9	Industry leader	Tina	No	CEO, arts funding body
10	Industry leader	Cathy	No	CEO, Industry partner
11	Carer	Morag	No	Carer, Raylene
12	Artist	Raylene	Yes	Performer, with disability
13	Artist	Moses	Yes	Performer, with disability
14	Staff	Nathan	No	Company Manager
15	Staff	Mary	Yes	Artistic director, with disability
16	Staff	Bessie	No	Marketing and fundraising executive
17	Staff	Rosemary	No	Artistic Manager

Artistic Development

Respondents believed that engaging with therapeutic arts influences the artistic capacity of artists with disabilities (Dirth & Branscombe, 2017; Evans et al., 2017; Solvang, 2018). Artistic capacity is developed through funding accessibility and inclusive environmental settings. Mark, an external stakeholder, suggested that disability arts are a development of therapeutic arts. While not wishing to denigrate or belittle the value of therapeutic arts, as they create a supportive environment to enable artists with disabilities to develop their artistic potential, he recognizes their limitations.

> Disability arts has come from a place of therapy. Keep them busy, give them something to do. I don't want to disparage that there's therapeutic value. But it's more how we create an environment that supports deaf and disabled artists to flourish and grow.
> (Mark, stakeholder, director at a disability arts organization)

Five interviewees, including board members, external stakeholders, and artistic staff, explained that disability arts organizations are confronted with challenging factors in their efforts to move forward, beyond merely therapeutic or recreational arts, in developing artistic skills and capabilities. For example, there is a shortage of trained dancers while prejudice remains a barrier. Furthermore, Mary, an artistic director, was concerned that they need to train more young artists to improve their technical skills and quality of performance.

> We've had a stable group of young performers, up to 26. They are now becoming seniors. So, it's about working with those younger dancers, to build their technique and performance skill, so that they are the next cohort to come through.
>
> (Mary, staff, artistic director)

However, four interviewees agreed that financial support is a challenge for the sustainability of the artistic program. Tina, the CEO of an arts funding body, explains that the additional cost of having a paid carer to support artists with disabilities can be a financial challenge for them and their families, despite government funding (e.g., NDIS). For example, some artists with disabilities need personal assistance, such as personal care, drop-off, and pick-up. Such support is a key ingredient in empowering artists with disabilities. Professional capacity development of artists with disabilities might be limited without such assistance from their carers. "A simple challenge would be the financial cost of additional support workers" (Tina, stakeholder, CEO of an arts funding body).

Restless has provided consistent opportunities for artistic development despite these challenges. Rosemary, an artistic manager, and Mary, an artistic director, both suggest that Restless creates a supportive and positive environment for artists with disabilities by providing creative and broad opportunities within the company as well as externally. They also believe that Restless creates a direct or alternative pathway for young people with disabilities to become independent artists.

> The dancers would often follow a dancer without disability. Whereas, Mary [the artistic director] really encourages independence in the dance... encouraging them to become makers, artists in their own right, and be responsible for their programs.
>
> (Rosemary, staff, artistic manager)

Mary also notes: "Some of our dancers are starting to do work outside Restless. They can see a direct pathway in the arts for people with disability as performers" (staff, artistic director).

Raylene and Moses, both artists with disabilities, believe that their experiences working with Restless, as well as other national and international resident opportunities, have not only improved their artistic skills but also enhanced their professional careers. For example, Raylene points out that her skills have expanded from dance performance to also add teaching dance. She is now studying at the university to challenge herself further. Morag, the carer of Raylene, adds that Raylene now enjoys improved independence, self-confidence and self-determination. "Restless enhances my skills to do teaching as well as dancing in the theater area. I've been doing teaching at Restless" (Raylene, artist with disability). "It [Restless] offered Raylene the opportunity for independence . . . it adds self-confidence. . . . It helped her to make changes" (Morag, carer for Raylene).

Janet, a former chair of Restless, and Mary both agree that some partnership between parents of artists with disabilities and a professional tutor is critical in order to extend the artistic skills of the individual artists with disability. Janet, however, states that the company should not be expected to function as quasi-parents of children with disability in order to improve their professional development.

> Our performers need to have the highest skilled tutors, to build on technique. If we feel we need to have a conversation with the parents, to see if there's a holistic approach for both families and us, we do so. They become independent.
>
> (Mary, staff, artistic director)

"There had to be a lot of letting go of some of the functions of the parent that we typically see in parents with children with disability" (Janet, stakeholder, former chair).

In summary, there are four significant findings regarding artistic development at the individual and organizational levels: (1) The company provides creative and performing opportunities for artists with disability as a pathway to developing their professional practice; (2) the company creates opportunities for artistic skills and technique development not only by involving professional tutors but also by working collaboratively with parents of artists with disability; (3) the company and individual artists with disabilities aim to deliver quality and authentic performances to audiences at a professional level; and (4) individual artists build their independence, self-confidence, and self-determination through their artistic development as independent artists.

Establishing Reputation and Recognition

The findings indicate that establishing the reputation of, and recognition of, artists with disability as professionals is a critical component of professionalization in disability arts at both individual and organizational levels. The essence of establishing recognition as professionals depends on how artists with disabilities identify themselves since showcasing the artistic value and integrity of artists with disability can improve public perceptions of disability. Mary and Nathan, company manager, argue that artists with disability identify themselves as artists rather than as individuals with disability who participate in the arts. "Participants envisage themselves as professional dancers, which wasn't possible before" (Nathan, staff, company manager). "At Restless, they are seen as artists. And that's something that I have quite a passion about. I joke saying I get wheeled out. I get asked to talk quite regularly, if someone's dealing with disability" (Mary, staff, artistic director).

Janet, a former chair of Restless, explains that artists with disability do not deny having a disability or feel ashamed of identifying themselves as such; they are proud of disability as part of their identity. "They were not trying to reform or reshape the person with disability into something else. They were celebrating the person with disability, for their expression to be witnessed and observed as something that was as eloquent as mainstream ballet" (Janet, stakeholder, former chair).

Restless commits to offering a diverse creative experience for audiences through performances presented collaboratively by artists with and without disabilities; this is something that mainstream dance companies are unable to do. Sam, a board member, proudly describes the quality of performance that Restless delivers to audiences as authentic and professional rather than as primarily an artistic outcome of therapy. Bessie, a marketing and fundraising executive, agrees with Sam and argues that the quality of the performance genuinely reflects the artists' disabilities. "Restless, it's a place to give people with disability that don't necessarily get opportunities in mainstream dance companies to perform with creative integrity. It's not just therapy for people with disability but a legitimate forum to perform" (Sam, board member). "The works that we make come from the performers" (Bessie, marketing and fundraising executive)

At the organizational level, financial management and ways of utilizing funding are significant in relation to building reputation and recognition as a professional arts organization. Depending on how the organization funding has been spent, management intent can be interpreted in different ways, but the outcome of funding usage can also be varied. Tina, CEO of an arts funding body, explains that the funding body assesses a group's financial needs based on the expenditure plan for artistic development, including artistic programs, management, and administration for artistic projects. "They present a budget and a program to us each year. We manage an assessment process which examines the quality of the artistic program, management decisions and governance" (Tina, stakeholder, CEO at an arts funding body). Funding is supposed to be spent on the artistic development of artists with disability rather than on care or support for specifically disability matters. Nash, a board member, explains that the company aims to create a high-level reputation as a professional dance theater under the guidance of the qualified artistic director. He adds, proudly, that the company has been nominated for multiple awards.

The role of Restless can't be fulfilled by any one individual. Restless' role is to create high quality dance theater informed by disability. Restless is getting stronger and stronger under the guidance of the artistic director. The artistic quality that's coming out of the company is incredible. We've been nominated for numerous awards.

(Nash, chair of the board)

Celine, a board member, also states that the company pursues the consistent development of artistic potential to raise the artistic quality of performances and to reach broader audiences in events at national and international stages.

We never envisioned it being exactly what it is today, but it continues to grow and develop. It hasn't yet hit its potential. It continues to push the boundaries. *Intimate Space* and the Commonwealth Games are good examples of that.

(Celine, board member)

Establishing a high-level, professional reputation for any company is challenging, but it is an important component of building professional value at the individual and organizational levels. In this study, we found three significant approaches by which individual artists with disabilities and the company integrate in order to build their reputations and recognition as professionals: (1) Individual artists identify themselves as artists with artistic integrity; (2) management seeks to be well-structured in terms of finance, funding expenditure, and artistic programs, including those for professional artistic staff; and (3) individual artists with disabilities and the company pursue the consistent development of artistic potential by presenting their artistic performances in national and international events.

Changing Perceptions by Breaking Stereotypes

This study demonstrates that for the process of professionalization in disability arts, changing the stereotypical perceptions of the public toward disability in term of its professionalism is significant. There is a gradual positive change toward the better understanding of disability and greater social inclusion, although public perception of disability is still strongly rooted in socially devalued images of people with disabilities as incapable or dysfunctional (Aubry et al., 2013; Solvang, 2012). Sometimes stakeholders bring their own stereotypical views on disability to a performance. Restless sees its role as changing such views by enabling them to view joyous, quality performances, thus overcoming what is expected through unique storytelling and even sometimes the imperfection of performance. This approach creates an aesthetic value for their performances. For example, Mary, the artistic director, explains the audience's emotional journey to overcome the tendency to focus on the performers' disabilities rather than on their art. Nash, chair of the Board, shares his thoughts about how the label of disability becomes a social stigma, which tends to lower audience expectations of the artistic quality of performances by artists with disability. He points out, however, that audiences are surprised at the quality of artistic performance when they experience it. "They do have an emotional journey. The performance made the audience question their perception of art, but also of disability" (Mary, artistic director).

> Disability has a stigma in society, and so people going to a performance that's informed by disability or viewing art by people with disability come to it not expecting as much. And universally, when I've been in the role of audience, or in a place where I'm viewing the audience's reaction, people are universally surprised at the quality.
>
> (Nash, board member)

Sam, a Board Member, shares her views as an audience member by explaining that people in general do not expect people with disabilities to be proficient at dancing; rather they might come to Restless to see more than just ballet.

> You're coming to it with a different perspective. I, as an audience member, I'm just being honest. Sure, I hope I don't come across as being putrid or anything like that but I suppose I'm not going to a Restless Dance piece to see the ballet.
>
> (Sam, board member)

Another viewer, Cathy, points out that audience's perceptions will be improved by having more opportunities to see performances by artists with disabilities who might have particular physical and mental characteristics. Cathy suggests that anyone who makes art is an artist, and audiences eventually begin to identify artists with disabilities as professional artists rather than persons with disability working in the performing arts. Nathan agrees that the aim of broadening the public's perception of diversity in dance can create greater opportunities to come into contact with people who do not expect to see artists with disabilities.

> She provides audiences with a broader opportunity of who artists are, and what they might look like. . . . It's the audience that gives people a broader look at who they can identify with, as an artist. . . . People have different definitions of the term artist, but certainly, everyone performing onstage, or engaging in making art, is an artist.
>
> (Cathy, stakeholder)

> So that means that in terms of being able to widen people's perceptions of what dance can be, it put us into contact with more people. It put us into contact with people who were not expecting to see us. . . .
> I'm always really impressed by the people without disability who come

to Restless. They are extraordinary people. They're not scared of disability, they usually have some familiarity with disability, probably for family reasons. But they are open and supportive.

(Nathan, company manager)

Vicky, CEO of an inclusive arts organization, explains the nature of the culture in the arts sector as a "competitive cannibalistic culture" and laments the lack of innovation and collaboration that prohibits the inclusion of artists with disabilities and the cultivation of their professional careers. Such a view, held at least by some leaders in arts organizations, highlights the tensions that exist in arts organizations that need to be navigated by those who seek to make their careers in them. It also indicates that professionalization is still developing in the arts ecology, including in disability arts organizations. Lilly, chair of an inclusive arts organization, points out despite Australia being a culturally diverse nation, there are few artistic roles for people who do not fit traditional views of normality. "The arts are based on a competitive cannibalistic culture where one survives on the back of another's failure. There is a lack of innovation in the sector to collaborate" (Vicky, Stakeholder, CEO of an inclusive arts organization).

We are a culturally diverse nation. Why aren't the diverse people in our society getting artistic roles? They aren't seen. . . . The arts are integral to the way you look at the world. It's not about telling stories or something you watch. There is a disjoint in our society.

(Lilly, stakeholder, chair of an inclusive arts organization)

Breaking the stereotypical perception of disability is the greatest challenge to improving the professional status of artists with disability. Professional artistic staff and stakeholders interviewed, including artistic directors and board members, agree that the key to making the change is presenting high-quality artistic performances by artists with disability. Restless provides a high-quality artistic experience, including performances by artists with and without disabilities and diverse artistic interpretations. Mary, the artistic director, emphasizes that presenting and celebrating diversity in mainstream theater is an important step for the Australian artistic landscape.

The role of Restless, is to celebrate diversity on stage. We have an important role, in mainstream theater, to have people with disability represented. But also, to present work where the artists are celebrated in the best possible light for their skill. It has a role in the Australian artistic landscape.

(Mary, Artistic director)

Janet, a former chair of an inclusive arts organization, states that professional, quality performance and creative expression by artists with disabilities play a key role in shifting people's attitudes and changing prejudices toward disability in society. Amy, a philanthropy manager, also comments that the high level of the artistic work performed by artists with disabilities is inspirational and can challenge people's perceptions.

> Professional, quality performance and creative expression by people with disability is helpful in society. We can provide a retrospective gaze on that, if we look back at some of our famous composers and visual artists. It plays a key role in shifting people's attitudes towards disability, shifting prejudice.
>
> (Janet, former chair)

> What Mary does in terms of her choreography is amazing. They're on a world stage, they're in festivals and they just lift the soul. So then, we're not talking something where they're just doing, and it's not, the whole principle they do is not to educate, just to educate, it's to inspire. They are presenting work at a level that is actually inspirational and does make you think and does challenge your perceptions.
>
> (Amy, philanthropy manager)

Celine, a board member, points out the importance of positive interactions between people from diverse backgrounds, including social, cultural, physical, mental, and sexual diversity. Celine also argues that people should stop looking at disability as a tragedy since living with an impairment is not tragic or something to feel sorry about.

> It's having that interaction. That's one of the things that Restless does. . . . And it stops people looking at disability as being a tragedy, which is one of the key things I teach. Living with an impairment is not a tragedy, it's not something to feel sorry for, we don't want pity.
>
> (Celine, board member)

Changing perceptions of disability is a long-term project for individuals with disabilities as well as for the community. This study identified three significant suggestions or arguments from the interviews with professional staff and stakeholders. Those suggestions entail changing public perceptions by (1) creating more opportunities for artists with disability to perform and present to audiences; (2) presenting quality artistic productions and creative expression by diverse artists with and without disability in mainstream theater; and (3) creating opportunities for positive interactions between audiences and artists from diverse backgrounds, including those with social, cultural, physical, mental, and sexual diversity.

Discussion

The findings identified commonalities and differences in the ways in which professionalization in disability arts was reviewed compared to earlier studies. These themes emerged when conducting interviews with a variety of people with and without disabilities. Four components of professionalization in the arts were identified: education and training; career progression; action of creation; and cultural capital (Bain, 2005; Svensson, 2015; Throsby & Petetskaya, 2017; Wyszomirski & Chang, 2017). The themes of artistic development and establishing recognition and reputation identified in our findings align with the two components of education and training and career progression in professionalizing the careers of artists with disabilities at the individual and organizational levels. The key agenda in disability arts is to shift the perception of disability from being culturally devalued to being socially and culturally valued through the professionalization of disability arts at individual and organizational levels.

Developing professionalization in disability arts can be an effective way to shift negative perceptions of disability (Collins et al., 2022; Fujimoto et al., 2013). The study discovered two significant differences in order to develop professionalization in the disability arts compared to professionalization in the arts more generally. First, the role of an inclusive arts organization is critical and must operate in a multifunctional manner for artists with disabilities. Inclusive arts organizations are not only employers for artists with disabilities but also provide professional training services as an alternative career pathway, replacing colleges and universities. They support the artistic development of artists with disabilities by providing training, mentoring, and networking. They also play a producer role in creating performing opportunities nationally and internationally through marketing and promotion. Second, the involvement of individual supporters (e.g., paid carers and family members) of artists with disabilities is significant because these artists may require extra personal support given their physical condition or (and) cognitive challenges.

The study found that the public understanding and perceptions of professionalization in disability arts require improvement. Furthermore, longitudinal research on the progression toward developing public perceptions of disability arts may be valuable for the professional development of disability arts at the individual and organizational levels.

Conclusion

Based on a case study of Restless Dance Theatre, this chapter highlights the important role that inclusive arts organizations play in promoting the professional development of artists with disabilities. The role of inclusive arts organizations is complex and multifunctional and is intertwined with that of their personal supporters, paid carers, or family members of artists with disabilities in the promotion of their professional artistic careers. The nature of disability is complex, and the role that these other stakeholders play in alleviating the physical and cognitive challenges of artists with disabilities is critical. Nevertheless, the artistic quality of performances presented by artists with disabilities cannot be compared or reviewed based on the physical or cognitive conditions of the artist. The professional recognition and reputation of artists with disabilities should be based on the artistic value and quality of the individual act of creation, not on the disability with which artists live.

Finally, the study argues that improving public understanding and perception toward disability is a major long-term project and one that constitutes a significant challenge in relation to the development and professionalization of disability arts. All interviewees emphasized the need to create more opportunities to demonstrate the artistic and cultural value of disability arts to a wider audience. Understandings of professionalization have broadened and varied as cultures and structures of society have changed. Public perceptions of disability, however, have not improved in line with this wider social change. These are two facets of professionalization juxtaposed one against the other in the realm of the arts and disability. Similar challenges may confront emerging contemporary artists who are still developing their reputation and struggling to build professional careers (Fillis et al., 2015; Lee, Fraser et al., 2018; Lee, Fillis et al., 2018). Diversifying arts and culture can be an effective way of improving public perceptions and familiarizing people with the diversity of humankind by presenting artists working with diverse social, cultural, and physical conditions.

References

Argyle, E. (2003). Care study: Art for health describes a scheme to use art therapy to help those at risk of mental illness. *Mental Health Nursing, 23*(3), 4–6.

Aubry, T., Flynn, R. J., Virley, B., & Neri, J. (2013). Social role valorisation in community mental health housing: Does it contribute to the community integration and life satisfaction of people with psychiatric disabilities? *Journal of Community Psychology, 41*, 218–235.

Bain, A. (2005). Constructing an artistic identity. *Work, Employment and Society, 19*(1), 25–46. https://doi.org/10.1177/0950017005051280

Barnes, C. (2003). *Effecting change: Disability, culture and art* [Conference presentation]. Finding the Spotlight Conference, Institute for the Performing Arts, Liverpool.

Chandler, E., Changfoot, N., Rice, C., Lamarre, A., & Mykitiuk, R. (2018). Cultivating disability arts in Ontario. *Review of Education, Pedagogy, and Cultural Studies, 40*(3), 249–264. https://doi.org/10.1080/10714413.2018.1472482

Cohen-Gewerc, E. (2013). *Serious leisure and individuality*. McGill-Queen's University Press.

Collins, A., Rentschler, R., Williams, K., & Azmat, F. (2022). Exploring barriers to social inclusion for disabled people: Perspectives from the performing arts. *Journal of Management & Organization, 28*(2), 308–328. https://doi.org/10.1017/jmo.2021.48

Currie, G. (2010). Actual art, possible art, and art's definition. *Journal of Aesthetics and Art Criticism, 68*(3), 235–241. https://doi.org/10.1111/j.1540-6245.2010.01415

Dickie, G. (1974). *Art and the aesthetic*. Cornell University Press.

DiMaggio, P. J. (1987). *Managers of the arts: Careers and opinions of senior administrators of US art museums, symphony orchestras, resident theaters, and local arts agencies.* Seven Locks Press.

Dirth, T. P., & Branscombe, N. R. (2017). Disability models affect disability policy support through awareness of structural discrimination. *Journal of Social Issues,* 73(2), 413–442. https://doi.org/10.1111/josi.12224

Eisenhardt, K. M. (1989). Building theories from case study research. *Academy of Management Review, 14*(4), 532–550.

Evans, T., Bellon, M., & Matthews, B. (2017). Leisure as a human right: An exploration of people with disabilities' perceptions of leisure, arts and recreation participation through Australian community access services. *Annals of Leisure Research,* 20(3), 331–348. https://doi.org/10.1080/11745398.2017.1307120

Fillis, I., Lee, B., & Fraser, I. (2015). Measuring the cultural value of the royal Scottish academy new contemporaries exhibition as a platform for emerging artists. *Cultural Trends, 24*(3), 245–255.

Fokt, S. (2017). The cultural definition of art. *Metaphilosophy, 48*(4), 404. https://doi.org/10.1111/meta.12251

Fujimoto, Y., Rentschler, R., Le, H., Edwards, D., & Härtel, C. (2013). Lessons learned from community organizations: Inclusion of people with disabilities and others. *British Journal of Management, 25*(3), 518–527.

Lee, B., Fillis, I., & Lehman, K. (2018). Art, science and organisational interactions: Exploring the value of artist residencies on campus. *Journal of Business Research,* 85, 444–451. https://doi.org/10.1016/j.jbusres.2017.10.022

Lee, B., Fraser, I., & Fillis, I. (2018). Creative futures for new contemporary artists: opportunities and barriers. *International Journal of Arts Management,* 20(2), 9–19.

Lee, B., Rentschler, R., & Park, S. E. (2022). Connect2Abilities: Staging virtual intercultural collaboration during COVID-19. In *Curating access* (pp. 45–58). Routledge.

Monseré, A. (2016). The charge from psychology and art's definition. *Theoria, 82*(3), 256–273. https://doi.org/10.1111/theo.12093

Pitman, A. (2012). Professionalism and professionalisation. In E. A. Kinsella & A. Pitman (Eds.), *Phronesis as professional knowledge* (pp. 131–146). Brill.

Rentschler, R., Lee, B., & Fillis, I. (2021a). Towards an integrative framework for arts governance. *International Journal of Arts Management, 24*(1), 17–31.

Rentschler, R., Lee, B., & Subramaniam, N. (2021b). Calculative practices and sociopolitical tensions: A historical analysis of entertainment, arts and accounting in a government agency. *Accounting History, 26*(1), 80–101.

Restless Dance Theatre. (2019). *Our company.* http://restlessdance.org/restless-dance-theatre/

Restless Dance Theatre. (2016). *Annual report.* www.acnc.gov.au/charity/charities/a8bff630-39af-e811-a962-000d3ad24a0d/documents/

Richards, M., Lawthom, R., & Runswick-Cole, K. (2019). Community-based arts research for people with learning disabilities: Challenging misconceptions about learning disabilities. *Disability & Society, 34*(2), 204–227. https://doi.org/10.1080/09687599.2018.1522243

Sandahl, C. (2018). Disability art and culture: A model for imaginative ways to integrate the community. *Alter, 12*(2), 79–93. https://doi.org/10.1016/j.alter.2018.04.004

Solvang, P. K. (2012). From identity politics to dismodernism? Changes in the social meaning of disability art. *Alter*, 6(3), 178–187. https://doi.org/10.1016/j.alter.2012.05.002

Solvang, P. K. (2018). Between art therapy and disability aesthetics: A sociological approach for understanding the intersection between art practice and disability discourse. *Disability & Society*, 33(2), 238–253. https://doi.org/10.1080/096875 99.2017.1392929

Stöckl, A. (2014). Common humanity and shared destinies: Looking at the disability arts movement from an anthropological perspective. *Anthropology in Action*, 21(1), 36–43. https://doi.org/10.3167/aia.2014.210107

Svensson, L. G. (2015). Occupations and professionalism in art and culture. *Professions and Professionalism*, 5(2), 1–14. https://doi.org/10.7577/pp.1328

Throsby, D., & Petetskaya, K. (2017). *Making art works: An economic study of professional artists in Australia*. Australia Council for the Arts. https://australiacouncil. gov.au/advocacy-and-research/making-art-work/#:~:text=Overview-,Making%20 Art%20Work%3A%20An%20Economic%20Study%20of%20Professional%20 Artists%20in,funding%20from%20the%20Australia%20Council

Vick, R. M., & Sexton-Radek, K. (2008). Community-based art studios in Europe and the United States: A comparative study. *Art Therapy*, 25(1), 4–10. https://doi.org/10.1080/07421656.2008.10129353

Wyszomirski, M. J., & Chang, W. (2017). Professional self-structuration in the arts: Sustaining creative careers in the 21st century. *Sustainability*, 9(6), 1035. https://doi.org/10.3390/su9061035

Yin, R. K. (2014). *Case study research: Design and methods* (5th ed.). Sage Publications.

13 Making a Buck Through Blockchain

Artist Entrepreneurship in the Artworld

Minha Lee

Introduction

This chapter considers how recent blockchain innovations might change the current practices of visual artists, especially since they provide entrepreneurial working solutions. Various changes in contemporary society increase the need to rethink whether existing meanings and principles in the visual arts field are suitable for the twenty-first-century context, and the meaning of "professional visual artist" is no exception. Discussion on how the term should be systemically constructed in the visual arts context in the modern world is limited (Carvalho et al., 2018; Chang & Wyszomirski, 2015; Thom, 2016a, 2016b; Wyszomirski & Chang, 2017). Additionally, fundamental questions regarding the support structure for the professional development of visual artists remain unaddressed (Thom, 2015, 2016a, 2016b; Wyszomirski & Chang, 2017). New discussions are necessary to define the meaning and processes of becoming a professional visual artist in the digital age and provide a more helpful environment for sustainable career development.

This chapter proposes emerging blockchain technology as an option to consider in these discussions. Since the adoption of blockchain is in its infancy and its application is in the experimental phase, this chapter introduces a discussion on the broader conceptual influences of blockchain in the visual arts field rather than an assessment of its technical performance or effectiveness. It proposes that the core philosophy of blockchain, namely decentralization (Reijers & Coeckelbergh, 2018), makes it possible to rethink the visual arts market system in the digital age. The application of blockchain in the visual arts suggests a new way for the production and distribution of artworks and provides a context to facilitate the creation of new types of business models for visual artists. This chapter underlines how blockchain helps artists take more direct control of their financial rewards by enabling direct artist-to-collector transactions without intermediaries.

Blockchain literally refers to a virtual chain of blocks used to store information that is operated by an online, peer-to-peer computer network (Tapscott et al., 2016). It gained its reputation as a "get rich quick" tool (Bambrough,

DOI: 10.4324/9781003138693-15

2019) through the foundational technology of the best-known cryptocurrency, Bitcoin, which recorded its highest price of nearly $65,000 in 2021. However, beyond the usage of blockchain as an investment tool or technical infrastructure, this chapter focuses on the basic feature of blockchain that challenges traditional centralized norms and standards in the exercise of power in the visual arts.

This chapter introduces emerging blockchain-based art projects for artists and arts managers, as well as researchers, to identify new opportunities associated with blockchain in the contemporary art market. It provides useful information for managerial practice, given that blockchain has a potential to be an alternative service platform for artists, offering not only a method of raising money but also opportunities to extend relationships with customers and other stakeholders. The content of this chapter is as follows: First, it explains how the concept of "the professional" has been constructed in the visual arts market system. Second, it explores the transformative impact of blockchain in terms of the development and expansion of the current art market. Third, it introduces blockchain-based art projects that are shaping new opportunities as exemplary case studies: DADA, a community platform for visual artists; CryptoPunks, a new form of digital art; and Maecenas, an online art auction platform. Finally, it discusses the implications of integrating blockchain into the visual arts field in terms of expanding entrepreneurial opportunities for artists in the changing landscape of a technology-rich environment.

Career Pathways of Professional Visual Artists

The meaning of the term professional varies, but in a broad sense, it is defined as a person who earns a living from a certain activity, as opposed to an amateur or hobbyist (Abbott, 1988; Stichweh, 1997). In a technical sense, professionals are generally required to have a license authorized by a governing body to prove a certain level of quality in their activities (Bagchi, 2011; Freidson, 2001; Noordegraaf, 2015; Svensson, 2015). In the field of visual arts, there is uncertainty regarding the types of capabilities needed to become a professional artist (Beck, 2008; Thom, 2016a). Someone who paints, draws, or makes sculptures can call themselves an artist because becoming an artist requires no official exam or certificate. What, then, does being a professional artists precisely mean?

While no official license is necessary, there exists a "professionalization" process in the visual arts field (Evetts, 2014; Flisbäck & Lund, 2015). Professionalization indicates an ongoing process through which members of a particular occupation try to prove special competencies to achieve the status of professional (Evetts, 2014). In the visual arts field, professionalization is strongly dependent on the norms and conventions of the so-called artworld (Danto, 1964; Dickie, 1974). The art world, consisting of artists, art galleries, collectors, critics, museums, and academics, functions as an "interpretive community" (Danto, 1964) that establishes particular criteria to assess both artists and artworks, influenced by its ideological, political, and economic beliefs (Bourdieu, 1993). These standards are operated as the "field of power" (Bourdieu, 1993) by which the exclusive boundaries of professional artists are defined and maintained (Svensson, 2015).

The place where the professionalization takes place is the art market. The art market is divided into a primary market, where an artist sells their artwork directly to dealers or galleries for the first time, and a secondary market, where the resale of artworks is usually made through auction houses (Chong, 2005; Goodwin, 2008). In the art market, the career of an artist progresses through a multi-level selection process carried out by the artworld elites, who validate and legitimize artworks through exhibitions, critical appraisal, and private and public purchases (McIntyre, 2004; Jyrämä & Äyväri, 2006). In this selection process, various forces, directed by the members of the artworld, shape the evaluation criteria that eventually affect the value and reputation of artists and artworks (Jyrämä & Äyväri, 2009). This applies particularly to "key" or "star" intermediaries in the art market who promote and connect their affiliated artists to collectors and institutions (McIntyre, 2004, p. 4), and exercise influence on building their artists' brand and market power (Heinlich, 2012; Jyrämä, 2002; Thom, 2016b). Thus, in visual arts, the term professional references the result of a particular nexus of interactions and relationships, and economic and aesthetic interests in the art market (Svensso, 2015). Consequently, for those who pursue a career as professional artists, it is crucial "to be seen, discovered, and recognized to be given an opportunity" in the art market (Svensson, 2015, p. 4).

Constructing a New Identity: The Professional Visual Artist

Because the visual arts market is controlled by those whose voices have a great influence on art trends and trade in contemporary visual art, only a few selected artists who meet the criteria of the art world find opportunities to show and sell their works (Abbing, 2002). Throughout the history of artistic endeavor, artists like Paul Cezanne, Vincent van Gogh, and Paul Gauguin, considered great masters today, were unrecognized by the art world in their time and died in poverty. Today's situation is not different. While many artists spend their time, money, and energy in creating artworks, the majority struggle to even show their works to audiences (Thom, 2016b).

Critics claim that the "winner takes all" (Thom, 2016b; Del Valle, 2019) structure of the contemporary visual arts market is the major reason for the unstable financial position of artists (Frenette, 2017; Gerber & Childress, 2017; Menger, 1999). Almost half of all recent post-war and contemporary art auction sales are by a small number of high-profile artists. In 2017, works by 25 renowned artists were sold for $1.2 billion, which accounts for 44.6% of the total $2.7 billion generated at public auctions of contemporary art worldwide. This phenomenon is driven by the increasing competition among wealthy buyers to acquire works by the most prestigious artists at the top of the market (Halperin & Kinsella, 2017). TBR's Creative & Cultural Team's report on Visual Artists Livelihood (2018) indicates that the visual artists' mean average total income in the United Kingdom was £16,500 in 2015 while that from art practice was £6,020, which represents 36% of total income. The report shows that only 3% of visual artists indicate that their income from art practice allows them to live comfortably, 7% state that it is "only barely" enough to support their living (TBR's Creative & Cultural Team, 2018, p. 2), and 90% state it is insufficient to live on. This situation explains why some authors categorize artists as "precariat" rather than professional (Flisbäck & Lund, 2015, p. 5). Artists have consistently shown poorer financial returns than other professionals, even if they hold multiple jobs (Throsby & Zednik, 2011).

The way the concept of a professional artist is developed might be the main cause of the trope of the starving artist (Abbing, 2002, 2015, 2019). To be a professional in the visual arts field is not just a case of possessing formal qualifications but also having access to the art market controlled by the art world (Thom, 2016b, p. 21). Therefore, artists need to be trained and prepared to deal with the logic of the art world that overtly highlights the symbolic value—art for art's sake—as a virtue of professional artists (Abbing, 2002; Lopez, 2015; Svensson, 2015; Throsby & Thompson, 1994).

Fine (2017) argues that an emphasis on artists' artistic identity has ironically made their professional position unstable by neglecting financial independence in the visual arts field. Abbing (2002) criticizes the fact that the myth of the solitary genius—that is, to be entirely immersed in artmaking without considering financial or material returns—is fully embraced as the ideal model of an artist. He also insists that powerful players in the art world created such myths for their own interest, thereby separating artists from the managerial and business procedures in the art market (Abbing, 2019).

Recently, some authors proposed a new discussion to redefine the identity and practice of professional artists (Flisbäck & Lund, 2015; Svensson, 2015; Thom, 2015). Contrary to the traditional notion of a professional artist, which emphasizes recognition and acceptance by the art world, this contemporary discussion centers on how artists themselves can finally survive in the art market system (Abbing, 2002; Tapscott & Tapscott, 2017; Throsby & Thompson, 1994). It proposes that being a contemporary professional artist entails not just a dedication to art but also a recognition that entrepreneurial skills are indispensable in the fiercely competitive art industry. Today's artists are urged to adopt a dynamic mindset regarding their professional identity and commitment, gaining a deeper understanding of the market's viewpoint to effectively harmonize their artistic personas with the prevailing norms, values, and expectations of the external market landscape (Wyszomirski & Chang, 2017; Thom, 2015). Through discussion, the traditional definition of the professional artist has clearly been questioned, and a suggestion has been made that entrepreneurial competencies should be considered one of the main components of professional education or training for artists (Phillips, 2010; Thom, 2015; Deresiewicz, 2015).

Considering that entrepreneurship is not only about launching a new business but also about generating new ideas and initiatives (Kaplan & Warren, 2009), artists should develop entrepreneurial skills and competencies to better recognize and realize business opportunities, as well as fine-tune their commitment and self-management strategies (Bridgstock, 2012; Pollard & Wilson, 2013; Roberts, 2012; Wyszomirski & Chang, 2017). In consideration of this, one important challenge arises—the issue of how to build up capacity for developing this new visual artist identity. This perspective has rarely been considered in the past entrepreneurial education and training research. Therefore, practical ideas on overcoming the current structural issues of the centralized art market have not been developed.

In summary, a discussion on the ways to define contemporary professional visual artists leads to a critical view on the current art market structure because the challenges and tensions in the career of artists, often posed by the artist-intermediary-collector triad, have been embedded in the art market system for a long time. Additionally, discussions on a market environment in which professional artists can reach broader audiences beyond the boundary of the current art market system are lacking. Thus, this study questions the specific environments that enable artists to access various channels to show their creative aspirations to wider audiences. It also emphasizes the need for research on the support structure, including training, identification, retraining, and reward systems, needed for the professional development of artists.

The next section, therefore, attempts to explore the solutions or recommendations that could be proposed to allow artists to identify new markets and resources for their entrepreneurial success. In so doing, the next section explores how technology assists in developing the careers of artists through case studies on blockchain-based art projects. These cases show how adopting new technologies may invigorate artists' relationships in the art market, as well as revitalize the art market itself in terms of innovation, expansion, and growth.

New Technology and New Relationships in the Visual Arts Field

Since Web 2.0 was popularized in the early 2000s, and has been influential in shaping new business models, it has involved strategies that have transformed the way in which products and services are received and consumed. Web 2.0 refers to a set of technologies that facilitate the sharing of information and knowledge online, including social media platforms, online collaboration tools, and cloud-based services, all of which are claimed to be characterized by openness, user participation, and collaboration (Murugesan, 2007). This phenomenon accelerates the disruption of the conventional business paradigm in various industries, paving the way for the development of a new business model called platform (Shah & Tripsas, 2007). Supported by numerous digital DIY tools, any individual can tap into entrepreneurial opportunities by forming a platform through independently creating and distributing new products and making a profit (Fischer & Reuber, 2011).

As such, these new technologies have provided a context facilitating new market opportunities and visions in the visual arts field. Web 2.0 has brought a new perspective to the structure of the art market by helping artists independently launch and manage their own brands. Free or low-cost digital DIY tools have helped artists directly reach collectors and generate sales without intermediaries such as galleries or dealers. Namely, the new technology has an important ramification for professional self-structuration in the art field: the ability to promote and cultivate enduring relationships with audiences and collectors is no longer the exclusive property of specific elite groups.

Nevertheless, there is a flipside. Critics of Web 2.0 question whether its applications are appropriate for putting its democratic vision into practice. As one of the representatives of Web 2.0, YouTube actively supports its users in the expression and creation of their thoughts and ideas; however, it eventually leverages these ideas and creations to strengthen its own brand (Van Dijck & Nieborg, 2009). While users seemingly have the freedom to create content and access wider opportunities to commercialize their works, in exchange for this access, social media companies sell their private data to advertisers for profit (McDonald, 2009). In essence, although the aim of Web 2.0 was to foster mutual benefits for all participants, the social media monopolies have dominated the market and distributed unfair benefits to users, resulting in inequality and imbalance (Goanta & Spanakis, 2022).

Against the backdrop of Web 2.0, expectations are growing for Web 3.0, which is seen by many as a response to some of the limitations and challenges of Web 2.0. While Web 2.0 has faced criticism for concentrating power and control among a handful of large tech corporations, Web 3.0 focuses on decentralized and distributed systems enabled by blockchain technology, artificial intelligence, and the Internet of Things (Bashir, 2018). Web 3.0 is widely recognized as having the potential to address imbalances in various sectors by eliminating intermediaries. One of the key benefits of this is the creation of new opportunities for creating, distributing, and monetizing digital content. Therefore, by leveraging blockchain technology and other Web 3.0 tools and platforms, artists are expected to gain more control over their creative output, connect with new audiences, and receive fair compensation for their contributions. This is made possible by dismantling the hierarchies that exist within the art market. The centralized power of the art market may be lessened by gradually de-linking artists from conventional norms and values of the traditional art market, and at the same time challenging the myth of professionalization in the visual arts field.

Features of Blockchain

Blockchain is an online database based on highly secure cryptographic algorithms. The core feature of blockchain is decentralization (Aitken, 2017) and it operates on a peer-to-peer computer network (De Leon & Gupta, 2017); anyone who has computing power and an Internet connection can participate in verifying and storing data in blockchain (Allen, 2017). Contrary to the traditional database controlled by a central institution, blockchain is managed by network participants, eliminating the need for an intermediary (Davidson et al., 2016). Once data are recorded in a blockchain network, the same copies of the blockchain are automatically shared by network participants globally (De Leon & Gupta, 2017). Therefore, deleting or modifying information is prohibited once information is appended to the blockchain (Deloitte & ArtTactic, 2019). Thus, blockchain has more benefits than traditional databases. Hacking blockchain is difficult because changing the content in one block is impossible without changing the whole chain of blocks (Ølnes et al., 2017). In addition, transaction fees can be cheaper than those normally managed by central authorities. The only costs incurred in blockchain are the nominal fees used to reward the participants who run a node on the blockchain network (Zhu & Zhou, 2016).

Besides its security and cost-efficiency benefits in data management, blockchain offers new solutions to traditional business models, namely smart contracts and tokenization. Smart contracts refer to computer protocols embedded in blockchain networks that automatically execute pre-arranged terms under pre-defined conditions (Nowiński & Kozma, 2017). Once smart contracts operate, revenues and funding flows are recorded in the blockchain and become open to all network users so that transactions between two parties can be made without intermediaries. Tokenization refers to the process of converting any sensitive information into specific digital codes called "tokens" (Wu et al., 2019). It enables a real-world item to have a virtual representation of itself on a blockchain for safe and secure transactions.

These technical features make blockchain an attractive technology to potentially "disintermediate and decentralize law, contracts, and government" (Allen et al., 2017, p. 3). Blockchain's potential is not constrained to its technical attributes but is increased by its philosophy, which leads "people across industries to reconsider how such an industry might be structured and organized" (MacDonald-Korth et al., 2016, p. 8). As an alternative control mechanism of data and information, blockchain could serve as an ideal setting for ensuring reliable and secure transactions. Thus, some envision that blockchain might revolutionize the existing market system and mechanisms, and provide new means to explore diverse opportunities in various fields, including the visual arts.

Blockchain and Art

The changes expected to result from blockchain in the visual arts market include (1) new ways of storing data and managing transactions; (2) new ways of monetization; and (3) new ways to invest. Traditionally, the visual arts field is relatively conservative and does not welcome change (Lopez, 2015); however, blockchain has recently gained momentum in the visual arts field when it comes to addressing problems around provenance (Deloitte & ArtTactic, 2019). Provenance refers to "the history of the whereabouts of an artwork from the day it was created by the artist to the present day" (Shindell, 2016, p. 407). Given that the authenticity of an artwork is directly related to its value, provenance is an important issue in terms of insurance, rent, and trade of artworks (Elhanani, 2018). However, the visual arts field has been a "notoriously opaque world," as it has never systematically recorded provenance (Schuetz, 2018). Considering that one of the major problems in the art market is how easily artworks can be copied and replicated, the improvement in authenticity can reduce the number of fakes and further increase the resale value of genuine artworks. Thus, blockchain is regarded as an efficient and reliable technology to ensure the provenance of artworks (Michalska, 2016; Zeilinger, 2016). Converting all the information related to an artwork into encrypted data and storing it on blockchain can keep a permanent record of the artwork and prevent it from being modified (MacDonald-Korth et al., 2016).

The leading auction house, Christie's, first announced a blockchain-based art auction in November 2018. In collaboration with Artory, a blockchain-secured art registry startup, Christie's used blockchain to register each artwork sold at the auction to track its provenance and title. Since then, discussion on the impact of blockchain on the art market has increased across media reports and public forums. New startup VerisArt launched a service that gives both sides of art transactions direct access to a history of ownership while ensuring the owner's identity remains secret, which is often an important issue for wealthy collectors with large collections. As a secure transaction solution, blockchain stores and verifies coded information across multiple computers, which replaces the role of intermediaries and helps avoid adverse effects that sometimes arise when information is managed by a single institution.

The use of blockchain to supplant intermediaries is of interest as blockchain could resolve the chronic problems of the art market structure (MacDonald-Korth et al., 2016). Most artists have been forced to go through intermediaries to participate in art transactions, including selling artworks, hosting exhibitions, and presenting artworks at art fairs, paying a commission to the intermediaries up to 50% of the sale price (Sherwin, 2012). However, by using blockchain, artists can self-organize the production and distribution process of artworks, rendering hub institutions no longer necessary (Swan, 2015). The following cases present blockchain-based alternative models for art creation and distribution.

1. DADA: A Decentralized Community Platform for Visual Artists

DADA (dada.nyc) was launched in 2017 and is built on the Ethereum blockchain, which enables the creation and trading of unique digital artworks that are verified and secured using cryptographic algorithms. DADA's main mission is to provide a decentralized platform that lowers the boundary between artists and audiences, amateur and professional artists, and high-end and popular arts by facilitating connections and collaborations for digital artwork. While other platforms primarily showcase finished artworks, DADA focuses on the artistic process, enabling users to collaborate on drawings and create shared works of art that can be minted as NFTs and sold on the platform. In this process, to ensure that artists receive their fair share of the profits, the Dada platform has created a smart contract that guarantees the artist receives 30% and the collector receives 60% of the sale price when an artwork is sold (Ramos, 2021).

One of the unique features of DADA is its focus on a new economic system for artists made possible by blockchain technology. DADA recently presented a new economic paradigm called "The Invisible Economy," which explores the potential for art-making to be radically separated from the market (Ramos & Mam, 2020). This allows artists to create without pressure to produce and sell while receiving a guaranteed basic income for their participation in the community. The basic income is funded by a portion of the revenue generated by the platform's sales of NFTs, with 100% of the revenues going to the DADA Fund, which is then distributed to contributing members of the community in the form of basic income. All financial and market interactions occur in the background and are managed by smart contracts. In this way, this blockchain-based community attempts to re-structure the art market, from a top-down hierarchy to a decentralized network, by encouraging artists to cooperate and co-evolve their capacities.

2. CryptoPunks: Tokenization as a New Model of Art Production and Distribution

CryptoPunks is a blockchain-based art marketplace. CryptoPunk is the name of a pixel art-style punk character created by John Watkinson, the co-founder of CryptoPunks, with no formal art education. Watkinson created 10,000 digital images of different punk characters, measuring 24 × 24 pixels, each with slightly altered hairstyles, clothes, and skin colors. Each character has certificates of ownership stored in a blockchain that is collectible and tradable. The CryptoPunks website exhibits these characters and provides a marketplace for buying, selling, or bidding on each CryptoPunk character (larvalabs.com/cryptopunks).

By using the NFT (non-fungible token) function of blockchain, CryptoPunks introduces a new model of art creation and circulation (Klein, 2019). Anyone can issue their own cryptographic token like Bitcoin through a simple smart contract running on a blockchain. While Bitcoin is a fungible token interchangeable with fiat money or other cryptocurrencies, NFT refers to a special type of token with a unique identity that is not interchangeable (Wu et al., 2019). NFT is also called "crypto-collectibles," as it is represented in various forms such as cats (cryptokitties.com) offered for trade and collection (Fenech, 2018). The rarer a crypto-collectible, the more valuable it is, driving up the price (Fang, 2019). When the CryptoPunk characters first came on sale, the average price of each character was $1 to about $30. However, in 2022, CryptoPunk #7523 was sold at a price of $11.75 million in Sotherby's sale. CryptoPunks have also made their debut in the mainstream art scene. The first exhibition of printed versions of CryptoPunks was held at Kate Vass Galerie in Switzerland in 2018, and the Centre Pompidou recently announced it was adding Cryptopunk#110 to its permanent collection in 2023. This is interesting because, traditionally, artists who do not have an artworld background or networks are likely to be isolated from the art market. The CryptoPunks case presents a benchmark for DIY art production, exhibition, and trade for aspiring or emerging artists. The concept of "digital scarcity," developed through the integration of art and blockchain, eventually leads to a new market niche.

3. Maecenas: Fractional Ownership as a New Model of Art Investment

Maecenas (www.maecenas.co/) is a blockchain-based art auction platform aimed at "making fine art more accessible" (Maecenas, 2019). In contrast to the traditional art auction, where the highest bidder receives a physical copy of the artwork, Maecenas introduces a new form of art trade. It converts the artwork into several digital codes recorded on a blockchain and offers certificates of these digital codes for bidding. In Maecenas' first auction in 2018, Andy Warhol's 14 Small Electric Chairs was sold in the form of distributed digital certificates. Over 800 people signed up to participate in the auction, and the highest bid was $6.5 million. Successful bidders received certificates of digital codes that grant a "fractional ownership" of the artwork (Adam, 2018). These certificates can be traded or used to collect interest when the physical artworks are leased to galleries or museums.

The idea of fractional ownership proposes a new means of art investment. By converting an artwork into digital certificates for joint purchase, the ownership of artworks has been expanded to include members of the general public. On the basis of the fractional ownership model, anyone can be an owner of a Picasso painting for only $10 once they pay for the fractional share (Maecenas, 2019).

The Rise of the Tertiary Market? The Potential of Blockchain for the Professional Development of Visual Artists

This chapter began with the proposition that the present boundaries of professional visual artists must be more reflective of changes and progress in a fast-moving society rather than being restricted by old, traditional conventions. In today's rapidly changing art world, artists at all levels, including hobbyists, recent college graduates, and established professionals, must skillfully navigate and adapt to internal and external shifts. Undoubtedly, the cultivation of innovative strategies within a contemporary context is of utmost importance for visual artists, as it empowers them to establish new and meaningful relationships within the dynamic art market. These strategies and relationships should not be about instant promotion or branding but about building a sustainable working environment to diversify artists' portfolios in order to further expand their professional competencies.

These three cases show us that blockchain drives new changes in the art market. With its decentralized nature, blockchain can provide artists with a tool that can tackle existing problems and constraints in the art market and hence expand and create new opportunities to show and sell their works. The potential changes expected from the adoption of blockchain in the art market are as follows: (1) Reconceptualizing the role of art intermediaries; (2) increasing opportunities to monetize artworks; and (3) increasing opportunities to develop new market segments.

First, the case of DADA and CryptoPunks shows that blockchain could contribute to reshaping the art market in the digital era by scaling down the role of traditional art intermediaries. For several decades, a few dominant players in the art market have historically wielded significant influence over the career trajectory of artists. The key lesson from these cases is that by using such an alternative platform, artists themselves can organize the production, distribution, and sales of their works free from the traditional ethos of exclusivity and elitism in the visual arts field. Blockchain enables such activities by replacing the traditional art intermediaries, strict gatekeepers who guard the concrete boundary of the art market, with technology. Blockchain-based platforms provide collectors and artists with an independent venue where certification and registration information is recorded on a digital ledger, making artists and art buyers easily accessible for verification and detection without traditional intermediaries.

Second, the CryptoPunks case demonstrates the possibility of expanding opportunities for artists to monetize artwork. By leveraging blockchain's tokenization capability (Samuel, 2019), CryptoPunks proves that blockchain helps artists take full control of the copyrights. Artists can now have their artwork converted into collectible digital assets, which allows anyone to buy and trade a portion of their artwork. On the basis of smart contracts that record all funding flows, artists can be paid fairly at lower intermediary costs. Young or emerging artists who were unable to negotiate deals with galleries or who were cheated by unfair contracts and low payments can be empowered with abundant entrepreneurial opportunities and functionalities to access useful resources to start launching and managing their own brands.

Finally, Maecenas demonstrates that blockchain can enhance opportunities to expand customer bases and diversify market segments. Art collections are regarded as "wealthy people's toys" because information and networks related to art trade and investment are likely to be limited to rich insiders (Reyburn, 2018). Art is a riskier investment than stocks and bonds due to its illiquidity. Additionally, it is impossible to predict the true annualized rate of return for a specific artwork because there is no transparent price index that allows collectors to make advance decisions for their collections. As the valuation of an artwork is made by influential intermediaries, it is impossible to know whether prices for a particular artwork will increase or decrease. Art investment also requires considerable extra costs, including commissions and insurance. Additionally, there is always a chance of forgery, theft, or damage. However, tokenization, one of the unique functions of blockchain, has the potential to overcome this situation by creating new concepts like fractional ownership and shared distribution (Whitaker, 2018). By providing fractional possession and token-based commerce, this new model of ownership becomes an entry point for new art buyers (Botz, 2018). According to the Hiscox Report (2019), a survey of 706 art buyers shows that almost half of survey participants under the age of 30 answered that they would consider investing in fractional ownership. Thus, the new technology helps the art market develop a wider buyer base, especially among young people (Garner, 2019).

The cases explained earlier suggest that the adoption of blockchain technology can create a new layer in the existing art market (Figure 13.1). In this new layer, blockchain provides new platforms, methods, and approaches to the way artworks are sold and bought, in which we can envision innovative business models that trigger new art ecosystems in four ways. First, for artists, blockchain provides them with DIY tools to self-organize and self-manage

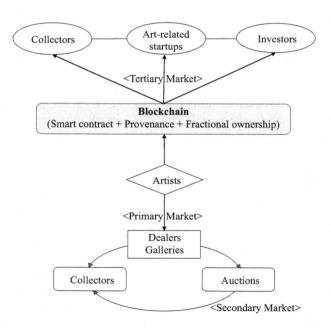

Figure 13.1 Blockchain-Based Art Market Platform

their brands. Once artists register their work on a blockchain platform with an in-built provenance system such as Artory or VerisArt, they can create a certificate, which allows them to prove the authenticity of their artworks. In addition, blockchain puts artists in direct contact with the buyers, thereby saving them the large commissions they usually have to pay galleries or dealers. New ventures like Pixura or Freeport enable artists to launch a smart contract, tokenize their own art, and sell it on their own marketplace with no computing skills. Second, art collectors can use blockchain to track the entire history of an artwork. Blockchain startups like VerisArt and Codex provide certification and gallery registration services with which details of artworks are recorded and stored in the digital ledger so that anyone can check and detect the artwork's data. Third, for the auction house, blockchain helps increase the long-term data transparency and security of information about artworks and guarantees a reduction in online auction-related fraud such as non-payment or non-delivery. Finally, art investors can benefit from blockchain as the costs and fees of transactions are lower. It can transform artworks worth millions of dollars into small digital units that are easily purchased and sold in real time without heavy fees.

Drawbacks and Implications

Despite the significant benefits, the application of blockchain in the visual arts field has side effects and drawbacks as well. First, whether the blockchain-based new ventures actually contribute to putting the vision of decentralization into practice is questionable. Smart contracts, one of the main features of blockchain, were expected to disrupt traditional art market structures by solving the intermediary issues. However, the art market still demonstrates an apparent gap between initial conceptualizations of blockchain's first instantiations, particularly around the idea of complete decentralization. It may be that the growth of blockchain might result in another centralization of institutional power (Mire, 2019). The role of blockchain in the art industry is not yet clear, as there is uncertainty regarding whether it will reinforce the existing monopoly of the traditional art world or provide greater opportunities for emerging artists to access new markets and customers. With blockchain's power to control and govern data, the question of who controls the system remains important. Further discussions of blockchain should focus on not only using the technology to empower individual actors in the visual arts field but also reducing the potential risks of the technology. For example, who controls an art object that has fractional ownership? Who has the residual rights for artworks? Can artists receive royalties or residuals for the later sales of their works in the blockchain-based art market?

Second, blockchain could provide positive impacts on entrepreneurial preparation and commercial benefit for artists accustomed to working with technologies or who have a deep interest in infusing technology into artmaking. However, a digital divide might emerge over access to blockchain that could eventually produce another kind of inequality and hierarchy (O'Dwyer, 2017). Effective use of any digital tool requires changes in artists' training, especially for the artists' new role as an entrepreneur. Especially with the advent of AI-powered tools like ChatGPT, which allow for the creation of original content by learning from existing data and generating new ideas and inspirations, it is important to incorporate new technologies and strategies into art schools' curricula. Rethinking the functions and training of artists to survive in the digital age will be critical. Additionally, there is an urgent need for new models that respond to the changing conditions affecting the art market by adapting to instability and unpredictability among art students who are more entrepreneurial, flexible, and alert to change.

Third, while the adoption of blockchain could lead to an increase in new capital inflows in the art market, it also gives rise to fear of speculation. The values of art-related cryptocurrencies have proven unstable with rapid rallies and sharp drops. For example, Maecenas' ART token reached its peak value of $2.58 in early 2018, but by 2020, it had dropped to approximately $0.03.

Such extreme price volatility questions the sustainability of the blockchain-based art market. Given that in the blockchain-based art investment landscape, where art buyers only obtain certificates rather than physical artworks, buyers tend to prioritize economic value as their main motivation for investment on art. However, although there are some success stories in developing new market segments to increase their chances to make a living, it is largely uncertain that blockchain has had a significant impact on developing new revenue sources for artists. Despite big expectations that this new technology could offer a range of options to expand their market access opportunities, it seems to be difficult for many artists to sell their works by just displaying them on blockchain. There must be additional resources and support to develop customers who are interested in buying their artworks as well as who know how to use cryptocurrency to become successful on blockchain-based platforms.

Finally, there is concern about the valuation of an artwork. In the blockchain-based art market, crypto-art or collectibles gain the status of art, and the boundary of art is even expanded to popular meme characters (Garner, 2019). Apart from its positive impact of reducing the elitism and authority in art production and distribution, blockchain raises an issue on how valuation on artworks could be carried out (Hiscox, 2019). Since both blockchain art production and investment operate on a decentralized platform, the lack of a decision-making group in charge of making decisions about "what is art?" and "what is good art?" will be an important consideration for the long-term sustainability of the blockchain art market.

Various projects and start-ups in recent years have experimented with new aesthetic, economic, and social visions of visual arts using blockchain. Newly proposed blockchain-based art initiatives show an alternative perspective on how artworks can be produced and traded, potentially serving as templates for the digital age. Blockchain opportunities are derived from the technology's capacity to access diverse portfolios that the existing system was unable to satisfy (Aitken, 2017). Thus, blockchain technology encourages a new type of opportunity for artists by creating opportunities that enhance social and economic wellbeing for traditionally excluded members of the visual art community. However, opponents of blockchain point out that it is merely an ideal narrative or a temporary phenomenon that may not be able to reach an optimal solution as many expect (Deloitte & ArtTactic, 2019; Iansiti & Lakhani, 2017). Yet, most of these are still in their infancy and still experimental. A wide range of institutional changes across economic, industrial, and social sectors are required to actively integrate blockchain into daily life.

Currently, it is necessary to be wary of using art as a tool for new business experiments that will eventually be absorbed by market mechanisms. Whenever new technology emerges, both research and policy concerns tend to concentrate on directly implanting the grammar of technology into business models without considering its drawbacks and side effects. A deep understanding of the potential risks and threats resulting from the novel technology is needed to develop more proactive strategies for reliable investment and/or policy attention.

References

Abbing, H. (2002). *Why artists are poor?* University of Amsterdam Press.

Abbing, H. (2015). *Inner art world exploitation of poor artists* [Conference paper]. Cultural Economics Conference, Tehran and Shiraz, Iran.

Abbing, H. (2019). *The changing social economy of art: Are the arts becoming less exclusive?* Palgrave Macmillan.

Abbott, A. (1988). *The system of professions: An essay on the division of expert labor* (1st ed.). University of Chicago Press.

Adam, G. (2018). Blockchain: Hot stuff or hot air? *The Art Newspaper*. www.theart newspaper.com/feature/blockchain-hot-stuff-or-hot-air

Aitken, A. (2017). How blockchain technology is "disrupting" the art economy as we know it. *Forbes*. www.forbes.com/sites/rogeraitken/2017/08/17/how-the-blockchain-is-disrupting-the-art-economy-as-we-know-it/#3f53a68574fe

Allen, D. (2017). *Discovering and developing the blockchain cryptoeconomy*. https://ssrn.com/abstract=2815255; http://dx.doi.org/10.2139/ssrn.2815255

Allen, D., Berg, C., Lane, A., & Potts, J. (2017). *The economics of crypto democracy*. https://ssrn.com/abstract=2973050; http://dx.doi.org/10.2139/ssrn.2973050

Bagchi, S. (2011). *The professional: Defining the New standard of excellence at work*. Portfolio, Penguin.

Bambrough, B. (2019). A bitcoin "millionaire" is planning to "resurrect" $20,000 per bitcoin by 2020. *Forbes*. www.forbes.com/sites/billybambrough/2019/06/10/a-bitcoin-millionaire-is-planning-to-resurrect-20000-per-bitcoin-by-2020/?sh=3341df0de47b

Bashir, I. (2018). *Mastering blockchain: Distributed ledger technology, decentralization, and smart contracts explained*. Packt Publishing.

Beck, J. (2008). Governmental professionalism: Re-professionalising or de-profession alising teachers in England? *British Journal of Educational Studies*, 56, 119–143.

Botz, A. (2018). *Is blockchain the future of art? Four experts weigh in.* www.artbasel.com/news/blockchain-artworld-cryptocurrency-cryptokitties

Bourdieu, P. (1993). *The field of culture production.* Polity Press.

Bridgstock, R. (2012). Not a dirty word: Arts entrepreneurship and higher education. *Arts and Humanities in Higher Education*, 12, 122–137.

Carvalho, T., Correia, T., & Serra, H. (2018). Guest Editorial. Professions under suspicion: What role for professional ethics and commitment in contemporary societies? *Sociologia, Problems e Practicas*, 88, 9–25.

Chang, W. J., & Wyszomirski, M. J. (2015). What is arts entrepreneurship? Tracking the development of its definition in scholarly journals. *Artivate: A Journal of Entrepreneurship in the Arts*, 4(2), 11–31.

Chong, D. (2005). Stakeholder relationships in the market for contemporary art. In I. Robertson (Ed.), *Understanding international art markets and management* (pp. 84–102). Psychology Press.

Danto, A. (1964). The artworld. *Journal of Philosophy*, 61(19), 571–584.

Davidson, S., De Filippi, P., & Potts, J. (2016). *Economics of blockchain.* http://ssrn.com/abstract=2744751

De Leon, I., & Gupta, R. (2017). *The impact of digital innovation and blockchain on the music industry.* Inter-American Development Bank.

Deloitte & ArtTactic. (2019). *Art & finance report 2019.* https://www2.deloitte.com/content/dam/Deloitte/ch/Documents/privatemarket/deloitte-ch-private-art-and-finance-report-2019.pdf

Del Valle, G. (2019). *Why is art so expensive? The $64 billion, "winner take all" global art market, explained.* www.vox.com/the-goods/2018/10/31/18048340/art-market-expensive-ai-painting

Deresiewicz, W. (2015). The death of artist and the birth of the creative entrepreneur. *The Atlantic*, 315(1), 92.

Dickie, J. (1974). *Art and the aesthetic: An institutional analysis.* Cornell University Press.

Elhanani, Z. (2018). How blockchain changed the art world in 2018. *Forbes.* www.forbes.com/sites/zoharelhanani/2018/12/17/how-blockchain-changed-the-artworld-in-2018/#65dcbc5e3074

Evetts, J. (2014). The concept of professionalism: Professional work, professional practice and learning. In S. Billet, C. Harteis, & H. Gruber (Eds.), *The international handbook of research in professional and practice-based learning.* Springer.

Fang, S. (2019). *Blockchain trends explained: What are crypto collectibles?* www.bitcoininsider.org/article/68676/blockchain-trends-explained-what-are-crypto-collectibles.

Fenech, G. (2018). Unlocking a $200 billion dollar collectibles market on the blockchain. *Forbes.* www.forbes.com/sites/geraldfenech/2018/11/08/unlocking-a-200-billion-dollar-collectibles-market-on-the-blockchain/#3f3d011e5554.

Fine, G. A. (2017). A matter of degree: Negotiating art and commerce in MFA education. *American Behavioral Scientist*, 61(12), 1463–1486.

Fischer, E., & Reuber, R. (2011). Social interaction via new social media: (How) can interactions on Twitter affect effectual thinking and behavior? *Journal of Business Venturing*, 26(1), 1–18.

Flisbäck, M., & Lund, A. (2015). Artists' autonomy and professionalization in a new cultural policy landscape. *Professions and Professionalism*, 5(2), 1–16.

Freidson, E. (2001). *Professionalism, the third logic: On the practice of knowledge.* University of Chicago Press.

Frenette, A. (2017). Arts graduates in a changing economy. *American Behavioral Scientist, 61*(12), 1455–1462.

Garner, B. (2019). *10 ways blockchain technology is changing art.* https://coincentral.com/blockchain-technology-art/

Gerber, A., & Childress, C. (2017). I don't make objects, I make projects: Selling things and selling selves in contemporary artmaking. *Cultural Sociology, 11*, 234–254.

Goanta, C., & Spanakis, G. (2022). The commercial unfairness of recommender systems on social media. In *Artificial intelligence and the media* (pp. 148–170). Edward Elgar Publishing.

Goodwin, J. (2008). *The international art markets: The essential guide for collectors and investors.* Kogan Page Limited.

Halperin, J., & Kinsella, E. (2017). *The "winner takes all" art market: 25 artists account for nearly 50% of all contemporary auction sales.* https://news.artnet.com/market/25-artists-account-nearly-50-percent-postwar-contemporary-auction-sales-1077026

Heinlich, N. (2012). Mapping intermediaries in contemporary art according to pragmatic sociology. *European Journal of Cultural Studies, 15*(6), 695–702.

Hiscox. (2019). *Hiscox online art trade report.* www.hiscox.co.uk/online-art-trade-report

Iansiti, M., & Lakhani, K. (2017). The truth about blockchain. *Harvard Business Review.* https://hbr.org/2017/01/the-truth-about-blockchain

Jyrämä, A. (2002). Contemporary art markets-structure and actors: A study of art galleries. *International Journal of Arts Management, 4*(2), 50–65.

Jyrämä, A., & Äyväri, A. (2006). *Shaping the practices: Role of different actors within the context of contemporary art market* [Conference paper]. IMP Conference, Milan.

Jyrämä, A., & Äyväri, A. (2009). Marketing contemporary visual art. *Marketing Intelligence and Planning, 28*(6), 723–735.

Kaplan, J., & Warren, C. (2009). *Patterns of entrepreneurship management.* John Wiley & Sons.

Klein, J. (2019). *How CryptoPunks' creators charmed the art world and paved the way for blockchain art.* https://breakermag.com/how-cryptopunks-creators-charmed-the-art-world-and-paved-the-way-for-blockchain-art/

Lopez, A. (2015). *New paradigms for artists in the marketplace: Artists as entrepreneurs?* [Conference paper]. European Forum Biennial Conference, Poznan, Poland.

MacDonald-Korth, D., Lehdonvirta, V., & Meyer, E. (2016). *The art market 2.0: Blockchain and financialisation in visual arts.* University of Oxford & The Alan Turing Institute.

Maecenas. (2019). *White paper: Maecenas, the decentralised art gallery.* www.whitepaper.io/document/241/maecenas-whitepaper

McDonald, P. (2009). Digital discords in the online media economy: Advertising versus content versus copyright. In P. Snickars & P. Vonderau (Eds.), *The YouTube reader.* National Library of Sweden, Wallflower Press.

McIntyre, M. H. (2004). *Taste buds: How to cultivate the art market.* Arts Council England.

Menger, P. M. (1999). Artistic labor markets and careers. *Annual Review of Sociology, 25*(1), 541–574.

Michalska, J. (2016). Blockchain: How the revolutionary technology behind bitcoin could change the art market. *The Art Newspaper*. www.theartnewspaper.com/anal ysis/blockchain-how-the-revolutionary-technology-behind-bitcoin-could-change-the-art-market

Mire, S. (2019). *What are the challenges to blockchain adoption in the art industry? 5 experts share their insights*. www.disruptordaily.com/blockchain-adoption-challenges-art-industry/

Murugesan, S. (2007). Understanding Web 2.0. *IT Professional*, 9(4), 34–41.

Noordegraaf, M. (2015). Hybrid professionalism and beyond: (New) forms of public professionalism in changing organizational and societal contexts. *Journal of Professions and Organization*, 2(2), 187–206.

Nowiński, W., & Kozma, M. (2017). How can blockchain technology disrupt the existing business models? *Entrepreneurial Business and Economics Review*, 5(3), 173–188.

O'Dwyer, R. (2017). Does digital culture want to be free? How blockchains are transforming the economy of cultural goods. In R. Catlow, M. Garrett, N. Jones, & N. Skinner (Eds.), *Artists: Rethinking the blockchain* (pp. 302–316). Torque Editions.

Ølnes, S., Ubacht, J., & Janssen, M. (2017). Blockchain in government: Benefits and implications of distributed ledger technology for information sharing. *Government Information Quarterly*, 34(3), 355–364.

Phillips, R. J. (2010). Arts entrepreneurship and economic development: Can every city be "Austintatious"? *Foundation and Trends in Entrepreneurship*, 6(4), 239–313.

Pollard, V., & Wilson, E. (2013). The "entrepreneurial mindset" in creative and performing arts higher education in Australia. *Artivate: A Journal of Entrepreneurship in the Arts*, 3(1), 3–22.

Ramos, B. (2021). *Beyond resale royalties*. https://powerdada.medium.com/beyond-resale-royalties-18508683da46

Ramos, B., & Mam, Y. (2020). *Introducing the invisible economy*. https://power-dada.medium.com/the-invisible-economy-db46897d4f07

Reijers, W., & Coeckelbergh, M. (2018). The blockchain as a narrative technology: Investigating the social ontology and normative configurations of cryptocurrencies. *Philosophy & Technology*, 31, 103–130.

Reyburn, S. (2018). Art is becoming a financial product, and blockchain is making it happen. *New York Times*. www.nytimes.com/2018/06/08/arts/art-financialization-blockchain.html

Roberts, J. (2012). Infusing entrepreneurship within non-business discipline: Preparing artists and others for self-employment and entrepreneurship. *Artivate: Journal of Entrepreneurship in the Arts*, 1(2), 53–63.

Samuel, E. (2019). *SMART(ER) ART: Valuing artists by the atom*. https://newlab.com/stories/smarter-art-valuing-artists-by-the-atom/

Schuetz, M. (2018). *Startup codex brings blockchain to art with backing from Pantera*. www.bloombergquint.com/markets/startup-codex-brings-blockchain-to-art-with-backing-from-pantera

Shah, S., & Tripsas, M. (2007). The accidental entrepreneur: The emergent and collective process of user entrepreneurship. *Strategic Entrepreneurship Journal*, 1, 123–140.

Sherwin, B. (2012). *Art gallery commission: Complaining about the "split" is a waste of time*. https://fineartviews.com/blog/49269/art-gallery-commission-complaining-about-the-split-is-a-waste-of-time

Shindell, L. M. (2016). Provenance and title risks in the art industry: Mitigating these risks in museum management and curatorship. *Museum Management and Curatorship*, *31*(5), 406–417.

Stichweh, R. (1997). Professions in modern society. *International Review of Sociology*, *7*(1), 95–102.

Svensson, L. (2015). Occupations and professionalism in art and culture. *Professions & Professionalism*, *5*(2), 1–14.

Swan, M. (2015). *Blockchain: Blueprint for a new economy*. O'Reilly Media.

Tapscott, D., & Tapscott, A. (2017). Blockchain could help artists profit more from their creative works. *Harvard Business Review*. https://hbr.org/2017/03/blockchain-could-help-artists-profit-more-from-their-creative-works

Tapscott, D., Tapscott, A., & Kirkland, R. (2016). *How blockchains could change the world*. www.mckinsey.com/industries/high-tech/our-insights/how-blockchains-could-change-the-world

TBR's Creative & Cultural Team. (2018). *Livelihoods of visual artists: 2016 data report*. Art Council England. www.artscouncil.org.uk/sites/default/files/download-file/Livelihoods%20of%20Visual%20Artists%202016%20Data%20Report.pdf

Thom, M. (2015). The suffering of arts entrepreneurs: Will fine art students be educated on how to become successfully self-employed? *Journal of Education and Training Studies*, *3*(1), 64–77.

Thom, M. (2016a). Crucial skills for the entrepreneurial success of fine artists. *Artivate: Journal of Entrepreneurship in the Arts*, *5*(1), 3–24.

Thom, M. (2016b). *Fine artists' entrepreneurial business environment* (Working Paper). www.researchgate.net/publication/309733620_Fine_Artists'_Entrepreneurial_Business_Environment

Throsby, D., & Thompson, B. (1994). *But what do you do for a living? A new economic study of Australian artists*. Australia Council for the Arts.

Throsby, D., & Zednik, A. (2011). Multiple job-holding and artistic careers: Some empirical evidence. *Cultural Trends*, *20*(1), 9–24.

Van Dijck, J., & Nieborg, D. (2009). Wikinomics and its discontents: A critical analysis of Web 2.0 business manifestos. *New Media & Society*, *11*(5), 855–874.

Whitaker, A. K. (2018). *Blockchain, fractional ownership, and the future of creative work* (CFS Working Paper Series). Goethe University, Center for Financial Studies (CFS).

Wu, X., Zou, Z., & Song, D. (2019). *Learn Ethereum: Build your own decentralized applications with Ethereum and smart contracts*. Packt Publishing.

Wyszomirski, M. J., & Chang, W. J. (2017). Professional self-structuration in the arts: Sustaining creative careers in the 21st century. *Sustainability*, *9*. https://doi.org/10.3390/su9061035

Zeilinger, M. (2016). Digital art as monetised graphics: Enforcing intellectual property on the blockchain. *Philosophy & Technology*, *31*(1), 15–41.

Zhu, H., & Zhou, Z. Z. (2016). Analysis and outlook of applications of blockchain technology to equity crowdfunding in China. *Financial Innovation*, *2*(29), 1–11. http://dx.doi.org/10.1186/s40854-016-0044-7

14 Epilogue
Challenges for Creative Professionalism

*Margaret J. Wyszomirski
and WoongJo Chang*

Impact of COVID-19 on the Creative Sector

The societal shutdown triggered by the COVID-19 pandemic that started in early 2020 prompted multiple crises in global society regarding healthcare, the economy, and the social contact that impacted all sectors and industries. While the pandemic displayed aspects that were shared globally, it also was experienced differently by different sectors, various kinds of workers and professions, varying demographic groups, and different communities. The creative sector both endured broad shocks generally and encountered particular challenges that tested its resilience.

Basically, resilience implies a capacity to absorb and bounce back from shocks and/or disruptions (Holling, 1973). COVID-19 triggered an unusually complex set of shocks that were global, multiple, sequential, and unpredictable. In the United States, layered onto pandemic disruptions, the summer of 2020 saw a second deep social shock when police arrested and murdered George Floyd and there was a surge of protest in the streets by the Black Lives Matter movement and its allies against police racism, brutality, and lack of accountability. Their calls for greater social justice and an end to systemic racism, though hardly new, impacted U.S. society in ways that seemed unprecedented. By the end of 2022, the pandemic seemed to end in the North American and European countries, which began a transition to the endemic era. Yet, as of this writing in early 2023, China has ended its Zero COVID policy and is experiencing another wave of COVID-19 infections and deaths. Thus, societies globally remain vulnerable to successive waves of the pandemic and need to foster social, economic, and cultural resilience.

Although we are still in the wake of the social disruptions caused by the pandemic and the virus remains a threat, in the interests of brevity and for the United States, the term "COVID era" will be used to refer to the dramatic and unprecedented ruptures of the two-year period between March 2020 and March 2022 when the disease was most active. The "bouncing-back" sense of resilience sounds relatively straightforward, suggesting a return to a condition of the status quo ante. But, in reality, resilience can refer to many targets

DOI: 10.4324/9781003138693-16

of "return"—ranging from survival and restoration to recovery, adaptation, and sustainability and can stretch beyond to thriving and transformation. Furthermore, resilience is not a static capacity but one that needs to be dynamic and flexible depending on the nature and severity of the shock; the capacity of individuals, organizations, or sectors to absorb and cope with the shock; as well as the extent of panarchy—that is the scope of ecological components simultaneously and interactively disrupted by the shock (Walker et al., 2004). The dimensions of resilience discussed earlier can be combined with the indicators and processes of professionalization that have been established and applied earlier in this volume to provide a framework for discussing the interrelationships and impacts of resilience, COVID-era disruptions, and creative professionalism.

Resilience: Absorbing the Shocks of COVID-19

The first stage of creative sector resilience involved absorbing the sudden effects of the pandemic: the broad economic shutdown, which, although it exempted certain essential industries, set strict limitations on the social contact and movement that the creative industries depend on. As public policymakers ordered the shutdown in early 2020, they defined the creative industries and their workers as non-essential as well as a potential threat to public health due to the difficulties in enforcing social distancing both among creative workers and with their audiences. As a consequence, most creative activities and organizations—from movie theaters and film and TV production to Broadway plays to museums and galleries—closed down immediately and completely. This led to widespread layoffs or furloughs for creative workers. Added disruptions for creative professionals came from the shutdown of other sectors in which artists commonly sought portfolio employment, such as restaurants and bars, festivals, and touring. As schools switched from in-person teaching to virtual, online classes, another common set of portfolio jobs for artists as arts educators were eliminated.

The designation of the creative sector industries as nonessential dealt a disheartening psychological blow to their workers' professional identities and sense of public value. This caused at least one professional association in the arts to contest the designation. Dance/NYC launched #ArtistsAreNecessaryWorkers, an online campaign demanding acknowledgment, representation, and integration into planning for the post-pandemic future (Blake et al., 2021, p. 4). Since it was government regulation at national, state, and local levels that declared and treated the creative sector and its workers as nonessential, this could also be seen as a de facto deprofessionalization rather than diminished official validation of the public value of the arts and the work of creative professionals.

However, other activities of governments, professional associations, and foundations tried to help workers and organizations in the creative sector gain access to survival relief programs by offering technical assistance and application information, providing updates and instructions on health and safety measures, and providing technical assistance regarding alternative digital programming options. Public arts agencies at the federal, state, and local levels worked with grantees to renegotiate the expectations and goals of grants in process, turning many into planning grants for virtual rather than live programming. This happened not only in the United States but also in other countries in Europe and East Asia. Public arts agencies, professional associations, and private foundations undertook new initiatives to provide small, emergency financial support grants, especially for individual artists, for small arts organizations, and for culturally specific minority arts organizations. Such efforts sought to maintain field networks and activate them as sources of vital information about formal relief efforts and communication on how colleagues were coping with the shutdown, with adopting digital programming activities, and sharing experiences and encouragement. Thus, even though most creative professionals were not working, these networks supported their sense of shared professional identities.

Additionally, many arts professional associations and advocacy groups began collecting information documenting the impact of the pandemic shutdown on the sector. Such efforts not only helped inform the sector about changing COVID-19 health precautions but also built a foundation of data concerning likely recovery needs (American Alliance of Museums and Wilkening Consulting, 2020; Blake et al., 2021). Americans for the Arts, the premier U.S. national art advocacy organization, maintained an up-to-date online listing of relevant information concerning news and resources for the arts and cultural field—the Coronavirus (COVID-19) Resource and Response Center (AFTA, n.d.). These webpages covered health precautions and practices, listed scores of links to arts agency and arts professional association resource pages, field tools, and relevant research, as well as equity and mental health tools, news, and resources to support equity and diversity concerns. State and city governments and arts agencies, particularly those with large and thriving creative sectors like New York and California, began to document the economic impacts and projected organizational and individual losses that followed the COVID shutdown. These effects included job losses, wage losses, unexpected business expenses, losses to local, state, and national economies, decreases in arts audiences, expected permanent closings of arts organizations, and projected arts organizational deficits (NYCDCA et al., 2020; Otis College of Art and Design, 2021; Office of the New York State Comptroller, 2021).

Resilience: Relief and Reopening

A second stage of resilience focused on relief and reopening efforts. Both individual arts organizations and individual artists engage in survival efforts.

Unsure of how long the shutdown might continue, many arts organizations furloughed their employees without pay. Broadway venues closed shows and cancelled expected openings. Most dance and orchestral companies cancelled seasons, some with a rolling series of closures and tentative re-openings followed by subsequent closings or cancellations (see Wyszomirski, 2022).

The U.S. federal government provided a series of both general and targeted relief assistance. These started with the March 2020 Coronavirus Aid, Relief, and Economic Security (CARES) Act, which allocated $2 trillion to be spread across a set of programs that were relevant to creative sector workers and businesses, including direct assistance to artists, assistance to small businesses to pay their workers, disaster loans, and emergency grants from federal arts and cultural agencies.

As many of the relief funds were expiring, Congress approved the Consolidated Appropriations Act of December 2020, which extended the first three CARES programs listed earlier (with some changes) and added a $15 billion targeted fund—the Shuttered Arts Venues Fund—to be distributed by the Small Business Administration to applicants such as live independent arts venues, movie theaters, and museums to replace up to 90% of lost revenues. In March 2021, the Shuttered Venue Operators Grant program received an additional $1.25 billion, bringing the program's total to over $16 billion.

The third wave of federal relief assistance was marked by the American Rescue Plan (ARP), signed into law by President Joseph Biden on March 11, 2021. ARP relief expanded general unemployment assistance, health insurance coverage, and food and rent assistance. It also widely distributed direct stimulus checks to many workers, including creative sector workers. Additional funds were allocated to federal cultural agencies (NEA, the Institute of Museum and Library Services, and the Corporation for Public Broadcasting) to support organizations and jobs impacted by the pandemic in the creative sector. An NEA press release on ARP noted that these earmarked allocations represented "a strong commitment from President Biden and Congress to the arts and a recognition of the value of the arts and culture sector to the nation's economy" (NEA, 2021). The NEA directed 40% of its ARP allocation to be distributed to state arts councils and regional arts organizations. The other 60% was to be distributed in the form of competitive grants. In efforts to achieve more equitable funding distribution, eligibility was not limited to previous NEA grantees. Also welcomed were applications from underserved populations, arts organizations with small and medium sized budgets, rural and urban communities, and from first timers (NEA, 2021). Thus, federal arts relief funds went to directly support workers in the creative sector, to support jobs in the sector, and to help nonprofit arts organizations and local arts agencies to keep their doors open nationwide. They also helped to sustain the incomes of creative professionals and protect field structuration from the economic ravages of the pandemic and its impacts.

Subsequent phases of resilience saw the interplay of reopening and audience hesitancy as COVID-19 vaccines became available and infection rates fell, allowing the American economy and society to begin to reemerge. Bouncing back from COVID shutdowns presented challenges beyond reopening; it also presented challenges for encouraging audiences to come back. For instance, when Broadway began to reopen in the summer of 2021, most required both vaccine checks and mask mandates. When the vaccine checks were done away with at most theaters in Spring of 2022, many theater patrons felt uneasy about the safety of attending live theater without such protocols. Thus, health adaptations continued to present problems for live performing arts attendance (Stevens & Sherman, 2022). Furthermore, even as the performing arts returned to their stages, their audiences did not fully return. For example, the Metropolitan Opera saw its paid attendance fall to 61% of capacity from 75% before the pandemic. Overall Broadway ticket sales for the 2021–2022 season were 40% lower than in the last fall season before the pandemic. The number of performances of Broadway shows dropped from 13,590 in 2018–2019 to just 6,860 in 2021–2022, and gross ticket revenue fell from $14.8 billion to $845 million (Paulson & Hernandez, 2022). Diminishing international tourism also aggravated these difficulties, as can be seen from restrictions on tourists from countries with high infection rates. For many arts organization leaders, it was unclear when and if the pre-pandemic audience would fully return or if they had developed other habits and concerns during the pandemic. Questions concerning the return of arts audiences will be a continuing factor in reestablishing sustainability within the creative sector and for the future of creative professionals (Hernandez, 2021).

Resilience: Diversity, Equity, and Inclusion Demands for Change

Other profound impacts occurred as the Black Lives Matter movement surged in May 2020 and spurred national activism demanding recognition and confrontation of systemic racism and a quest for greater concern for diversity, equity, and inclusion. This movement for racial and social justice made it clear that the post-pandemic reopening could not simply aim for the restoration of cultural activities, organizations, and industries to pre-pandemic conditions. Rather, new professional and field associations were formed to advocate for change. A few field examples illustrate the shape and agendas of such efforts.

In mid-June of 2020, the formation of Black Theatre United was announced as a spontaneous effort to activate Black artists and allies for racial justice (BTU). BTU brought together professionals from all areas of theater—from theater owners to producers and creatives to casting and unions. Their stated mission was to

> stand together to help protect Black people, Black Theatre, and Black lives . . . [and to raise their united voices] to educate, empower and

inspire through excellence and activism in pursuit of justice and equality . . . [and] tell our stories, preserve our history and ensure the legacy
of Black Theatre as American culture.

(Black Theatre United, 2023)

BTU embarked on a series of video messages, town hall meetings, panel discussions, political activism to get out the vote, created internship programs
for aspiring black theater professionals, and convened a series of field forums
to develop an agenda for needed changes. The forums were funded by the
Ford Foundation and resulted in a document called "A New Deal for Broadway," which was released in August of 2021 just as Broadway shows were
beginning to reopen. The 41 signatories of the pact included owners and
operators of all 41 Broadway theaters, the Broadway League (of producers), and the Actors' Equity Association. The pact called for a commitment
that creative teams (which include directors, writers, composers, choreographers, and designer) should never again be all white, but should be diverse.
Each of the three major theater owners promised to name at least one of
their theaters for a Black artist. The signatories also pledged to create a new,
mandatory, industry-wide training program for equity, diversity, inclusion,
accessibility, and belonging, to engage in ongoing mentoring and sponsoring
of Black talent in the industry, and to implement various contractual and
staffing procedures to ensure these changes (Paulson, 2021b). Clearly, BTU
represented a variety of organized interests in the theater field that were acting in alliance to make changes in professional opportunity structures and
operations to advance social justice and diversity. This multi-professional
coalition motivated by a hybrid of all three types of interest groups identified
in the literature on interest groups: those motivated by tangible interests (like
professional associations); those motivated by Solidary/Solidarity reasons
(those with a shared social identity such as ethnic or cultural heritage); and
those motivated by a central cause to take purposive action to achieve change
(Wyszomirski & Cherbo, 2001).

The breadth of collective action mobilization exhibited in the creative sector in this movement for greater social justice was not confined to the Black
community. Parallel activities could be seen among Asian American performers who had formed the Asian American Performers Action Coalition
(AAPAC). AAPAC had been compiling and annually publishing *The Visibility Report: Racial Representation on NYC Stages* since its founding in 2011
(see AAPAC, 2021). The 2021 edition documented the "lack of diversity
among those who make artistic, financial, and hiring decisions in New York's
theaters," and called for "a fundamental paradigm shift" away from dispro-
portionate control of American theater by white people (Paulson, 2021a).
In addition to Black people, Indigenous peoples, Latinx, and Asians were all
active in seeking a more equitable place in American society as well as recognition that none of these groups should be considered ethnically homogeneous
(García, 2020). In the wake of growing activism against racial inequity in the

American theater, an opinion article in the *New York Times* drew attention to the underrepresentation of female writers, composers, directors, designers, producers, and advocates that had been documented by a data report dating back to 2015. Through a partnership with the Dramatists Guild, this led to the 2010 creation of the Lilly awards, which recognize "extraordinary women in theatre." Thus the long overdue transformation for racial justice resounded with a call for "a gender reckoning, too" (Rebeck, 2021).

Other creative industries and professions were also dealing with calls for greater diversity, equity, and inclusion. In 2020, a group of Black artists, songwriters, managers, record label representatives, attorneys, and other music executives formed the Black Music Action Coalition (BMAC) as an advocacy organization to address systemic racism in the music business (Hissong, 2020). The BMAC pursued action through programming, policy advocacy, voter and election initiatives, philanthropy (including a COVID RELIEF Fund, and paid internship and mentoring programs), and research and media campaigns. It also developed a Music Industry Report Card to track how well the music industry was meeting its promises to change (Sisario, 2021). Meanwhile, the Academy of Motion Picture Arts and Sciences (which overseers the Oscars) announced that nominees for the best picture category would have to meet increasingly high standards for representation and inclusion in actors, storyline, and creative controllers. Clearly, these requirements have the potential to induce many changes in the stories, workforce, and management of the film industry, thus changing professional opportunities and norms.

Finally, museums, as both a field and as specific institutions, also grappled with DEI issues. Perhaps the most profound change saw the International Council of Museums revise its definition of what a museum is for the first time in 50 years to advance the cause of racial and social justice. The new definition held that:

> A museum is a not-for-profit, permanent institution in the service of society that researches, collects, conserves, interprets, and exhibits tangible and intangible heritage. Open to the public, accessible and inclusive, museums foster diversity and sustainability. They operate and communicate ethically, professionally, and with the participation of communities, offering varied experiences for education, enjoyment, reflection and knowledge sharing.

Thus, the members of this international professional association added principles of diversity and inclusion to the very identity of museums globally and set in motion professional efforts to set out next steps for implementation and adoption (Seymour, 2022).

At the level of individual museums, many created new administrative positions as diversity officers "to increase the number of people of color on the staff and board, but to also broaden their programming and address acknowledged patters of systemic racism" (Pogrebin, 2021). *Culture Type*, a newsletter focused on the visual arts from a Black perspective, reported that 47 black museum curators, educators, conservators, and leaders stepped into new appointments during the first half of 2022 (Valentine, 2022). Additionally, many long-tenured, white executive directors of arts and cultural organizations in a variety of fields have resigned or announced their retirement since 2020, some of them explicitly noting that they wanted to make room for women, a younger generation, and/or more diverse successors (Jacobs, 2021; Kourlas, 2021). In December 2020, Congress approved the establishment of a National Museum of the American Latino and appointed its first permanent director (Jorge Zamanillo), with an expected opening in ten to 12 years. A second new Smithsonian institution was also announced—a national museum of women's history (Bahr, 2022).

In a different initiative, the Library of Congress with the support of a $15 million grant from the Andrew W. Mellon Foundation announced a new initiative called Of the People: Widening the Path. This was a three-pronged initiative: (1) The library's American Folklife Center would award fellowships to support ethnographic documentation of contemporary cultural activities among people whose experiences might not otherwise be included in the national record; (2) increased outreach to students at tribal and historically Black universities through internships to help "develop a new generation of diverse talent for cultural heritage organizations"; and (3) a grant program to cultural heritage institutions to encourage them to use materials from the Library's digital collection in digital exhibits concerning people of color (Moynihan, 2021).

Keeping It Going on Zoom: Technology and Connection

While technology has become increasingly important in the creative sector since the 1980s, the pandemic lockdown dramatically accelerated the decentralization of artistic encounters. Digital and Internet technologies for video conferencing, real-time music jamming, co-working, and virtual musical ensemble production allowed artists and audiences isolated in their own homes to connect personally and musically with each other. The survival of a viable creative sector in a profoundly disrupted world was in many ways due to video conferencing apps, of which Zoom was by far the most common. Those arts and music festivals and music camps that didn't simply cancel their events in 2020 and 2021 shifted to online presentations. Artists whose concert tours and gigs were abruptly canceled turned to Zoom and other streaming platforms (e.g., Facebook Live) to reach their audiences. Contra and square dances were held on Zoom, as were plays, poetry, and book readings.

According to Rentschler and Lee (2021), the pandemic has resulted in three major shifts in the ecology of the art world, and technology has played a pivotal role in each. The first shift has been to localism, in which surviving arts and cultural events moved from national and international venues to local venues. The second shift was from competition to collaboration in response to the changing needs of multiple stakeholders in the art world ecology, including different government bodies, artists, audiences, and festivals. The final shift entailed a digital transformation that saw the art world respond to the global pandemic through online live performances and workshops and streaming international events, which, in contrast to the pandemic's localizing action, made many events available globally. All in all, the landscape of devastation created by COVID-19 also opened up heretofore unimagined possibilities and opportunities as technology was leveraged to connect audiences with artists in an experience of the arts that, though undeniably different, was sometimes actually improved. There were certainly boons on the meta scale since suddenly there was a mass audience, many of whom had not been familiar with Zoom, who became tech-literate, digital culture consumers overnight. This created an unprecedented level of *glocalism*, which presented not only unforeseen opportunities for artists but also new kinds of national and international engagement for audiences; geographic and economic barriers to attending live events evaporated when those events went online. Ticket prices were dramatically reduced, and since the event could be enjoyed in the participants' living rooms, travel expenses were nonexistent.

Thus, the COVID-19 pandemic has had transformative impacts on the arts sector. To say that these impacts have been negative and profoundly challenging is an understatement. Yet, the challenges have also brought unparalleled opportunities. On the one hand, artists abruptly lost venues, audiences, and income. On the other hand, many were able to leverage digital technology to reach their fans and gain new audiences while still others took advantage of their unexpected downtime to pursue learning opportunities and develop new creative projects. Community musicians who were accustomed to gathering in person for jamming or song circles were forced to take their activities to the musically problematic platform of videoconferencing apps such as Zoom and WebEx. For musicians who wanted to present performances, there were a number of livestreaming apps to choose from, such as Facebook Live or Instagram Live, Vimeo Live, YouTube Live, and Twitch. Musicians who wanted to play or sing together without the latency problem of video streaming apps used more technically challenging online jamming apps, such as JamKazam or Jam Studio, which required a microphone, an audio interface, hardwired Ethernet connection, and considerable tech savvy to set up.

Final Thoughts

Pandemic shifts to digital technology have highlighted the dynamics of professionalization and jumpstarted a profound revision of artists' relationships with their audiences. The increased centrality of digital tools has both facilitated and necessitated a new level of self-structuration of their portfolio careers, potentially ameliorating financial precarity in the long term, despite the hit their income streams have taken in the short term. COVID-19 has also reshaped the field structuration of the arts and creative sector, as novel forms and levels of support for artists and the arts have been improvised.

Indeed, the processes of professionalization we have examined in this volume have been rendered in high relief by the pandemic. Originally, this book sought to explore the professionalizing processes of collective action, public policy, and field institutionalization. Using these lenses has helped us gain a deeper understanding of how these processes work and their impacts on creative professionals. It has also brought another process of professionalization in the creative sector into clearer focus—entrepreneurial self-structuration as undertaken and practiced by individual creatives.

The COVID-19 pandemic exploded into the broader context of an expanding globalization and a growing focus on diversity, inclusion, and social justice, all potentiated by tectonic shifts in digital technology that have reshaped our daily lives, scope of awareness, and aspirations. The already emerging transformations to the potential for professionalization and improved social position and financial prospects for workers in the creative sector were accelerated and intensified by the unique stressors of the pandemic. The ongoing processes and influences that have driven professionalization in the creative sector persist have been profoundly redirected and reshaped by this unprecedented global disaster. Through the interplay of our immutable human social needs with our astonishing resilience, the tension between our desire for safe sameness and our drive to explore the unknown, and the limitations and capacities of digital technology, elements of a surprising new landscape are emerging, the full implications of which we can only guess at now. At this juncture, our task is to seek to shape the future toward our best understanding of the public good. Toward that end, the work our authors have done here to explore the multiple and specific trajectories of professionalization, their histories, and current state set the stage for the creative sectors' response to COVID-19 and gives an invaluable ground from which to launch a world in which human creativity is a central and respected force for the public good and artists are recognized as the inspirational leaders they are. The profound challenges and unforeseen opportunities of recent years require us to face the future with bold imagination, expanding vision, and irrepressible hope, and present possibilities we can barely grasp now. No sector of the art world will be the same going forward, not the nonprofit arts, not the commercial entertainment industry, not the community arts. It is up to us, individually and collectively, as artists and arts workers, as entrepreneurs and managers, as professionals and amateurs, as private foundations and government agencies, to meet the coming day ready to innovate in the new landscape. For this, we need professionals in the creative sector, and we need to understand their role and how to support them. It is to this effort that we hope this volume has made an essential contribution.

References

AAPAC (Asian American Performers Action Coalition). (2021). *The visibility report: Racial representation on NYC stages, 2018–2019.* www.aapacnyc.org/2018-2019. html

AFTA. (n.d.). *Coronavirus (Covid-19) response and resource center.* Americans for the Arts. www.americansforthearts.org/by-topic/disaster-preparedness/coronavirus-covid-19-resource-and-response-center

American Alliance of Museums and Wilkening Consulting. (2020). *National snapshot of COVID-19 impact on United States museums.* www.aam-us.org/wp-content/uploads/2020/11/AAMCOVID-19SnapshotSurvey-1.pdf

Bahr, S. (2022, February 5). Smithsonian names first director of Latino Museum. *The New York Times,* p. C7.

Blake, C., Youdan, G., & Cifuentes, A. D. (2021). *Coronavirus dance impact study: A dance sector in peril.* Dance/NYC.

BTU (Black Theatre United). (2023). *Who we are.* www.blacktheatreunited.com/portfolio/who-we-are/

García, I. (2020). Cultural insights for planners: Understanding the terms Hispanic, Latino, and Latinx. *Journal of the American Planning Association, 86*(4), 393–402.

Hernandez, J. C. (2021, June 22). Charting a future for orchestras. *The New York Times,* p. C2.

Hissong, S. (2020, June 22). Meet the music industry's new black music action coalition. *Rolling Stone.* www.rollingstone.com/pro/news/black-music-action-coalition-record-industry-1018726/

Holling, C. S. (1973). Resilience and stability of ecological systems. *Annual Review of Ecology and Systematics, 4*(1), 1–23.

Jacobs, J. (2021, July 26). New directors at Steppenwolf. *The New York Times,* p. C3.

Kourlas, G. (2021, December 20). School of American ballet appoints new leaders. *The New York Times,* p. C3.

Moynihan, C. (2021, January 28). New diversity efforts at the library of congress. *The New York Times,* p. C3.

NEA (National Endowment for the Arts). (2021, June 23). *NEA offers relief funds to help arts and culture sector recover from pandemic.* NEA Press Release. NEA.

NYCDCA (New York City Department of Cultural Affairs), Americans for the Arts, & SMU/DataArts. (2020, June). *COVID-19 impact on nonprofit arts and culture in New York city.* NYCDCA.

Office of the New York State Comptroller. (2021). Arts, entertainment and recreation in New York city: Recent trends and impact of COVID-19 (Report 12). Office of the New York State Comptroller.

Otis College of Art and Design. (2021). *2021 Otis college report on the creative economy.* Otis College of Art and Design.

Paulson, M. (2021a, June 19). White gatekeepers largely control New York theaters, a study says. *The New York Times,* p. C6.

Paulson, M. (2021b, August 24). Broadway seals a pact for advances in diversity. *The New York Times,* pp. C1, C6.

Paulson, S., & Hernandez, J. C. (2022, August 22). Stars return to fill stage, but gaze at many empty seats. *The New York Times*, pp. A1, A14.

Pogrebin, R. (2021, January 18). For diversity leaders in the arts, getting hired is just the first step. *The New York Times*, pp. 1, 5.

Rebeck, T. (2021, October 15). Theater needs a gender reckoning, too. *The New York Times*, p. A17.

Rentschler, R., & Lee, B. (2021). COVID-19 and arts festivals: Whither transformation? *Journal of Arts and Cultural Management*, 14(1).

Seymour, T. (2022, August 25). What is a museum? ICOM finally decides on a new definition. *The Art Newspaper*. www.theartnewspaper.com/2022/08/24/what-is-a-museum-icom-finally-decides-on-a-new-definition

Sisario, B. (2021, June 20). Race "report card" rates music industry. *New York Times*, p. C3.

Stevens, M., & Sherman, R. (2022, May 7). Vaccine check goes dark on Broadway. *The New York Times*, pp. C1, C7.

Valentine, V. (2022, August 8). On the rise: 47 museum curators and arts leaders who took on new appointments in first half of 2022. *Culture Type*. www.culturetype.com/2022/12/26/on-the-rise-27-museum-curators-and-arts-leaders-who-took-on-new-appointments-in-second-half-of-2022/

Walker, B., Holling, C. S., Carpenter, S. R., & Kinzig, A. (2004). Resilience, adaptability and transformability in social-ecological systems. *Ecology and Society*, 9(2). www.ecologyandsociety.org/vol9/iss2/art5/inline.html

Wyszomirski, M. J. (2022). Chasing resilience for the arts sector: American experiences of the COVID-19 pandemic. *Korean Journal of Arts & Cultural Management*, 15(1), 121–134.

Wyszomirski, M. J., & Cherbo, J. M. (2001). The associational infrastructure of the arts and culture. *Journal of Arts Management, Law, and Society*, 31(2), 99–122.

Index

Note: Page numbers in *italics* indicate a figure and page numbers in **bold** indicate a table on the corresponding page.

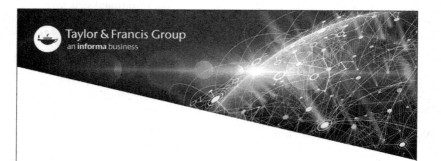

Printed in the United States
by Baker & Taylor Publisher Services